# Towards a Poetics of Fiction

# Towards a Poetics of Fiction

Edited by Mark Spilka

Essays from *Novel: A Forum on Fiction*, 1967-1976

INDIANA UNIVERSITY PRESS
Bloomington and London

Copyright © 1977 by Indiana University Press

Published in Canada by Fitzhenry & Whiteside Limited, Don Mills, Ontario

Manufactured in the United States of America

**Library of Congress Cataloging in Publication Data**

Main entry under title:
Towards a poetics of fiction.

A collection of essays which originally appeared in Novel:  a forum on fiction,
from 1967-1976.
1.Fiction—Addresses, essays, lectures.  I.Spilka, Mark.  II.Novel.
PN3331.T65  1977  809.3  76-48550
ISBN 0-253-37500-2  1 2 3 4 5 81 80 79 78 77

2985469

# Contents

*VI. Language and Style*

# Introduction

Ten years ago a group of fiction specialists at Brown University decided to establish a critical journal which would meet a number of pressing needs in the field. It would serve as a kind of clearinghouse for the conflicting theories of fiction which emerged in the decades following World War II; it would accommodate the novel's history in all literatures (something no other journal then attempted); and it would invite readings—comparative, comprehensive, historical—which would accommodate the novel's unusual breadth and depth and its strikingly varied forms. Out of such considerations *Novel: A Forum on Fiction* was born, in the Fall of 1967, and has since thrived and prospered.

The journal took as its chief justification the remarkable ferment in fiction studies in the postwar period. The novel had received more theoretical attention in those years, and more intelligent criticism, than in all its previous history. But the theories were at odds and ill-assorted, there was no way to mediate between them, and the amount of bad criticism they fostered threatened to submerge the good. The New Critical shift of attention then from poetry to fiction had brought with it an avalanche of image and point-of-view studies of uneven merit, and a penchant for treating novels as poems which proved more suitable to the poetic and hermetic strain in modern fiction than to novels of the past. The approach had accordingly generated one of those academic wars between ancients and moderns which takes decades to settle, and which is still very much with us. The New Critics had drawn support for their views from turn-of-the-century defenses of the art novel by James, Conrad, and Ford; from Percy Lubbock's reductive condensation of those defenses in the 1920's; and from the aesthetic justifications of Flaubertian novelists of the 20's like Joyce and Woolf—all of which were revived to advance their case for modern fiction. At the same time sociological realists like Ian Watt, and social and moral realists like Lukacs, Trilling, Raymond Williams, Erich Auerbach, and the New Critical renegade F. R. Leavis, were proffering strong defenses of past fiction, often in the form of selective "great traditions." Psychological and mythic theorists like Fiedler and Richard Chase defended still other traditions, as did the intentional and rhetorical moralist from Chicago, Wayne Booth. And time and space theorists like A. A. Mendilow and Joseph Frank, along with narrative and generic strategists like Scholes, Kellogg, and Northrop Frye, responded with new taxonomies and cosmographies. It was in this heady context that the editors of *Novel* proposed a series of essays which would unscramble the log-jam in theory, and which would hopefully lead "Towards a Poetics of Fiction" (the series' title) as workable as that which New Critics had more or less successfully devised for poetry; and with similar intent the editors called for criticism based on a more comprehensive sense of the novel's massive hybrid nature, its varied forms and functions, its historic development in many literatures, than previous novel criticism had exhibited.

The essays in this volume represent a decade of effort, then, in encouraging the kind of theoretical and critical support for fiction which poetry had received from the critical revolution in that field from the 1920's onward. Our initial series, "Towards a Poetics of Fiction," was an attempt to define a number of possible and useful approaches to fiction which any student of the genre might take into account. As such, it exemplifies the journal's function as a forum for debate on the novel's manifold nature, and for developing complementary perspectives through cumulative progress. Readers of this series will find contributors responding directly to previous arguments, accommodating previous approaches so as to go beyond them. Such give-and-take exchanges invest this series with a dialectical dimension which extends to the rest of the anthology, and which other "theory of the novel" collections often lack. Comparison, contrast, and increasing comprehensiveness in outlook are built-in features of this "forum" on the novel's nature.

In the first contribution to the series, for instance, the British novelist-critic Malcolm Bradbury sets the terms for further debate by defining the neo-symbolist and linguistic tendencies in New Critical approaches to fiction and the anti-literary, pro-life tendencies of the rival school of realists and empiricists. Scoring both approaches for excluding or minimizing what the other includes, Bradbury then offers a neo-Aristotelean solution: the way in which novelists *structure* their materials, work to persuade us to adopt certain attitudes toward characters and events and to reach gradual conclusions about them, allows us to take both verbal and mimetic effects into account and "to move freely between language and life" in all their relevant fictive dimensions.

In the course of his "Approach through Structure" Bradbury takes issue with another British novelist-critic, David Lodge, the next contributor to the series. Lodge returns the compliment in his "Approach through Language." Interestingly, he begins as a fellow novelist with a different view of structural prefiguring: in his own experience, the achieved structure of novels frequently displaces original prefigurations or radically alters them, so much so as to make genetic speculation an unreliable basis for a poetics of the novel. Then, surprisingly, Lodge denies the neo-symbolist label Bradbury gave him, says he too believes in worked persuasion through the effects of language; but since language is the novel's "all-inclusive medium"—and not merely "one of a variety of elements which the writer must dispose of," as Bradbury holds—Lodge prefers to work as richly as possible through that medium. He sees it, moreover, as both a realistic medium for fiction and one devoted to *pattern*—which seems to be his word for what Bradbury calls "structure." In discussing the tension between pattern and realism (or the unruly details and contingencies of workaday life) he invokes the next contributor to the debate, Frank Kermode, whose *Sense of an Ending* deals with a similar set of fictive tensions.

Kermode's essay, "Novel, History, Type," originally appeared without the series heading; but it appeared also as our third essay on poetics, so by the grace of hindsight it seems appropriate now to include it in the series at this point. Kermode joins Bradbury in taking the discussion of novel theory outside the novel: he wants us to compare fictional with historical narration for the facts and followability common to both, and he wants us to compare fictional with biblical types because they are "indices of contemporaneity" and because "the followability of any narrative depends on them." When the exegete, the historian, and the novelist are doing comparable things, it seems provincial not to compare them. Similarly, Barbara Hardy, in her "Approach through Narrative," emphasizes the connections between storytelling in life and narrative consciousness, between dreams and truth-telling as they figure in and outside novels. Her analysis of realistic novels which explode fantasies only to return to them at novel's end suggests a tension not unlike that which Lodge posits between pattern and realism.

Kermode and Hardy are the third and fourth British contributors to the series. The three American contributors who follow are like them in moving in and out of novels to find (or reject) a poetics. In his "Approach through Genre" Robert Scholes argues that it is the teaching of fiction—the need to justify what we do by some adequate literary explanation—which makes us want a poetics. He believes our explanations should be generic because both writing and reading are bound by generic considerations, as is criticism itself, where false norms and bad judgments may be traced to generic exclusions and misunderstandings. Thus, after developing his pie-shaped history of fictional forms, he makes a point of catching David Lodge taking necessary generic considerations into account before analyzing verbal patterns in specific texts.

In "The Novel as Chronomorph" Eleanor Hutchens narrows generic focus to a single fictive element, time, which she finds "constitutive" for the novel, and not merely as successiveness, but as "the matrix of life" as measured finally by "the human lifespan." Then, in a manner Kermode might approve, she tests her theory against the treatment of time in anti-novelistic novels past and present, short stories, histories, plays, films, poems, and biographies.

In "The Problem with a Poetics of the Novel" Walter Reed takes on all such theories by arguing that a poetics of fiction is neither possible nor desirable. Holding that a poetics tends to establish literary norms and canons, while the novel by nature and history opposes such norms with the forms of everyday life (or with James and many moderns, vice-versa), he makes what *seems* to be a nice generic distinction and shows how it applies to this most anti-literary of literary forms. It is a distinction, moreover, comparable to the tension between pattern and contingency, dream and truth-telling, which fascinates Lodge, Kermode, and Hardy, and which seems (to the editors of *Novel* at least) rich matter for a poetics.

The binding and distorting effects of arbitrary norms and canons generated by schoolmen troubles Reed; yet it is the hope of schoolman Scholes, and of his fellow editors on *Novel*, that useful distinctions will be liberating, will help us to understand and justify what we do when we teach this "outside model" inside academic walls. A working poetics more loosely pluralistic than fixed, constantly tested, revised, and modified by experience, and so kept tentative and flexible, can promote the best kind of novel criticism, that which takes into account the novel's manifold nature and history as it makes its inevitably selective and partial illuminations.

Accepting the risks and hazards of all such theorizing, the journal has also called for "second thoughts" by the authors of important books on novel theory; and it has invited reappraisals of current schools and theorists by other hands. These different kinds of reconsideration, appearing in sections II and III, are another unique feature of this anthology; they record and respond to the gestation of key positions in the great postwar debate on fiction, and so constitute a modest inventory of contemporary critical history found in no other comparable collection. The essays by Watt and Booth on their own books, their conception and reception, seem to us well worth the price of admission in this respect; they are crucial to study of the books themselves and to problems of critical reception raised by them which affect us all; and they are humane and funny and pluralistic in their treatment of those problems. The essays by other hands—on formalist and structuralist approaches to fiction, on the connections between Booth and his Chicago forebears, on the Marxist Lukacs' early Hegelian view of epic fiction as that view relates to current taxonomies, and on contested assumptions at work in Leavis's novel criticism—seem to us admirable assessments of particular "poetics," and thus (along with the self-assessments of Booth and Watt) extensions of our ongoing forum on the novel's nature.

The remaining sections of the anthology extend debate along lines of controversy already suggested by Bradbury's essay. Sections IV and V, on "Biography and Theory" and "History and Culture," relate novel theory to those mimetic reaches dear to empirical explorers; section VI relates it to form and language in New Critical or neo-symbolist ways—but then all these sections offer admirably pluralistic versions of their dominant mode. The biographical essays show the impingements of private considerations on the genesis of two famous defenses of the modern art novel by James and Woolf, each involving attacks on the previous crudenesses of realist poetics. The essays on history and culture pursue such extra-literary matters as historical perspectivism, communal speech, pastoral myths, matriarchal homes, and sexist fears with a fine eye for textual incarnations; and the essays on language and style show an appreciative sense of human contexts as they illustrate a range of verbal functions: poetic in Fielding, communal in Tolkien, corporeal in Rabelais, defusing in Flaubert, allotropic in Lawrence.

These examples of the comprehensiveness and scope which novel criticism should exhibit are also in many cases comparative essays, dealing with foreign literatures as Reed, Scholes, Good, and others have dealt with them in earlier sections. The journal's interest in comparative approaches is another instance of its attempt to cross boundaries and make connections useful to critical discourse; and it is another distinctive feature of this anthology that it makes such connections. The Anglo-American nature of the "poetics" exchange might be recalled here. Adding Williams, Bilan, and Good to the Anglos, there are a total of five British and two Canadian contributors to this volume, to say nothing of expatriate Ian Watt. There are also four novelists (adding Williams and Moynahan), five women (and here a cheer for the new feminist approaches to fiction in section V seems in order), at least six practicing comparatists, two historicists, and one staunch medievalist (Kirk). Our journal is pleased as Punch to have set going the many-sided dialogue which such contributors ably represent. We owe much of this diversity to our Anglo-American base at the University of Birmingham in England, manned by British Editor Park Honan (one of the journal's three American founders) and board member David Lodge; and to the diverse interests of our foreign, English, and American fiction staff at Brown, and to our distinguished advisors there and elsewhere. On behalf of these fictionists, and with particular thanks for their advice and assistance with this volume to fellow founder and Senior Editor Edward Bloom, Associate Editor Roger Henkle, and former Book Review Editor (and current board member) Robert Scholes, let me welcome all fellow and sister fictionists to our tenth-anniversary forum on the liveliest, if most elusive, of literary genres.

MARK SPILKA, for the Editors
of *Novel: A Forum on Fiction*

# I.

# Towards a Poetics of Fiction

# An Approach through Structure

MALCOLM BRADBURY

The study of the novel has emerged as one of the great growth-industries of modern criticism. Fiction—and particularly modern fiction—has taken on a comparatively new importance in literary study. Indeed it is effectively only over the last twenty years or so that many of the familiar reputations in the modern novel—Joyce, Lawrence, Forster, Conrad, Proust, Mann, Svevo, Faulkner, Hemingway, and so on—have really been secured. At the same time there has emerged a clearer critical consensus about the great novelists of the past, and there has tended to emerge something like an implicit aesthetics for the description and assessment of novels. Much of this has been founded on earlier work, but it has betrayed its own obsessions and interests, and the starting point of the argument that follows —an argument designed to start an argument and not conclude one—is a sense of considerable dissatisfaction with the present state of debate about the nature of the novel and the general practice of novel-criticism as it flourishes in the learned trade-journals. One important feature of the present wealth of critical activity is the comparative slowness with which it has developed. There was, as the modern period began, an abundance of sophisticated debate about fiction produced by practitioners of the novel—Flaubert, James, Howells, Conrad, Joyce, and others —of quite as good an order as the new self-consciousness in poetry, and involving similar aesthetic radicalism. But, for reasons hard to see, the new aesthetics in poetry penetrated into the academies with much greater speed than the corresponding movement in fiction. The consequences of this for novel-criticism have been considerable, and do much to account for its present disarray. For the aesthetics based on poetry made literary language, its symbol-making and tension-making power, the main new point of attention. It characteristically saw works of art as total symbolic objects, single concrete wholes which could not be changed in any detail without changing total meaning. This view of literature was best ascertained if the object of demonstration was a short or lyric poem. As one obvious result, many of the most pressing of modern critical assumptions are founded on the mode of working of that exemplary object.

The consequent orthodoxy about literature that developed is familiar enough and still influential enough not to require extensive discussion. But a number of central points need disentangling if we are to approach the present impasse in fictional criticism. The first point is that the New Criticism, as we call it, has been easiest with intensely concentrated works, lacking directly represented characters or anything resembling a narrative line. The second is that this criticism has tended to regard works of literature as closed systems; it is anti-causal or solipsistic. It tends to concern itself primarily with a single unit of art—the poem—and to see this existing independently of its creator or reader in its only ascertainable form:

words on a page. This primary unit is usually studied in terms of methods for attaining verbal coherence—processes of repetition and contrast in the use of language (hence "imagery," "theme," "tone," "tension," "paradox"). These elements are usually taken as parts of a whole whose character is normally defined by maximum use of poetic language—a language of concrete instances transformed by the interplay of verbal resonances into something universal. This does not mean that the work imitates types in general nature; the theory is not neo-classic. Nor does it mean that it is the product of intense awarenesses within the creative power itself about the vital springs in things; it is not romantic. Rather the view is linguistic and neo-symbolist; it holds that language itself has the inherent power to project wide possibilities which can take the form of a concrete universal. Works of art are thus verbal constructs in which all the material necessary for their appreciation and elucidation is contained; they are distilled thought-feeling complexes in which the verbal procedures for creating progression derive from the properties of heightened, literary, non-discursive language (hence their essential features are best defined by grammatical terms, like paradox, antithesis, metaphor, symbol, not by mimetic terms like character, description or plot). The main assumptions of this aesthetic for my purposes are these: 1) that works of art are autotelic discourse, concrete representations in heightened language of an experience which can only be abstracted by criticism from the complete work, 2) that because a work of art exists in this way, we should be less interested in its structure than in its overall texture and its verbal modes of unity, and 3) that literary language is the distinctive feature of such works, and the procedures which distinguish that language from other forms of language are a crucial part of the critical accounting.

In consequence, the critical approach derived from this view is not conceived as a means of reference to objects imitated by literature; it finds no inherent universals in the external world—only those in the  metaphoric or symbolizing function of language itself. Thus "content" must be subsumed into "form" and be seen usually as a species of verbal or thematic recurrence. The general inference is, therefore, that when we confront human experience and relationships in literature, we do so within a broad framework of composition which creates a sense of universality through the given powers of language itself. Hence, inevitably, this kind of criticism concerns itself more and more with devices of presentation, rather than representation, and in doing so has claimed superior critical logicality. This logicality has rightly enough been applied to the criticism of fiction, as of longer poems, and it has in many respects proved profitable. Though New Critics often tend to distinguish poetic from prose language categorically, it has become more and more familiar to suppose that there are close analogies between the modes. Indeed, in a recent excellent book (*Language of Fiction*, 1966), David Lodge has argued that most of the attributes the New Criticism applies to poetic language apply quite precisely to prose language in fiction as well. Hence, he argues, it is only logical to regard novels as pieces of autotelic discourse; if they differ from poems by virtue of their dimension and their prose form, they do not differ radically and we must therefore apply the same kind of stylistic analysis to them as we have to poetry. In fact, many of the assumptions about the unitary nature of the work of art, the relation of form to content, and parts to wholes, have been long adopted into the study of fiction. The two main consequences of this fact have been that a) much of the criticism of fiction has had a submerged symbolist aesthetic behind it, and b) a large amount of fictional criticism has devoted itself to finding stylistic or verbal unities in literary matter inherently more discursive than most poetry.

But since novels do have an enhanced referential dimension, and since any discussion of linguistic unity is likely to leave that dimension unsubsumed, so there is, in criticism of this sympathy, a tendency to see a kind of subtext of representation beneath the process of presentation. The compositional scale must be one appropriate to the complexity of life; technique must be discovery. Hence the effort of such essays as Mark Schorer's justly influential "Technique as Discovery" to capture as much for rhetoric and composition as can be got without sacrificing some mimetic or representational dimension altogether. But the presence of an unreconciled element—the element of empiricism, of attention to workaday reality, that we associate with the novelty of the novel, for instance—makes the case seem incomplete and leaves us divided between two divergent poetics. However, the compensatory emphasis provided by critics who stress the referential quality of fiction, its capacity to particularize, its closeness to life, seems often equally misleading. Ian Watt, in *The Rise of the Novel* (1957), advances an argument of this kind, finding the distinctive nature of the novel in its empirical disregard of traditional conventions and structures. Other critics have intensified the possibilities of this approach by suggesting that what most typifies the form is what Henry James would call its "illustrative" nature—its singular attentiveness to life, its empirical curiosity, its instinct for the luminous rendering of the particular. But whether this emphasis moves toward Barbara Hardy's view (in *The Appropriate Form*, 1964) that the ideal form for the novel is like that of *Anna Karenina*—"an assertion of dogma in an undogmatic form, the last pulse of a slow and irregular rhythm which is a faithful record of the abrupt, the difficult, the inconclusive"—or whether it moves toward F. R. Leavis's view (in *The Great Tradition*, 1948) that "an unusually developed interest in life," a humane and moral concern, constitutes fineness in a novel, such arguments tend to be weakened first by the fact that there are many novels which have other ends in view (so Ian Watt stumbles with Fielding, Leavis with late James and Joyce) and second by the fact that lifelikeness is only one aspect of mimesis, and hence is conditioned by larger purposes operative in the novel. Further, by attributing the capacity to render life to some moral quality in the author, Leavis tends to see the novel as a literary situation in which the author transfers sincerity or maturity by direct correspondence to the reader. The ontological argument, on the other hand, tends to divest itself entirely of questions about the way in which fiction affects us, and also ignores questions about the imitative function of literature, its relation to that which inherently it must imitate.

These two views, the two most familiar views of the novel we have, thus diverge in a variety of respects. But they are alike in their unwillingness to describe the novel formally, and to determine the disposition of elements other than verbal structure or the incremental addition of scene to scene. The neo-symbolist view, which sees all literature as verbal procedure, finds difficulty in suggesting any features which make novels recognizably novels; and the realistic view, which typifies novels by their special degree of interest in life, tends to classify them as an a-generic genre. Yet a full description of the novel is not really possible if we concentrate only on those characteristics which create an effect of verbal unity, nor if we concentrate only on those which make for lifelikeness and solidity of specification, or regard the novel as an undefinable because empirical species. At the same time both of these views have an implicit poetics—one symbolist, the other realist —which can only lead to radically different critical emphases and preferences; and this in itself must create the desire for a more inclusive typology.

What surely is needed is an approach to fiction which concerns itself with the special complexities of novels and the distinctive kinds of artifice and imitation employed in their creation. We can only achieve this by recognizing that the novel is not a traditional literary genre, like tragedy or comedy, but a general form like poetry or drama; a form recognizable, moreover, to writers when they write one and to readers when they read one, but subject to broad and narrow uses and not to be defined even as clearly as poetry and drama. There is no generic theory which will enable us to define closely the kind of matter it is likely to imitate or the kind of effect it seeks to produce; nor can we define it clearly by its diction or mode of presentation, as we can define poetry and drama. Though we can say that novels are usually presented to us in prose, as bound books for private reading, and are fictive and hence autotelic, this will give us little guide to the matter presented in them, to the kind of action they will contain or the kind of effect they will produce. The result is that any attempt at generic classification is likely to end up with some monstrosity of definition, like Henry Fielding's "comic epic poem in prose." On the other hand, if we deduce from this that novels are intrinsically a-generic, typified by their revolutionary nature, their freedom from convention, and their stress on the novel and the individual in human experience, as some critics have, we are apt to define them rather by their place in history, in a history of style or the evolution of modes. So we can, following Ian Watt's lead, identify them socially with the middle class, see them as literary vehicles of burgher individualism, and characterize them further by a complex of realism founded in philosophic empiricism, fascination with material environment, and a new kind of demanding intercourse between the individual and society. We can thus find a place for them in history and the social world, see their method of depiction as low mimetic, and their prevailing obsession, the unveiling of illusion and hypocrisy. But from the point of view of a poetics, a more profitable approach is to recognize that while the novel has no *typical* action, certain compositional problems and features do exist, distinctively and inherently, in novels, in their fictive nature, their character as prose, and their magnitude or epic dimension.

A novel is a fictional prose discourse that is, in the Aristotelian formulation, "necessarily of a certain magnitude." The problems of the magnitude and hence of the necessary range of the novel—the problems that derive from "our inability to possess a novel as a picture or a lyric can be possessed," as E. K. Brown puts it— seem fundamental, since they determine the essential conditions of our engagement with the medium, whether we are readers or writers. They oblige the critic to possess larger terms than many have for talking about the spatial and temporal extension of novels and the full worlds they explore. Equally they commit the writer to a certain scale of attention, an epical dimension whose action, as Henry Fielding describes it, is "more extended and comprehensive" than that of tragedy, contains "a much larger circle of incidents," and introduces "a greater variety of characters." The fact that the novel is written in prose also significantly determines its matter. Prose, as compared with poetry, has an accentuated referential dimension: it is our normal instrument of discursive communication, is associated with our ways of verifying factuality, and is thereby subject to a complex of social uses not imposed on verse. In compositional terms, an extended piece of prose will inevitably use forms of discursiveness and persuasion not normally available to poetry, will have a different tonal and structural engagement with the reader, and so will emerge as a different species of persuasion, usually involving extremely varied use of language (ranging from reportage to extreme poetic effects) and large-scale rhetorical strategies of the kind explored so well in Wayne Booth's *Rhetoric of Fiction* (1961). As for the fictive nature of novels, this can indeed be seen as a feature common to all forms of invented discourse, but it can also be distinguished as that matter for invention appropriate to this scale and this mode of discourse, so that a writer will choose to develop it through prose fiction and no other form: and that matter is typically characters and events, presented to us by verbal means and shown in extended interaction. Thus the novel is a complex structure by virtue of its scale, prose-character, and matter, being more extended than most poems, dealing with a wider range of life, appealing to the reader through a broader variety of approaches, having a different relationship to working language, and above all stating its character, intentions and conventions with less immediate clarity and a greater degree of gradual, worked persuasion. It will tend, then, to be more discursive than poetry, and its stronger referential dimension will be shown not only by attentiveness to people as they talk and think and act, and places as they look and institutions as they work, but also to large processes of human interaction as they take place over a long chronological span, or spatially over a large area of ground or a large sector of society.

The structural principles deriving from these features are various and cannot be closely defined in terms of a subject-matter. There is no necessary kind of hero, though there is usually a hero; and there is no necessary kind of action, either in substance or shape, as in tragedy or comedy; but frequently there are structures like those of classical comedy, in that the diction tends to be mean, the range of characters wide in classes and social types, and the social and moral worlds discordant, though moving toward harmonious resolution. Still, if there is no necessary structure, almost any fictional structure must necessarily consist of certain things—primarily a chain of interlinked events unified by persuasive discourse and by those materials in life which, transliterated as discourse, take on for the author a character of interconnectedness. We cannot provide a total typology of such a structure, but we can, and need to, seek empirical means for describing what is inevitably present in a novel. Now it seems to me that any effective account of such structures, which are not prior typologies but compositional constructs deriving from rhetorical and mimetic sources, must be concerned both with discourse, in this particular form, and that which in life determines and organizes an author's interest in such discourse. For if we say that the character of a work of fiction is primarily verbal, is a linguistic effect, we will tend to be committed to questions about the role of language, and find the order and unity of the work lying in that; and if we say that the nature of the novel is primarily to render, to make vivid, to give a sense of life as lived, we may primarily be involved in judgments about life and society, and find order and unity lying in some typology in the world. But if we say that the novel is determined by conditions within the medium itself and outside it in life, then we may move freely between language and life, and find order and unity in the kind of working that a novel has to have, and that any given novel *has* had, in achieving its persuasive ends; and we may further allow, by this approach, for the book's referential dimension as an account of life, its rhetorical dimension as a species of language, its sociological dimension as an exploration and crystallization of a cultural situation, and its psychological or mythic dimension as an exploration of personal or social psychic experience.

Let me now make it clear that I have no wish to disparage or reject stylistic questions, or the analysis of verbal and rhetorical procedures. I believe that they have done much to enlarge our sense of the workings of fiction, and to dissipate many traditional illogicalities in the criticism of literature. My gratitude is only tempered by the fact that they have made us suspicious of talking about the referential dimensions of literature at all. There is a quiver of unease that comes over us when we sit down to talk about a novel and use mimetic words like "plot," "character" or "incident"—a fear that we are imposing unwarranted demands upon what is, after all, essentially a block of words. We are therefore inclined to assume that if we can show that the imagery of cash and legality runs through a Jane Austen novel, or that a whiteness-blackness opposition runs through *Moby-Dick*, we can show more about the real being of the book than by showing that it deals with a society, with dispositions of character and relationship, so as to create a coherent moral and social world and an attitude toward it, steadily worked from page to page, which condition our responses. We *may* be interested in such things, but we will be tempted to regard them as more diffuse versions of the essential linguistic relationship which words create between writer and reader. It is perhaps not unfair to claim, at this point, that there are very few writers who appear to have felt that it is only through language that they communicate. They are, I would suppose, always conscious that they are mediating verbally a devised succession of events; and that the organization of those events, their relations one to another, their selection and their disposition are primary to their task as writers and are utterly crucial to the effect of their work. Most writers would consider, I think, that they are making verbal approaches to the reader which engage him with a shared reality, and which create in him expectations and values, sympathies and repulsions, appropriate to the comprehension of that reality. We may then take the writer's language in this essential activity as an enabling feature, one of a variety of elements which the writer must dispose of in producing a work. If we take this position, we will find the author's signature not simply in stylistics, as neo-symbolists do, but in his urging upon us, through verbal means, a particular complex of matter for persuasion.

To provide an adequate account of the structure of fiction, then, we must honor the fundamental recognition of modern criticism that all things in a novel are mediated through words, yet acknowledge that certain things are logically prior to those words, a matter which they mediate. We cannot, I think, isolate these things as a species of prior content seeking an appropriate form, since they will include ideas, insights and compositional commitments not definable as content. Rather we are concerned with the process of inventing or making a world, with the dynamics by which that world is shown and evaluated by forms of rendering and distancing, ordering and urging, which are the larger blocks of fictional persuasion. The trouble with such matters for enquiry is that, though we may accept them as a necessary condition of literary creation, there is no really satisfactory method of ascertaining what they are except *through* the words which finally express them. On the other hand, our successful reading of those words is surely a kind of process by which we hypothesize the sort of decisions of relevance made in order to put this material to us in this way. What we are concerned with, then, is not the projection of some matter or action prior to the writing which has produced it, but a steady appreciation of the way in which a writer has shaped and been shaped by his undertaking. We might project the situation back in Aristotelian terms, or neo-Aristotelian terms, in the form of a prior working out of the action in the mind of the writer, which the compositional process then imitates; but it is only meaningful to do this if we say that the action imitated exists simultaneously as that which has to be written (that which motivates and directs the compositional process) and that which is worked, achieved, realized in the writing. For any novelist will admit that the prefigured novel is not the same as the novel achieved, but that nonetheless it is the interaction between what is prefigured and the obligations of achieving it that "create" a novel. A novel is inevitably determined by prior intentions and choices (the most significant being the choice of the novel as the right narrative form), but the crucial selection, and rejection, lies in finding a means for persuasion compatible with the author's prior interests and the conditions of the novel-form itself as a species of working and persuading. Hence we will not want to define the structure of a novel as a prior typology, but on the other hand we will not want to say, I believe, that it is formed only by the aesthetic logic of the literary structure alone, which is the neo-symbolist tendency.

But if, therefore, we avoid looking for a prior action, a story to be told, we can still derive from a novel a causative hypothesis, a unifying purposefulness which sets the aesthetic logic into action and which perpetually shapes it. In this way we may discover how the novelist limits, by formalizing it, the total environment offered by life, how he creates a conditioned world with its own laws and probabilities, a world in which experience can only assume certain shapes and characters only assume certain dimensions, in order that "structure" may have its existence. By this view structure would be that devised chain of events that, presented by narration, conditions the successive choices, made sentence by sentence, paragraph by paragraph, chapter by chapter, and constitutes not only an entire narrative but an attitude toward it; it is thus the substantive myth that we can derive from the novel without regarding it as something independent of it. It is therefore a compositional achievement, *this* action existing in *that* social and moral environment and in *that* context of rhetorical effects designed to control and represent *that* world for us. These effects thus exist less in the realm of style *per se* than in the realm of persuasion, to the end of producing a logic or a response in readers which is the proper outcome of the ordering and selecting process, those decisions about technique and stylistic base and pattern about which criticism is capable of talking so well (*e.g.*, Booth). Now in novels this synthesizing process will normally, though not always, emerge as a dynamic action about persons in a society (frequently one we recognize as analogous to our own) and will usually advance through unfolding events to which we are continually being given an attitude, a response (so that they are never *neutrally* events). And since each novel is, for reasons already given, a unique conjunction of variables, not having a definable generic nature, we must be particularly attentive and responsive if we are to project our sense of what this structure might be.

In any novel of more than incidental interest, then, we must assimilate and respond to a world with its own defined conditions and conventions (however lifelike these may seem), and at the same time judge, estimate and evaluate what is being urged to us. In a complex way, we must dispose and relate parts and elements in order to form a growing hypothesis about the total action, and we must group blocks of experience according to standards of judgment whose aesthetic and evaluative terms are given by the text. We are guided in this process by a narrative pattern which both places and conceals elements in the action. So we are encouraged to make all sorts of provisional assessments, and provisional *classifications;* so we assemble characters in groups and classes, estimate the status of particular values in relation to other values, and acquire a conditioned sense of moral appropriateness, a conditioned sense of choice. In doing all this we are not, I think, engaged with life as such, nor committed only to tests of realization, by which passages or scenes may be analyzed for lifelike texture. Nor, I think, are we engaged only with something that can be described simply as discourse and analyzed only as an image-system or a rhetoric independent of writers and readers. My case is that, while there is no single dynamic that is generically characteristic of the novel, its main structural characteristic lies in a developing action about characters and events conducted in a closed—that is to say, an authorially conditioned—world containing principles, values and attitudes by which we may evaluate those events. To talk about this structural dimension, we need to be able to open up that closed world by asking questions about causation and effect, a procedure that does not seem at all fallacious if we raise the questions and answer them from cruxes within the work. To do this is to elevate into prominence those conscious or intuitive choices which every writer must perpetually make, and to regard not only the discourse but the structure—which can be distinguished from the discourse as a species of imitation—as part of the matter to be persuaded. It also means that, while we regard novels as verbal constructs, we must see the nature of what is constructed not as a self-sustaining entity but a species of persuasion, the writer handling material for the reader so as to engage him properly with the world of this single work. And one point now needs firm restatement: it is only if we have some such theory of structure, however empirical, that we are likely to acquire a meaningful descriptive poetics of fiction; and the absence of that, the current weakness of critical terminology, is a central cause of the inadequacy of much of the present wealth of novel criticism.

# An Approach through Language

DAVID LODGE

I must begin with an apology, to Malcolm Bradbury, who initiated this series with his thought-provoking "An Approach through Structure" in *Novel*, I (Fall, 1967), 45–52, and to all those who may feel that I have taken advantage of his coming before me to argue with his case instead of formulating a parallel case of my own. My excuse must be that following the latter course would have entailed my repeating a great deal of what I have said in a book called *Language of Fiction* (1966). If I felt that I had nothing to add to or subtract from what I said there, I should not have accepted the invitation to contribute to this series. But inevitably I write as one defending a position already occupied, rather than as one throwing down a challenge. This procedure is the more difficult to avoid because Malcolm Bradbury cites my book in connection with an approach to the novel which he finds (while acknowledging its usefulness) to be in some ways inadequate and misleading.

That approach he characterizes as "symbolist" or "neo-symbolist," tracing its derivation from the principles that modern criticism developed in the study of poetry, especially lyric poetry. In this perspective novels like poems "are verbal constructs in which all the material necessary for their appreciation and elucidation is contained." Elucidation and appreciation are conducted primarily in terms of verbal analysis, and the novelist's art is seen as one of "presentation, rather than representation." Bradbury finds this approach wanting in its failure to accommodate the referential character of novels or their "attention to workaday reality." But the kind of criticism which *does* undertake to deal with this element he finds equally unsatisfactory. This is the "realist" approach, which characterizes the novel by its special interest in "life," whether this is seen (as by Ian Watt in *The Rise of the Novel*) as the expression of historical changes in human experience and modes of perceiving it, or (as by F. R. Leavis in *The Great Tradition*) as the mediation by author to reader of a more or less mature and life-enhancing scale of values in concretely realized instances.

Neither of these critical approaches, in Bradbury's view, offers the basis for a "poetics" of the novel; neither is capable of giving a comprehensive formal account of the novel's peculiar identity. To reconcile "these two divergent poetics" Bradbury proposes a more inclusive one, which he calls "structural." Our series-title rather plays into his hands here, for his approach is essentially neo-Aristotelian. The novel "is a complex structure by virtue of its scale, prose-character and matter." This, he concedes, does not yield a structural typology, but "still, if there is no necessary structure, almost any fictional structure must necessarily consist of certain things—primarily a chain of interlinked events, unified by persuasive discourse and by those materials in life which, transliterated as discourse, take on for the author the character of interconnectedness." It is the last part of this sentence that is crucial: Bradbury is seeking to accommodate within the concept of novel *form* that *matter* which is the special concern of the realist critics. "If we say that the novel is determined by conditions within the medium itself and outside it in life," he writes, "then we may move freely between language and life, and find order and unity in the kind of working that a novel has . . . in achieving its persuasive ends; and we may further allow, by this approach, for the book's referential dimension as an account of life, its rhetorical dimension as a species of language, its sociological dimension as an exploration and crystallization of a cultural situation, and its psychological or mythic dimension as an exploration of personal or psychic experience."

The inclusiveness of the poetics sketched here is indeed appealing, but I rather doubt whether the concept of "structure" can be made to bear the strain of so many different applications. The word "structure" in literary criticism is, after all, a metaphor, which describes a temporal medium in spatial and visual terms, and it can be no more inclusive analogically than it is literally. For example to describe the structure of a cathedral is to describe its overall shape, its balancing and distribution of large masses and spaces, not the texture of its stone, or the carving of its gargoyles, or the coloring of its windows. Thus it is not surprising to find Bradbury later defining the concept of structure more narrowly as "that devised chain of events that, presented by narration, conditions the successive choices, made sentence by sentence, paragraph by paragraph, chapter by chapter, and constitutes not only an entire narrative but an attitude towards it. . . ." This is much more like the concept of "plot" in Aristotelian and neo-Aristotelian criticism. Bradbury is shrewd enough to see the pitfalls inherent in such a theory, but not, I think, to avoid them altogether. "We might project the situation back in Aristotelian terms, or neo-Aristotelian terms, in the form of a prior working-out of the action in the mind of the writer, which the compositional process then imitates; but it is only meaningful to do this if we say that the action imitated exists simultaneously as that which has to be written (that which motivates and directs the compositional process) and that which is worked, achieved, realized in the writing." The two parts of this sentence cancel each other out: priority cannot be logically reconciled with simultaneity. Yet some notion of priority—of crucial choices and decisions being made by the novelist prior to the verbal articulation of them in the novel—is essential to Bradbury's theory, since it is in this way that he aims to incorporate an account of an author's particular engagement with "life" into a formal poetics, by seeing selection and ordering of experience as "the larger blocks of fictional persuasion." As he recognizes, "the trouble with such matters for enquiry is that, though we may accept them as a necessary condition of literary creation, there is no really satisfactory method of ascertaining what they are except *through* the words which finally express them." This is, in fact, an argument I have used myself to urge primary attention to the novelist's use of language. Bradbury's answer is that "successful reading of those words is surely a kind of process by which we hypothesize the sort of decisions of relevance made in order to put the material to us in this way." He buttresses this by what I must take as an *argumentum ad hominem*: "there are very few writers who appear to have felt that it is only through language that they are communicating. They are, I would suppose, always conscious that they are mediating verbally a devised succession of events. . . ."

Now, whatever novelists "feel," it is axiomatic that it is only through language that they are communicating, since there are no other means of communication at their disposal. What Bradbury means, I think, is that novelists feel it is not language *that* they are communicating: that, in other words, they are conscious of selecting and arranging non-verbal "life-stuff," which is gradually rendered more and more concrete and particular in the process of verbalization. In this view, while it is acknowledged that only through the final verbalization do we apprehend the gross structure, the gross structure also conditions the final verbalization; and a meaning or persuasive power inheres in this gross structure which cannot be accounted for by direct reference to the language alone, but only by working back from the language to construct a hypothetical picture of the initial non-verbal process of selection and ordering.

"It is the interaction between what is prefigured and the obligations of achieving it that creates a novel," is Bradbury's elegant formulation. But that second "it" is an ambiguous word. As Bradbury says, "any novelist will admit that the prefigured novel is not the same as the novel achieved." And this difference, it must be emphasized, is not merely a matter of detail or density—it is also in Bradbury's terms "structural." If we are to appeal to the experience of novelists (my own certainly bears this out) it will be found that in many, if not most cases, major decisions regarding the pattern of events, the behavior of characters and so on, are made or significantly revised at an advanced stage of composition—at the point, very often, when the ongoing process of composition compels a decision upon the writer. Let me explain what I mean by a hypothetical and very stylized example.

For a novel consisting of three chapters, I "prefigure" a character X who undergoes experience *a* in Chapter I, performs action *b* in Chapter II, and is left in situation *c* or *d* (I haven't decided which) in Chapter III. In the process of articulating $Xa$ I shall discover things about X that I didn't "know" before—he will be a much more fully defined and at least to that extent a different X from the prefigured X. And this difference will suggest to me when I begin Chapter II that action *e* would be a more natural development for Chapter II than action *b*; furthermore, *e* will prepare much more satisfactorily for situation *f* that I have just thought of for Chapter III, and which I am very excited about. Accordingly I will proceed to articulate $Xe$ for Chapter II, and $Xf$ for Chapter III, and go back over Chapter I to strengthen the links between $Xa$ and $Xe$ (a process I will denote by $Xae$). Thus while the structure of the prefigured novel might be represented as

$$Xa + Xb + Xc?d?$$

that of the achieved novel would be represented as

$$Xae + Xe + Xf$$

In the light of this example the prefigured structure of a novel seems less like the framework of pillars and arches which holds a building in a certain shape, than like the scaffolding, without which indeed the building cannot be started, but which is altered and dismantled in the process of construction. If we examine Bradbury's statement that "it is the interaction between what is prefigured and the obligations of achieving it that 'creates' a novel," we now see that the second "it" cannot refer to "what is prefigured," though this is what the grammar of the sentence suggests. More meaningfully one might say that "the interaction between what is prefigured and what is achieved creates a novel." In this interaction what is achieved is certainly conditioned to some extent by what is prefigured, but in a more significant sense what is achieved, as it is achieved, *displaces* what has been prefigured, and alters the prefiguration of what is not yet achieved.

Furthermore, the devising of a chain of events is accorded very different degrees of priority by different novelists and is by no means as constant a feature of the prefiguring process as Bradbury's theory seems to require. His theory would probably fit *Tom Jones* very well, but hardly *Madame Bovary*:

> *Flaubert said to us today: "The story, the plot of the novel is of no interest to me. When I write a novel I aim at rendering a color, a shade. For instance, in my Carthaginian novel, I want to do something purple. The rest, the characters and the plot, is a mere detail. In* Madame Bovary, *all I wanted to do was to render a grey color, the mouldy color of a wood-louse's existence. The story of the novel mattered so little to me that a few days before starting on it I still had in mind a very different Madame Bovary from the one I created: the setting and the overall tone were the same, but she was to have been a chaste and devout old maid. And then I realized that she would have been an impossible character.*[1]

The genetic study of works of literature is indeed a fascinating and rewarding branch of literary criticism, but the processes of composition vary so much between one writer and another (and often between one book and another by the same writer) that genetic study will not yield enough reliable generalizations on which to erect a poetics of the novel.

It will be noted that I am not denying that novelists make choices and decisions regarding the kinds and disposition of characters, events, backgrounds, themes, moods to be handled in a given novel, nor that these decisions are (in a provisional and variable sense) made prior to their articulation in the actual work. What I am

---

[1] From Edmond and Jules Goncourt, *Pages from the Goncourt Journal,* ed. and translated by Robert Baldick, (1962), reprinted in *The Modern Tradition,* edd. Richard Ellmann and Charles Feidelson, Jr. (New York: Oxford University Press, 1965), p. 126.

denying is that these things have any substantive existence somehow "outside" language, that in Bradbury's words, "the structure . . . can be distinguished from the discourse as a species of imitation." To make this point clear I must dissociate myself both from certain assumptions about language implied in Bradbury's theory, and from those he attributes to "symbolist" criticism.

To begin with the latter point, I would reject the symbolist theory as he describes it, as "anti-causal or solipsistic"—and not only with regard to the novel, but with regard to verse. I take language to be a shared system of sounds and written symbols for sounds, by which meaning is conveyed between people who share the system. This excludes the possibility of a private language and of a literature of "pure" sound (sound without meanings). It means that I would not regard a novel as "something which can be analyzed only as an image system or a rhetoric independent of writers and readers." In fact I am in complete agreement with Bradbury in seeing the art of the novelist as "persuasion"—as effects achieved in order to persuade the reader to view experience in a certain way. But I must protest when he says that "these effects exist less in the realm of style *per se* than in the realm of persuasion." If style means (as I presume) literary language here, there can be no such thing as style *per se* (that is, words considered apart from the meanings they bear and the persuasive purposes they serve) and no persuasion without style. In my view the crucial fallacy in Bradbury's argument, and in most neo-Aristotelian theory, is that it regards language as, in his words "one of a variety of elements which the writer must dispose of in producing a work," and not as the all-inclusive medium in which whatever "elements" we may choose to discern and categorize in a work of literature are contained and communicated.

Fundamentally, my position rests on the assumption that consciousness is essentially conceptual, i.e. verbal. There is of course such a thing as non-verbal or pre-verbal *experience*—the whole life of sensation, for example—but we cannot be conscious of that experience without verbal concepts. This position would only imply solipsism if language was a private and arbitrary affair. It is not, but the notion that, in Wittgenstein's words, "the limits of my language are the limits of my world" is apt to be resented because it seems to deny the reality of non-verbal experience. In this latter view meaning resides in experience, in things, in "life," which we use language merely to refer to. But this is to confuse meaning with reference, it is, as Wittgenstein says, to confound the *meaning* of a name with the *bearer* of a name. Meaning, we might risk saying, resides in the application of a concept to a thing in particular circumstances. "Just as a move in chess doesn't consist merely in moving a piece in such and such a way on the board—nor yet in one's feelings and thoughts as one makes the move: but in the circumstances that we call 'playing a game of chess,' 'solving a chess problem,' and so on."[2]

It is true that this leaves us problematically situated in relation to "reality." We "know" that there is a reality outside language, but we have no means of describ-

---

[2] Wittgenstein again. I have taken these philosophical hints at second hand from John Casey's *The Language of Criticism* (London, 1966), pp. 2–3. For a fuller argument that consciousness is dependent on verbal concepts see J. M. Cameron's essay "Poetry and Dialectic" in *The Night Battle* (London, 1962), especially pp. 142–46.

ing it except through language: language, as someone succinctly put it, is an experiment without a control. This makes the practice of criticism particularly difficult, but it is evidently the price we pay for being human.

It follows from what I have been saying that there is no mental act involved in the creation of a novel, however far one projects back, which is not conducted in language. There is no point at which we can say: up to this point the author was sorting out the basic life stuff, and then afterwards he began to put it into words; because it has been in words all the time. To be sure, the words change, and are incremented, as the novel acquires body and definition in the ongoing process of composition, but "it" is changing and being incremented *pari passu*. There is in fact no substantive "it" which remains constant throughout the creation of a novel. "It" is only available for observation when the compositional process is temporarily or finally arrested, and "it" is never the same at any two such points. The final text of a novel is not therefore evidence from which we infer how the author saw, and how he meant us to see, a certain complex of experience; it is the criterion—the only criterion—of what he is seeing, and how he is seeing it, and how he means us to see it.[3]

I must emphasize that I do not wish to prohibit Bradbury or anyone else from discussing the "structure" of novels; I am merely affirming that he can usefully do so only by virtue of his responsiveness to their language, and that, conversely, explicit critical attention to language does not, as he implies, involve the neglect of "structure," and what he includes under that category. Let me take the question of the "devised chain of events" to which he attaches cardinal importance, or in other words, plot. Plot I take to denote the invention and arrangement of events to show their sequence in time and their connections of cause and effect. In a sense every work of literature must have a plot, since language, being itself extended in time, cannot stand still, despite the efforts of some modern poets to create that illusion. Plot, however, is especially significant in narrative literature, where it characteristically operates to arouse and appease our hopes, fears and curiosity about the fortunes of certain characters. At first sight plot, and the skill necessary to create one, seem to have nothing to do with language, but this is an illusion. It is certainly possible to communicate a plot by non-verbal means—in a silent movie, for example—but scarcely without the assistance of language. For, to take the example of the silent movie, by what other means is the story to be devised and the contributions of those concerned to be coordinated?

The case of the novelist is still more clear-cut. He is committed to language all along the line: the first glimmer of an idea, the first hesitant vague shaping of a possible story, requires not only a lexis with which to name things, but a grammar with which to relate them, and this dependence on language can only become

---

[3] I borrow this formula from John Casey (*op. cit.*, p. 106): "Shakespeare's language is (in some wide sense) a *criterion*—the central criterion—of how he is seeing and feeling, not evidence on the basis of which we can make an inference. When what is seen and felt is essentially bound up with a mastery of language, the language is the only criterion. Macbeth's capacity to feel as he does when he hears of his wife's death is bound up with his capacity to speak as he does: the feelings 'expressed' by the 'tomorrow and tomorrow and tomorrow' lines are inseparable from a mastery of language. To try and speak about these feelings apart from their expression would be to try and talk about a non-entity." In the theatre, of course, the "expression" is not entirely linguistic. But this problem does not concern the novel.

more pressing as the compositional process proceeds. We might indeed in a stylized way describe the prefigured plot as a single, simple sentence which in the
creative process quickly becomes a complex sentence through the insertion of
subordinate clauses carrying further ramifications until the weight of subordination makes these clauses break off into independent complex sentences of their
own, which in turn produce further sentences, and so on, each new development
burgeoning and branching from another, not evenly or predictably, but (the favorite organicist analogy is irresistible) like a tree, until it stands, fully grown, one
huge complex feat of language from root to blossom.

> *O chestnut tree, great-rooted blossomer,*
> *Are you the leaf, the blossom or the bole?*

Well, we all know the answer to that one, and it certainly isn't the seed. So that
when, for the purposes of describing a plot, we try to reduce the innumerable
sentences through which it is communicated—if not to a single, simple sentence,
at least to a few complex ones—we shall not produce anything resembling those
first *ur*-sentences of the foreshadowed novel. Nor shall we produce anything that
in itself conveys the quality or value of the reading experience.

Thus, if we say that it was very clever of Jane Austen to invent a situation in
which Emma thinks that Mr. Elton is courting Harriet when he is really courting
Emma, and Mr. Elton thinks that Emma is leading him on when she is merely of-
ficiously trying to promote Harriet's prospects, we can't mean that this situation
is inherently significant, has any persuasive power, merely as a situation in which
any three people might find themselves. We can only mean that it is significant
and persuasive because it happens to three characters who have been richly realized for us in other ways, because it grows out of and adds to what we already
know of them, and because it is not presented to us as a bald fact, as it appears
in our summary, but as a process, subtly and delicately rendered for us in a sequence of small, perfectly-judged effects. And if pressed to substantiate this argument we should inevitably end up by indicating and analyzing linguistic maneuvers on the author's part.

Now in actual critical practice such explicit demonstration is not necessarily
binding on the critic, but it must always be implicit and, as it were, producible on
demand. Consider for example Percy Lubbock's justly esteemed book *The Craft
of Fiction* (1921). This follows what one might call a structural approach, in that
Lubbock takes "the whole intricate question of method in the craft of fiction . . .
to be governed by the question of the point of view—the question of the relation
in which the narrator stands to the story," and that question is one that, usually,
is decided early in the compositional process and conditions the range of effects
available in a given novel.[4] Using this approach, Lubbock examines very perceptively a dozen or so major novels and enhances our understanding and appreciation of them in the process. He does so without, I believe, giving a single illustrative quotation from his texts. Yet we cannot say that the narrative strategies he
is examining have any life except insofar as they are embodied in these texts, in

---

[4] I say *usually* because it is always possible to introduce a new point of view at a late stage—as late as an epilogue—and thus open up an entirely new range of effects.

language; and he carries us with him precisely to the degree that his own sensitive and delicate use of language conveys to us, or revives in us, a sense of that life. Similarly, our differences with him must appeal to the same criteria, in matters both major and minor. When Lubbock asserts that we never for a moment move outside Strether's point of view in *The Ambassadors*, we must point, for instance, to the explicit appearance of an authorial "I" in the first chapter, and the description of Strether's physical appearance through the eyes of Maria Gostrey in the same place. And when Lubbock claims that the narrative method of *The Ambassadors* is the "ideal" method, implying that it has some inherent virtue which would be conferred upon any novel that used the same basic strategy, we must protest, no, you have only shown us that it is the ideal method for *The Ambassadors*.

To summarize: my position is that all good criticism is a response to language—that it is good insofar as it is a sensitive response—whether or not there is any explicit reference to language in the way of quotation and analysis. This applies not only to the "structural" approach, but to the moral, mythical, historical, psychological and thematic approaches too; and it explains, I believe, why we can profit from criticism using radically different approaches from our own. Does this mean that any approach is as good as any other? Not quite—I must believe that criticism responsibly aware of its engagement with language is less likely to go seriously wrong than criticism which is not so aware, or which denies the primacy of language in literary matters. But I think we have to admit that any given method is justified by the use made of it by a particular critic. Critical methods do not compete with each other *as methods* (they may of course conflict over the interpretation and evaluation of a particular work)—they complement each other. We can see them as competing only if we pursue some phantom of total accounting. There is no satisfactory total account of a work of literature except the work itself. It is only the work itself that presents *all* its meanings in the most significant and assimilable form. We therefore cannot ask the critic to tell us the "whole truth" about a novel, any more than we can ask a novelist to tell us the whole truth about life. Criticism does not—cannot—aim to reproduce the work it contemplates. It sets beside this work another work—the critical essay—which is a kind of hybrid formed by the collaboration of the critic with the artist, and which, in this juxtaposition, makes the original yield up some of its secrets.

Criticism, then, cannot avoid being partial and selective. Percy Lubbock's discussion of *The Ambassadors*, for example, which slices a thin layer off the whole surface of the novel, is no less selective than Ian Watt's article on "The First Chapter of *The Ambassadors*" which cuts deep into one small part of it. They are selecting differently, to different ends. Furthermore, Watt's article presupposes a knowledge of Lubbock's, or rather an equivalent acquaintance with and understanding of the novel's total scope and narrative strategy. And if I am asked why I personally choose, in discussing this novel, to follow Watt's approach rather than Lubbock's, it is partly because Lubbock has more or less exhausted the possibilities of his approach, whereas Watt has not.

"We are inclined to assume," Bradbury complains, "that if we can show that the imagery of cash and legality runs through a Jane Austen novel, or a white-ness-blackness opposition runs through *Moby Dick*, we can show more about the real being of the book than by showing that it deals with a society, with disposi-tions of character and relationship, so as to create a coherent moral and social world and an attitude towards it, steadily worked from page to page." I would say, rather, we assume that the fact that each novel deals with a society, with dis-positions of character and relationship, can be taken as common ground between readers; that we cannot afford to ignore this common ground, but we can afford to allude to it; and that the "steady working from page to page" by which the so-cial and moral world is created and by which our responses are controlled is pre-cisely what the tracing of iterative imagery and the like is designed to explain and illustrate. Such tracing can give us a model, a clue, a key—call it what you will—that enhances our response to the complex original.

It will be evident that a rather misleading flag is flying over this essay. Perhaps it should have been called "Against a Poetics of Fiction." I am certainly skeptical of the possibilities of formulating a poetics of the novel analogous to that which Aristotle formulated for the tragic drama of his time, not only because the novel is a much more amorphous genre than fifth-century Greek tragedy, but because so many of the philosophical assumptions underlying Aristotle's descriptive ap-paratus have been undermined. Furthermore, in the present state of modern knowledge, we cannot expect to agree upon any descriptive or analytic scheme which will serve all the purposes literary criticism may apply itself to. I am far from claiming that the fundamental axiom that novels are verbal constructs yields any foolproof or exclusive prescriptions for critical procedure.

I do believe, however, that if, in Aristotelian fashion, we try to define the novel as a genre by reference to its distinguishing characteristics, we shall find its way of using language the most promising area for inquiry. Bradbury suggests that the novel is distinguished as a genre by "its scale, prose character and matter." It is evident, however, that there is nothing we can say about the scale and matter typical of novels that cannot be matched in poems (like *Don Juan*) or in non-literary narrative fictions such as movies and TV serials. We are left, then, with "prose-character."

Now of course the use of prose for narrative is not peculiar to the novel, but I think we can say that the emergence of the novel as a literary phenomenon—the way it defines itself against earlier forms of prose fiction and, once established, exerts a magnetic attraction over all forms of prose fiction—is closely associated with the use of a certain kind of prose language, designed to render experience in a certain way, for which our handiest term is "realism." This, of course, is Ian Watt's argument in *The Rise of the Novel*, and it seems to me substantially cor-rect. It is, I think, reconcilable with the scheme more recently proposed by Scholes and Kellogg in *The Nature of Narrative*, according to which the novel is seen as a modern synthesis of "fictional" and "empirical" modes (romance and allegory on the one hand, history and fictional realism on the other) which were originally held together in the synthesis of the primitive oral epic, but which fragmented and developed separately in late classical and medieval literature. For while the novel certainly includes all these modes in various ways, and therefore cannot be properly regarded as antithetical to any of them, there is little doubt that realism (what Scholes and Kellogg call, rather confusingly, "mimesis") is the dominant or synthesizing mode. Modern prose fictions with a marked romantic or allegorical character (*The Blithedale Romance*, *The Trial*, and *Giles Goat-Boy*, for example) are distinctly different, in the kind of response they invite, from classical or medieval allegories and romances, even when the latter are written in prose. And this difference, I suggest, resides in the kind of "illusion of life" with which such modern texts invest their actions, however fantastic, and which they derive from the more orthodox novel tradition and the kind of language used in that tradition. I am not saying that all novels are realistic; I am saying that realism conditions all novels.

Let me return to something I said earlier: that the notion that consciousness is dependent on verbal concepts is resented because it seems to deny the reality of non-verbal or pre-verbal experience. This is because as living, acting, responding individuals we are conscious of our sensations, desires, fears, and choices, but we are not usually conscious of our consciousness of them, and to be doubly conscious in that way, at least all the time, would appear to dissipate the unique significance of what we are experiencing. Thus when we fall in love, we are not conscious that it is only by virtue of possessing a common concept of "falling in love" that we do so, and if this is pointed out to us we are likely to feel that the spontaneity and integrity of our emotion is impugned. This is a natural reaction, and it may well be that without the illusion from which it derives we should be paralyzed as regards action. It does not, however, affect the actual state of affairs.

The case of literature is rather different. In most traditional literature, especially poetry and poetic drama, the "double consciousness" I have spoken of is deliberately brought into play—the verbal conceptualization of experience is overtly stressed in verbal artifice; so that in reading a Shakespeare sonnet, or beholding a Shakespeare play, for instance, we are simultaneously conscious of being put in touch with a bit of life, and of having this bit of life presented to us in a particular way, which imposes aesthetic distance on it. Among the various literary forms, this distance is, notoriously, most foreshortened in the novel. No other literary form immerses us so completely in the life it presents; no other form takes such pains to disguise the fact that it is an artefact. There is no need to dwell on the devices and strategies it uses to this end—solidity of specification, continuity with history, etc.—except to note that they naturally require as medium that kind of written language which we use to record and describe actual events, namely the prose of historiography, essays, letters, diaries, and so forth.

At the same time, the novel, being fictive, is committed to rendering experience with an enhanced sense of order and harmony, and this obligation pulls the novelist in the opposite direction, towards a heightened version of experience and a heightened use of language. Thus the novelist is constantly divided between two imperatives—to create and invent freely, and to observe a degree of realistic decorum.[5] And it is precisely this dynamic tension that has made the novel the dominant literary form in an age when, as Frank Kermode has pointed out,[6] the paradigms that we impose—that we *must* impose—upon discrete "reality" come under the maximum degree of skeptical scrutiny.

Arnold Kettle has called these two opposing tendencies within the novel "life" and "pattern";[7] and the history of the novel is very much the history of the compromises novelists have struck between them. "Pattern" certainly includes those deliberate arrangements of events to which Bradbury attaches great importance, but as I have already argued, we cannot ultimately dissociate such arrangements from verbal arrangements. It is language—specifically the language of prose— which has to bear the strain of reconciling the life and the pattern; and the great novelists are those who in very different ways have managed to stretch their medium to encompass both ends simultaneously. I therefore maintain that the explicit analysis of the language of novels is likely to be a particularly fruitful approach. In the case of those novels (perhaps the majority) which accord a high degree of respect to the demands of realistic decorum, such analysis will be mainly concerned with demonstrating how language that appears to serve only the purpose of "life" also serves the purpose of "pattern." (This might take the form of, for instance, exposing the submerged imagery of cash and legality in a Jane Austen novel. But imagery is only one—perhaps the most obvious and accessible—kind of linguistic patterning which we can examine: the more closely we look, the more apparent it becomes that there is no aspect of Jane Austen's language that is innocent of persuasive purpose, that her choices of diction and syntax are at every point creating, ordering and judging the experience she offers to us.) As, particularly in the twentieth century, the notion of "reality" on which the novel's realism was based, is called more and more into question, that kind of prose language which, I have suggested, is the staple of the novelist's medium, is more and more thickly overlaid with "poetic" kinds of linguistic patterning, in an effort to render the flow of interior consciousness, or the operation of the individual and collective unconscious, or the life of visions, hallucinations and dreams. Joyce's progress from *Dubliners* to *Finnegans Wake* epitomizes the movement, and with fiction that belongs to the latter end of this spectrum there is not likely to be any argument that the critic is dealing with verbal artefacts. Indeed, with many such works, the critic is likely to find his earlier task inverted: that is, he may now be concerned to show that language which appears to serve

---

[5] What I mean by this second imperative can be illustrated by another quotation from Flaubert, writing to a friend in 1856: "Try, my good fellow, and send me by next Sunday, or sooner if you can, the following morsels of medical information. They are going up the slopes, Homais is looking at the blind man with the bleeding eyes (you know the mask) and he makes him a speech; he uses scientific words, thinks that he can cure him, and gives him his address. It is, of course, necessary that Homais should make a mistake, for the poor beast is incurable. If you have not enough in your medicine-bag to supply me with the material for five or six sturdy lines, draw from Follin and send it to me." From J. C. Turner, *Gustave Flaubert as seen in his Works and Correspondence* (1895), reprinted by Ellmann and Feidelson, *op. cit.*, p. 243.

[6] See Frank Kermode, *The Sense of an Ending* (London, 1967), especially chaps. 5 and 6.

[7] See Arnold Kettle, *An Introduction to the English Novel* (London, 1951), I, chap. 1.

only the purpose of "pattern" also serves the purpose of "life." I hope this makes it clear that in recommending an approach to the novel through language I am not seeking to deny or sever its connection with "life," but merely asking that the crucial role of language in presenting life to us in literary fiction be adequately recognized.

# An Approach through History*

FRANK KERMODE

There has been a great expansion in the number of books about the novel as a genre, but so far as I can see they stick to the prescribed terms of reference, working within the limits of the "subject" rather than asking how this kind of literature matches other activities of the modern mind. Ours is peculiarly the subject which can intensify linguistic perception, but it is nevertheless a subject which has open frontiers with almost all others. We cannot allow the traversing of these frontiers to be a matter of daytrips.

Our procedures are likely to be changing in so far as they are healthy and useful. It is certain that we do, and that as writers and teachers, we ought to erect and abandon explanatory and evaluative terminologies rather freely; they have no absolute value, and if fossilized they tend to enclose us in the subject, diminish the relevance of literature to anything else, and close our eyes to the change which is integral to our studies. Since we cannot simply dismiss this as an inexplicable movement of taste, we may often need new terminologies to explain our preferences. It seems to me to make very little sense to argue that we can read *Middlemarch* better than Leslie Stephen or Henry James, or *Women in Love* better than Eliot (or even that Eliot could not read it because he was not *echt* English as Dr. Leavis suggests). We change our critical language to explain our higher valuation, but are aware that we are thinking about the same book. How can we assume this? Presumably because there is somewhere an accessible *Middlemarch* structure, or a *Women in Love* structure, a radical set we all know, and which may suit us better than it did earlier readers. If so, it might help to consider such novels in their *historical* and *typical* aspects. I will try to explain what they are.

There are some obvious ways in which a novel resembles an historical narrative. A narrative is a structure imposed upon events, "grouping some of them together with others, and ruling out some as lacking relevance."[2] How do we know whether or not an event would lack relevance and so be excluded either by novelist or historian? The relevance is determined by the interests and knowledge of the maker; it may be part of his business to establish it where it had not been suspected before. For instance, a medieval historian will relate dancing-madness, by hindsight, to the symptoms of ergotism, a diagnosis formerly impossible; or the collapse of the feudal system to the labor shortage following the Black Death. The barest chronicle is animated by some such sense of relevance, an ascribing of cause or motive. The historian postulates some kind of story, on the basis of a set of records, and then

---

[1] This article formed part of one of the Alexander Lectures given at Toronto in 1967.

[2] Arthur C. Danto, *Analytical Philosophy of History*, 1965, p. 132.

*Originally published under the title "Novel, History, Type."

seeks further supporting evidence. The narrative link between such events is an historical explanation. It is peculiarly the work of a mind contemplating discrete events. At the time nobody knew that there was a link between diseased rye and insane dancing; and so far as the *OED* knows, nobody ever spoke of the "feudal system" before Adam Smith. Behind such explanations lie general laws. As Gilbert Ryle observes, to find the motive of an action is to classify it as being of a certain type.[3] Explanations are not only stories; they embody some plausible view of the world accepted by the historian as in accordance with known types. They are what come between the beginning and an end of a story; the middle is an explanation, and its structure necessarily conforms to some type or set of types.

Thus it appears that we shall often ask of an historical narrative whether it fulfills or qualifies or controverts a type. Under it there will be some "organizing scheme." The same is true of science, though the determination of philosophical analysts to abolish the difference between historical and scientific explanation won't do. Unlike science, history tells stories.

The affinities between history, thus considered, and novels, are touched on by W. B. Gallie.[4] What we ask of story and of history, he says is *followability*. In a story this involves, as it does in a history, coherence; and we shall not want to follow it unless it has certain other qualities, notably theoretically predictable conclusions which contingencies or the manipulation of contingencies prevent us from predicting. This is what makes narrative explanations differ from scientific arguments and from prophecy. A different kind of *following* is involved. The logical structure of stories matches not that of scientific argument, but that of everyday life. In "following" them we accept or discard suggestions and leads in relation to an acceptable end. Thus the middle though at first it may appear so, is never arbitrary; contingency is humanized (made to fit a human "set"): "there is something . . . due to the peculiar set and structure of our basic interhuman feelings," says Gallie, "involved in the following of any and every story."[5] So insofar as a story works, whether it is invented or based on a set of documents, we shall find that the narrative implies historical explanations, and that these embody human topics and assumptions.

But of course there are also simple *differences* between histories and novels. They are both stories, but novels are made up, contain material which differs from the historical explanation in that it is not hypothetical but fictive. (Too sharp a distinction, of course; *War and Peace* contains historical hypotheses.) And although this material is subject in the end to the same laws of *followability* as historical matter, the criteria of followability are different and probably more various, simply because by association with other kinds of art it is possible for novels to be relatively inexplicit; they do not have to be so overt about whatever relationship between facts they may be establishing. There is a kind of novel from which fact, "history," practically disappears. There is another kind which as far as possible does away with the "end" and so blurs the purpose of the historian's middle.

[3] *The Concept of Mind,* 1949, pp. 86 ff.

[4] *Philosophy and the Historical Understanding,* 1964, pp. 22 ff.

[5] *Ibid.,* p. 45.

All this is true, but not simple. The fact in fiction is a vexatious matter, as critics have lately been remarking. For Fielding *Tom Jones* was a "history," but nobody would without premeditation call *The Waves* a history. The novel is palpably betwixt and between. As Ian Watt says, the demands of realism required the novel to break with other "abiding literary values"; it lost some of the old right to a highly selective criterion of relevance, for example, since "a patent selectiveness of vision destroys our belief in the reality of a report."[6] Others might say the break with abiding literary values came later and in a different manner—for instance with the "open form" twentieth-century novel; Alan Friedman observes that the abandonment of conventional "resting places, eminences and consummations"—the expression is Virginia Woolf's—is what we attribute to such writers as Lawrence.[7] Others would argue that a progressively "open form" is a reflection of historical necessity, either relating it with Georg Lukàcs, for instance, to the conditions of twentieth-century capitalism, or claiming with others, including René Girard, that a certain ironic allusiveness to the narrative types is our only way of asserting continuity under the conditions prevailing.[8]

The fact remains that a degree of "historical" fidelity is something most people still ask of novels. Commending it in Scott, Lukàcs speaks of that writer's faithful account of the realization of historical necessity through indeterminable human passions;[9] and most people would feel this to be a good, even if they disliked the Marxist language and said something else instead of "necessity." Mary McCarthy, in an essay that is probably too sharp in its brilliance,[10] speaks of the novelist as one who has "a deep love of fact, of the empiric element in experience"; fact, she says, "must be present in fairly heavy dosage" and there must be an absence of what shocks the sense of fact: Krook exploding is wrong and damaging, Zossima smelling is right. Krook belongs to another mode, the fable; it would be all right to have that kind of event in, say *The Dream Life of Balso Snell*, but not in *Bleak House*, which invites us to consider the kind of historical explanations for which we prepare ourselves when we are reading a novel. *Factuality* is an essential of the novel, and its characteristic explanations depend upon it. We make the narrative as like an historical narrative as possible, and impose upon it by whatever means relatedness, coherence of a kind that depends on plausibility; the logical situation must resemble that of life.

This is evidently true of *Middlemarch*, for example, and also, I think, of *Women in Love*, despite the differences between them.[11] These differences lie in a reduced confidence that historical narrative can match the historian's (novelist's) own "set." Or, to put that in another way, Lawrence's set is more remote from acceptable his-

[6] *The Rise of the Novel*, 1957 (1963 ed.), p. 31.

[7] *The Turn of the Novel*, 1966, pp. 130–131.

[8] René Girard, *Mensongs Romantique et Vérité Romanesque*, 1961, pp. 314 ff. See also Harry Levin, "Towards a Sociology of the Novel," *JHI*, XXVI (1965), pp. 148–154.

[9] *The Historical Novel*, trans. Hannah and Stanley Mitchell, 1962.

[10] "The Fact in Fiction," *On the Contrary*, 1961, pp. 249–270.

[11] See my forthcoming article on these novels in *Critical Quarterly*.

torical explanations because it contains elements tending to deny ordinary criteria of followability. Thus *Women in Love* has a thematic rather than a narrative structure. The point, touched on long ago by Forster, is made clearly by Anthony Cronin in a recent essay. Why, he asks, should creative prose-writers be enslaved to *plot*? Coherence need not mean more and more fabrication, more and more vulgar concatenation, at the expense of "surfaces, fabrics or personalities."[12] There are necessary explanations which are not narrative at all, and he thinks they are the business of the novel. He is saying, against Gallie, that the logic is *not* that of everyday life; that as art the novel must deal alogically in static images, which are trivialized when inserted into a narrative. There is confusion between "images which exist in their own entelechy" and those "which a necessary motion of the narrative demands"—and no doubt, since he is silent on Lawrence, he would find such confusion in *Women in Love*. He wants to do away with "the trumpery of causation"; his novelist will find what suffices in the random flux, eschew the "merely narrative," the "kinetic." Freed of the photograph and followability, he can render certain types of reality more immediately. We are not to have our attention "teleologically guided," as in Gallie (p. 64), but to contemplate discrete epiphanies or types.

But there may be less difference between these views than at first appears. Historians seek their epiphanies in fact, arranging minor events around a central incident, unique but complying with a type. Novelists can dwell more on the situational logic. Let us look at a specimen, Chapter IV of *The Secret Agent*. Chronologically it follows III after a gap in time, during which Stevie has been blown up. The novelist chooses not to recount this, the historical event upon which the story is founded. Instead he sets his scene in a small café of bizarre décor. Ossipon enters and asks the Professor for information about the Greenwich explosion. But at first we do not know what he is asking about. "Unless I am very much mistaken, you are the man who would know the inside of this confounded affair," says Ossipon. What affair? For answer, a player piano bursts into life, playing a waltz "with aggressive virtuosity." Ossipon is strong and yet weak-minded; the Professor fragile but endowed with the destructive power of a fanatic. This contrast is dwelt upon. They discuss the Professor's policy with his explosives, and his imperfect detonator, and how he has made himself safe from arrest. He could, he explains, in twenty seconds blow up the café. The piano mysteriously plays a mazurka. The Professor expounds absolute anarchism, and his contempt for partial anarchists and policemen. But at last they get to the topic of the Greenwich explosion. The Professor and Ossipon assume that it is Verloc, to whom the Professor has given explosives, who has blown himself up. Ossipon's misinformation, incidentally, is not corrected until he actually sees Verloc's body with the carving knife in it, near the end of the book. As the Professor is leaving, the piano strikes up with "The Bluebells of Scotland." Ossipon follows him into the sordid street: "a raw, gloomy day of the early spring . . . the grimy sky, the mud of the streets, the rags of the dirty men . . . the posters maculate with filth. . . ."

---

[12] "Is Your Novel Really Necessary?" *A Question of Modernity*, 1966, p. 50.

Now of course Conrad was habitually oblique, but this is not one of the novels in which the reader finds himself bewildered about the narrative sequence—it is not *Lord Jim* or *Nostromo*. On the other hand it is hardly the sort of narrative we find in the most progressive historian. The first we hear about the accident at Greenwich is gossip, and we are not even certain that Verloc was not carrying the bomb; later we remember many hints and ironies that implied his plan to use Stevie, but we probably need to read the book again to pick them all up. Nor does this, the central episode in the book, seem to be given high importance. It happens offstage, and we study the evidence—the fragments—with Inspector Heat. Perhaps it isn't important; part of the point is the mindless stupidity of the attempt, the propriety of its having been bungled by a mental defective acting on the orders of a vain diplomat, by the agency of an informer with pretensions to respectability. It takes place, though little is made of this, at the dead center of the human world, at meridian zero. But we are clear that it belongs not to a world marked off by meridians—are they reduced to Stevie's pointless, endless circles?—but to a world entirely without coherence, a world which already echoes the hopes of the anarchists. The chapter ends with another allusion, one of dozens planted throughout the book, to the filth and greyness, the hideous agglomeration of brick and dirt, that make up the great city at the heart of the world's darkness, eater of its light. We shall even discover that the absurd attempt took place in fog. But we first hear it discussed against the background of irrelevant frescoes ("varlets in green jerkins brandishing hunting-knives") and irrelevant, mechanical music. The frescoes and the player-piano have of course no information to convey in narrative terms. Nor are they simply descriptive. They establish emblematically the utter incoherence of the anarchist's world, bringing out a bizarreness new to Conrad (Nostromo cutting off his silver buttons is almost allegorical by comparison; the moon in the sky over the gulf, like a silver bar, plainly so). The relation between these properties and the thematic design of the book is an occult one.

Yet after all it is an extremely informative scene, and in its way a plausible one. It makes us *see*. It explains. It takes us into a region of historical explanation from which historians feel themselves debarred by their primary adherence to the documents. Yet it is recognizably historical; Gibbon would have admired it. Before he ventures, in his final chapter, to set down the four causes of the decay and destruction of Rome, he describes what Poggio said of it in 1430. Poggio's vision takes in the Tarpeian rock first in its original savage state, and then as it was for Virgil, crowned by the golden roofs of a temple. Then Poggio looks at the Palatine Hill, seeking "among the shapeless and enormous fragments the marble theatre, the obelisks, the colossal statues, the porticoes of Nero's palace." Thereupon Gibbon reflects upon the necessary retrogression of human affairs that do not go forward. Then he adds his own detailed account of the ruins: another layer of imperial imagery. But he starts from a chaos of marble, an image of ruin, and imposes on it other images, the same milieu before, and during, its glory. No doubt it is what any historian might do in the circumstances. And he goes on to bridge the gap between his narrative and this image with an explanation, a theory. Conrad simply leaves you to infer a theory, or to collect what is said elsewhere in the book about the structures of civilization and the dark of evil. But there is a theory, somewhere in *The Secret Agent,* a theory which resembles Gibbon's in that it involves imperial decline, "the injuries of time and nature," the hostile attacks of barbarians, the use and abuse of materials. It predicates the retrogression of what ceases to go forward. Only Conrad deliberately falsifies the imperial type, the *urbs aeterna* at the heart of the world. Instead of marble gleaming in the sun, instead of the battered triumphal arch, we have raw London brick and the fog, the absurd fresco and the sinister piano, the government of the dark world conducted in a foggy ditch. The historian gets his effects by explanations of which the narrative content is much reduced and by chronological conflations; the novelist does it more freely. Mr. Cronin's ideal novel would not have the story, even obliquely, of an attempt on the Observatory, only the frescoes and the piano, the jingling crazy cab, Stevie's circles. But for all their differences, Conrad is closer, in this highly wrought novel, to the historian than to the poet.

It seems, then, that philosophy of history is the business of people who teach novels. There are perhaps distinctions we need to make, relating for instance to the difference between hypotheses and fictions; but we cannot allow them to cut us off completely from a neglected aspect of our discipline. We can say that narrative is explanation, and that behind every narrative there is some element related to the human set: some type.

I must now explain why I have been using this word so much. I don't, of course, have in mind mythical archetypes, but use the term in a simple way. General thinking, whether historical or not, has a typological basis, the reduction of experience to some flexible pre-existing set, rather as an alphabet reduces words to its set, or a computer reduces information to its binary terms or analogues. Historians use types whenever they explain anything, as I have suggested; and the followability of any narrative depends upon them.

Thus considered, of course, types may be extremely unimportant and obvious, but before we get to that stage of atomic reduction we have to allow for more organized types, formulae of explanation or coherence which have a certain molecular quality. When of this magnitude they are less easily reconcilable with random events. Thus we have great difficulty with such historical concepts as *Renaissance;* the difficulty is one of matching, and also one of proliferation, for the concept is originally periodic, but acquires, from contact with the documents, stylistic overtones. It is a familiar problem, and I suppose I am at present inadvertently illustrating the difficulty of solving it.

The kind of typology we need in the present instance is a feature of all secular narratives, but we understand it best as it occurs in theology. The authentic Christian typology is actually borrowed by some poets and novelists, such as Péguy and David Jones and Muriel Spark, which makes their books something of a special case, since the ordinary secular novelist has to validate his types in terms of his story, and not in terms of a transcendent model.

The types of the New Testament have of late been a more or less regular part of literary discussion, and what I have to say about them is limited to the question of their relevance to secular narrative of a kind that does not imply a direct mimesis of them. The function of Old Testament events, on a typological view, is simply that their full meaning is available only when they are "completed" by something in the New Testament; this is implied in the New Testament expression, "that it might be fulfilled." Ends give meaning to events which, considered rawly as they occur "in the middle," are either apparently random or have been wrongly or imperfectly explained in terms of a different and less valid philosophy of history. (It is the powerful historical element, of course, that distinguishes New Testament types from the mythological.) Before Christ nobody could know the full significance of the Exodus, or indeed of Jewish ceremony and liturgy. The plot was incomplete; the past takes on a glow of remarkable meaning from the radiance of the end. And a good deal of modern scholarship is intended to show that the New Testament was shaped by this purpose: to the fulfillment of types.

A. C. Charity in his illuminating book, *Events and Their After-Life* (1966) invokes Rudolf Bultmann's distinction between *historisch* and *geschichtlich*—that which can be established by historical criticism of the past, and that which has a vital existential reference to the present (p. 14n). On this distinction, the authors of the New Testament were entirely concerned with those parts of the Old Testament which could be shown to be *geschichtlich*. It is for this reason that we can say the novelist is closer to the New Testament author than to the modern historian, for he too is concerned with the *geschichtlich*, whereas the historian has to concern himself with the *historisch*.

But this must not of course persuade us that the novelist has no care for the *historisch*, nor the historian for the *geschichtlich*. That has been my concern here —the overlapping. As Conrad remarked, "Fiction is history, human history, or it is nothing. But it is also more than that; it stands on firmer ground, being based on the reality of forms."[13] But the historian must also concern himself with the reality of forms. His is a world in which myth and ritual are no longer relevant except as material; but the radical requirement of coherence, the need for explanation, is still with him, and he cannot avoid his types.

An illustration of the *historisch* that must underlie every novel: the moment in *Middlemarch* when Mrs. Cadwallader strangely conjectures that Ladislaw might be a natural son of Bulstrode, a teaparty nonsense that could well have drifted away into the vast limbo of events, rejected as merely *historisch*—as, in *Middlemarch*, the cholera which was originally to have been important is dropped out. But Mrs. Cadwallader's remark stays in because she is able to say, after it has been refuted, that "the report might be true of some other son," which makes it a mock-oracular prefiguration or type of something that does happen in the end. The *historisch* survives because touched by the *geschichtlich*. An historian confronted with a pure piece of *Geschichtlichkeit*, such as the identification of Napoleon with the Beast from the Land, treats it as *historisch*: it tells you that people sought a particular scheme for their feelings at the time. It is when he adds that the tendency to do so has always been very strong, and perhaps speaks of other such identifications in

---

[13] "Henry James: An Appreciation" (1905), *Notes on Life and Letters* (1921), 1949 ed., p. 17.

the past, referring for example to Frederick the Great and Nero, that he begins to use, as a mode of explanation, a typology, though a typology related to historiography rather than to myth.

The exegete, the novelist and the historian are all doing their own things, and we easily see very sharp and obvious distinctions between them; so we rarely think of them all together, rarely consider the remarkable and complicated resemblances. At a time when we are required to give scrupulous attention to factuality, to the *historisch*, the novelist still has a certain license in respect to types. It may be that his structure of type is in some ways analogous to a mythic event, suggesting the degree of social or psychological stability we are prepared to put up with in a reality we try to think of as structureless, the amount of cosmos we will allow in what we take to be chaos. More positively, he is concerned with "what suffices" when "romantic tenements of rose and ice" are no longer habitable. And this means that there are resemblances to biblical typology, especially in its modern form (which is as much like its medieval form as *Ulysses* is like a Gothic cathedral). But we may also reflect that the novel belongs to an epoch of history; we may say of it what Charity says of the Jews, that it has emigrated from myth into history.[14] Like the New Testament, it is on the side of contemporaneity; but it is the types that make it possible for the past to possess contemporaneity alike for the Jews, the New Testament, and the novel. Types are indices of contemporaneity, not of mythical content. Mr. Charity observes that this typology "brought man into encounter with God not to restore the *status quo*, but to make present to him an altogether new status, which takes him away from natural into historic existence, investing him with a new freedom and a new burden of responsibility."[15] The patterns of Old and New Testament typology are repeated in the novel—the form of narrative most sensitive now to change and to contemporaneity, most involved with new problems of freedom and responsibility, with explanations of the unfollowable world. In it things happen as they happen, though they can be made typical; its motto might be St. Paul's "all these things happened . . . symbolically [*typikos*] . . . upon us the fulfillment of the ages are come." But its second motto is Conrad's, "Fiction is history, *human* history, or it is nothing."

It follows, I think, that the study of the novel ought to involve more than structures of research or terminology proper to itself. In the limited instances under discussion it appears already that the novel ought also to be considered a branch of a wider subject, involving other kinds of fiction, other historical and typological enquiries. Perhaps it should even be considered in relation to the typologies of the sociologists and the psychologists, even the mathematicians. It seems possible that we have been somewhat provincial in determining the scope of our critical interests.

---

[14] *Events and Their After-Life*, p. 17.

[15] *Ibid.*, p. 56.

# An Approach through Narrative

BARBARA HARDY

My approach through *narrative* is set forward neither as primary nor comprehensive but as locally illuminating. My argument is that narrative, like lyric or dance, is not to be regarded as an aesthetic invention used by artists to control, manipulate, and order experience, but as a primary act of mind transferred to art from life. The novel merely heightens, isolates, and analyzes the narrative motions of human consciousness. One might say that the novelists have been more concerned with this element of fiction than the critics, and indeed the main point of this essay is to suggest that we go to novels to find out about narrative. Novelists have for a long time known enough about the narrative mode to be able to work in it, criticize it, and even play with it. Sterne juggles, shows off, and teases us in a form which draws special attention to its own nature—and ever since, novelists have been dislocating, inverting, attenuating, and analyzing narrative. The uses and dislocations exist in a pre-aesthetic state in routine acts of human consciousness, and the "analysis" is not narrowly literary but extends to the whole range of psychic narratives.

I take for granted the ways in which storytelling engages our interest, curiosity, fear, tensions, expectation, and sense of order. What concern me here are the qualities which fictional narrative shares with that inner and outer storytelling that plays a major role in our sleeping and waking lives. For we dream in narrative, daydream in narrative, remember, anticipate, hope, despair, believe, doubt, plan, revise, criticize, construct, gossip, learn, hate, and love by narrative. In order really to live, we make up stories about ourselves and others, about the personal as well as the social past and future.

I set out this long, incomplete, and highly obvious list not simply to point to the narrative structure of acts of mind but to suggest the deficiency of our commonly posited antagonism between dream and realistic vision. Educationalists still suggest that the process of maturation involves a movement out of the fantasy-life into a vision of life "as it is." Teachers have even constructed syllabi on the assumption that we begin with fairytales and daydreams and work gradually into realistic modes. John Stuart Mill, with his feelings restored by the poetry of Wordsworth, took the love of narrative to be characteristic of the infancy of men and societies. F. R. Leavis and his followers are stern about immature and indulgent fantasy in literature. There is a widespread and, I suggest, dubious but understandable assumption on the part of wishful believers in life-enhancement that human beings begin by telling themselves fairytales and end by telling truths.

If we apply some introspection it looks rather more as if we go on oscillating between fairytale and truth, dream and waking. Fantasy-life does not come to an end at eighteen but goes on working together with the more life-orientated modes of planning, faithful remembering, and rational appraisal. We can distinguish the extremes of cut-off indulgent fantasy and faithful document, but the many inter-mediate states blur the distinction and are compounded of fantasy and realism. The element of dream can be sterile and dangerously in-turned; it can also pene-trate deeply and accept a wide range of disturbing and irrational experience that cannot easily, if at all, be accepted, ordered, understood, or reconstructed co-herently and dispassionately. Dream can debilitate, but its subversive discontents are vital for personal and social development. It can provide escape or a look at the unwished-for worst. It lends imagination to the otherwise limited motions of faithful memory and rational planning. It acts on future, joining it with past. It creates, maintains, and transforms our relationships: we come to know each other by telling, untelling, believing, and disbelieving stories about each other's pasts, futures, and identities. Dream probes and questions what can be the static and overly rational stories about past, future, and identity, and is in the process itself steadied and rationally eroded. We tell stories in order to escape from the stub-bornness of identity, as Randall Jarrell reminds us:

> *What some escape to, some escape: if we find Swann's*
> *Way better than our own, and trudge on at the back*
> *Of the north wind to—to—somewhere east*
> *Of the sun, west of the moon, it is because we live*
>
> *By trading another's sorrow for our own; another's*
> *Impossibilities, still unbelieved in, for our own. . . .*
> *'I am myself still?' For a little while, forget:*
> *The world's selves cure that short disease, myself,*
> *And we see bending to us, dewy-eyed, the great*
> *CHANGE, dear to all things not to themselves endeared.*

Here, in "Children Selecting Books in a Library," he argues the paradox that to be mature involves escape, or rehearses a non-attachment to self which is perfected in death. Thus we may be engaged in telling ourselves stories in a constant attempt to exchange identity and history, though many of us stay in love with ourselves, sufficiently self-attached to rewrite the other stories for our own purposes. But "escaping" and "escaping to" form only a part of narrative activity and function. We tell stories in order to change, remaking the past in a constant and not always barren *esprit d'escalier*. The polarity between fantasy and reality is another in-stance of convenient fiction: we look back to go forward or to stay in a past-centered obsession. Like most works of fiction, personal history is made up of fantasy and realism, production and idling.

We often tend to see the novel as competing with the world of happenings. I should prefer to see it as the continuation, in disguising and isolating art, of the remembering, dreaming, and planning that is in life imposed on the uncertain, attenuated, interrupted, and unpredictable or meaningless flow of happenings. Real life may have the disjointedness of a series of short stories, told by someone like Katherine Mansfield, but seldom has the continuity of a novel. Recollection of happenings, which removes certain parts for various conscious and unconscious motives, is the best life-model for the novel. We do not grow out of telling stories.

What consequences are involved in seeing fictional narrative as continuous with narrative action and reaction? One might be the erosion of our favorite distinction between fantasy and reality. The best fantasists, as we know from introspection or from *Emma,* work in starkly realistic terms, staying in the drawing-room, using the minutiae of everyday dress and dialogue. Another consequence would be an increased attentiveness to the combination of reminiscence and anticipation, interpenetrating each other and complicating the temporal relations of beginning, middle, and end as they do indeed in our play of consciousness, which is more like the loose-leaf novel than the Aristotelian progress. Another consequence would be the recognition that while twentieth-century interior monologues are more realistic in form than their Victorian predecessors, earlier novelists represent or symbolize the inner narrative in indirect and less mimetically accurate modes. Joyce and Proust and Beckett use the stream of consciousness in ways which force us to acknowledge the continuities of narrative I have spoken of, but eighteenth and nineteenth-century novelists use the multiple plot, the shifting point of view, the combined impersonal and personal narrative, the person-centered third-person novel, and so on, to represent the same confused and complex fluency of recording. Such earlier novels mime the sheer variety of mental narration, often most explicitly.

Out of many such interests, I take the self-conscious representation of narrative as a starting-point. Art-forms frequently and unsurprisingly discuss and explore the subject of their own mode. Narratives and dramas are often *about* making up stories and playing roles. The novel is introverted in this sense, not because novels tend to be about novels, but because they tend to be about the larger narrative structure of consciousness, and the value and dangers involved in narrative modes of invention, dream, causal projection, and so on. Sterne shows this introversion in a highly literary way, and his play, like most, is based on certainties, or at all events starts off from theories which are locally or temporarily entertained as exploratory hypotheses. When in *Tristram Shandy* he plays with the complexities of authorial voice, generality, omniscience, completion, chronological order, and biography, he reveals the complexities of such conventions by exaggeration, distortion, suspension, and isolation. Our attention is engaged with such narrative means in a play which temporarily and wittily presents them as ends. In order to perform such virtuoso acts of distortion and separation Sterne has had to identify, judge, and analyze as persistently and closely as any Hypercritic. Narrative—analyzed and judged in the chronological displacements—is revealed as a coherence and a solicitation of curiosity, a movement towards completion. The very incoherence, the tantalizing, and the incompleteness unbare characteristics of narrative and also mime the complexity of the process in the primary act of consciousness. Tristram is both a novelist and an informal presenter, his medium close to the medium of interior monologue. He "unrealistically" interrupts his story over and over again, refuses to let us read straight through, frustrates and plays with our desire to learn, know, keep to the point, and come to a conclusion. The form is only unrealistic or artificial when contrasted with other narratives; set beside the multiplicity and complexity of psychic narration it is close to life. Unrealistic, rather, is the story that has its say for good long stretches, the story that is isolated, the story that gets finished. One characteristic of most novels is the sheer number of narratives they contain, and *Tristram Shandy's* many anecdotes, stories, tall tales, travelogues, and so forth are small and artificial conventional stories that draw attention to the fidelity of the main wayward stream.

Beckett is perhaps the novelist closest to Sterne in his marvelous combination of anecdote with discontinuous, self-defeating story. Joyce seems to me to mime the life-narrative much less well, and to impose too great a control on fluency and incompleteness, though I know this is open to argument. But all three provide us with lucid criticism of narrative as well as with great narratives. They have analyzed well enough to play. Less realistic novelists, like the Victorians, seem to be caught between the assured conventionality of an earlier age of fiction and the assured brave dislocations of the next. They too are sufficiently in touch with the forms of narrative in consciousness, using them implicitly and analyzing them explicitly, to be worth a look in this context. Fielding and Sterne, in their individual ways, contrast the neatness of artistic narrative with the flux and fits and starts, the untidiness and incompleteness of inner action. The Brontës, Thackeray, early Dickens, George Eliot, and even Henry James, tend to divide action evenly between many stories, and to avoid an encapsulated model of artificial narrative like Sterne's anecdotes or the comic epic or the inset story. Their interest in narrative tends to show itself in discussion. But there may be less obvious connections between their narrative forms and narrative acts of mind. Charlotte and Emily Brontë sometimes drive a lyric wedge between the narrative parts of their novels, and their use of different narrators or points of view shows some reflection of the tension between dream and actual vision, between wishing or praying, and accepting events. The socially directed novels of Thackeray, Mrs. Gaskell, and Dickens show an insistence on the connections and collisions between separate stories, though this is sometimes blurred by the Providential pattern. George Eliot and Henry James, for all their differences in intensity, can combine a deep central core of complex inner narrative—Dorothea's or Rowland Mallett's—with a briefer treatment of another opposing or antagonistic story. James of course differs from all the others I have mentioned in the way he centers the narrative on one register of consciousness while avoiding a first-person novel. Charlotte Brontë and Dickens are especially attached to narrative based on memory; George Eliot and Henry James to the reports of immediate apprehension. Taking in the present might be said to be the basic stance in their major novels. But all the novelists I have mentioned not only reflect narrative forms but also discuss them.

James likes to show the working of sensibility and intelligence in the present happening, but as he so often centers the interest in a spectator, he can show and

exploit a slight but subtle and important gap between happening and interpretation: the narrative contains a narrative of what happens counterpointed on a narrative of what seems to be happening, or what the spectator tells himself is happening. The gap is also present but on an enormous scale and with vast irony in
*Tom Jones* and *Wuthering Heights*. One of James's great achievements is to narrow the gap so that many readers never see it at all, and all readers have to work
uncomfortably hard to see it. One of his major themes is the relation between what
happened and what was reported, expected, believed, dreamed, and falsified. The
self-contemplating narrative of fiction is nowhere subtler and more explicit than
in *The Ambassadors*.

Let us begin with the *locus classicus*, Strether by the river:

> *What he saw was exactly the right thing—a boat advancing round the bend
> and containing a man who held the paddles and a lady, at the stern, with a pink
> parasol. It was suddenly as if these figures, or something like them, had been
> wanted in the picture, had been wanted more or less all day, and had now
> drifted into sight, with the slow current, on purpose to fill up the measure. They
> came down slowly, floating down, evidently directed to the landing-place near
> their spectator and presenting themselves to him not less clearly as the two
> persons for whom his hostess was already preparing a meal. For two very happy
> persons he found himself straightway taking them—a young man in shirt-
> sleeves, a young woman easy and fair, who had pulled pleasantly up from some
> other place, and being acquainted with the neighborhood, had known what this
> particular retreat could offer them. The air quite thickened, at their approach,
> with further intimations; the intimation that they were expert, familiar, frequent
> —that this wouldn't at all events be the first time.*

David Lodge, in *Language of Fiction*, quotes Wittgenstein's saying, "The limits
of my language are the limits of my world." Mediated through the limits of
James's language are the limits of his narrative, but he is explicitly aware of such
limitations, and they form at least a major part of his subject. Our narratives are
of course limited by our sensibility, inhibitions, language, history, intelligence,
inclinations to wish, hope, believe, dream. *The Ambassadors*, like most great
novels, is concerned with the powers and limitations of narrative, and so Strether
is shown here, as elsewhere, as seeing and telling. He has been seeing these same
characters and telling himself stories about them for a long time, and here he is,
seeing them for the first time with the truly alienated vision of the stranger. He is
therefore made to show his sensibilities as narrator. We are about to see—not for
the last time, indeed, in this novel that goes on moving—a climactic collision between what he wants to tell and what he has to see. We see his impulse to order
and his impulse to praise, first in the pure form of a vision of people who mean
nothing to him. The imagery is pictorial and even impressionistic, deriving as it
does from the generalized imagery of painters, painting, and aesthetic vision, and
from the localized context of the remembered unbought Lambinet. But this is the

kind of picture the impressionists did not paint, the kind that tells a story. James, like Lawrence, seems often to write about artists so that he may and yet need not be writing about novelists. Here the implications, for all the trembling visual delicacy and radiance, are plainly narrative. The figures are "as if" wanted in the picture but they come to break down the picture's static composition, do not stay, like figures cut through by the frame, on the edge of the impressionist landscape. They continue to move, to come nearer and loom larger, they cease to be compositionally appropriate to the picture and become people. The stories Strether tells are elegant configurations, and who should know more than Strether's creator about the special temptations of aesthetic arrangement in narrative? But Strether is also moved to tell stories out of curiosity: he does not know enough, he is kept guessing, there are secrets and mysteries. He is lied to by Little Bilham and left by Maria Gostrey, who runs away rather than lie or stop telling the story. Maria says at the end that Strether has been vague. He has also, of course, been benevolent. He is more like a Dickens than a James, trying to see the best in people, wanting his characters to be moral as well as dashing. James's method is to show the special bent of Strether's vague and curious benevolence almost unobtrusively set in a routine process of consciousness. What is there in this passage that is colored by the viewpoint of Strether and his storytelling? He straightway takes the couple for "very happy persons" on the pretty slight evidence of their dress, their youth, the day, the boating, and nothing else. He sees them as having pulled "pleasantly" from somewhere else. But much of what he says and thinks is rightly inferred from what is before him. Strether is not a narrator like Emma, who projects her wishful fantasies and interpretations on to highly intransigent materials. Strether needs more malleable stuff to work in. Just as Jane Austen tells us, as well as shows us, that Emma is an imaginist, so James gives us many explicit clues, long after we might have ceased to need them. Here he tells us that Strether's inventiveness is active: "the air quite thickened, at their approach, with further intimations." The scene is of course created for a narrator by a narrator and the last stroke of irony is that the air was indeed quite right to thicken.

Strether is not the only narrator, only the chief one. Most novels concerned with the nature of narrative—that is, most novels—create tensions between narrators. In *To the Lighthouse* we have Mr. Ramsay, the realist who will not use fantasy and lies even to comfort a child, and Mrs. Ramsay, who will, but who also tells James the terrible fairy-story of *The Fisherman's Wife*, thus making it clear that she is no mere sentimental protector of the child. In *The Mill on the Floss* we have the narrow moralizing realism of Tom Tulliver, the narrow, powerful fantasy of Stephen's desire, and the strengths and weaknesses of dream, moral scheme, and emotional continuity, in Maggie. In *The Ambassadors* Strether's benevolently colored vagueness is contrasted with Marie's truthtelling, Little Bilham's kind lies, and Chad's dazzling evasions and omissions, which show him a master of the kind of narrative that will make him succeed in advertising. We also have within single characters the attempt to attend to what really happens and the desire to change by the pressure of wish and faith. This often takes the most subtle form of the benevolent story: Strether, Isabel Archer and Dorothea Brooke do not move from selfish fantasies towards life as it really is but from self-abnegatory fantasies towards a different story. There is a conflict between the story they tell themselves—about marrying Casaubon, helping society, marrying Gilbert Osmond, not marrying Lord Warburton, living hard no matter how, and so forth—and the harder, more realistic story their author has written for them. Yet in a sense the story these heroic characters try to live does shape their lives too. The ironies are blurred and complex. Dreams are productive when they lead to productive conflicts. Stories need not be just lies.

But there are novelists who show a larger discrepancy between the inner narrative and the novel. Gissing and Hardy write about characters very like the heroic figures in James and George Eliot—but characters who do not succeed in making their fantasy in any sense productive, who indeed fail most bitterly by the imaginative energy involved in telling the story of life as they wish to lead it. Tess is a passive instance, involved and manipulated by her family's narrative, in all its socially significant and pathetic crudeness, rather than by her own energies. Jude is the classical instance of failure of imagination, since the tale he tells himself can have no substance and would have been better untold. Gissing's heroes are often like Hardy's. In *Born in Exile* the hero creates an enterprising narrative and role, explicitly and intelligently attempting to give society what it wants in order to take what he wants. Gissing shows the social impulse to lie, in the extreme inventiveness of the man who is essentially a novelist's creation, who researches for his lie, dresses for it, moves into the right environment, and acts it out, right to the point of collapse. He shows here, as in *New Grub Street*, the failure to impose and sustain a certain kind of story, though in *Born in Exile* the breakdown is weak, coming out of accidental, though probable, discovery, rather than out of socially and psychologically expressive action. Gissing diverts the interest and misses a fine opportunity, failing to finish his story properly, like his hero. Indeed, the two failures may be related. Gissing may fail because he cannot carry through a story about a man who lives a lie—or rather, about a man of such imagination and humanity. His novels are indeed full of more simplified minor characters, like some of the successful writers in *New Grub Street*, who lie successfully by finding the right formula and telling the right story to themselves and others in the right place at the right time and in the right style.

There are also novelists and novels who are more optimistic about the stories people tell, who show the productiveness of fantasy. In Joyce and Beckett we see the healing power or the sheer survival of mythmaking, of telling stories about past and future and identity, even in the face of a dislocation of time and identity. The nostalgias and unrealities and comfort of the dream of youth, love, and past happiness, for instance, are set against Molly Bloom's sexually obsessed repetitions—another narrative novelists did not invent—and against the harshness of infidelity and impotence and the grander nostalgias of the *Odyssey*. In Beckett the human beings tell stories in the least promising circumstances, in the mud, dragging the sacks, jabbed and jabbing: they tell the incoherent story of life as they feel its pressures, with the odd sweet flash of what seems to be memory. The novels of Beckett are about the incorrigibility of narrative, and indeed the pessimistic novelist who wrote a story in which narrative as an act of mind had collapsed would clearly be telling lies about the relation of his own creativity to his own pessimism. Novelists are expected to show the story going on. But in Beckett the productiveness of story, joke, memory, or dream is rudimentary, spasmodic, often absurd. Narrative survives, no more.

There are novelists who are less clearly in command of the relation between the storytelling of their characters and the novel in which the stories are told and discussed. Jane Austen creates novels in which characters learn to imagine scrupulously, and feel correctly, in response to the sense of probability. Her novels might be said to describe the difference between writing a Gothic novel and a novel by Jane Austen, to reveal the assimilation of so much parody and criticism of the wrong kind of story. But Mrs. Gaskell, Dickens, and George Eliot write novels which set out to show a similar process of learning how to dispense with fantasy but which in the end succumb to fantasy after all. And here too, as in Gissing, is a kind of understandable inconsistency: they are attempting what they know, even if they fail.

In *North and South* we have a *Bildungsroman* in which Margaret Hale tells herself a story, a fable about North and South. The novel tests, corrects, and dispels this story and others. The narrative is full of supporting cases, not just of blatant and apparently deliberate instances of differences between North and South, but of people telling stories. Bessy Higgins tells the common story of Heaven, which her father sees as the sustaining fantasy she needs. Mr. Hale tells himself a story about leading a new life in the North. Mrs. Thornton tells a story about North and South too, and a more interesting and personally-colored story about her son and the marriage he may make. Margaret also tells other stories. One is about saving her brother's reputation and bringing about a family reunion. Whenever character comes up against character there is an immediate narrative reaction, and the marked social and regional contrast encourages social fable, though the significant narratives that are tried and dispelled are moral and psychological. Mrs. Gaskell is often said to be a rather mechanical and sensational plot-maker, but I have been struck by the way the heavily plotted parts of this novel (almost like sensation-novels in capsule form) eventually have the effect of showing up the falsity and sensationalism of the stories the characters tell. The story about Margaret's brother brings out not only her fantasy of rescue and reunion but also the lie that she has told herself about her own moral principles and the lie that Thornton has told himself about her moral nature. Mrs. Gaskell was clearly interested in the way we tell high moral tales about ourselves and each other. This novel takes us and the characters through the complex process of adjusting and rejecting untrue and unreal stories.

Yet it ends with the reconciliation of Margaret and Thornton which subsidizes his new liberalized attitudes and activities, with the fabulous story of the financial failure and the legacy. The novel which criticizes sensational narrative ends with the plotting of the sensation novel, and we run up against a concluding fable after all, one which resembles the stories that have been tested and found wanting, in its falsity and its ready usableness.

Such a self-division is not a weakness peculiar to Mrs. Gaskell. We find it in Dickens and George Eliot too. They write novels about growing away from the romantic daydream into a realistic acceptance, but most of their novels—except perhaps *Middlemarch*—end with the dream-conclusion and wish-fulfillment. *David Copperfield* tells the story of a novelist who learns to discipline his heart, and though there is an interesting lack of connection between his development as a novelist and his development as a man, he certainly thinks he learns to stop dreaming by hearing other people's stories and finding the traps and dangers of his own. This is to express the course of the novel too simply and lucidly. The brilliant parodies of calf-love are anticipations, both literary and psychological, of David's blindness, and we follow him into the "real" world. Unfortunately, neither the Wordsworthian imitation of natural sublimities in Switzerland nor the saintly and rocklike qualities of Agnes act convincingly to clear the heady air, and the final harmony of financial, professional, moral, and domestic successes seems more dreamlike and unreal than anything that has gone before. Not only do we move towards a concluding dream after criticizing the dangers of dreaming, but we move further and further away from the real world, while more and more is salvaged by plot and idealized invocation. *David Copperfield* is Dickens's most divided novel, I believe, but a similar self-destructiveness and contradiction exists in most of his other books.

Dickens's attempt to criticize fantasy may often fail because of his personal dependence on sexual fantasy, and because he seems to have been caught between a fairly common Victorian antagonism between faith in the individual and despair about society. Almost the reverse might be said of George Eliot, but she too illustrates the attempt to supplant fantasy by realism, and an interestingly uncontrolled reversion to fantasy. As in Dickens, her characters tell stories to each other, to themselves, try to impose the stories, try to live by them, try to "escape or escape to." She puts an enormous energy of imagination and intelligence into a critical analysis of the stories we tell about life. There is no doubt about the life-enhancing realism she sees as her end: it is unfantastic and realistic. She speaks of gradually losing poetry and accepting prose, and all her novels explore the moral consequences of sterile dreaming and productive realism. She shows the interpenetration of many narrative modes that do not come into earlier English novels: the social myth, the literary fantasy, the sustained and culture-fed fantasy, the imaginative fantasy (Maggie's), the ethically noble fantasy (Dorothea's), and the feeble but still potent fantasy (Hetty's), and the tempting nightmare (Gwendolen's). As an analyst of narrative she stands with Stendhal and Flaubert. But in one novel she too succumbs as Mrs. Gaskell and Dickens succumb.

I neither want nor need to follow Maggie Tulliver's story through in order to bring out the clash between analysis and dénouement. We follow Maggie's progress through the dreamworld of a child's fantasy-life, responding to varied deprivations, sufficiently individualized and sufficiently common. We follow her through the solicitations and failure of the fantasies of literature, myth, music, religion, and sexual desire. George Eliot not only analyzes the individual qualities of the different stories Maggie listens to and tells herself, she most subtly shows their mutual influence, correction, tension, and interpenetration. Maggie's fantasies are not knocked down like ninepins, but leave their traces even when they have been explicitly discarded: we see her giving up the nourishing fantasies of wishfulfilling childish story, Romantic poetry and Scott, and Thomas à Kempis, but eventually each is shown to be a remaining influence, both for good and evil. But at the end, after such a searching and scrupulous analysis, and after taking her heroine into a solitude few Victorian fictional characters ever know, she too falls back into fantasy: the answer to prayer, the healing flood, the return to the past, forgiveness, the brother's embrace, and—most subtle illusion—forgiveness and understanding newborn in Tom's eyes. The novel refuses the prose realities, and saves its heroine from the pains of fresh starts and conflicts by invoking the very narrative consolation it has been concerned to analyze and deny.

Are such failures Victorian weaknesses? The proximity of Providence? We might perhaps look again at Proust, Forster, Virginia Woolf, and even Joyce, and find something like the narrative solution which retreats into fantasy. How often do we as students of politics, self, or literature, make the move from realism back to fantasy again, and translate the despair and pain as stoicism, the madness as aesthetic eloquence, the disorder as a new order? It is hard to stop telling stories.

# An Approach through Genre

ROBERT SCHOLES

In this "age of suspicion" the opening phrase of Aristotle's *Poetics* must provoke a nostalgic sigh, as we contemplate the earnest confidence with which he began—that confidence born of almost Adamic innocence with which he prepared to name the denizens of his circumscribed world: Περὶ ποιητικῆς αὐτῆς τε καὶ τῶν εἰδῶν αὐτῆς . . . (About poetry itself and the species of it . . .). How tentative, in comparison, is our timid "*towards* a poetics of fiction." And how nice it might be if we could paraphrase Aristotle's entire opening paragraph in this manner:

> *About fiction itself and its various genres, with the characteristic function of each genre and the way it must be structured to succeed, and with the number and character of the parts of a fiction and other relevant matters, let us inquire, beginning as nature directs, with first principles.*

But "nature" does not give us directions so plainly any more, and here we are, arguing about first principles before moving hesitantly in the direction of a poetics of fiction.

My own contribution to this argument will be to make the case for generic study as the central element in a poetics of fiction. But before beginning my argument, and at the risk of being stiflingly methodical, I wish to inquire into the purpose of such a poetics. After all, fiction has got on without one fairly well for some centuries; so why bother now? We feel the need for such a thing, I believe, for reasons primarily pedagogical. The spread of higher education has resulted in more and more teaching of literature to less and less interested students, by teachers less and less certain of what they are doing. At present the liberal arts—and especially literary studies—are under strong pressure to justify their existence in terms of practical value to the student and social value to the community. This means we must choose between offering a pseudo-scientific justification of what we are doing in literary studies—with all the deceit and dishonor that implies—and offering a genuinely literary and imaginative justification of the study of imaginative literature. Here is where we feel the need of a poetics. We need to be able to say much more clearly what we are doing with such a thing as the undergraduate major in English—and we need to *do* it better. My own feeling in this matter is that we can no longer justify ourselves in an Arnoldian way. We

---

[1] Robert Scholes' approach through genre was preceded in this series by Malcolm Bradbury's approach through structure (Fall 1967), David Lodge's approach through language (Winter 1968), and Barbara Hardy's approach through narrative (Fall 1969).

cannot say that we are presenting "the best that has been thought and said" so as to equip the student with moral strength and conservative values. Seen clearly, such a system amounts to a kind of brain-washing in which students are presented with ideas about literary texts but never equipped to criticize those texts or produce comparable ones themselves.

How, then, do we justify our teaching and study of literature? We do it partly on the pragmatic grounds that we are teaching valuable linguistic skills, and that literary works, being the most powerful and complex kinds of verbal experience, are appropriate and natural materials with which to develop such skills. And we add to this our claims for literature as a developer of the imagination—the best available means of encouraging sensitivity and enlarging sympathies. If the formal study of English is to maintain its place as a liberal art, of value to a man as citizen or as person and not just as a kind of professional training, it must take as its end the equipping of its students to encounter literary works after graduation, in the midst of non-literary careers and other public and private distractions. Our graduates in English should be, simply, literate—capable of making an adequate response to the best contemporary literature and the literature of the past, and capable of exercising real judgment in reacting critically to the works they read. They should also be sincerely anxious to read—turned on, not turned off, by their education.

In recent years we have made some strides in developing a poetics for the teaching of lyric forms. After I. A. Richards' *Practical Criticism,* a real revolution in the teaching of poetry began—and though that revolution is unfinished and in some aspects wrong-headed (in my view), it has placed poetry clearly ahead of fiction in that many teachers of poetry know what they are doing when they teach a poem, while very few teachers of fiction have an adequate idea of what they are doing when they teach a novel. This, I wish to suggest, is why we feel so pressing a need for a poetics of fiction; and this is the need that a poetics of fiction should fill. It should help us to teach fiction better, so that our students will read it better after they have graduated and left our hands. Incidentally, it will have to make better readers of us in the process.

Now I want to argue that a poetics such as the one I have mentioned should be essentially generic in character. And this means I want to argue that our instruction in the classroom should also be essentially generic. My argument will take up two aspects of the question: first, the reasons for basing a poetics on genre-study; and second, the nature of a generic study of fiction really adequate for the purpose I have sketched out. In making my initial case for the study of fictional genres and modes, then, I should like it understood that I am not advocating the simple-minded, pigeonholing operation which has sometimes presented itself as genre-study in the past.

To begin with, the notion of a poetics of *fiction* is already generic. We have assumed, at least provisionally, that fiction does not work the same way that lyric poetry does, and beyond that, that imaginative literature does not work the way that certain other verbal constructs—which are not imaginative—do in fact work.

The very pressure for a separate poetics for fiction suggests that we feel it to be a distinct genre, with attributes, problems, and possibilities all its own. I agree that this is the case. And I would go farther. I would say that this is so because the two essential things we are concerned with—the reading process and the writing process—are fundamentally generic in nature.

The writing process is generic in this sense: every writer conceives of his task in terms of writing he knows. However far he may drive his work into "things unattempted yet in prose or rhyme," like Milton himself he must take his departure from things already attempted. Every writer works in a tradition, and his achievement can be most clearly measured in terms of the tradition in which he works. The hack or journeyman—whether writing TV westerns in the 1960s or Elizabethan romances in the 1590s—takes his tradition for granted and cranks out works according to formula. The master, on the other hand, makes a new contribution to his tradition, by realizing possibilities in it which had gone unperceived, or by finding new ways to combine older traditions—or new ways to adapt a tradition to changing situations in the world around him. A writer may claim, like Sidney, to look in his heart and write, but he will actually, like Sidney, see his heart only through the formal perspectives open to him. In *Astrophel and Stella*, the Petrarchan sonnet sequence provided Sidney with the occasion to look into his heart, and it lent its coloring to the picture of Stella he found there.

If writing is bound by generic tradition, so is reading. Even a little child must come to learn what stories *are* before he likes listening to them. He has, in fact, to develop a rudimentary poetics of fiction before he learns to respond, just as he develops a grammatical sense in order to speak. In the adult world, most serious misreadings of literary texts and most instances of bad critical judgment are referable to generic misunderstandings on the part of reader or critic. In his book *Validity in Interpretation*, E. D. Hirsch has argued persuasively that

> an interpreter's preliminary generic conception of a text is constitutive of everything that he subsequently understands, and that this remains the case unless and until that generic conception is altered.

The context in which we read the language of a literary work, Hirsch insists, is generic. As we begin reading we postulate a tentative genre, which we refine upon in the course of reading, as we approach the unique nature of the work by means of its affinities with other works that use language in similar ways. For example, if a word or a passage or an episode is to be taken ironically—in a sense opposed to its apparent meaning—the reader must perceive appropriate generic signals in the text. Hirsch's view of the reading process finally persuades me because it squares with my own sense of what happens when I read. It also casts some light on the problems of literary evaluation.

A recurrent tendency in criticism is the establishment of false norms for the evaluation of literary works. To mention a few instances in the criticism of fiction, we can find Henry James and Co. attacking the intrusive narrator in Fielding and Thackeray; or Wayne Booth attacking the ambiguity of James Joyce; or Erich Auerbach attacking the multiple reflections of consciousness in much modern fiction. The reasons for these critical aberrations are most clearly diagnosable when we see them as failures in generic logic. Henry James set up his own kind of fiction as a norm for the novel as a whole, because he was unable or unwilling to see the term novel as a loose designation for a wide variety of fictional types. In a similar though opposed fashion, Wayne Booth set up eighteenth-century rhetorical-didactic fiction as *his* norm. And Erich Auerbach set up nineteenth-century European realism as his. The moral of these exempla is that unconscious monism in literary evaluation is a real danger, capable of bringing the whole enterprise of evaluation into disrepute—which is exactly where a vigorous branch of critics led by Northrop Frye would like to have it. Frye argues that all evaluative criticism is subject to distortion by personal prejudice and passing fashions in literary taste; and is therefore fraudulent or sophomoric. From the same data and premises I should prefer another conclusion: which is, that since even the very best critics of fiction—men of sensitivity, learning, and acumen—can go wrong when they seek evaluative principles that cross generic boundaries, we should consciously try to guard against monistic evaluation by paying really careful attention to generic types and their special qualities. Among works that have real affinities in form and content, a genuine comparative evaluation is possible.

Now I wish to turn my attention to the kind of theory that will answer to the needs and possibilities that I have been discussing. Space is limited, but that cannot stand as an excuse. Either the examples I am about to present will argue powerfully for the uses of genre-theory in the teaching and study of fiction, or my presentation must be counted a failure.

Traditional genre theory has two facets, almost two separate methods. In one, specific works of literature are referred to certain ideal types, in which reside the essence of each genre and its potential. In the other, a notion of general types is built up from data acquired empirically, based on historical connections among specific works, and traditions that can be identified. One is essentially deductive, the other inductive. An ideal theory of fictional genres should work toward a reconciliation of these two approaches, which are equally necessary, and in fact complementary. For clarification, I wish to call my theory of ideal types a theory of modes, using the term genre in a narrower sense for the study of individual works in their relationship to specific, historically identifiable traditions.

A theory of modes should work toward a general overview of all fiction, providing a framework for discussion of literary affinities and antipathies. It should also prove amenable to historical perspectives, indicating broad relationships among the specific fictional genres which have established themselves as literary traditions. With an almost Aristotelian hubris, I will found my modal theory on the notion that all fictional works are reducible to three primary shades. These primary modes of fiction are themselves based on the three possible relations between any fictional world and the world of experience. A fictional world can be better than the world of experience, worse than it, or equal to it. These fictional worlds imply attitudes that we have learned to call romantic, satirical, and realistic. Fiction can give us the degraded world of satire, the heroic world of romance, or the mimetic world of history. We can visualize these three primary modes of fictional representation as the mid and end points of a spectrum of possibilities. Like this:

satire                          history                          romance
|_____|_____|

If we think of history as representing a number of fictional forms which take the presentation of actual events and real people as their province (journalism, biography, autobiography, etc.), the basic fictional forms which existed before the rise of the novel can all be located on this spectrum. But where should the novel itself be placed? Is it more satirical than history or more romantic? Clearly, it is both. Thus, the novel belongs on both sides of the fictional spectrum—a satirical novel between history and satire, and a romantic novel between history and romance. Bringing our knowledge of the actual development of fictional modes to bear on this scheme, we can make one more useful subdivision among fictional shades at this point. The satirical novel can be divided into picaresque and comic forms. And the romantic novel can be divided into tragic and sentimental forms. This more elaborate spectrum will look like this:

satire   picaresque   comedy   history   sentiment   tragedy   romance
|_____|_____|_____|_____|_____|_____|

Here a word is no doubt necessary on the arrangement of these subdivisions. In using traditional terms for the modal divisions, I run the risk of creating confusion because these terms are used in so many different ways. Let me repeat, then, that terms like tragedy and comedy here are meant to refer to the quality of the fictional world and not to any form of story customarily associated with the term. In this modal consideration, what is important is not whether a fiction ends in a death or a marriage, but what that death or marriage implies about the world. From the relationship between protagonists and their fictional surroundings we derive our sense of the dignity or baseness of the characters and the meaningfulness or absurdity of their world. Our "real" world (which we live in but never understand) is ethically neutral. Fictional worlds, on the other hand, are charged with values. They offer us a perspective on our own situation, so that by trying to place them we are engaged in seeking our own position. Romance offers us superhuman types in an ideal world; satire presents subhuman grotesques enmeshed in chaos. Tragedy offers us heroic figures in a world which makes their heroism meaningful. In picaresque fiction, the protagonists endure a world which is chaotic beyond ordinary human tolerance, but both the picaresque world and the world of tragedy offer us characters and situations which are closer to our own than those of romance and satire. In sentimental fiction, the characters have unheroic virtues, to which we may well aspire; in comedy, human failings which we, too, may strive to correct. Comedy is the lightest and brightest of the low worlds; it looks toward romance frequently, offering a limited kind of poetic justice. And sentiment is the darkest and most ordinary of the high worlds. It looks toward the chaos of satire, and it may see virtue perish without the grace of tragic ripeness. In a sense, comedy and sentiment overlap—in that comedy suggests a world somewhat superior to its protagonists and sentiment offers us characters somewhat superior to their world.

This modal scheme, crude as it is, can help us to perceive some affinities and antipathies in fiction. For example, considering a crucial century of English fiction, we could locate the names of some major figures on the spectrum in this way:

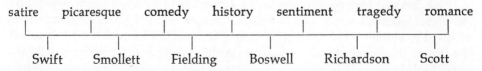

The anxieties that result from this pigeonholing are a measure of its inadequacies. They can be relieved somewhat by locating specific works more precisely. Fielding's *Jonathan Wild*, for instance, belongs well over toward satire; *Joseph Andrews*, on the picaresque side of comedy; *Tom Jones*, on the historical side of comedy, and *Amelia* well over toward the sentimental. Richardson's *Pamela* and *Clarissa* have clear affinities with sentiment and tragedy respectively. But then, what do we do with Jane Austen's blend of comedy and sentiment, or Sterne's blend of sentiment and satire? Clearly this spectrum cannot be turned into a set of pigeonholes, but must be seen as a system of shades that writers have combined in various ways.

To facilitate a consideration of fictional mixtures, and for some other reasons, I would suggest one further change in this modal system, and that is a change in its shape for graphic representation. If we bend the spectrum at its midpoint—history—we can produce a figure shaped like a piece of pie:

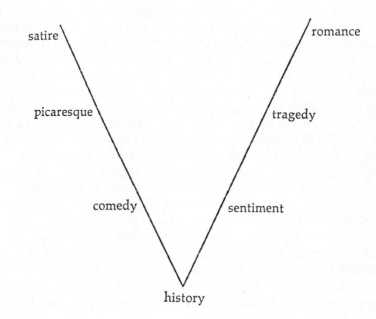

Using this scheme we can not only begin to designate more complicated fictional mixtures, like that of Cervantes in *Don Quixote*, which seems to partake of all the attributes named here; we can also trace certain interesting developments in the history of fiction. Before the novel was developed as a fictional type, both satirical and romantic fictions flourished. We can, in fact, see the rise of the novel as a result of a flow of fictional impulses from both romance and satire, attracted toward history by a growing historical consciousness in the later Renaissance and the Age of Reason. In the course of this movement, the rogues and whores of picaresque became the rakes and coquettes of comedy. The heroes and heroines of romance and tragedy became the men of feeling and women of virtue who populate sentimental fiction. (Fielding and Richardson drew from both sides of the spectrum, but in different ways.) Realism as a fictional technique, then, can be seen as the curbing of satirical and romantic attitudes in response to scientific or empirical impulses, which were also taking shape as journalistic, biographical, and full-blown historical types of narrative. In English fiction of the eighteenth century, we can see persistent traces of one or the other of the pre-novelistic fictional modes. Sterne, for example, holds sentiment and satire in suspension; even though he mixes the two, they never unite in a single solution. In fact, this persistence of primitive narrative modes continues in the English novel into the nineteenth century and beyond. In a sense, a realism which really unites these two broad fictional traditions never establishes itself completely in England. The difference between Stendhal and Balzac and their predecessors in both England and France—and their English contemporaries as well—is that Stendhal and Balzac bring these two modal lines into a much tighter fusion than the others. We can compare Stendhal's blend of sentimental and picaresque elements in *The Red and*

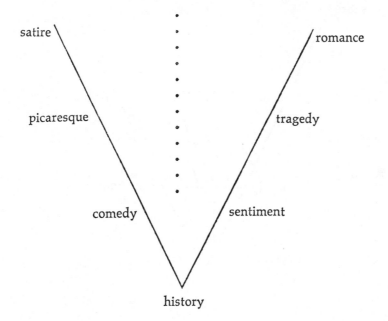

*the Black* with Smollett's in *Roderick Random,* for instance, to see the difference between merely mixing and really fusing the two modes. There is, I think, a value judgment implied here, but a real value judgment must take into account many more factors than a broadly modal consideration provides.

Because the novel as a fictional form has tended to draw from both sides of the spectrum, we can finally reintroduce it into the scheme by representing it as a vague, dotted line slicing the center of our piece of pie (see diagram on p. 107). This will enable us to make a further interesting refinement or two. If realistic fiction first established itself (in the form we now recognize as the novel) as a result of a movement from satire and romance in the direction of history, we can then see the subsequent development of the novel in terms of its movement away from the initial point of conjunction. If the novel began in the eighteenth century as a union of comic and sentimental impulses which we may call realistic, in the nineteenth century it moved toward a more difficult and powerful combination of picaresque and tragic impulses which we have learned to call naturalistic. The realistic novels tended toward stories of education, amelioration, integration. The naturalistic novels have been concerned with alienation and destruction. The novel reached its classic form in the nineteenth century when it was poised between realistic and naturalistic modes. We can represent the area of the classical novel by shading a segment of the graphic scheme in this way:

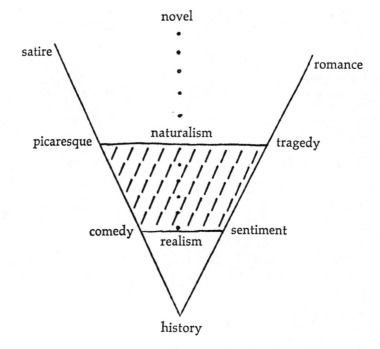

Stendhal, Balzac, Flaubert, Tolstoy, Turgenev, and George Eliot all work near the center of this area. Dickens, Thackeray, Meredith, and Hardy tend more toward the edges and corners.

In the twentieth century, fiction has tended to continue moving away from realism, going beyond naturalism. In this development, the novel has had difficulty holding together as a form in the face of such extremely divergent satirical and romantic possibilities. If this scheme has any historical validity, the natural combination for our era would seem to be precisely those two divergent poles of fiction, satire and romance. Here we would expect a combination of the grotesque in characterization and the arabesque in construction. Allegory would be a likely vehicle for fiction because it traditionally has offered ways of combining satire and romance. In fiction of this sort the world and its denizens would appear fragmented and distorted, and language would be tortured in an attempt to hold the satiric and romantic views of life together. Is this, in fact, the present literary situation?

I think it is. I think the description I have just set forth represents the state of fiction as practiced by our best writers from Joyce and Faulkner to Barth and Hawkes. This modal scheme, then, can help to tell us where we are and to explain how we got there. In doing so, it should serve to make us more sympathetic and open to the varieties of fiction, old and new. It can also serve us pedagogically as a way of teaching literary history as a living and ongoing process, and as a way of putting historical learning in the service of interpretation. A theory of modes and genres is, in fact, the natural meeting place of scholarship and criticism, since both are absolutely required by it.

So much, for the moment, for fictional modes. To come down from the heady, conceptual wheeling and dealing of modal criticism to the painstaking historical study of generic traditions is a descent indeed. It is so demeaning, in fact, that many theoreticians never make it. The weaknesses in Northrop Frye's clever discussions of fictional genres and modes—both of which are modal in the sense used in this discussion—seem to me clearly traceable to his reluctance to face the intractable actualities of specific types and historical relationships. My own consideration of fictional modes is intended to be superior to Frye's parallel treatment (from which I have learned a good deal) because it is more aware of specific and historical generic considerations. But this does not solve the problem of adequately illustrating generic procedure in a poetics of fiction. Modal criticism, because it starts at the center of things with a limited number of ideal types, is readily demonstrable. Generic criticism, on the other hand, begins in the thick of the phenomena, trying to organize them in such a way as to make a glimpse of those ideal types possible, without doing injustice to a single individual work. In the ideal act of critical reading we pass through insensible gradations from a modal to a generic awareness, to a final sense of the unique qualities of the individual work, as distinguished from those most like it. Generic criticism finally requires more learning and more diligence than modal criticism, a deeper and more intense kind of scholarship. No student has finished a proper initiation into a generic poetics of fiction until he has experienced the gap between generic knowledge and modal ideas, and has some notions of his own about how to reshape modal theory to close that disturbing space.

As an example of refined and subtle generic theory in action, I wish to turn to the country which has given us the word "genre." Northrop Frye, in chiding us for our failure to develop a useful theory of literary genres, pointed out that "the very word 'genre' sticks out in an English sentence as the unpronounceable and alien thing it is." Perhaps we can learn something about how to domesticate the term from those who pronounce it naturally. One of the nicest—in both old and new senses of the word—examples of generic criticism that I have encountered is contained in the modern Édition Garnier of Prévost's tragi-sentimental novel, *Manon Lescaut*.

The editors of this work, Frédéric Deloffre and Raymond Picard of the Sorbonne, include in their introduction a section called *"Sources Littéraire et Histoire du Genre."* In it they draw upon earlier work by C.-É. Engel and M. H. Rodier to place Prévost (incidentally along with Richardson whom he translated) in a tradition exemplified by a lesser writer of fiction named Robert Challes, in a work called *les Illustres Francaises,* which was translated into English in 1727 by Penelope Aubin (and softened and sentimentalized in the process) under the title: *The Illustrious French Lovers, being the histories of several French Persons of Quality . . ."* The editors document with care and skill Prévost's knowledge of both the English and French versions of this work in particular, and beyond that, they trace the history of this specific genre from Boccaccio through Challes, emphasizing the way in which it was modified by acquiring attributes we now recognize as realistic. This genre, which they call simply *"l'histoire,"* received a new impetus with the decline in popularity of fictions of the romantic and the marvelous that became noticeable after 1670. Such "histories" of two lovers, which had been a traditional feature in earlier Spanish fiction, usually appearing as separate narrative units inserted in longer works, became more popular and almost took on a life of their own in collections like that of Challes, invariably retaining from their heritage in Boccaccio and Margaret of Navarre as well as from their status as inserted tales, the apparatus of a frame which introduces the narrator of the "history" itself.

From their careful historical sketch—itself a summary of larger studies—which I have clumsily tried to summarize here, they derive a list of attributes of the tradition before Prévost's contribution to it, which they call "the unformulated rules of the genre." In summary the attributes are:

1. The framing of the tale.
2. The presence of a narrator whose character lends resonance to the style, radically affecting its texture.
3. The development of a narrative prose which has the familiarity of conversation—especially important in a country where the elegant aims of a vigilant academy acted as a barrier to the use of living language in serious writing.

4. Selection of ordinary characters—of "*condition moyen.*"
5. Exactness in the rendering of dates, places, and manners ("*moeurs*").
6. Plausibility in the incidents.

The editors conclude their generic investigation with these words:

> *If we add the influence exerted by* les Illustres Francaises *in showing* [Prévost] *what degree of emotion the genre could attain in its better productions, we will have defined the preliminary conditions which made possible the* chef-d'oeuvre. *It remains to examine the work itself in order to recognize its richness and originality.*

And they devote some seventy additional pages to an exploration of this originality and richness, examining texture and structure with care and sensitivity. Their generic study was merely the indispensable preliminary to a consideration of the work itself—indispensable because it provided the necessary background for perceiving and appreciating the richness and originality of Prévost's achievement.

In a similar fashion David Lodge, a vigorous advocate for giving consideration of fictional language the primary position in a poetics of fiction, finds it indispensable to establish Wells's *Tono-Bungay* as a "Condition of England novel" before demonstrating its stylistic effectiveness; and to refine on coarser notions of "romantic novel" and "novel of manners" in order to treat the texture of *Jane Eyre* and *Mansfield Park*; and to designate *Hard Times* a "polemical" novel which is therefore especially dependent on Dickens' rhetoric of persuasion. Generic investigation is in fact the most precise and legitimate way into the vexed question of the intentionality of a work. It makes possible not only the comparative evaluation of works in the same tradition, but also consideration of the extent to which a work succeeds in accomplishing what it suggests by generic signals to be its aims.

From the broad generalizations of modal theory to the precise discriminations of genre study, generic theory provides a rigorous intellectual discipline, which can hold its head high as an area of academic study, without compromising the essentially personal and imaginative qualities of individual response to literary texts. Considered pedagogically, genre-study has the great advantage of being a clear and orderly procedure, teachable to the neophyte and infinitely perfectable for the expert. It requires both learning and sensitivity, and, unlike some kinds of literary study, it bends all its efforts toward the proper end of a literary education—generating appropriate responses to individual works of literature.

# An Approach through Time*

ELEANOR N. HUTCHENS

The identification of time as the constitutive element in the novel moves us close to a tenable poetics of the genre.[1] Despite our excursions into the extra-literary temporalities of sociology, history, theology, physics, philosophy, and theoretical psychology, and despite the inclination of some of us to lump the novel with other forms of prose fiction when speaking of time in literature, we are beginning to get at the generic secret that yields the peculiar pleasure of reading a novel. Much work lies ahead, however, to show us clearly how the novel takes on the form of time. Two questions in particular stand in the way: what about the apparent exceptions? and what about other forms, especially the short story, in which time seems decisively operative?

When we consider the novels that seem to defy temporal control, it becomes evident that they make up the body of the anti-novelistic novel: that is, every test of the novel is a temporal test. From Sterne to Robbe-Grillet, the writers who strain the genre strain it by flouting a temporal norm. The more defiant they are, the more they call attention to the primary importance of time. Mrs. Shandy's ill-timed question—about a clock, of course—interrupts an action which, like a simple narrative, is expected to go directly forward to its conclusion. As a result,

*Originally published under the title "The Novel as Chronomorph."

[1] Georg Lukás *Die Theorie des Romans* (Berlin: P. Cassirer, 1920) heads the lengthening bibliography of this idea, though it only recently entered the mainstream of Anglo-American novel criticism. Some important later contributors are Georges Poulet, *Studies in Human Time* (Baltimore: John Hopkins University Press, 1956) and *The Interior Distance* (Baltimore: Johns Hopkins University Press, 1959), both translated by Elliott Coleman from the French editions of 1950 and 1952 respectively; A. A. Mendilow, *Time and the Novel* (London and New York: P. Nevill, 1952); Hans Meyerhoff, *Time in Literature* (Berkeley and Los Angeles: University of California Press, 1960); Jerome Buckley, *The Triumph of Time* (Cambridge, Mass.: Harvard University Press, 1966); Archibald C. Coolidge, Jr., *Charles Dickens as Serial Novelist* (Ames: Iowa State University Press, 1967); Frank Kermode, *The Sense of an Ending* (New York: Oxford University Press, 1967); J. Hillis Miller, *The Form of Victorian Fiction* (Notre Dame: University of Notre Dame Press, 1968); and John Henry Raleigh, *Time, Place, and Idea* (Carbondale, Illinois: Southern Illinois University Press, 1968), a collection of essays some of which began having their influence years before appearing in the book. This list represents more a convergence of thought than a line of descent, several of the critics on it evidencing unawareness of their predecessors. Most of them do not, as Lukács does, assert the primacy of time in the exclusive generic identity of the novel, but all offer support to the hypothesis.

Tristram is constitutionally unable to finish any story without mind-boggling interruptions that wreck whatever time-scheme the reader may be trying to cling to, making him more keenly aware of the interrelation of time and action than if he were proceeding peacefully through a chronicle. The opening incident, reinforced by frequent subsequent teasing, goads the reader into seeing his own impatience for conclusions as a brand of concupiscence. He is finally schooled to perceive that time passes significantly not from an action to its sequel but within each action, however small. He is broken of the habit, essential in reading romances and picaresque tales, of reading to find out what happens next, and is taught to read for its own sake the page before him, where the action is not abstracted from time and time does not pass without action but the two make each other possible. Time is not mere successiveness; it is the matrix of life. When the reader comes at last to the Widow Wadman, he is not disturbed to note that her fateful question was asked years before Mrs. Shandy asked hers at the beginning of the novel. He has long known that each action in the book is encapsulated within its own bubble of time, which is clustered with other bubbles to form the mind of Tristram, which thus takes its shape from units of significant time. The reader has learned to pass from one to another through the quirky valves of Shandean association. That these bubbles are ordered not clockwise but Shandy-wise only emphasizes on the one hand their temporal identity and on the other Tristram's characteristic inability to put things in conventional order. Time, then, shapes the book more conspicuously than if events were chronologically ordered. The fact that they are temporally located, so that a true chronological order is implied and can be reconstructed, endows them with the novelistic life that distinguishes them from, say, the episodes in a series of *Spectator* papers. Anyone who doubts the pertinence of such a well-hidden chronology should consider the effect of C. P. Sanger's "The Structure of *Wuthering Heights*,"[2] which, by reconstructing the accurate underlying chronology felt all along by the sensitive reader to be there, did a great deal to validate the book as a novel instead of the wild romance some had taken it to be. Romance or romantic poem: in its chill Lockwoodian frame it may seem to work inward to a center of hot intensity and then out again to the cold, like "The Eve of St. Agnes"; but the book asserts its authentic power with the dream-Cathy's wail—"Twenty years!"—when we first glimpse the workings of time behind the strange Heathcliff household of the present, and it is the assured sense that time has held and shaped everything in the book that gives it the solid novelistic relish we find in it. So with the earlier criticism: as long as it remained blind to the temporal structure, it could not accredit *Wuthering Heights* as a novel.

Much the same thing is true of twentieth-century novels that play with temporality. We come gradually to see Leopold Bloom and Clarissa Dalloway, not each on a single June day in middle age, but as what has happened to the Bloom of Howth Head and the Clarissa of the garden at Bourton—and as what is likely to happen from the present day forward, to those who have come to terms with

---

[2] This landmark in Brontë criticism was first read at a meeting of the Heretics, Cambridge University, and later, in 1926, published by the Hogarth Press as Essay XIX, by C.P.S.

time. In Robbe-Grillet's *The Voyeur*, the central character not only is a watch salesman but must be intent upon time in order to fabricate an alibi; the repeated superimposition of past and possible future scenes on the present only sharpens our sense of time, and the chronology of the alibi underscores the temporality of the present in much the same way as the sounding of Big Ben in *Mrs. Dalloway* and the movement toward and away from four o'clock in *Ulysses*. As in *Tristram Shandy*, the concern with time in these books is obsessive, substituting overt emphasis for the slow cumulative sense of time's power we get in *Middlemarch* or *War and Peace*.

Another seeming exception is the kind of novel that in retrospect appears not to have been set in time at all but to have floated in some realm of the spirit. Yet if we go back to such a book, we are surprised to find that its transcendental effects have been prepared and given their power over us by an unusual attention to time. About two thirds of the way through *The Brothers Karamazov*, Dostoyevsky prepares to introduce a new character, the boy Kolya Krassotkin. After a short paragraph telling the reader that the present time is early November, he begins:

> Not far from the market-place, close to Plotnikov's shop, there stood a small house, very clean both without and within. It belonged to Madame Krassotkin, the widow of a former provincial secretary, who had been dead for fourteen years. His widow, still a nice-looking woman of thirty-two, was living in her neat little house on her private means. She lived in respectable seclusion; she was of a soft but fairly cheerful disposition. She was about eighteen at the time of her husband's death; she had been married only a year and had just borne him a son. From the day of his death she had devoted herself heart and soul to the bringing up of her precious treasure, her boy Kolya. Though she had loved him passionately those fourteen years, he had caused her far more suffering than happiness.[3]

Of those seven sentences, five contain specific information about time. The rest of the chapter relates, at first largely in summary, then in dramatic detail, the life of the fatherless boy up to the present time of the novel, when he is to become Alyosha's disciple and thus complete the young hero's emergence from his own pupilage under Father Zossima. Dostoyevsky's task is to give this conquest impressive meaning, to convince the reader that Alyosha really has attained spiritual authority in the two-month time span of the novel. A character sketch showing Kolya's impulsiveness and egotism, even with the aid of dramatic episode, would not authenticate him as belonging in this novel; nor would his thematic relevance as a father-seeker bring him into its narrative stream with sufficient momentum to move in the Karamazov world. He must have a history giving him both temporal depth and an acceleration of willed action by which he can arrive, alive and self-propelled, in Alyosha's orbit and add his own impetus to the forward thrust of the novel. When the two meet outside the dying Ilusha's

[3] Modern Library Edition (New York, 1950), p. 625.

house, Kolya has acquired full novelistic life in his own right, and we see the meeting in its great importance to him, an importance essential to our acceptance of Alyosha's new status.

The introduction of a new character so late in the book is not the most difficult test of novelistic assimilation in *The Brothers Karamazov*. Temporal specificity goes far toward convincing us that any newcomer, whether an active character or not, has really been alive all the time we have been with the others. Perhaps the hardest test, not only of the author's assimilative skill but of the importance of time in conferring novelistic life, comes with the creatures of Ivan's imagination, especially the Devil. The Grand Inquisitor appears in a prose poem Ivan had made up "about a year ago" and is assigned to the sixteenth century, which in turn is invoked by the citing of certain religious poems of the time—the time being broadly conceived as reaching from Dante to Peter the Great. So, although the Inquisitor enters the time of the novel only as an expressly imaginary character, he is in a sense temporally accredited. The Devil, on the other hand, who appears to Ivan toward the end of the book, would seem timeproof, whether he is actually Satan or only a figment of Ivan's troubled brain. Nevertheless, Dostoyevsky proceeds to endow him with temporal shape:

> *This was a person or, more accurately speaking, a Russian gentleman of a particular kind, no longer young,* qui faisait la cinquantaine, *as the French say, with rather long, still thick, dark hair, slightly streaked with grey and a small pointed beard. He was wearing a brown reefer jacket, rather shabby, evidently made by a good tailor though, and of a fashion at least three years old, that had been discarded by smart and well-to-do people for the last two years. His linen and his long scarf-like neck-tie were all such as are worn by people who aim at being stylish, but on closer inspection his linen was not over clean and his wide scarf was very threadbare. The visitor's check trousers were of excellent cut, but were too light in colour and too tight for the present fashion. His soft fluffy white hat was out of keeping with the season.[4]*

Thus is the apparition domesticated into the temporal embrace of the novel: his hair is *still* thick, he is *no longer* young, he has been wearing his present clothing for some time. He materializes on Ivan's sofa in his own right, entering the Karamazov world fully four-dimensional and ready to fend for himself in one of the characteristic debates of the book, bringing to the discussion far more novelistic life than it could attain either as a struggle within Ivan or as an encounter with a being untouched by time.

Everything in a novel must of course be located in a time scheme that brings it into relation with everything else in the novel. The movement of time, which is realized in the progress of thought, perception, action, and—above all—change, gives everything its peculiarly novelistic life as distinguished from the life it might have in any other genre. To say, as Proust says of his work, that the novel has the form of time is to say that its materials are both temporally fixed (in

---

[4] *Ibid.,* p. 772.

relation to each other) and in flux, taking their successive shapes from the significant passage of time, and that the reader's sense of their actuality derives from his conviction that time has brought them to birth and is taking them on to some maturity. This illusion is essential and, once skillfully created, is hard to destroy: even when Thackeray tells us he is shutting up his box and his puppets, we continue to feel that not he but time has created and ruled Becky Sharp, the Crawleys, the Sedleys, and the rest; even when we return to the point of beginning in *Finnegans Wake*, we have only substituted circular for linear time and are no less impressed with its supremacy; and even when successiveness is discarded as in some current experiments, we go on thinking of time as container and matrix. We hang on to time as the *sine qua non* of novelistic life, and the novelist who tries to wrench us loose is only felt to be trying to see how far he can go before his work ceases to be a novel.

Since all narrative moves through time and any shaped narrative is likely to be temporally shaped, it would seem that the short story or at least some short stories might share the novel's chronomorphism and thus disqualify this as a generic distinction. But in the novel, time contains and molds not only events but all other materials and, perhaps most important, the reader's consciousness. There is a qualitative difference in fictional life between Faulkner's Miss Emily and Dickens's Miss Havisham, although both, arrested in time, live with pathological intensity while normal lives flow past them, and although our understanding of both comes from seeing them at various points in this flux. The difference is that we share a temporal frame with Miss Havisham. "A Rose for Emily," though drenched in the sense of time, still has the shape of Miss Emily, while *Great Expectations* has the shape, not of Miss Havisham nor even of Pip, but of the time of his maturation. Miss Emily is like a monument, observed from time to time but outside the time that passes significantly for her townsman the observer and thus for the reader; Miss Havisham, in one way equally stationary, is very much inside Pip's growing time, advancing and receding and re-emerging in importance as that time proceeds in its shaping of the novel and the reader's knowledge of everything in it. The short story isolates for scrutiny; the novel assimilates for comprehension, with time as the mold. "A Rose For Emily" comprises many elements often found in novels: the strong sense of history, the opposition of the individual and society, the illustration of a turning point in prevailing manners, and the embodiment of all these in the large symbol of the house, one of the persistent central images of the novel. But one has only to set the story beside *The Sound and the Fury* to perceive the difference between time in which a subject is dipped and time in which subject and reader swim together.

Although Miss Emily exists, fictionally, for her curious relation to time, it is the stance she takes, and not the time within which she takes it, that gives the story its form. Could the same be said of Emma Bovary? We do study her as one who has adopted an attitude; or do we? Is the experience of reading *Madame Bovary* one of scrutinizing a static object? Only a reader who has abstracted himself from the flow of the novel and regarded it from afar, as a form in space, can think so. The reader who includes in his idea of the novel the experience of reading it—and if this be fallacy, then art exists only to be thought and talked about—knows that at the core of that experience is the sense of moving through the time that gradually shapes Emma's fate by a series of collisions with her will. Time is reality in the novel and gives reality to all it contains. It is Emma's life, a shape in and of time, that constitutes *Madame Bovary* in whole and in part, the framework of Charles's life providing temporal bounds within which the significant time does its work. Emma Bovary in a short story would appear as a portrait, as does Félicité in "A Simple Heart" although this story spans a long life; in a novel her will, seeking to shape the content of time, must move her into one losing battle after another with time the real and invincible shaper. Again and again, Emma gets what she wants on the short term; it is the long term that brings her successive defeats. Thus time makes all the difference.

The combined sense of enclosure and movement within time, a sense that holds the reader in a kind of symbiosis with the materials of the book, generates a teleological impression that distinguishes the novel from history except insofar as history is written novelistically, that is, under the assumption that time is a shaping force. When Fielding in *Tom Jones* calls novelists the registers of the grand lottery of time,[5] he happens to be arguing his right to treat periods of time at lengths proportionate to their significant content, but in so defining his function he is identifying time with fate in the novel. Whatever in a novel escapes from the strict governance of time—for example a passage of exposition, description, or dialogue either not located in time or too long sustained to seem subject to the action of time—loses novelistic life, though it might flourish in another genre. Characters created on principle, insofar as they are embodiments of ideas and thus immune to the modifying temporal flow, are novelistically inert, because time cannot mold them or their destiny. A novel may contain them, but at its own risk and then only as markers of reference points along the course of its real people. The weakness of the thesis novel is that its action is felt to be decided by an idea, which is timeless, rather than by time. The weakness of formula novels, pleasing though they may be as entertainment, is that the formula (the solution of the crime, the working of the Western code), rather than time, is in command.

In a novel, things happen when it is time for them to happen. For this reason, the genre accommodates coincidence and the unprepared event much more comfortably than does any other. Time brings them; they are time at work. Time will bring many things before the end. Ripeness is all; and ripeness arrives when time and the will of the characters have fought out the matter between them and time is seen to have prevailed, having devoured many of its antagonist offspring but perhaps decided to let some survive—bearing its image, of course.

The supremacy of time over will in the novel can be tested by a book that seems at first to be working out according to carefully documented shifts in human volition. C. P. Snow's *The Masters*, which chronicles an academic election, proceeds along a narrative line that appears to be determined by changes in conative thrust; yet all along this line, one is pre-eminently aware of the movement of time toward an unknown but inevitable election day. Held sooner or later, the

[5] II, i.

balloting might result differently; but time, shaping events toward a temporally defined end, decides the outcome. It is time that transforms Jago from a possible master, a potential imaginative leader, to a defeated colleague, and Crawford from a somewhat alien entity to master. The characters of these men and of those who choose between them exert pressures that only result in their own temporal molding, as material that swells within a container takes its shape. Time presents an outcome that, given the temporal enclosure of the whole, at last seems inevitable. The immersion of the will in the temporal finite yields the authentic novelistic pleasure.

When *The Masters* was made into a play, the pressure of time in the form of a deadline must have remained. Time must have had the same mechanical importance it had had in the novel. What makes the difference between novel time and dramatic time? Is it only that time is the very grammar of narrative, holding everything firmly in the grip of tense? Not only, but perhaps largely, with the addition that the novel elevates time from grammar to rhetoric, summoning not only tense but the full resources of changing imagery and the subjective persuasions of psychological time to enclose the reader as he cannot be enclosed by a play, even one read in Charles Lamb's study, and to maintain a persistent flow of meaning between time and its content. In the drama, wills clash with other wills, the focus being on speech and action. The will of fate or of divinity may shape the end, but time cannot, because the drama does not possess the crucial novelistic means of making the sense of time fundamental. A narrative the length of *Antony and Cleopatra* and spanning the same stretch of time could not be a novel; there simply would be room for the words to weave the temporal web. Conversely, to turn a novel into a play one  must tear away the web and liberate the will. It was perhaps the failure to deal with this fact of genre that kept James from succeeding as a playwright, though others have made successful plays of several of his narratives. The neoclassical unity of time in the drama makes more sense when seen in this light, as supporting a generic quality, than when judged on the ground of credibility. It seeks to poise action on a temporal point so as to deny the effect of time and bring into unrelieved prominence the will and action of the characters. A play is preeminently an action shaped by will, human or superhuman or both, the will making itself felt in speech, action, and event. A novel is preeminently a time-span shaping a variety of time-products, the pressure of time making itself felt through the grammar of narrative and the rhetoric of temporal change, the whole being long and complex enough for this rhetoric to figure forth the experience of passing time. In a play, the major changes that time brings must take place offstage; a character youthful in the first act may reappear with gray hair in the third, or a house new in the first may be dilapidated in the third. What happens in between is the body of the novel, and it cannot happen before our eyes in the 45 minutes of Act Two. It can be much more strongly suggested on film, where the changes made by time can be represented gradually, sometimes in a way beyond the power of human senses, as in time-lapse photography. Much of the intermediate section called "Time Passes" in *To the Lighthouse* could be reproduced faithfully on film, because there is little internal experience in it: the most notable part, the tracing of changes in an unoccupied house, seems to be recorded by some such impersonal medium as a camera, because no human senses are present. The same is true of some of Dickens's temporal treatments of interiors in *Bleak House*. The camera could do them almostly perfectly. Yet, while it can evoke the sense of time with considerable power, film cannot give us the fundamental conviction that its subjects have their origin, existence, and destiny in time. Perhaps because film presents the spatial dimensions to our sight, the temporal one cannot be present in such force as it is when the medium of language gives it, through tense, supremacy over space. The novel is sometimes likened to dream, but this comparison is much more appropriate to drama; the novel is more like memory, a stretch of experience edited by and embalmed in time.

There remains narrative poetry. To reverse Fielding's definition, is the epic a grave novel in verse? No; its elevation requires that something not so permissive as time shape its men and events. The theory has been advanced that time in the novel has replaced old beliefs in powers that ruled mankind from outside of time and society. This is a sociocultural theory as much as a literary one, and it may be socioculturally true. But I think the operative difference for the reader is that whatever allows things to happen in the novel is more liberal than whatever allows them to happen in the epic. In a lesser degree of stringency, the same is true of other long narrative poems that are shapely enough to be compared with the novel: their teleology, matching their prosodic regulation, is too strict to be the work of time. Even *The Prelude*, which in a novel-dominated age might have been *A Portrait of the Artist as a Young Man*, must live up to the claims of blank verse by being supradiurnal—by placing its materials *sub specie aeternitatis* rather than *sub specie temporis*. Wordsworth's memory of getting drunk in Milton's old room at Cambridge is rich novel material, but his choice of form forces him to render it so that he sounds more like one of the ageless sons of Belial, subject to sonorous Olympian (or Sinaic) reproach, than like a particular green undergraduate sprouting in the tolerant nursery of time. And even *Don Juan*, in which I don't suppose anyone detects a governing belief in transcendent powers, is nevertheless held to a standard by its brisk metrical form, which will not let its action slow to the pendulum swing of time and admit the small, casual events that would complete a temporal fabric. The ritualistic quality of verse, generated by its incantation, pulls its materials toward the archetypal, independent of time: part of our pleasure in poetry lies in the sense that it is taking us into an extraordinary mode of apprehending experience, a mode that enlarges or intensifies the particular into the universal, whereas the peculiar pleasure of the novel demands that we feel its particulars to exist in their own right, within the limitations of ordinary human observation, and only by the cumulative processes of time to achieve anything like general or absolute meaning.

The assumption of poetry is that we can beat our way to truth: that by setting up rhythms of sound and imagery we can conjure up the archetypes of meaning. The assumption of drama is that we can mime our way to truth: that by acting out our beliefs we can make the god appear. The assumption of the short story is that we can see eternity in a grain of sand: that a single human situation, properly contemplated, will crystallize into a replica of an ultimate truth. The assumption of the novel is that truth is the daughter of time. The novel avails itself of rhythm, of mimesis, and of the microcosm; but its rhythms are those of time, the great action it imitates is the process of time, and its microcosmic moment renders an image not of the eternal but of a temporal macrocosm—namely, the human life-span.

No matter what length of time the human action of a novel takes—whether it be a day or several generations—its paradigmatic structure is the normal human lifetime. Hence the most durable kind of novel is the *Bildungsroman*, which concentrates on the formative period of life, the youthful experience that sets the trajectory for the rest of the span. Biography, although it is often novelistically conceived and written, exploits for its primary pleasure the love of authentic record, especially the record of a human life that succeeded in adding up to something. Boswell articulates the details that express an overpowering personality; Henry Adams relates his struggles with the actualities of an old and a new society, seeing himself philosophically as a Rasselas testing the claims of the world rather than as an organism growing and decaying by the action of time itself. The life span of a biographical subject dictates the formal structure for the documentation of his existence, and we read biography as document, time being among the facts documented. In the novel the life span is not temporal fact but temporal archetype. The historical novel, which delights at first because its subjection of all things to the sense of temporal period yields a spurious version of the true novelistic pleasure, inevitably fades except in cases like *Henry Esmond* and *War and Peace* where individual human lifetimes achieve and retain an autonomous and decisive interest. In every novel the age of a character, his place on the time-line between birth and death, is of the utmost importance, and the kind of truth is revealed to and by him and the manner of its revelation must have something to do with his age. The Oedipus of Sophocles could be any age compatible with the external facts of his history. So could King Lear, though the pity and terror of his condition are intensified by his being old. Not time but willed action brings revelation in tragedy. The perception of the novel character is gradually changed by the probable experience that time brings, and our judgment of him takes his age into account in an essential way. Mr. Micawber at age 20 would not be absurd; we should not expect him to know that his optimism was ill-founded; but in middle age he is a figure of fun because time has taught him nothing. His young counterpart Richard Carstone in *Bleak House* is not funny but pathetic, the victim of a monstrous system that paralyzes his ability to learn the relation between present and future. The Court of Chancery holds out to him the false hope that time will bring him wealth. Because *Bleak House* is a very serious treatment of irresponsiblity, embodying it in the central image of the Court of Chancery, which destroys lives simply by letting time pass, the result to Richard is fatal. If the tone of *David Copperfield* were darker, the plight of the Micawbers would be seen as sad, like that of Skimpole's family in *Bleak House*, instead of comic; but even in *Bleak House* Skimpole himself, the middle-aged child, is seen as comic. These characters, Richard and Mr.

Micawber and Skimpole, are cases of temporal maladjustment, their dealings with time being decisive in showing them to us as the characters they are. Thus time shapes not only the obvious person in a novel—the hero of the *Bildungsroman*, for instance—but our conception of secondary characters who seem not to develop in time. Such characters are seen as odd for the very reason that they are out of phase with time, whereas other odd characters must be provided with pasts and futures in which time produces their oddness and takes it to its destination. A miser out of Molière or Ben Jonson becomes a Silas Marner in the novel; Nora's husband in *A Doll's House* becomes a Soames Forsyte in the novel; the ruthless conqueror in myth and legend becomes a Gatsby—all submitting to the mitigating power of time.

If the novel is generically chronomorphic, it follows that the best novelists are those who best impose the shape of time. The seasonal patterns and accompaniments; the counterpoint of durability and change, often worked out between a house and its occupants or some such rigid institution as a school or any army and the young people who mature in its grip; the sense of period, openly exploited in the historical novel but also apparent in any novel of manners; the whole impulse and design of the *Bildungsroman*; the cyclic rhythm of the family or regional chronicle; the constant weaving together of past and present through memory, and the steady movement toward an end that seems temporal even in the most radical of our contemporary experiments: through all these the novel gratifies our sense of experienced time, of life as it can be apprehended within a lifetime. Here our sense of time is not of time philosophically conceived but of the passing of time as we know it and yet can never, in the living of life moment by moment, grasp it as the novel enables us to do. The novelist, because he must know how time shapes life, is characteristically middle-aged, as the Romantic poet is characteristically young. Many young writers attempt novels now, but they would probably do better at poetry or parody; the novels that have survived the past have nearly all been those of older writers, and this fact supports the thesis that human time gives the novel its proper form.

Whether genre is really just the shape of an experienced reader's expectations or, as Aristotle assumed, a natural form to be gradually discovered, the persistence of genre in literary history suggests that a work must succeed in its genre in order to attain permanence. The fringes of literature abound in works which, because they adopt some conventional rather than essential feature of the genre they lay claim to, are all but forgotten. Romantic poems pretending to be plays, short stories forced to be poems, and tracts, dialogues, character sketches, and periodical essays masquerading as novels litter the edges of graduate work—often interesting in esoteric ways but only thinly alive. The appropriate form must be found by the writer, and it must be recognized by the critic who attempts a satisfactory answer to the basic question of criticism: "What makes the work good?" What makes a novel good, I submit, is the success with which its materials are molded by time: that is, the degree to which it is convincingly chronomorphic.

# The Problem with a Poetics of the Novel

WALTER L. REED

There have been a number of attempts in the last ten years to arrive at or point the way toward a poetics of the novel, a systematic account of the forms of prose fiction.[1] I should like to add to this discussion by raising the question of whether a poetics of the novel, properly speaking, is possible or even to be desired. Since the critical path is beginning to be much travelled, I should like to post a sign of warning along the way, proposing at least a detour from the route. In a round-about way, a better understanding of the problems inherent in a poetics of the novel can lead to a better understanding of this problematical literary form. Of course many recent poetics are more broadly conceived, dealing not simply with "the novel" but with "fiction," "narrative," or "prose." But as most of these schemes give the novel a place of prominence in the conceptual spectrum, it seems fair to address oneself to this historically significant type of prose fiction and ignore for the time being the wider reaches. It is also true that the term poetics may be loosely used, applied simply to a group of essays on different aspects of the novel by different hands. Even in this case, a clarification is worthwhile.

The term "poetics," as is well known, comes from Aristotle's *peri poetikes*—"on the poetic (art)"—and has become the generic name for a certain kind of literary study. Like Aristotle's treatise, later poetics have involved two distinctive elements: "a tendency toward system or structuration," as Claudio Guillén puts it,[2] and a tendency to establish literary norms and a literary canon. The full Aristotelian system was lost when the second book of the *Poetics*, on comedy, disappeared, but as Guillén has shown, European poetics have continually conceived of themselves in terms of totalities and hierarchies of genres, not simply as series or enumerations. Thus there is a difference between a poetics, such as Frye's *Anatomy of Criticism*, and a work of criticism, such as Brooks's *The Well-Wrought Urn*.

The Aristotelian practice of aesthetic judgment, based on a work's approximation to an ideal form, and the practice of indicating canonical examples (the *Iliad*, *Oedipus Tyrannos*) have also been part of the tradition. Since the later eighteenth century, as the Princeton *Encyclopedia of Poetry and Poetics* points

---

[1] In addition to articles by Malcolm Bradbury, David Lodge, Barbara Hardy, Robert Scholes, and Eleanor N. Hutchens, in *Novel* 1, 2, and 5 (1967–68, 1968–69, 1972) in the series "Towards a Poetics of Fiction," see *Zur Poetik des Romans*, ed. Volker Klotz (Darmstadt, 1965); *Romananfänge: Versuch ze Einer Poetik des Romans*, ed. Norbert Miller (Berlin, 1965); Robert Scholes and Robert Kellogg, *The Nature of Narrative* (Oxford, 1966); Tzvetan Todorov, *Poetique de la Prose* (Paris, 1971); Robert Scholes, *Structuralism in Literature* (New Haven, 1974), pp. 59–141; Jonathan Culler, *Structuralist Poetics* (Ithaca, 1975), pp. 189–238.

[2] "Literature as System," in *Literature as System: Essays Toward the Theory of Literary History* (Princeton, 1971), p. 376.

out, there has been an emphasis on the descriptive, classifying element, after an over-emphasis on the prescriptive and the canonical in Neoclassical poetics. But there is a difference between a theory of literature (or some branch of literature) and a poetics, just as there is a difference between a poetics and a piece of literary criticism.[3] If a theory of literature is primarily descriptive and largely assumes the questions of norms—what is literature and what isn't—it is not a poetics in the true sense of the word. Staiger's *Grundbegriffe der Poetik* is a poetics; Wellek and Warren's *Theory of Literature,* as the authors point out, is something different. The distinction revolves around the question of literary value. Explicitly or implicitly, a poetics is concerned with judging literature according to some standard of aesthetic good and bad—whether the judgment is elitist and restrictive, as in the case of Staiger, or democratic and expansionist, as in the case of Frye. The recent Structuralist *poetiques* of literary discourse, with their claim to a more value-free systematics, may challenge this traditional conception, but I should like to leave this question until the end of my essay.

A final distinction must be made on the historical side. Since the later eighteenth century many poetics have assumed a genetic or historical orientation, static taxonomies giving way to dynamic models of evolution, as in Hegel's *Aesthetik.* But though poetics have been influenced by literary history, they have not been subsumed by it. Renato Poggioli used the phrase "unwritten poetics" to refer to the fact that literary genres and forms inevitably exist in the minds of authors and audience before being codified by critics and theorists.[4] Greek tragedy existed, after all, before Aristotle anatomized it. But once written down, the "unwritten poetics" loses its collective, historical character; an actual set of general habits is transformed into an ideal set of specific rules. It is with the fully articulated systems that we are concerned here. Furthermore, and this brings us to the question of the novel, while there have been many implicit or partial sets of rules available to people writing novels, the novel has generally tried to keep its methods from explicit recognition, or has delighted in flaunting its own conventions. As Guillén puts it elsewhere, "the modern novel, . . . from Cervantes to our own time, could be described as an 'outsider' model that writers insist on regarding as essentially incompatible with the passage from an unwritten poetics to an 'official' system of genres."[5]

It is this sense of itself as "outsider," in fact, that I would single out as the most basic feature of the novel as a literary kind. The novel is a deliberate stranger to literary decorum; it insists on placing itself beyond the pale of literary tradition. The ethos of opposition is fundamental and should not be ignored. It is one reason that the term 'novel' (from the Latin *novellus,* 'news') has proved so difficult to define, a term not even available in most modern European lan-

---

[3] This difference has little to do with any distinction between verse and prose, since Aristotle had specified that either might be termed poetry. A distinction should perhaps be made between "poetics" without any article preceding it, which as René Wellek suggests "in a wide sense is identical with theory of literature" ("Closing Statement," *Style in Language,* ed. Thomas A. Sebeok [Cambridge, Mass., 1960], p. 411), and *a* poetics, with the indefinite article, which is a particular kind of discourse about literature.

[4] "Poetics and Metrics," *The Spirit of the Letter* (Cambridge, Mass., 1965), p. 345 ff.

[5] "On the Uses of Literary Genre," *Literature as System,* p. 127. Guillén has been referring before this to Poggioli.

guages, which unlike English do not distinguish between 'novel' and 'romance.' [6] Most definitions strike one as overly vague (Forster's "a prose fiction of a certain extent . . . not less than 50,000 words") or overly specific (Frye would limit the term to fiction whose narrative and dialogue are "closely linked to the comedy of manners" and whose characterization attempts to approximate "real people"), or else avoid the issue by a historical pluralism, as with Ralph Freedman's suggestion that "it is simpler to view all of prose fiction as a unity and to trace particular strands to different origins, strands which would include not only the English novel of manners, or the post-medieval romance, or the Gothic novel, but also medieval allegory, the German *Bildungsroman* or the picaresque." [7] Nevertheless, the term does continue to mean something to educated readers, as the title of this journal attests. It is the idea of a novelty opposing itself to literary tradition that seems to me of the essence.

The novel, I would argue, is a long prose fiction which opposes the forms of everyday life, social and psychological, to the conventional forms of literature, classical or popular, inherited from the past. The novel is a type of literature suspicious of its own literariness; it is inherently anti-traditional in its literary code. The dialectic of "literature" and "life" is of course relative—"life" may not always have the last word—and it is historically conditioned. As Borges notes of *Don Quixote*, the antithesis that Cervantes posits between the idealism of the chivalric romances and the reality of contemporary Spain has been confused by our historical distance from the text. But Borges also acknowledges that a novelist of our own time would use details equivalently mundane, like filling stations, to oppose the literary.[8] The term *nouveau roman* is a redundancy (now redoubled in *nouveau nouveau roman*), necessary in mid-twentieth century French culture and language, perhaps, but stating nothing really new in the traditions of the novel as it has existed over the last four centuries. From *Don Quixote* onward the novel has adopted an antagonistic stance both toward the literary canon and toward its own precursors—even in novels like *Joseph Andrews*, written in mock-Neoclassical "imitation" of *Don Quixote*.

The problem of accommodating the experience of the present to the authority of the literary past is of course not unique to the novel. All kinds of literature, since the later Middle Ages at least, have felt and responded to the demands of representation, the need to modify or transform the inherited types and formulae the better to approximate the contemporary experience of author and audience. But the novel is distinctive in the prominence and autonomy it gives to forms which are unliterary or uncanonical. I say 'forms' because I do not consider that anything in a novel is truly formless. I agree with critics like Martin Price who argue that there is little "unshaped" material in the most realistic novel, that

---

[6] See Edith Kern, "The Romance of Novel/Novella" in *The Disciplines of Criticism*, ed. Peter Demetz, Thomas Greene, and Lowry Nelson, Jr. (New Haven, 1968).

[7] Forster, *Aspects of the Novel* (London, 1927), pp. 14–15; Frye, *Anatomy of Criticism* (Princeton, 1957), p. 304; Freedman, "The Possibility of a Theory of the Novel," *The Disciplines of Criticism*, p. 65. Freedman does go on to offer a unifying definition of the novel, but his terms become overly abstract and general.

[8] "Partial Magic in the *Quixote*," *Labyrinths*, ed. Donald A. Yates and James E. Irby (New York, 1962), p. 193.

what we find is "relevance expanding to acquire new detail, and the irrelevant detail becomes the boundary at the limit of expansion." [9] However, it seems to me crucial to distinguish between forms which acknowledge their literary standing and forms which claim to lie beyond the conventional literary repertoire: forms of speech (the peasant proverbs in *Don Quixote*), forms of commerce (the inventories and contracts in Defoe), forms of architecture and landscape gardening (the country estates of Jane Austen), forms of the landscape itself (the archeology of Wessex in Hardy)—not to mention the subliterary forms of journalism, the detective story, comic books and dirty jokes which find their way into novels of today in Mailer, Robbe-Grillet, Pynchon, and Barth.

The novel creates the illusion of a dichotomy by establishing different fictional levels, "so separated," as Richard Predmore says of *Don Quixote*, "that the difference which separates them seems to the reader to be the difference between literature and life." [10] It is in these terms that I would rephrase the critical commonplace that the novel deals with the difference between appearance and reality. The novel explores the difference between the fictions which are enshrined in the institution of literature and the fictions, more truthful historically or merely more familiar, by which we lead our daily lives. If we adopt the term fictions in its older, less pejorative sense of 'that which is fashioned or framed' and use it to include not only stories or texts which have been designated, honorifically, as literary, but also the numerous structures of culture and behavior which are demonstrably fictive or mind-made,[11] we can say that the novel is the literary genre which gives the greatest weight to those human fictions— economic, political, psychological, social, scientific, historical, even mythical —which lie beyond the boundaries of the prevailing literary canon. Literary paradigms are not simply modified in the novel, they are opposed by paradigms from other areas of culture.

A more extended example of this opposition might be useful at this point. There is the famous passage in *Middlemarch* in which George Eliot focuses her authorial attention on the match-making activities of Mrs. Cadwallader; she raises the question of motivation and of plot. "Now why on earth should Mrs. Cadwallader have been at all busy about Miss Brooke's marriage; and why, when one match that she liked to think she had a hand in was frustrated, should she have straightway contrived the preliminaries of another? Was there any ingenious plot, any hide-and-seek course of action which might be detected by a careful telescopic watch?" Not at all, the author answers, and uses the image of the telescope, figurative of the conventionally panoramic perspective of the Victorian novelist, as a means of introducing an explicitly unliterary image of point of view:

*Even with a microscope directed on a water-drop we find ourselves making*

---

[9] "Irrelevant Detail and the Emergence of Form," *Aspects of Narrative*, ed. J. Hillis Miller (New York, 1971), p. 75.

[10] *The World of Don Quixote* (Cambridge, Mass., 1967), p. 3.

[11] I adopt this term from Alvin Kernan, who uses it (with no particular reference to the novel) in "The Idea of Literature," *New Literary History*, 5 (1973–74), pp. 31–32, 38–40.

*interpretations which turn out to be rather coarse; for whereas under a weak
lens you may seem to see a creature exhibiting an active voracity into which
other smaller creatures actively play as if they were so many animated tax
pennies, a stronger lens reveals to you certain tiniest hairlets which make
vortices for these victims while the swallower waits passively at his receipt of
custom. In this way, metaphorically speaking, a strong lens applied to Mrs.
Cadwallader's match-making will show a play of minute causes producing what
may be called thought and speech vortices to bring her the sort of food she
needed.*

The "scientific" analogy here appeals to a model of vision outside the literary
even as it acknowledges its own metaphorical quality. The sweeping overview of
Eliot's predecessors—Dickens or Thackeray, for example—is opposed and
criticized by the more limited but more discerning point of view of the biological
researcher; a literary convention is criticized by a scientific one. There are many
other examples in *Middlemarch* of this formal dialectic: the medical procedures
and habits of mind in Lydgate conflict with his melodramatic perception of the
French actress Laure and his sentimental vision of Rosamond; the threads of
Reform politics picked up by Mr. Brooke confound the grand generality of his
Johnsonian view of human nature ("Let observation with extensive view . . .");
these same politics and his journalistic rendering of them transform Will Ladislaw
from a "Shelleyan" aestheticism to a position as an acknowledged legislator of
the world; Dorothea's hero-worshipping view of Casaubon as a Milton or a
Pascal is shattered by the formalization of his jealousy in the codicil to his will.

This unliterary material which Eliot brings into the novel (on the basis of
careful research, one might add) is not simply raw content or subject matter; it is
a fund of structures or codes quite apart from the structures and codes of literature as Eliot knew them. When Milton describes the "Optic Glass" of Galileo in
Book I of *Paradise Lost*, the formal possibilities of the telescope are subordinated
to the forms of poetry, to the epic simile, in this case. When Newton demands
the Muse somewhat later, his theories must submit to the formal requirements
of poetic tradition. Poetry or drama may include a good deal of extraliterary or
subliterary material, but these genres retain a much greater commitment to their
own aesthetic protocol. As a novelist, George Eliot is concerned with "reform-
ing" the novel reader's cultural perception, with expanding literature's repertoire
of forms to achieve a broader representation of human life in society. At the
same historical moment that Matthew Arnold was reemphasizing the literary
canon in *Culture and Anarchy*, Eliot was trying to move her readers toward a less
exclusive conception of civilizing form. This is not to say that *Middlemarch* is a
formal anarchy. As a number of critics have shown in the last dozen years, there
is considerable coherence and unity in the design of the novel as a whole. But this
is a "higher formalism," an organizing pattern which functions on a different
level. It may synthesize the literary and non-literary paradigms in a more appropriate form, but the significance of the synthesis cannot be appreciated with-

out a recognition of how this novel, in its own cultural moment, moves dialecti-cally back and forth between literature and other human institutions.

It should be obvious by now that a poetics proper of the novel proper is a highly problematic undertaking, attempting, as it must, to systematize the anti-systematic and to canonize the anticanonical. The opposition is often implicit, there are of course exceptions to the rule, and it is an opposition which might be related to more fundamental antinomies of the human mind, but I would offer the following generalization: the novel characteristically opposes itself to the view of literature that a poetic implies. Not only does it oppose itself to types of literature more traditional than the novel. As I have already mentioned, a novel characteristically opposes itself to other novels. This is not to say that novelists are not formally indebted to other novelists, but that the rules of the game forbid overt acknowledgement of this debt, except in the form of parody; such is not the case with poetry or drama. "There is need of a book showing in detail that every novel bears *Quixote* within it like an inner filigree, in the same way as every epic poem contains the *Iliad* within it like the fruit its core," Ortega y Gasset wrote.[12] There is a good deal of truth to this assertion, but the difference between the way the epic relates to its ancestor and the way the novel does to its great original is extreme.[13]

This basic incompatability between the novel and a poetics has been obscured and complicated by certain developments in the literary history of the last two hundred years, two developments in particular, both of them specialized but influential. The first was the reaction against the Neoclassical canon by certain German Romantics, who used the novel as one of the banners of their revolt. For a number of reasons, the popularity of Fielding, Richardson, Sterne, and Diderot being a significant one, German Romantics like Goethe and the Schlegels elevated the novel to a new prominence in their counter-canon. Goethe compared the novel to the drama in *Wilhelm Meister* in a way that placed the two genres on a par. Friedrich Schlegel spoke of the novel as "a Romantic book," the epitome of Romantic literature as distinguished from the Classical, and his brother August saw it as the genre which included all other genres. The other development was the creation of a modernist aesthetic which elevated the novel not so much by comparison to other types of literature as by comparison to the other arts, particularly music, painting, and architecture. In a sense, the novel is here projected beyond the older humanistic arena of Literature into a higher, more sacred precinct of Art, just as in German Romanticism there is a tendency to ground the novel not simply in Literature but in a more basic conception of Myth. The most influential figure in this latter development is of course Henry James, although one might mention Proust and Mann as well. Although he is wary of prescribing it, James insists on the high seriousness of the art of the

---

[12] *Meditations on Quixote*, trans. Evelyn Rugg and Diego Marín (New York, 1961), p. 162.

[13] Recent novels like Barth's *The Sot-Weed Factor* and Fowles' *The French Lieutenant's Woman* and older ones like *Joseph Andrews* are exceptions, self-conscious and deliberate, which prove the rule. Cf. Barth's "The Literature of Exhaustion" where he speaks of his own works as "novels which imitate the form of the Novel by an author who imitates the role of Author" (*The Atlantic*, August, 1967, p. 33). Borges' "Pierre Menard, Author of the Quixote" makes a similar point in a more imaginative and elliptical way.

novel. His famous image of "the house of fiction" reveals his desire to establish the novel as a solid and enduring institution, at least as important to the present age as poetry and the drama. In part James is responding to Victorian critics like Arnold, who were not disposed to include the novel in the best that had been thought and said. James demands that the novel be admitted to the privileged circle of culture in response to those who would keep it beyond the pale.

As far as the definition of the novel itself is concerned—the novel as outsider model which opposes other forms of life to the forms of literary tradition—one would have to make some adjustments for the novels of German Romanticism and the novels of European Modernism. In both these movements, the novel now claims more centrality for itself within the sphere of literature and culture, and the opposition is now one between the forms of a semi-sacred myth and/or art and the forms of a meretricious life. However, the forms or fictions of everyday life are still represented in breadth and detail, even as they are being criticized or subsumed by the forms or fictions of art. Goethe shows the petty financial and erotic troubles behind the company of actors in *Wilhelm Meister* as well as their production of *Hamlet;* James insists on the particulars of Strether's Woollett character as well as on the synthesizing power of his imagination of Paris; Proust presents the redemptive world of art deeply imbedded in the snobberies of contemporary French society. Only in what Ralph Freedman has called the "lyrical novel," in Hesse, Gide, and Virginia Woolf and certain German precursors, has there been a significant weakening of the novel's commitment to the extra-aesthetic world.[14]

Furthermore, even in many earlier novels, the opposition between inherited and experienced fictions is not as one-sided as in works of realism like *Moll Flanders, l'Assommoir,* or *One Day in the Life of Ivan Denisovitch.* In *Don Quixote* the literary fictions often come out ahead of the over-confident assumptions about "truth." The barber and the curate, those figures of normative sobriety, turn out to be avid consumers of romances themselves, and Sancho's proverbs are applied with the same imaginative irrelevance as Quixote's chivalric scenarios. A similar ambivalence toward the structures of "reality" (a word that should always be used in quotation marks, as Nabokov says) can be found in *Tristram Shandy, The Confidence-Man,* or *Lolita.* What is different for Goethe, James, and their heirs is that "culture," to follow Raymond Williams' argument, had begun to be seen itself as a form of opposition, opposition to the increasingly dominant forces of democratic and industrial society.[15] Some novelists preferred to join forces with a canon increasingly on the defensive rather than continue to oppose a less influential establishment. Some, and some of the greatest, but by no means all.

As far as a poetics of the novel is concerned, there were no real attempts at official classification until the twentieth century. James was adamant in refusing to lay down rules for the art of the novel. Schlegel's *Brief Über Den Roman* was

---

[14] *The Lyrical Novel* (Princeton, 1963).

[15] *Culture and Society, 1780–1950* (London, 1958). Williams only discusses English writers, but his analysis is relevant to the broader European context.

cast not as a systematic treatise but as a dialogue, a Romantic form which "rebels against systematic order" and which Schlegel himself called "chaotic." [16] Schlegel also ignores the formal distinction between the novel (*Roman*) and Romantic literature in general, in which he includes Dante and Shakespeare. In Percy Lubbock's *Craft of Fiction*, however, we have a genuine poetics of the novel based on James's practice, and in Lukács' *Theory of the Novel* we have a historical poetics of the novel based on German Romantic methods, particularly those of Hegel. The inadequacy of Lubbock's system and canon, with *The Ambassadors* and *The Wings of the Dove* as his *Oedipus Tyrannos*, has generally been realized by now; it was most fully exposed by Wayne Booth's *The Rhetoric of Fiction*, which unfortunately tended to set up a counter-poetics of its own, based not on Lubbock's dramatic model of representation but on a rhetorical model of narration, and which proscribed, in turn, James and other modern novelists for their "confusion of distance." The limitations of Lukács' theory are less obvious; it has been less influential than that of Lubbock, it is more catholic in its tastes, and it recognizes more fully the novel's negative ethos. But while Lukács begins with a direct contrast between the novel and the epic, he attempts to find a synthesis of the two genres in novelists like Goethe and Tolstoy. Lukács expresses his own dissatisfaction with this Hegelian poetics in the preface he wrote for a reissue of the book in 1962. "Suffice it to point out that novelists such as Defoe, Fielding, Stendhal found no place in this schematic pattern, that the arbitrary 'synthetic' method of the author of *The Theory of the Novel* leads him to a completely upside-down view of Balzac and Flaubert or of Tolstoy and Dostoevsky, etc., etc." [17] Both Lukács and Lubbock have particular difficulty in assimilating Tolstoy's work to their systems.

It may be true, as Graham Good claims in a recent issue of NOVEL,[18] that the epic-oriented theory of Lukács is a healthy corrective to the drama-centered theory of Lubbock and others, but as both try to reunite the novel with the more regular, more tradition-minded forms of epic and drama they falsify the nature of the genre. "The want of a received nomenclature is a real hindrance," Lubbock complained, "and I have often wished that the modern novel had been invented a hundred years sooner, so that it might have fallen into the hands of the critical schoolmen of the seventeenth century." [19] The teaching of literature in schools in fact has been an important stimulus to the creation of poetics throughout the ages, as E. R. Curtius has observed.[20] As schoolmen of the twentieth century, dealing with a genre increasingly studied within the academy, we must resist the temptation to order and norm which can easily distort the nature of the material we are trying to teach.

The existence of this ancient quarrel between the novel and literature does not

[16] *Dialogue on Poetry and Literary Aphorisms*, trans. Ernst Behler and Roman Struc (University Park, Pa., 1968). p. 16.
[17] *The Theory of the Novel*, trans. Anna Bostock (London, 1971), p. 14.
[18] "Lukács' Theory of the Novel," NOVEL, 6 (1973), pp. 183–84.
[19] *The Craft of Fiction* (London, 1921), p. 22.
[20] *European Literature and the Latin Middle Ages*, trans. Willard R. Trask (New York, 1953), p. 247 (cited by Guillén in "Literature as System").

mean that the idea of a poetics is simply irrelevant to the novel and should be discarded by all critics concerned, however. It is an idea against which the novel, since it is after all literary in the wider sense of the word, must struggle. If we think not of a poetics *of* the novel but of poetics *and* the novel we may understand better both these antithetical categories. "The theoretical orders of poetics should be viewed, at any moment in their history, as essentially mental codes— with which the practicing writer . . . comes to terms through his writing," Guillén has suggested.[21] If we adopt this more phenomenological view, we can see this coming to terms as an important aspect of a novel, and a significant constituent of its meaning.

Without pretending to be exhaustive or systematic myself, I would say that there are three fundamental ways in which the novel comes to terms with the alien order of a poetics. The first is the realist strategy of rejection: the novel asserts its place not within the literary universe but within the "real" world of non-literary discourse. *Moll Flanders* is "a private history" in which the author has merely edited the style and diction of the woman who lived the life. *Pamela* is a series of letters "which have their foundation in Truth and Nature" and are assembled by an editor. Twain posts the "Notice" at the beginning of the colloquial narrative of *Huckleberry Finn*: "Persons attempting to find a motive in the narrative will be prosecuted; persons attempting to find a moral in it will be banished; persons attempting to find a plot in it will be shot." Form and function are not ostensibly conditioned by literary priorities, as they are in *Paradise Lost*, Pope's *Pastorals*, or, in a subtler way, Wordsworth's lyrics; they are dictated by the types of persons and places involved. In Robbe-Grillet's *Jealousy* the rejection of literary form is dramatized by the discussions of the African adventure novel which take place in this strangely neutralized and non-eventful narrative.

The realist strategy in *Jealousy* shades off into the second way in which the novel declares its independence of poetics, the fictionalist strategy of incorporation and transcendence. Here the novel becomes its own poetics, in a parodic and subversive way, including encyclopedically within itself examples of other genres along with critical discussion of them. The best example of this tactic is *Don Quixote*, which mocks in its preface the absurdities of Aristotelian classification, but which incorporates a great variety of genres—epic, pastoral, ballad, Greek romance, picaresque novel, Moorish history and others—alongside Quixote's chivalric romances and which includes a number of learned debates on literary subjects. Fielding follows Cervantes' lead. Where Richardson declined to write a preface for *Pamela*, letting nature speak for itself, Fielding writes a mock *Poetics* for *Joseph Andrews*, taking up where Aristotle left off and defining the novel, with tongue-in-cheek Neoclassicism, as a "comic epic in prose." Throughout the novel Parson Adams is made to find that nature and Homer are not, in fact, the same. *Tristram Shandy* devours, digests, and regurgitates the whole eighteenth-century system of the arts in its eccentric and unbalanced *paedia*. In *Ulysses* this need to free oneself from another's system by creating one's own

[21] "Literature as System," p. 390.

becomes an obsession; Homer himself is subsumed and redistributed in Joyce's fictive universe. Barth's *Giles Goat Boy* attempts a similar incorporation of the ancients in the modern, though, one may feel, with less success.

The third way the novel has resisted the embrace of a poetics—used by Barth and Joyce as well—might be called the populist strategy of vulgarization. Popular literature, beneath the contempt of a poetics if not beyond its pale, is made to challenge the canonical, as in *Great Expectations*, where Mr. Wopsle's recitation of Collins' "Ode on the Passions" and his ill-fated performance in *Hamlet* compare unfavorably with Pip's obsessional acting out of the patterns of the fairy tale, or with Miss Havisham's reenactment of the creature-creator dialectic of Mary Shelley's *Frankenstein*. Or popular literature may stand in for the canonical and reveal the emptiness of the literary universe itself, which is how I read Emma's immersion in the popular romances and keepsakes in *Madame Bovary*—not as a criticism of this trivial literature alone but as an exposure of the literary imagination in general. More explicitly, Pynchon reduces Classical and Renaissance tragedy to the paranoia of mass culture in *The Crying of Lot 49*.

I would not go so far as to say that all novels resist the claims of a poetics in one or more of these ways. The pressure of classifying and canonizing systems has not always been felt by novelists as needing such specific resistance.[22] I would also grant that for any writer in any genre, coming to terms with the theoretical order of poetics requires a certain amount of struggle and assertion of independence. But the novel arose, first in Spain and then in England, out of the attempt to create a vernacular literature addressed to the middle classes that neither submitted to the Classical ordering of genres and forms nor acknowledged the superiority of that ordering by a traditional cultivation of native and popular modes. The rise of the novel in eighteenth-century England is generally acknowledged and has been much discussed. The rise of the novel in late sixteenth and early seventeenth-century Spain is less widely recognized.

In *Don Quixote* and the numerous picaresque novels of this earlier period we have the first fully developed examples of an extended prose writing which opposes the fictions of everyday life to the fictions of a literary tradition. In *Lazarillo de Tormes*, *Guzman de Alfarche*, *El Buscón* and other Spanish picaresques, the injunctions of the Counter-Reformation against the idealizing and entertaining literature of the Renaissance bore fruit. The prose of the world is played off against the prose of belles-lettres, out of a basically religious reaction against the Renaissance celebration of the nature and dignity of man.[23] In a rather different spirit, Cervantes' ironic genius reacted to the strictures of the Neo-Aristotelians against the popular romances of chivalry, strictures that would

---

[22] Indeed, some novelists—Cervantes and Dostoevsky, for example—profess a great respect for poetry if not poetics, for the orderly, the harmonious and the classical in literature, which seems curiously at odds with their own creative practice. The problem of intention such apparent inconsistency raises—the conflict between genre and individual genius, between precedent and theory, theory and practice—is unfortunately too complicated to be dealt with here, but it should be acknowledged. Although my argument here may suggest it, I by no means believe that the literary code of the novel as a genre acts as the sole determinant of a particular novel's ethos.

[23] See esp. Alexander Parker, *Literature and the Delinquent: The Picaresque Novel in Spain and Europe 1599–1753* (Edinburgh, 1967).

limit the freedom of the artist to imagine, observe, and above all involve the reader in an imaginative world.[24] At a time when many theorists were subjecting the romances to a new poetics—an attempt Cervantes himself was to make in *Persiles and Sigismunda*—*Don Quixote* gave the uncanonical and the unliterary fictions of the day a major voice in literary politics.

Thus at the same historical moment Cervantes and the authors of the Spanish picaresque novels subjected the literary humanism of the Renaissance to its first major critique from within the province of literature more broadly conceived. At the same time that Poetry was winning its battle against philosophy and religion, as in Sidney's *Apology* with its Aristotelian basis, the Novel was launching the literary tradition of the new which was to make serious inroads on Literature, in the classical, canonical sense of the word, in the nineteenth and twentieth centuries. The novel, of course, has undergone a great many changes since Cervantes' time, most notably in the way it has risen in literary prestige. And poetics have changed a good deal since Sidney, becoming less dogmatic, and less influential as well, in their prescription of literary laws. Nevertheless, the basic antagonism has persisted. Now, it would seem, the novel itself is being challenged by a new imaginative medium, the film—though it would be unwise to proclaim the death of our exemplary modern genre. As Wellek and Warren remind us, the evolution of aesthetic forms is not like the evolution of biological species. Old genres never die, they just reach a relatively smaller audience, which may expand at a later time. New genres never take over the earth, they just create new and larger audiences for their art—which may not prove as lasting over the years.

An adequate *theory* of the novel, then, would have to be something more than a poetics; it would have to combine a poetics with a semiotics in order to describe the interaction between the existing conceptions of literature and the conceptions of the non-literary which are brought to bear upon the literary. It is in this context that I would like to raise the question of the adequacy of the poetics of the French Structuralists and their Russian Formalist predecessors for the novel. Critics like Tzvetan Todorov and Roland Barthes have certainly been making efforts in this direction which need to be taken seriously. Robert Scholes has been one of the most enthusiastic about these developments, asserting that "formalism and structuralism have indeed made significant contributions to the poetics of fiction," [25] and claiming that the future of a poetics of fiction from this quarter is large, if not immense.

In the first place, one might well question the applicability of the term 'poetics' to the Structuralist analysis, a term used primarily by Todorov. At issue is not merely the apparent lack of concern with a canon or with aesthetic value

[24] See the excellent discussion of the Italian background of this controversy and its presence in *Don Quixote* by Alban K. Forcione in *Cervantes, Aristotle and the Persiles* (Princeton, 1970).

[25] "The Contribution of Formalism and Structuralism to the Theory of the Novel," NOVEL, 6 (1973), p. 134. This argument is incorporated in the chapter "Toward a Structuralist Poetics of Fiction" in *Structuralism in Literature*, although Scholes is considerably more cautious here in his recommendations of the Structuralist, as distinct from the Formalist, poetics. Jonathan Culler's chapter "Poetics of the Novel" in his more recent *Structuralist Poetics* is ostensibly supportive of the French Structuralist contribution, but ends up demonstrating the inadequacy and/or inconsistency of most of the Structuralist systems as such.

judgments, but the lack of focus on the *literary* specificity of the texts that are being analyzed. Todorov cites Jakobson as a precedent for his use of the term poetics, but where Jakobson insists that "the main subject of poetics is the *differentiae specifica* of verbal art in relation to other arts and in relation to other kinds of verbal behavior," [26] both Todorov and Barthes are more concerned with illuminating literary structure by analogy with linguistic structure. Instead of taking up Jakobson's question, "What makes a verbal message a work of art?" Todorov tends to ask, "How is a work of art like a verbal message?" The terms of his "Poetique" are a curious mixture of categories taken from linguistics and logic and categories taken from traditional theorists like Aristotle and Henry James. In spite of his claims to the contrary, he offers no satisfactory definition of the literary *specificum*, something that Jakobson has been able to provide. Barthes' "L'introduction à l'analyse structurale des récits" elaborates the different levels on which a text and the exposition of it may operate, but the term *récit* effectively levels the distinction between the special and the general use of language that poetics is usually concerned with making.[27]

Nevertheless, one may use the term 'poetics' to describe the systematics of Structuralists like Todorov and Barthes if one realizes that there has been a transvaluation of critical values. The literary humanism of traditional poeticians like Aristotle, Sidney, Staiger, or Frye, is replaced by a scientific holism which explicitly rejects the humanist assumptions. Rather than a defense, the Structuralists offer an attack on poesy, a counter-poetics which takes as its field not "poetry" or "literature" but a much broader range of narrative discourse —popular, classical, informal, formal, oral and written. This is a valuable contribution in its own right and a serious challenge to traditional methods of literary study, but as it deliberately ignores the inherited notions of literary form against which the novel has struggled, it would not seem able to grasp the novel's dialectical nature. In fact, in its opposition to the idea of a literary canon and to the idea of literary value judgment, the Structuralist *poetique* can be seen as a novelization of traditional poetics—a poetics by the novel, or at least by the *nouveau roman*.

In Jakobson himself and in some of the Russian Formalists—Shklovsky, Eichenbaum, and Tomashevsky—there is a more adequate dialectical sense of the interplay between art and the non-aesthetic which could prove fruitful for a comprehension of the novel's ambiguous literary standing. In Shklovsky's notion of "defamiliarization," in Eichenbaum's theory of the evolution of genres,

---

[26] "Linguistics and Poetics," *Style in Language*, ed. Sebeok, p. 350. Todorov also cites Valéry as a source for his use of the term 'poetics,' but admits (in "Valéry's Poetics," *Yale French Studies*, 44 (1970), pp. 65–71) that Structuralist poetics ignores Valéry's emphasis on the creative activity of the artist. Culler more persuasively redefines Valéry's poetics of authorial creation in terms of a poetics of reader response (p. 117), but in doing so he would seem to undermine the systematic and—for the Structuralists—the scientific status of the term.

[27] Todorov's essay appears in *Qu'est-ce que le structuralisme?* ed. François Wahl (Paris, 1968), Barthes' is in *Communications*, 8 (1966), pp. 1–27 and has been translated in *New Literary History*, 6 (1975), pp. 237–72. Both Barthes and Todorov have applied these methods more specifically to individual texts and genres (*S/Z*, *Grammaire du Décaméron*, *Introduction à la littérature fantastique*), but in all of these applications the definition of the literary remains elusive. The works of A. J. Greimas and Claude Bremond, as Scholes points out (p. 96), are even less successful in dealing with the "aesthetic dimension" of their material.

and in Tomashevsky's conception of "thematics" there is an important recognition of the way novels transform not only "reality" but literary conventions as well. Jakobson's "synchronic poetics" would allow for a discrimination between conservative and innovative literary forms in any period. But none of these insights has ever been developed into an adequate theory of the novel per se, let alone a poetics of this radical and protean literary form.[28] It may be, as Frank Kermode has suggested, that the idea of the novel is a provincialism which we should leave aside in favor of a more comprehensive notion of how stories are told.[29] But provincialisms have a way of persisting in spite of reasonable efforts to wish them away. My own suggestion is that we leave aside the question of a poetics of the novel for the time being and look more closely at the way novels place themselves in literary—and extra-literary—history.

[28] The relevant essays are available in English in two anthologies, *Russian Formalist Criticism: Four Essays*, ed. Lee Lemon and Marion Reis (Lincoln, Neb., 1965) and *Readings in Russian Poetics*, ed. Ladislaw Matejka and Krystyna Pomorska (Cambridge, Mass., 1971). The inadequacy of the Russian Formalist theories for the novel, as opposed to shorter narrative forms, is argued by Fredric Jameson in *The Prison-House of Language* (Princeton, 1972), pp. 71–75. Jonathan Culler shows a dialectical subtlety akin to that of the Formalists in his concern with the raising and defeating of narrative expectations, but does not seem prepared to be systematic or comprehensive himself at this point.

[29] *Novel and Narrative*, The Twenty-fourth W. P. Ker Memorial Lecture (Glasgow, 1972). pp. 5–9.

# II.

# Second Thoughts on Theory

# The Rhetoric of Fiction
## and the Poetics of Fictions

WAYNE C. BOOTH

I

*The Rhetoric of Fiction* has been praised and blamed for saying many things that it does not say, and I am naturally tempted now to set everybody right about it. The invitation to reconsider my book and the responses to it is not likely to be repeated, and it would be pleasant to tick off the many misreadings, affecting the tone of those happily anonymous *TLS* reviewers who always have the last say:

Mr. X (his name is Legion) *has called me a moral reactionary, because I talk about "norms." Yet Mr. X himself has shown, in his own review, that he cannot escape norms, try as he will....*

Mr. Y *has praised me for finally providing a systematic terminology for the criticism of fiction. If he had read more closely, however, he would have discovered that I am not quite so naive as to believe in the possibility of....*

But even if I could make such corrections interesting, which is unlikely, I doubt very much that I could make them convincing, and they would almost certainly sound petulant: "That is not what I meant at all." Those who saw the book as a quarrel with fiction, or with modern fiction, or with up-to-date morality and post-Jamesian fictional techniques are not likely to be swayed by my asserting, however passionately, that they are wrong. Any reader who can believe that the book asks novelists to return to the Victorian period, that it deplores all irony, that it requires the novelist to state his position clearly in authorial commentary, or that it implies a demand for censorship, has developed subtleties of interpretation that would keep him immune from whatever could be said in a short article.

Another tempting direction would be to revise the book instead of admonishing its readers. I could try once more on that troublesome last chapter. I could recast the section on beliefs, as Stuart Tave (and David Hume) have convinced me I should, and I might either rewrite the clumsy sections on *The Aspern Papers* and *Journey to the End of the Night* or find examples which would lead fewer readers astray. There might even be a kind of masochistic thrill in public confession and correction of stylistic horrors.

But it should be more useful, writing for a new journal like *Novel*, to resist these forms of self-indulgence and try instead to say something about where we stand, in the profession, as we try to write to each other about "the novel." Do the six years of discussion of my book suggest any reasons for our failure to "get anywhere" in our criticism of fiction? I think I detect a sense of stagnation and futility in the journals, as we discover that the more we publish the less we understand. If I am right in this—if my own sense of having been more often than not misunderstood is shared by most authors who receive public comment—then many of our controversies are meaningless and much of our busy publication is fraudulent. It is fraudulent not primarily because, as non-academics think, it is done only to get and keep our jobs, but because it pretends to be public discourse when it is really little more than self-titillation.

The reasons for any such widespread failure must lie very deep, and they may often be moral and personal; if the seven deadly sins could be conquered (I think especially of sloth, pride, and envy) a good many of our controversies would evaporate. But not all. If my experience is any guide, our failures to understand cannot be cured with simple tolerance or generosity or hard work; to me the kindly energetic critics have seemed only slightly more relevant than the cruel and the lazy. The reasons for intellectual misunderstanding on the scale exhibited in America today must finally be intellectual, and though improved habits of courtesy and mutual respect no doubt would help, they are more likely to follow on improved standards of intellectual rigor and penetration than the other way round.

Let me illustrate from my own successive difficulties with one of the most extensive critiques *The Rhetoric of Fiction* has received, "The 'Second Self' in Novel Criticism," by John Killham (*British Journal of Aesthetics*, July, 1966). Both in the irrelevance of what he says of me and in the inadequacy of my first response to him, I see something lake a parable of our plight.

I discovered Mr. Killham's article through a citation by another critic (in manuscript) who had made me angry by what seemed almost a deliberate effort to misrepresent. When I found Mr. Killham saying that my influence in spreading the term "second self" was pernicious; that I had completely misunderstood the relation of authors to their works and readers; that the very term "second self" must be "utterly banished and extinguished, exorcized from the house of criticism," I was of course annoyed. When I found further, in that quick first reading, that Mr. Killham had distorted what I had originally meant by the term, and had, in fact, attacked me for beliefs I had specifically repudiated, using arguments I myself had used, I was quite naturally tempted to dismiss him as not worth bothering about.

Ordinarily I would in fact have done so. But I had promised an article to *Novel*, and Mr. Killham looked to be a good springboard. So I went through the piece somewhat more carefully, though still intent only on defending myself by showing him up. Then I wrote the following "refutation":

> Mr. Killham of Keele sets out to correct my views on the "author's second self," but the views he corrects are not mine. I thought I had made a distinction among (1) the real author, (2) various forms of narrators, "reflectors," dramatized tellers, and (3) the author implied by the totality of a work, a kind of second self that is the reader's picture of a creator responsible for the whole. Mr. Killham sets me straight by making precisely the same distinction: (1) "au-

thors, seated at tables with pens, or typewriters, or tape recorders," (2) "the imaginary persons whom they may invent as the supposed tellers of their stories," and (3) "the idea we have of the authors' literary character when we speak of reading 'Thackeray' or 'Dickens' and so on." Having thus done no more than reject my language, Mr. Killham then systematically—or so it almost seems—sets out to make a hash of disjointed and contradictory opinions in order to show the deleterious effects of the term "second self." I had written "Our sense of the implied author includes . . . the intuitive apprehension of a completed artistic whole." Within a page, Mr. Killham has translated this into the claim that I "prefer to think of a work as a person rather than a pot," and has of course dismissed my "false analogy"; and from "our sense of the implied author" he has eliminated "sense of," inventing an identity I had not intended: "Thus to make the term 'second self' stand for our 'intuitive apprehension of a completed artistic whole' . . . is quite self-defeating." Yes, indeed, it would be—had I done so.

And so Mr. Killham goes on, telling me that "the sort of second self an author creates" is "produced just as inevitably by one aspiring to 'drama' or 'impersonality' as by an early novelist boldly offering to tell a tale." Precisely— as I tried to argue at length in my book. I spend about a third of my book dealing with ways in which narrators differ from their authors, and Mr. Killham hectors me for forgetting "what has been well put by Professor Kathleen Tillotson: 'The narrator . . . is a method rather than a person: indeed the 'narrator' is never the author as man." Finally he decides that the term rhetoric is the trouble, because it means didacticism, and "no work of art, no novel, can be rightly considered rhetorical, for rhetoric is inimical to the freedom within the law a lifelike impression demands. . . . A work may attempt to teach, but only by being lifelike enough for that end: and this precludes rhetoric."

Can Mr. Killham have read so much as five pages of my book and still believe that this refutes anything I have to say? Mr. Killham's view of the invariably pejorative connotations of the word rhetoric is his own affair, and he may want to teach me a better word. But where can he and I begin in our discussion, if his notion of how to discuss leads him, whenever I use the word "rhetoric," in a sense that has a long and respectable intellectual history, to choose another meaning entirely and then blame me for the conflict between "rhetoric" and "art" that results? The deformations are indeed so frequent and so gross that I am almost tempted to guess at hidden motives. Have I attacked him somewhere, or one of his friends, without knowing it? Was he once bitten by a Chicago critic?

Having written that much as a draft, I pulled myself up short. Could I really fall back on bias as explanation here? After all, even in his garbled report on me, there is considerable evidence, ignored in my account, that Mr. Killham has worked seriously at his job. He has read and thought a good deal about the relations of authors to their works, and much of what he says makes sense. Most important, there is no reason to believe that my defense will convince him, no matter how carefully he reads it, if the original book could not do so. What, then, has gone wrong?

Courtesy alone might at that point have dictated a decision not to talk about Mr. Killham at all. Tolerance (what some people mistakenly call pluralism) might dictate a quick run-through to find some *good* things to say about him, to balance the bad, so that he and I might continue to live together in peace. But surely only one motive can finally prove adequate to the situation: the desire to understand Mr. Killham in order to explain his misunderstanding of me in terms that might promote genuine discussion. And that motive dictated my return to his essay for a few more hours, thinking about his problem and forgetting for awhile my own.

## II

What I found is that given the nature of *his* problem and given his way of taking hold of it (both of which are entirely respectable in themselves), Mr. Killham had an impossible task when he was confronted by my book. The topic of the second self is common to us both, but only as material in solving quite different problems. Mr. Killham's problem is that of reconciling what he calls the "autonomy" of a novel—a doctrine attributed to the New Critics—with his knowledge that any novel is, after all, written and read by human beings; he seeks—and he thinks that I seek—a reconciliation between the autonomous "well-wrought urn" and the world of the author's biography and psychology and intentions. In pursuing the reconciliation, he is concerned throughout with the processes of the imagination that account for how the author expresses himself in his work and yet is somehow never found directly in it. His talk is thus mostly in the expressive rather than the rhetorical mode—it is all about how authors "express what *they* think worth expressing," about the "psychology of literary invention," about "the attempt to find in a personal form and style a means of expressing the sense of self or inner being," about the transformation "of an artist's personality and experience . . . by the very act of writing."

Here, then, is an aesthetic problem seen in polar terms by a critic who accepts some truth in both poles. A work of art can, at one extreme, be seen as autonomous, divorced from the author's intentions; it can, on the other hand, be seen as the expression of the author's creative powers, of a kind of enveloping imagination, the author's creative self. Now along comes a book which seems to attempt to solve this problem by claiming that the author creates a "second self" which in turn works on the reader, turning *him* into a second self. But clearly this is a poor solution, a "too easy way of disposing of difficulties." The better way—predictable once the problem is set up in neat dichotomous form—is to recognize that true autonomy in a novel comes from our recognition of its independent "sense of life," which is, in fact, what the total creative act of the author, with *his* sense of life, gave it. "In other words, a novel never imitates life . . . but only depends upon our sense of life for the *creation* of its autonomy." "Autonomy" and the sense of the author's life (identical now with "the author's sense of life") are thus reconciled in the reader's "imaginative capacity" to enter the author's world.

Clearly there is no place, in such a synthesis of polarities, for the second self as

I describe it, or for the notion of rhetoric as I tried to develop it. It is true that Mr. Killham cannot and does not ignore the problem of what I would call rhetoric: how the author's vision is transmitted. He even finds it impossible to avoid using rhetorical terms when he talks about how the author's world and the reader get together: the novel must be "life-like enough for us to be *persuaded* to enter it, but only to the end that we may see what the author *makes us believe . . .*" (my italics). But though the rhetorical process (in my definition) thus cannot be ignored, "rhetoric" must be dismissed since it is "inimical to the freedom within the law a life-like impression demands."

The reason it is inimical is thus found strictly in the relations of Mr. Killham's central concepts to each other. His original polarity admitted only three main positions, left, right, and center—autonomy, personal expression, and a reconciling view of their true harmony. But as in most dialectical schemes, there are good and bad versions of each polar position: harmony results from seeing the good versions and uniting them; error, from choosing the bad versions. On the expressive side, there is an incorrect way of talking about how the author imposes his creative vision—"rhetorically," "didactically," "telling" rather than expressing. It is inevitable that Mr. Killham should labor to fit me into this naughty position, inventing doctrines out of fragments of misunderstanding (e.g., "the presence of a 'teller' in many novels is not a sign [as Booth believes] that all novels are pieces of the author's mind, parable-like illustrations of views he wants to make his readers accept, sophisticated specimens of 'communication' "). On the autonomous side, there is also a major corruption: the New Critics "went too far," cutting the work off from its life source. But in trying to answer the extreme partisans of autonomy, Booth has taken a false grip on the only other horn available; in building a didactic theory, turning "expression" into "rhetoric," he has left unanswered "those critics who argue for the entire independence of a work from its author's intentions."

It is easy to see that no author holding Mr. Killham's views uncritically—that is, without thinking through their implications for method—could possibly grasp my way of going about things, let alone accept it. Even if he had worked very hard to understand me he still would have only so many places where I might fit on his implied chart of possible aesthetic views. Since it is clear that I sometimes deal with the work as in some sense autonomous, and since it is even clearer that I treat fiction as rhetoric, I must be trying awkwardly to solve the same problem *he* is trying to solve, failing in the effort at synthesis because I have used the wrong grip on each horn. If I am right in this, it is not wrongheadedness or ill-will that led him to his irrelevancies. If he had decided to become tolerant and fit me into his views, the same essential distortions would result. Even if he had decided to grant the courtesy of rereading and had discovered and removed the grosser misrepresentations, the essential incompatibility of problems and methods and assumptions would remain. In short, unless he could come to the point of enriching his repertory of possible positions, unless he could make his simple schematism more complex, he could hardly avoid reducing me to fit it.

But it is not only that my problem and method fall off his chart. Our notions of how alternative charts might work are radically different. He seems to believe that the critic should seek the one proper synthetic view of what the work of fiction *is*, and of how the author and reader relate to it. It is *either* autonomous, *or* it is an expression of the author's personality or imagination, *or* it is some subtler synthesis of the two. It is scarcely surprising, then, that when I come along believing that a novel is *both* autonomous (a concrete whole, a well-wrought urn) *and* a piece of self-expression (a lamp, a passionate cry), *and*—now moving off his chart entirely!—a work of rhetoric (a gesture, a plea to accept, an imposition by one man on another), *and* an embodiment of the social and literary forces of its times (a convention-carrying vessel, a mirror), *and* a statement of moral or philosophical truth (an argument, a philosophical dialogue, a sermon), and what not?—when I come along with such pluralistic assumptions, mostly unstated, and explore pragmatically what will turn up in one neglected mode, the rhetorical, of course he is lost. And he will remain lost unless he is willing to think about method, mine and his own.

Any novel, good or bad, "really is" many different things, and no critical language can engage it in its totality. A novel "really is" an autonomous construct, for some critical purposes, as a whole corpus of modern criticism has shown. But it is just as really the expression of the author's intentions, capabilities, and psyche; and a representation of historical realities, social, economic, political, literary; and an embodiment of world views or moral concepts that can be thought of *sub specie aeternitatis*. If I wanted to write a rhetoric of fiction, I was neither obliged nor able at the same time to write a "poetics" of fiction, analyzing some of the forms of great fiction in their autonomous purity; or a psychology of fiction, exploring the grounds of creativity in the novelist or of creative response in readers; or a sociology of fiction, tracing the history and social forms of reading publics; or a philosophy of fictional realism, testing fictional worlds against various views of the real world or against universal truths. Fragments of each of these subjects will of course appear, in distorted form, under various heads within my rhetoric. And consequently, to anyone totally committed to any other problem, it may appear that I have struggled with his problem and lost.

I did not deal with the pluralistic theory of such modes directly; that would have taken a book in itself, and besides it seemed to me to have been done already by Chicagoans like Crane, Olson, and McKeon, by M. H. Abrams in the opening of *The Mirror and the Lamp*, and in a broader sense by much of post-Kantean philosophy, with its talk about multiple languages and models and categories of perception. I wish now that I had at least tried to discuss more fully how a critical language treating fiction as rhetoric differs from or relates to other modes. To do so would have helped me, and consequently my readers, by leading me to discover my own true subject sooner than I did. The book's major fault, which I still would not quite know how to remove, lies in the confusion of focus between rhetoric as what I called "the more easily recognizable appeals to the reader" (rhetoric as overt technical maneuver) and rhetoric as the whole art of fiction, viewed in the rhetorical mode. A defense of direct forms of "telling" could be made, I think, from almost any critical position. But I tried to make it from two quite different positions, and I supported my move by stretching and contracting at will the area covered by the term rhetoric. "Even if there are permanent, universal responses embodied in the work, then, they are unlikely to move us strongly and they may be unclear—without the author's rhetoric." What does the word *embodied* in this sentence mean? According to my expanded definition of rhetoric, any act of embodiment can be treated as rhetoric. Yet the phrase, "the author's rhetoric" at the end of the sentence seems to mean simply overt rhetoric, like commentary and obvious technical manipulations. On the one hand, it means whatever the author does to make his "embodiment" clear to the reader—but the "embodiment" itself serves to do that. . . . This circularity would never have satisfied me, I think, if I had pushed myself earlier and harder on the question of how my "rhetoric" related to other modes, and especially to poetics.

## III

The book began as an attempt to show that Gordon and Tate (among many others) were radically confused about point-of-view and so-called objective narration; it was originally to be what parts of it still are, a polemical essay accepting the main premises of the various "schools of autonomy," and defending the artistic respectability of the visibly "rhetorical" elements that have been under attack at least since the time of Flaubert. It grew into a book on the rhetorical dimension of all fiction. In the original conception, the word rhetoric did not even appear. But I soon found myself using it to describe those obvious appeals to the reader which critics had attacked as inartistic excrescences. And then it took me some years to discover that it was not enough (though it was something) to accept the objectivist definitions of art and tuck the Greek chorus (as Aristotle manages to do), Iago's soliloquies, or Fielding's intrusions inside. Though I thought I could show, following Aristotle and others, that a radical purging of the author's voice need not follow from seeing fiction in its aesthetic autonomy, it became clear that a more interesting new view of the craft of fiction would come from a new definition. Despite extensive revision in the light of the new conception, the earlier book is still discernible, attempting still to answer in aesthetic terms an aesthetic question: "Is there any defense that can be offered, on aesthetic grounds, for an art full of rhetorical appeals?" Well, of course there is, and the book is in part a long footnote to what Aristotle says about "thought" and about "manner," and especially to that invitation in Chapter 19 of the *Poetics* to assume about "thought" what is said of it "in our Art of Rhetoric, as it belongs more properly to that department of inquiry."

If the author is considered, in that earlier conception, as *making a concrete form,* whether an imitation of an action or a system of symbols, a well-wrought urn, it is difficult (though not impossible) to justify evidences in his work of his efforts to make it accessible to the world. If on the other hand he is thought of as *making readers,* then of course his effort is visible in every moment, and one can forget about pejorative distinctions between rhetoric and pure drama. Every stroke is in this sense rhetorical, just as in the objective view every stroke is part of the concrete form, or in the expressive view every stroke expresses the artist's psyche, and in the art-is-truth view every stroke reflects a world of values or universals which the book is "about." In this view, even the most seemingly objective, intrinsic, "autonomous" elements, including the central events, the "hardest" symbols, can be fruitfully viewed as rhetoric—that is, they can be considered *as if* aimed at an effect on the reader (because in fact they produce that effect) regardless of the aesthetic theories or the actual writing practices of the author.

Now there has seemed to be something radically confusing to some critics in this pragmatic device of trying out a definition to see what it will yield. If "rhetoric" is used to cover the whole work of art, then I surely must be saying that the work of art *is* rhetoric, and everybody knows, as Mr. Killham says, that "no work of art, no novel, can be rightly considered rhetorical." A work of art *is* either one thing or another. Have I not heard of the law of non-contradiction?

But it is rather late in the day for us to ignore in this way how our categories of perception help determine what we see. It is true that the page on which I write cannot both be in the room and not in the room at the same time. *As a physical object* it really is in the room, and there's an end on it, even for the most ardent pluralist. But *as an object of my perception* it is an unlimited number of things, scrap paper, psychological threat, material for a fire, a product of American commerce, and even something that can be both outside the room (in my imagination) and inside the room (in physical presence) at the same time.

In exactly the same way, though more deceptively, the work of art *is* many things. Some definitions of what it is are admittedly of little help to a critic trying to understand artistic qualities. If I were to argue, for example, that works of art are *really* natural products, because man is simply a product of the natural world and nature has thus produced man's novels, my redefinition would be sound enough, and it might prove useful in an argument about the nature of the universe or of God. But it will be of no use to me in dealing critically with the art of this or that work. And there are limits, very real limits: it would be hard to do much, even metaphorically, with the claim that novels are really electric fans or chicken coop roofs. Thus there are many things that art for all practical purposes is *not*, and pluralism cannot lead us to a bland tolerance of all views, as long as they are developed coherently. But there are also many things that any work of art *is*, and one of the things that all literary and—with especial obviousness—fictional art *is*, *really is*, is an action that authors and readers perform together. There need be no argument about whether this view or the view of a novel as a poetic construct is true. Both are true, and both are useful because true. If someone asks, "Yes, but which is it, really?" he will have asked a question which a pluralist (of my kind) thinks unanswerable. It is really both, or really (but not exclusively) either, just as it is really (but not exclusively) an expression of the author's personality; and so on. One is philosophically and critically naive if he spends time debating such modes of perception in absolute terms.

It is not a waste of time, however, to show how a consistent and habitual use of one definition or perspective leads critics to distort or overlook or ban elements that in other views become quite natural. A generation had come to accept without thinking that a true "poem" (including fiction) should not mean but be. With the author ruled out under the "intentional fallacy" and the audience ruled out under the "affective fallacy," with the world of ideas and beliefs ruled out under the "didactic heresy" and with narrative interest ruled out under the "heresy of plot," some doctrines of autonomy had become so desiccated that only verbal and symbolic interrelationships remained. I had been taught what still seems to me by comparison an especially rich version of objectivist doctrine, derived from the *Poetics*; it had a way of talking about effects on readers and audiences, and it believed in the author's intentions as determinative (in a carefully limited sense) of the critic's quest. But it was objectivist nonetheless: the "poem" was an imitation of an action, composed as a beautiful object, designed to be excellent in its kind. Though an effect on audiences was implied by its form, the critic pursued the internal nature of the poem by analysing its parts in relation to the whole work.

This version of objectivist aesthetics has always tended to slide over into rhetorical study, as Bernard Weinberg has shown about renaissance "Aristotelians." Within the Chicago school there has been a steady drift, as I now see it, toward the "corruption" of objective views in the rhetorical direction. What I have done, it seems to me, like Sheldon Sacks working quite independently, is to make this tendency explicit. *The Rhetoric of Fiction* asks, as Kenneth Burke had been doing in a different way, that we think of the poem not primarily as *meaning* or *being* but as *doing*. In place of analyses of poetic form, descriptions and interpretations of types of action or plot (with their power to produce an effect indicated, but not exclusively dominant), I look at effects, at techniques for producing them, and at readers and their inferences. In place of a classification of literary kinds, I give an analysis of *interests* and (as in the *Emma* chapter) manipulations of interests. In place of an analysis into the poetic elements of the internal structure (plot, character, thought, diction) my elements become identical with the three that one finds in all rhetorics, author, work, audience: authors and their various surrogates and spokesmen; works, and their various arrangements for effect; audiences, and their preconceptions and processes of inference.

I did try to avoid ruling my conclusions, unlike some earlier rhetoricians claiming to work from the *Poetics*, according to the peculiar demands of particular audiences. But I did not (and would not now) surrender the insights that come when the work is viewed not as a formed object, eternally what it is, beautifully whole in its form, but as something designed, or at least suited, to impose itself upon us (not, be it noted, to communicate *themes* or *norms*, as Mr. Donald Pizer and many other readers have taken it, but *itself*). Study of what the work *is*, what it has been made to *be*, will yield a "poetics," and I hope someday to produce a poetics of some kinds of fiction.[1] What the work is made to *do*—how it is de-

---

[1] The editors have called my attention to the confusion that this use of the word "poetics" is likely to produce, since many other critics are using it differently these days. "Your use of the term 'poetics' jars with the way we've been using it, in our brochure and our first-issue editorial, to mean a theoretical account of the nature and function of literary genres. Malcolm Bradbury is also using it that way in his essay, "Towards a Poetics of Fiction: An Approach Through Structure," in our first issue. The notion of a poetics which pulls together many different approaches seems to be common—seems to correspond in fact with your plea for pluralism, and with the Chicago view of Aristotle's *Poetics* as a many-sided approach. So we are troubled by your confinement of poetics to matters of craft, to the inner nature of the art object, its isness versus its doesness." Though the present draft may not be quite so confusing as the one that elicited this comment, I can see that the term is so ambiguous as almost to be useless. For me a genuine poetics would *include* a "theoretical account of the nature and function of (some) literary genres," and it would "pull together many different ap-

signed to communicate itself—will yield a rhetoric. The two differing aspects will not be incompatible if they are done well, since a work *does* what it does because of what it *is,* and vice versa. But they will start and end at different points, and they will certainly deal with different elements in different proportions along the way.[2]

In theory, once I had grasped my subject as the rhetorical aspect of fiction I should have then written "the whole rhetoric of fiction." Such a work would have been different in many ways. It would have had the chapter on the "rhetoric of symbols" that John Crowe Ransom rightly demanded. It would have had much more on style, in the manner of David Lodge's excellent *Language of Fiction* (though avoiding his assumption that language is all). It might well have had a comparison of the rhetoric of literature, in this conception, with more directly rhetorical forms. Rereading it now, I am especially distressed by how little I wrote about the "rhetoric of event"—the way in which the synthesis of incidents determines how we respond. But it is clear why this was so. I still had my original polemic on my hands: of all the weapons in the writer's arsenal, only overt commentary, only "telling," had been attacked. And so the book has a great overload of defense of the author's voice. Indeed I sometimes feel that though I set out in part to undermine those who would make manipulation of point-of-view the whole art of fiction, my own polemical stress on narrators and voices has strengthened this one-sided view of the art of fiction. I occasionally receive manuscripts by critics claiming my influence, and they are always point-of-view studies, never studies of plot construction viewed as rhetoric.

If I had wrestled harder with the rhetoric of character and event, I hope I would have been led to the kind of thing done brilliantly by Sheldon Sacks in *Fiction and the Shape of Belief.* I am thinking not only of his central chapters on how Fielding's minor characters serve to shape our beliefs even as they amuse us, but even more of his carefully argued distinctions among three modes of narration: satire, apologue, and "action." Against the advice of R. S. Crane, I deliberately avoided systematic distinctions between works of explicit rhetorical intent, like *Gulliver's Travels,* and "mimetic" works like *A Passage to India,* and I would still hold to this indiscriminate grouping, on the twin grounds that my general case applies to all fiction, regardless of form or effect, and that any judgment of elements within a given work must be specific to that particular work and its needs.

---

proaches"—at least in the sense of trying to comprehend linguistic, technical, structural, and "affective" questions in a unified view. But it would by no means be "confined to craft," it would not be a compendium of all possible approaches, and its theory would be subordinated to the effort to give a practical account of how good works are in fact made and how we can talk about their special (autonomous) qualities without analogizing them to other human arts (like rhetoric, psychology, politics, etc.). Clearly someone should do a taxonomy of current definitions of *poetics,* before we all end up quarreling pointlessly about this term as we do about so many others.

[2] To dwell as I am doing on distinctions among dimensions or aspects or modes is of course once again to choose one way of doing things rather than other possible ways. A critic might well prefer to deal synthetically with questions of similarities among things, and he would have good reason then to ignore the distinction between rhetoric and poetics. A good example is the procedure of Frank Kermode, in his fine recent book, *The Sense of an Ending;* he dwells on the similarities among all "fictions," including myths and sociological and philosophical accounts, and our perceptions of the shape of life itself. Nothing could be less relevant to his profound pursuit of how the shapes of literature and life resemble each other than for me to complain that it gives no help to a critic pursuing rhetorical questions.

At the same time, it is quite clear that the rhetoric of fiction must finally deal, as Sacks does, with differences *of kind* among formal intentions. Such differences are implied throughout my book, but they are never discussed for more than a few sentences. Sooner or later the rhetorical critic must face them full-on. As he does so, he will of course move into the territory of what I am calling poetics, but he will do so as a stranger in a foreign land, discovering that the *kinds of actions authors perform on readers* differ markedly, though subtly, from *the kinds of imitations of objects they are seen as making,* in the poetic mode.

## IV

The position I have just described can be discovered in my book, but since it is largely implicit, I can hardly blame readers who missed it. But even as I write such self-criticism I must confess that I cringe in anticipation of what some readers will do with it. "Booth has himself admitted that the book is confused to the core. . . ." Mr. Killham, who has no room on his chart either for a poetics in my sense *or* a rhetoric will simply be further confused. Mr. Donald Pizer, who claims that in my "ethical conservatism" I am less interested in "how fiction communicates than in what it should communicate" (*College English*, March 1967), will perhaps conclude that the book as I revised it would be even more of a didactics of fiction than the one he discerns. The further I go in the direction of consistency in the rhetorical mode, the more I shall invite the charge of didacticism, and that final chapter, which has upset many readers, will when revised upset even more.

It may be true—to touch briefly on that chapter—that my interest in rhetoric springs from my being more morally conservative, and more given to imposing general standards, than I like to think. But just as there is an ethics of rhetoric, as everyone from Plato to Kenneth Burke has recognized, so there is a moral dimension to fiction as rhetoric. It does not dictate in any simple way a set of doctrines that fiction should communicate, and even in that "tendentious" final chapter my interest was not in *what* should be communicated; I ask only *that* the work communicate itself, that the author "be as clear about his moral position as he possibly can be" and that he "do all that is possible in any given instance to realize his world as he intends it." It is not hard for me to see how readers could take this, out of context, as an effort to ban ambiguities; after all, I did not underline "all that is possible in any given instance." To discover that I admire many great works that are both ambiguous and ironic and—to some degree—unclear, the reader would have to go back through earlier chapters with perhaps more care than one has a right to expect from one's readers. My attack was simply on the assumption that all the arguments favor a rhetoric of ambiguity.

But to deal with that final chapter would require another essay. Rather than trying here to answer or accept every possible objection to my book, I am trying simply to ask whether Mr. Killham and I belong as critics to a profession in which there is any chance whatever of cumulative discourse. Must we forever shout slogans at each other from distant armed camps? Presumably we must if, as Mr. Killham implies, there is one true aesthetic view which all must come to or perish. If on the other hand, there are many legitimate questions based on differing assumptions and definitions and amenable to differing methods, progress of a limited kind should be possible for those willing to share a mode, an interest, a language.

"Until you understand a writer's ignorance," Coleridge wrote, "presume yourself ignorant of his understanding." Most of my critics cannot "explain my ignorance," since they cannot really explain, in terms relevant either to their own interests or my own, why I do the strange things I do. They are thus reduced to assuming that temperament or moral bias or sheer stupidity has led me astray, or that happy chance has led me to their own conclusions. Inevitably such critics prove useless to me (as I to them) because even when they praise me we simply do not connect. What is disappointing is that with all the thousands of words written about the book, no one has tried, so far, to wrestle with the whole conception of the rhetoric of fiction and improve it, clarify it, make it more useful to more people. Nothing surprising in that, I suppose; it is our way of dealing with each other.

I must regularly disappoint other authors in the same way. New books on the novel come out almost every week. I buy them, and I "read" them—that is, I go through them quickly, first peeking to see what, if anything, they say about my own work, then, only slightly less shamefully, skimming for agreements and disagreements. It is only by an effort of will that I can resist using the results as if they had some value to myself and others as reflections of the real books. They do not. I am told by Mr. W. J. Harvey that *character* should be given primacy in dealing with the novel (*Character and the Novel*), and by Messrs. Robert Scholes and Robert Kellogg, in *The Nature of Narrative*, that *narrative shape* is central. Are they then in conflict with Mr. Lodge, who says it is all language, and with each other? They may be, but it is more likely that when I finally get inside their books I will find not only such obvious differences but more basic differences of method and principle that will allow me to accept the legitimacy of their attempt and Mr. Lodge's too—once they have been purged of their claims to exclusive truth. As claimants to the whole truth they may even turn out to be bad books; as complementary inquiries, they could nourish each other.

In any case, it is absurd to tell them—on this superficial acquaintance—that one of them must be wrong because they "disagree," or because Michael Raimond has shown that the novel is to be seen as a *way of dealing with reality* (*La Crise du Roman*), or because Ihab Hassan has taught us (*Radical Innocence*) that the basic question in dealing with the novel is metaphysical or because R.-M. Albérè (*Métamorphoses du Roman*) says that the basic question is moral. Of all these works I have just "placed" so glibly, which have I really read, which have I made my own? None, and I thus stand now exposed, not for the first time, as sinning against my own sermon. Well, I've been busy, of course, like you, and this promised article has to be completed by day before yesterday, and besides, I'm really quite sure that none of these authors will have a lot to say to.... No, no, that's not it exactly, but there are so many books, so many articles....

Must we forever rush through all these books, demolishing each man's shelter to provide materials for our own? Is each new position merely a fashion to be outgrown as soon as possible? Why not change our figure to something like a series of climbing expeditions, attempting different peaks or different faces of the same peak? If we could do so, most of us would discover that most of what we have said about other critics is flatly irrelevant. Take, for example, that stuff in *The Rhetoric of Fiction* on Ortega y Gasset, based on one reading of two of his short books, and in translation too! I know from that little raid that Ortega is not just worthless but aggressively misleading about the rhetoric of fiction. But what about *his* problem? What could a man of such obvious intelligence and sensitivity have been *doing*, that could lead him so far astray? The least I can do is take an oath of silence on Ortega until I have him cold, until I can explain his "ignorance" so well that it is no longer ignorance about my problem, but a form of knowledge about his.

# Serious Reflections on
# The Rise of the Novel

IAN WATT

Having, long ago, grimly refrained from posting sundry devastating retorts to a few of the original reviewers of *The Rise of the Novel*, I didn't at first find the attractions of contributing to the present series sufficient to warrant discomposing my posture of heroic abnegation. It wasn't as though, stumbling gamely along towards my centenary, I couldn't any longer risk passing up one final opportunity to provoke incredulous outrage among those still elbowing their way up the professorial ladder: " 'Sblood! Not buried yet?" Nor, certainly, had I any rankling sense that *The Rise of the Novel* had received less than its due—quite the contrary. However, I finally decided that a few rather miscellaneous reflections about the composition, the reception, and the shortcomings of the book, which had dimly glimmered in my mind from time to time, might have enough general interest to justify exposing myself to the charge of self-important anecdotage.

Retracing the stages of composition of *The Rise of the Novel* makes me realize how my operative, though largely unformulated, premises were intricately connected with the way the book was eventually received; and it also illustrates how academic writing, in its small way, is also subject to the processes of history.

Work on *The Rise of the Novel* began in 1938, when I held a Strathcona Research Fellowship at St. John's College, Cambridge. The war diverted me to other studies from 1939 to 1946; but when peace broke out I went back to work and finished a first draft early in 1947. I then laid the subject aside, and began various other more or less abortive projects; in 1951, however, I went back to the eighteenth-century novel, and the sixth revised draft was finally accepted for publication in 1956.

The main direction of the interminable and painful process of revision, forcibly stimulated in the last two years by the comments of various readers, stipendiary and otherwise, was towards making the book much shorter. This drastic reduction of scale primarily affected the beginning and the end.

Originally there was a long methodological first chapter. Having struggled through a good deal of Vaihinger, Wittgenstein, Carnap, Neurath, and other philosophers, I wanted not only to show it, but also to theorize about how literary history and criticism ought to be combined through what I then called the hypothetico-deductive method. Briefly, it seemed that the natural and social sciences had the advantage of beginning with objectively-demonstrable data; and the equivalents of these data in literature—the written records—could also be made the starting point of inductive study along the lines of traditional biographical and bibliographical scholarship. But in the larger critical and historical area which interested me the case was quite different. Here my procedure would have to be largely deductive; and so the nearest I could get to objectivity would be to start from a hypothesis that was based, not on my own opinion, but on that of the majority of qualified observers.

That was the gist of my original thirty-five page heavily-footnoted methodological introduction. Successive revisions eventually boiled it down to one word: the "if" in the opening paragraph which introduces the clauses "if we assume, as is commonly done, [that the novel is a new literary form], and that it was begun by Defoe, Richardson and Fielding, how does it differ from the prose fiction of the past . . . and is there any reason why these differences appeared when and where they did?"

There is, I have since discovered, nothing exceptional about such drastic cutting; indeed it seems to be the rule rather than the exception that introductions begin by being infinitely expandable and end by proving equally expendable. But I probably wouldn't have cut quite so drastically for economy alone. Another reason was certainly a growing disenchantment with all theory, even with my own. The decisive factor, however, was probably my slow-dawning realization that all those messy sheets of paper were in process of turning into that improbable object, a printed book. At once the question of my likely audience—even of my possible reviewers—became much more real; and this introduced all kinds of new considerations. One of them was the lurking (and unworthy) notion that it would be impolitic to affront the known prejudices of my main audience—students and teachers of literature—by flaunting the stigmata of my long fraternization with logical positivists and social scientists.

The deletion of the first chapter certainly made the book more palatable to publishers and readers; but it had an unexpected result—the whole of my cherished hypothetico-deductive method, which for me had continued to be immanent in that initial "if," passed quite unnoticed, and laid the book open to two general criticisms.

First, that its basic thesis was not original.[1] This, of course, was true; but originality would have been completely contrary to my chosen procedure.

Secondly, I was branded as a monocular modern, blind to the greatness of the ancients, and impervious to the legitimacy of other previous forms of fiction.[2] Here again, though the charge may be true, my methodological assumption had precluded any autonomous treatment of any forms of fiction other than those of early eighteenth-century England. The words "the rise of the novel," no doubt, looked as though I were making the much more unqualified assertion—that the only prose fiction which mattered began with Defoe; but such a supposition, I thought, was undercut not only by that initial "if," but also by my more modest and casual subtitle: "Studies in Defoe, Richardson and Fielding."

What conclusions can be drawn from all this I'm not sure. Perhaps that one's

[1] E.g., "Professor Watt *manages* [my italics] to challenge received opinion surprisingly little." J. Paul Hunter, *The Reluctant Pilgrim* (Baltimore, 1966), p. viii.

[2] E.g., "Ian Watt on the Novel Form," Appendix of E. M. W. Tillyard's *The Epic Strain in the English Novel* (London, 1958).

methodological assumptions have to be repeated very frequently if they are to remain active in the minds of readers; perhaps that some form of typographical emphasis—a *Ulysses*-like giant "IF" occupying the whole first page—would have
mediated my message better.

The second main cut during the process of revision was even larger in scale. It
came at the end. There were originally three final chapters—a further one on *Tom
Jones*, and one each on Smollett and Sterne. I cut out these chapters merely because
they would have made the book much too long; but although the omission helped
me to see how to give what remained a much firmer organization, it also damaged
the original proportions of the book. I had planned a structure in which the emphasis on "realism of presentation" in chapters two to eight was counterpoised by that
on "realism of assessment" in the last five chapters. When this original structure
was abandoned, the treatment of "realism of assessment" became so brief that,
perhaps inevitably, the book was read as rather more simple-minded in its advocacy
of "realism of presentation"[3] than it might have been otherwise. As a result I have
had to grow accustomed to figuring in some minds as a permanent picketer for the
Union Novel (International President H. James), carrying a sign which reads "Cervantes Go Home" on one side, and "Fielding is a Fink"[4] on the other.

Rereading *The Rise of the Novel* I can certainly detect a good many unhappy
relics of earlier drafts. Some are merely stylistic. The most masochistic reviser, I
imagine, finds it difficult not to succumb to the enchantment of his own prose, especially when it comes to him with the Mosaic authority acquired when the tablets
have been expensively retyped; much time, and a special frame of mind, and sometimes, alas, only the belated clarity of vision that comes when the words have been
set up in type, are needed before one finally recognizes all those ancient anal suc-
cubi, and blushes with shame to think that one was so long pleasured by such graceless imbecilities. There are also residues of a more programmatic adhesion to my
initial design than was wholly consistent with my final critical position. One of
these can be seen in the chaptering. As the years passed I had chafed more and more
under the restrictions of a positivist historical analysis of the elements of "new-
ness" in the novel form. This finally led me to decompose the original chapters on
Defoe and Richardson so that the social and historical approaches were separated
from a more autonomous literary treatment of particular works. Thus, although
*Robinson Crusoe* and *Pamela* were used mainly for thematic and illustrative purposes, *Moll Flanders* and *Clarissa* were given independent critical essays.

As far as I can now guess at it, my guiding impulse when I worked on the later
drafts was essentially rather simple—to write a book such as I myself would like
to read. Such a book would certainly have what are usually called the scholarly
virtues. I had long ago picked up the notion (I must not now speculate how or
where) that one should be serious at least about what one had freely decided to do:

---

[3] *E.g.*, "Watt's all-pervasive assumption is that 'realism of presentation' is a good thing in itself." Wayne C.
Booth, *The Rhetoric of Fiction* (Chicago, 1961), p. 41.

[4] *E.g.*, "Fielding is graduated without honors." *MLQ*, XXI (1960), 374. Here, and wherever else the need for
brevity made it impossible to present a critic's adverse judgment fairly, I have thought it more equitable to give
the barest reference, omitting names.

in Conrad's terms, one should be concerned about the cut of one's clothes even in a community of blind men. My experience in the graduate schools of U.C.L.A. and Harvard had opened my eyes to what responsible professional research should be; and I had attempted to incorporate these standards in the substance of the manuscript. But now the main emphasis changed. I came to see more clearly that my aim also implied various difficult, and to some extent conflicting, compositional imperatives. As regards scale, it involved not treating any topic at exhaustive length. As regards prose, it involved a much more rapid pace, and even more important, a whole style of writing that was responsive to two other unformulated premises: that writing about literature should somehow convey its awareness of that honor; and that it should also embody, though without buttonholing intimacy, the notion that it is the product neither of a card index nor of a divine oracle, but of a putative human-being communicating with other putative human-beings.

I must hurry on past these peculiarly delicate pretensions, pausing only at one paradox they suggest: that in their extreme forms scholarly and literary considerations are diametrically opposed.

At the scholarly pole we have a study which is in effect an organized collection of evidence, a meticulous concordance or catalogue of categorized citations, a corpus of texts with explanatory commentary. On some topics—as in Part III of H. T. Swedenberg's *The Theory of the Epic in England, 1650–1800* (1944), for example —this form can triumphantly justify itself; but for most subjects, quotations do not in fact speak for themselves; and if they are left to do so for very long, very few people keep on listening.

On the other hand, the more one departs from the exhaustive detailing of primary evidence, the more one is inevitably imposing one's own views and voice. For example, the literary need for prose of a reasonable pace requires much omission (a bore is a man who tells you everything) and, in particular, a severe pruning of quotations and qualifications. In addition, stylistic genuflections towards the literary nature of the subject-matter, and towards the presumably exhaustible attention-span of the reader, obviously demand various kinds of departure from plain declarative statement to more multi-vocal, or in other respects more complex, kinds of prose.

At the scholarly extreme, then, one discourages readers; at the other, one risks discouragement from the scholars. Omissions dictated by the need for pace, for example, will run up against the all-but-universal presumption that if you don't mention a book, you haven't read it.[5] As regards prose style, every departure from plain declarative statement increases the chances of being misunderstood. Ironical modes of statement, for example, can be made to look very silly when they are

---

[5] "... to assure ... readers ... that Defoe was being consciously ironic [in *Moll Flanders*] ... the critic must have read a good part of the five hundred and forty-seven items ... in Professor John Robert Moore's *Checklist of the Writings of Daniel Defoe* ... but this is precisely what none of the critics appear to have done." (Maximillian E. Novak, "Conscious Irony in *Moll Flanders*: Facts and Problems," *College English*, XXVI [1964], 199.) *Quippe peccavi*; but a good many footnotes and references were dropped during my revisions; and later the publishers asked for further drastic cuts. This horrified me at the time, but the cuts helped bring about what I now regard as a satisfactory balance between text and notes.

quoted as though they were meant literally;[6] fortunately one can always accuse the critic of having missed one's irony.

In any case, whatever the undoubted difficulties involved in trying to strike the right balance, and write both for the specialist and for what must pass nowadays for the general reader, I am still persuaded that there was—and is—nothing wrong with my basic compositional aim: trying to increase the exceptions to the rule that "scholarly" usually means "unreadable" and "readable" usually means "wrong."

## II

As far as the author is concerned, the reception of his book seems even slower and more painful than its gestation. First the elephantine parturition in publishing offices and printing houses. Next the onset of labor pains, usually announced by peremptory demands for corrected galleys or the index not later than last Monday. After many more months that seem like years, a few advance copies eventually arrive. The first thing one sees is a misprint. With sinking feelings one puts the book away, and waits. With luck a friend writes a review for one of the weeklies, and it comes out only a few weeks after the official date of publication. Then a long deafening silence, only interrupted by a press-cutting agency that sends funny little yellow paste-ups enshrining what the compositors of the *Brooklyn Daily* or the *Pomona Progress-Bulletin*[7] have made of the dust jacket, or of the notice sent out by Virginia Kirkus's Service. Finally, the numbing conviction that the grave will gape long before the learned journals allow themselves a majestically deliberate turn in your direction.

Whatever the delay, preparation for the majestic turn should begin much earlier than it usually does. If, for example, I had been advised to change my name at an early stage of authorship, and to adopt an intimidatingly sonorous *nom-de-plume*, it might have prevented my deep chagrin when the paronomastic insults to which my surname is so susceptible, and which had haunted me ever since first grade, relentlessly pursued my authorial reincarnation: the first printed notice of my work ended, with numbing irony, ". . . and now Watt."[8]

The century with which I co-exist has instructed me that the only way to handle such traumatic experiences is to convince oneself that they are universal. It is with this therapeutic orientation that I now offer a brief analysis—from which other authors may incidentally benefit—of the institution of reviewing.

Reviewing belongs to the large class of benevolent-aggressive dyadic relationships which are characterized, like dentistry, by an extreme asymmetry of roles.

---

[6] Thus George Starr's objection (*Defoe and Spiritual Autobiography* [Princeton, 1965], p. 120) to my writing, about the Friday-Crusoe relationship: "A functional silence, broken only by an occasional 'No, Friday,' or an abject 'Yes, Master,' is the golden music of Crusoe's *île joyeuse*," seems to me valid only if my statement is interpreted literally; and I had tried to write the sentence in such a way that it wouldn't be.

[7] "The novel has flourished in America since the growth of the lending library and the emancipation of women according to a study recently published by the University of California Press." (August 12, 1957.) The *Lodi News-Sentinel* echoed this laconic interpretation *verbatim* the next day.

[8] *PQ*, XXXI (1952), 266.

The transitive agent, the reviewer, is secure in the knowledge that his sitting duck can neither fly off nor hit back; despite this great freedom, however, reviewers seem to operate under a highly conventional set of institutionalized imperatives, all naturally directed towards producing the most pain with the least effort.

This expertise is highly valued whether it serves merely to maximize the personal pleasure of the reviewer, or, as more commonly, more to equip him for the effective discharge of his primary professional obligation—to teach the universe some of the discipline it so sadly lacks. The first principle of reviewing, then, is the law of Maximal Offense; and its main applications can conveniently be memorized under the rubric of the three "P's": *Sprezzatura;* Unacknowledged Paraphrase; and Benevolent Patronage.

No review, of course, is complete without pointing out at least one error, but decorum requires that it be done with glancing casualness—the mandatory strategy is to suggest "I really don't have the time to go through more than one or two pages in search of this kind of thing." Quotation or misquotation follows. Note that too copious or specific a listing spoils the effect of habitual but careless contempt which is the hallmark of true *sprezzatura.* For instance, the comment "three of Defoe's titles are incorrectly given"[9] would lose much of its force if the errors were illustrated; and the whole effect would certainly be ruined if the reviewer should add "and there is a dangling participle on p. 201."

So much for tone. As regards content, Unacknowledged Paraphrase is the standard pattern. It begins with something to the effect that "What poor Professor W * * * seems to have been trying to say," or "would have observed, had his maker endowed him with the wit, is . . ."—and there follows the required number of words in the form of a précis of the main point of the book with "immediacy of presentation," say, replacing the terms actually employed by the author—in this case "authenticity" or "realism of presentation."

The Unacknowledging Paraphrast usually employs Benevolent Patronage as his backstop. He is then in permanent possession of the useful option of being able to retort: "Why ever is that poor reviewee getting so bothered? After all I went out of my way to make the handsome concession that 'I imagine the book will be of considerable value to undergraduates' and may even 'remind [the specialist] of things he has forgotten.'"[10]

So much for Maximal Offense. The second law of reviewing is modeled on the Enclosure Acts, and is usually called the "One Man One Field Principle." The reviewer's pastoral role is, quite simply, to shoo writers back where they belong, if so dismal a pasture can be located. A simple example would be "If Mr. Watt had not attempted to combine literary history with criticism, his discussion . . . might have been of lasting value. . . . Unfortunately he has chosen a historico-philosophical approach, for which he seems less well equipped."[11] This is the egalitarian form of the law—"My Field—Keep Out"; but even after all fields have been equally al-

[9] *MLQ,* XXI (1960), 374.

[10] *Essays in Criticism,* VIII (1958), 433–437, 429, 437–438.

[11] *Birmingham Post,* Feb. 26, 1957.

lotted they must still be protected from dangerous pests; hence, the reviewer's pastoral role occasionally obliges him to put up a public notice for the protection of innocent wayfarers. One simple example of this "Beware the Dangerous Dog" posting is the reflection, "It seems to me that Mr. Watt gets a little 'Freudian' at the end."[12] "Seems," be it noted parenthetically, seems to be the reviewer's major lexical resource, possibly on legal grounds.

Some of the other established rituals of reviewing might at first seem to deserve the status of autonomous laws: the Law of Mandatory Regret (some always are); the "Quest for All-the-Earmarks-of Law" (on which see the latest brand-book of dissertations, or search the author's acknowledgments for any signs of telltale indebtedness to not-in influences); even the "Virtually Useless Index Law" (optional if there is no index). But further examination discloses that nearly all these are merely particular applications of the third basic principle of reviewing—the Law of Inevitable Disproportion. It can be put very simply: "If Not Too Many Then Too Few" (e.g., footnotes, quotations, jokes, ideas, friends, enemies, etc.).

Strictly speaking there is only one law for the intransitive agent, the reviewee: Forget it.

Unfortunately this law shares with most other forms of wisdom the sad truth that it is impossible to practice. It may, therefore, be useful to steel the patient for his ordeal by informing him of the main operative procedures as they affect the reviewee. They also are three in number.

First, there is the Law of Absolute Irrelevance. There is nothing which may not be introduced into public comment on any book. The author of a work on eighteenth-century fiction, for example, must never imagine himself safe from such no-doubt well-founded, if not transparently apposite, accusations as "Mr. Watt shows himself to be unaware of the work of philosophers like Augustine, Anselm, and Bonaventura."[13]

Secondly, there is the Law of Inverse Qualification, which states that the boiling point of malediction is inversely proportional to the age and professional status of the reviewer. It is really a special case of the universal law which states that the last acquired of Minerva's arts is charity.

Finally we have the Law of Mistaken Identity. No reviewee can ever recognize himself or his handiwork in the object which appears to have come under the reviewer's purview. This is true, unfortunately, even of laudatory reviews, for which the universally valid principle of Authorial Insatiability must be invoked. One might expect a reviewee to be satisfied, for instance, if he is placed on a footing with Gibbon and Hume:[14] actually he merely reads on, reflecting bitterly "Hm. He might at least have taken the trouble to *elaborate* his only valuable insight"; and exits muttering *Not a word* about that witty thrust in footnote 397. Criminal."

Lest any skeptical reader find this analysis lacking in objectivity, and be led to

---

[12] *Essays in Criticism*, VIII (1958), 438.

[13] *Essays in Criticism*, IX (1959), 206. Oddly enough there were in fact two references to the first, over-reverently indexed under St. Augustine.

[14] See Louis Kampf, "Review Essay" in *History and Theory*, VI (1967), 88.

surmise that I may be motivated by personal bias, I must also add that none of the above principles and practices actually produces the galloping *anomie* in the Republic of Academic Letters which might be expected: for they are all subject to the ultimate truth about reviewing, the Statute of Amnesic Limitation. The reviewee will probably never meet anyone who has read and remembers both the review and his book; and the wounds received from reviews heal unimaginably rapidly at the touch of time. The amnesia is equally functional for the reviewer: perhaps fortunately, since if any of his blows proved as deadly as they seem, they might sap his zest for battle.

## III

But I can no longer decently put off the only thing which may have been sustaining the interest of remaining readers—the always gratifying spectacle of public penitence. No prizes are offered for observing that a change of method and tone is called for. Anyone not utterly impervious to the possibilities of imitative form will be prepared for the logic which dictates that a first section which followed (admittedly at a great distance) Defoe's autobiographical mode, and a second which attempted to prove the writer not wholly deaf to Fielding's way of suggesting general principles by an ironic acceptance of their violation, should be succeeded by a third section which explores error and guilt in Richardson's copious manner.

What crows then shall I eat? How many have already been crammed down my recalcitrant gullet?

Professor J. C. Maxwell pointed out in charitable privacy a mistranslation of Aristotle on page 19 for which I can still find no explanation. As to the reviewers, some succeeded in convincing me that various confusions between British and American publishing styles had defaced the text with sundry reprehensible inconsistencies, while others demonstrated how I had misunderstood *Moll Flanders*.[15] But it seems better to use what space remains to confront, not my critics, but my own present sense of where my general intentions were mistaken, and how seriously my execution fell short of them.

The initial intention of the book is not, of course, unchallengeable. "Did the novel really rise?" To me, this question has the same kind of refrigerating generality as its much-mooted variant, "Is it now declining?"[16] Refrigerating because its meaning depends entirely on one's definition of the term "novel," and on the implications of the definite article which precedes it. My own title was really based on the current assumption in literary history, not on any personal or evaluative definition of "the novel"; and I take some modest comfort from the fact that the most widely-accepted view today about the development of prose narrative forms still seems to be the one I began to investigate, impossible as it now seems, nearly

---

15 I have discussed this elsewhere in an article, "The Recent Critical Fortunes of *Moll Flanders*," published in a new journal, *Eighteenth-Century Studies: A Journal of Literature and the Arts*, I (1967), 109–126.

16 I except Alan Friedman's excellent *The Turn of the Novel* (New York, 1966) from this generalization, since its title is, I suppose, obliquely ironical as well as allusive; and its subject is a specific historical change.

thirty years ago, and at a time when special permission was needed before one could take works of English fiction out of the Cambridge University Library.

Granted the premise, then, that in some qualified sense what are usually called novels first began to be written on a considerable scale in England and in the early eighteenth century, there seems no pressing reason to believe that my basic intentions were mistaken. I am certainly more convinced than ever of the value of what I suppose were the more original emphases in my treatment of the problem—roughly the sociological and the philosophic. It still seems to me that the whole question of the historical, institutional and social context of literature is very widely ignored, to the great detriment not only of much scholarly and critical writing, but of the general understanding of literature at every educational level. Secondly, though I can see more clearly now some of the inadequacies of logic and knowledge in the way I related philosophical ideas to the rise of the novel, the effort still seems to be preferable to the contrary, and still prevalent, tendency to write as though both ideas and novels existed independently of each other.

On the other hand I can see many ways in which my execution fell short of my intentions; and two of them, at least, seem worth considering in a little detail.

I've already alluded to the first—the truncation of my treatment of "realism of assessment." The omitted chapters on Fielding, Smollett and Sterne had attempted to show the various ways in which these later novelists got beyond "the tedious asseveration of literal authenticity" which characterized the formal realism of Defoe and Richardson, in order to bring the novel "into contact with the whole tradition of civilized values" (p. 288), which I took to be the ultimate aim of "realism of assessment." Something of the general range of these chapters can be surmised from the present concluding note (pp. 290–301): but many problems about the two realisms would have remained even if there had been no cuts.

To some extent the trouble was inherent in my method. I took over the commonest descriptive term applied to the novel—"realism"—and tried to clarify the issue by showing how the word was used to mean very different things. Nevertheless it seems clear to me now that I fell into the trap which awaits whoever employs the commonest of all Receipts to make an Academick Book—"Get yourself a couple of poles and turn 'em loose."

There was, to begin with, an unavoidable asymmetry in the terms: for one thing "realism of assessment" implied an evaluative—and implicitly approbative—moral judgment by its user, whereas "realism of presentation" referred to narrower and more technical matters; and for another, "realism of presentation" was specifically related to my subject, the novel, whereas "realism of assessment" was obviously a concept which was equally applicable to all forms of literature. Quite apart from this, however, my treatment assumed it was somehow possible to separate the two kinds of realism in a novel's structural elements—from the single word to the plot as a whole: and though this separation may be legitimate as an analytic construct, it is much more problematic than I realized.

As regards the smallest units—words and phrases—there is always a tension between the literal meaning, the bare denotation, on the one hand, and the connotations of the word on the other, to say nothing of its larger reference to the narration and to the whole pattern of the reader's expectations. This is true of the simplest word, and even, unfortunately enough, of the word "real." Thus when Tolstoy writes that, while Prince Vassily was telling the rich Princess Marya that he had always loved her as a daughter, "a real tear appeared in his eye" (III, iv), it is not just a question of the lachrymal-gland product as opposed to glycerine. A whole host of larger distinctions and assessments crowd in. Most obviously, Tolstoy is reminding us of the emotional falsity of the whole Kuragin clan at the very moment Vassily seems to be expressing his first disinterested sentiment: we expected false tears. Yet if we ruminate further, we see that Tolstoy is checking an absolute judgment—the Kuragins are also, and alas, human.

But if Tolstoy is the supreme master of the total and natural simultaneity of realism of presentation and of evaluation, some form of evaluation is always inextricably connected with any writer's presentation. Reading even the barest of Defoe's sentences in *Moll Flanders* we quite naturally go on from considering what is said to considering what is not said, and then to ask ourselves whether these conspicuous omissions are part of the picture of Moll's world or of Defoe's, or of both. That is, the reader finally concerns himself with Defoe's assessment of reality as it is implicit in words and phrases and sentences just as much as he does with Fielding. The difference is only that Fielding's words and phrases intentionally invoke not only the actual narrative event, but the whole literary, historical, and philosophical perspective in which character or action should be placed by the reader.

There is also a similar continual interplay of presentation and assessment—explicit or tacit—in the larger compositional elements of all narrative. This interplay can be briefly considered in relation to two of the larger compositional elements—the narrative episode and the plot as a whole.

The reader's impulse to make some kind of larger interpretation is quite independent of the author's wishes: it is a habit we have picked up from life. In every episode of *Moll Flanders* we develop our continuing judgment of the heroine as a criminal, as a woman, as a penitent, as an individual. Defoe, it is true, makes no very consistent effort to guide us as to what norms he intends us to use; but this merely makes the problem more difficult. There is a similar difficulty as regards Defoe's plot: we observe various elements of randomness and contradiction; and these finally become part of our final estimate of Defoe's view of life—we may decide, for instance, that the plot as a whole means something like: "If there is a pattern in human life it must be based on the single constant of individual biography and nothing else."

Here again Fielding is at the opposite pole; he really tells us that *Tom Jones* means what we can deduce from it: "This is the way I judge youth and goodness in general to be: and the general direction of life is towards the ordering of social groups, which are the supreme constants of the world as I see it." So with each of Fielding's narrative episodes: they are clearly responsible for whatever we can intelligently deduce from them.

My treatment did not go very far in this kind of analysis, perhaps because of my conceptual scheme. One major aspect of this problem has since been resolutely faced by Sheldon Sacks in his *Fiction and the Shape of Belief* (Berkeley and Los Angeles, 1964). But there are others: and a treatment of two of them, it now seems to me, might have clarified some of the larger connections of my subject.

"Realism of presentation" implies a narrative surface that is more or less identical with its meaning. But Fielding's novelistic technique is not primarily expressive in this sense. In his day the word "artificial" was still an approbative term though it was becoming obsolete (= "skilfully made"—1738; = "according to the rules of art"—1753. *OED*); and the elements of repetition, parallelism, and antithesis in Fielding's narrative pattern are intended to have an autonomous aesthetic appeal for their own sake—an appeal which is in its way similar to that of the combination of repetition and variation in sonata form, or to the sort of baroque narrative artifice which Casalduero has described in *Don Quixote*.[17]

Obtrusive patterning of this kind may do violence to the criteria of formal realism; but it is one way of solving another perennial problem for the novelist—that of detachment. Just as overtly as his generalized names or the multiple references of his diction, Fielding's plot invites the reader to detachment, and thence to conscious assessment.

In this and in many other ways, then, the relationship between the two realisms is more complicated than I thought. It was easy to show how realism of assessment, achieved through explicit authorial commentary, militated against realism of presentation; it was equally true, although less obvious, that emphasis on authenticity in itself makes it more difficult both for the reader and the author to achieve the aesthetic distance which encourages realism of assessment.

The second of the problems arising from the relationship between the two kinds of realism involves a rather different issue. If one goes a little further into the relationship between individual lives and actions and the social and moral norms by which they are judged, the relation between one aspect of eighteenth-century fiction and the later tradition of the novel becomes much clearer. Richardson and Fielding are alike in the sense that—in *Pamela* as in *Tom Jones*—the as-yet-undifferentiated ego of the protagonist is brought into contact with the various psychological, moral, and social norms of the author and his period. The very form of their basic plots enacts their normative assessment: and this helps one to see why the *Bildungsroman* has been one of the classic patterns in the tradition of the novel: the reader watches the individual being introduced to the general.

The insistence of Fielding and Richardson on normative standards was something they shared with their age. And it now seems to me that my failure to focus on evaluative fictional procedures which bore no direct relationship to later technical developments in the genre, was connected with my grossest substantive failure of execution. Briefly, through diffuse implication and assumption, rather than through explicit statement, I presented the "rise of the novel" as though it had been achieved in collusion with various changes in philosophical, moral and psychological outlook, and with something called the rising middle class (that restless

---

[17] Joaquín Casalduero, "The Composition of *Don Quixote*," *Cervantes Across the Centuries*, ed. Angel Flores and M. J. Bernadete (New York, 1947), pp. 56–93. See also my "Afterword" to *Joseph Andrews* (New York: Harper and Row, "Perennial Classics," 1966).

bunch). In so doing I tended to make it look as though the novel had emerged in consistent, though largely unconscious, opposition to the traditional social and literary establishment of the time.

Insofar as the main literary tendencies of the eighteenth century in England are labeled neo-classical, the contradiction is largely real: there was no convenient or prestigious place for prose fiction in the critical tradition that stemmed from Aristotle, Horace, and the Italian Renaissance critics; and most neo-classical critical theory was inimical to the particularizing, vernacular, and domestic kind of writing characteristic of the novel.

But for the writers of the time this contradiction was probably theoretical rather than operative; and in my concentration on "new" factors to account for a "new" form, I overlooked another set of common tendencies and traditions in eighteenth-century English life and literature, much more powerful than neo-classical theory, and only uneasily connected with it. These tendencies, which were reflected in many, though not all, of the features of the fiction of the period, are those which, for want of a better name, we call Augustan.

The term is admittedly vague, and can be misleading.[18] I use "Augustan" to denote the very substantial measure of general cultural continuity in England from 1660 to 1800, a continuity which seems to me to outweigh the period's admittedly enormous division of opinion. In this sense Augustan, like Georgian, is virtually a synonym for an elite outlook based on the defense of a civilized social order; and, quite as much as the card-carrying Augustans, all the major eighteenth-century novelists seem to me to belong to this movement, as did their successors, Jane Austen and Scott. They made stringent and wide-ranging criticisms of their age, but in ways and with accents which suggest that the Augustan norms seemed to them to have universal validity;[19] and these norms surely encouraged some of the special literary features which their novels had in common.

The political and religious settlements of 1660, 1689, and 1714 had brought about a very drastic reduction of the spectrum of literary attention: kings and courts, the military and heroic virtues, the intervention of God in human affairs— all these traditional components of classical literature, and especially of its chief narrative form, the epic, disappeared or at least occupied a much less prominent place. In *The Rise of the Novel* I related these changes to various aspects of individualism; but I should have added that much of the literary climate of the Augustan Age was determined by this drastic and pervasive reduction in the scale of human concerns. One result was to leave English literature free for a more intensive

---

[18] See James William Johnson, in his valuable article "The Meaning of Augustan": "it is the first four decades of the eighteenth century which are properly called 'Augustan,' " *Journal of the History of Ideas*, XIX (1958), 507–522; and Paul Fussell, *The Rhetorical World of Augustan Humanism: Ethics and Imagery from Swift to Burke* (Oxford, 1965).

[19] The fairly common view that Defoe and Fielding were in some sense radical dissenters from the class system of their day is only now being dispelled by such studies as Malvin R. Zirker's excellent *Fielding's Social Pamphlets* (Berkeley and Los Angeles, 1966). It is surely a move in the right direction to look at the similarities between the works of Richardson and Fielding, as William Park has recently done in his "Fielding *and* Richardson," *PMLA*, LXXVI (1966), 381–388.

and undisturbed cultivation of what was left—the social, personal and domestic life, and the application to it of what remained of traditional norms.

Of course we think of Augustan as denoting a primarily public demeanor; but the importance which the Augustans attached to private and social interests is actually very striking in contrast with France, where religious, political and intellectual divisions were so much more acute and imperative; and the assumption that the private life is man's major concern, which seems to me to be a characteristic Augustan attitude, in Temple and Congreve and Addison as well as in Pope, Johnson and Hume, points directly to the subject-matter of the novel.

In two main ways: to the novel's relatively detailed description of domestic life; and to the novel's interest in individual self-definition.

Minuteness of description was in some respects contrary to the neo-classical emphasis on generality and *la belle nature*. But although Swift and Johnson, for instance, mock detailed verisimilitude, and protest against numbering the streaks of the tulip, their own practice shows them to have been continually and successfully interested in the detailed presentation of the domestic scene. They did this mainly, it is true, in such peripheral literary forms as the journal and the private letter; but these are agreed to be modes of writing in which the Augustans were supreme. One could, indeed, reasonably argue that in the eighteenth century the most minute— and the most triumphant—descriptions of individual character in action against a fully presented environment are to be found, not in fiction, but in the various miscellaneous modes of the literature of experience. Thus Fanny Burney's novels hardly match the vividness of Horace Walpole's letters about social visits or parties of pleasure to Vauxhall, although her diaries almost do. Nor, I think, does even Richardson take us quite as close to the flux and reflux of consciousness as Boswell often does in his journals.

The question of individual self-definition is somewhat more difficult, since it is less characteristic of the English eighteenth-century novelists than it was to become later in France and Germany with Rousseau, Goethe and their successors. Still, one can certainly find the concern in many of the English novels of the period, from Defoe to Sterne, and it is central in Richardson. The identity crisis of Pamela,[20] for example, to say nothing of Clarissa's or Lovelace's, surely belongs to the same spiritual and psychological world as James Boswell's hectic pursuit of James Boswell.

There are, however, two general features of the Augustan attitude which seem to me to have been considerably less favorable to the emergence of what was later to be characteristic of the novel: the Augustan stresses on masculine and adult values. The two are, of course, functionally related; as when Chesterfield told his son that "Women . . . are only children of a larger growth" (September 5th, 1748). The pervasive importance of the Augustan attitude in the eighteenth-century novel suggests why it characteristically places much less emphasis on adolescent and feminine values than did later fiction.

---

[20] For one treatment of this, see my "Samuel Richardson," *The Listener*, Feb. 4, 1965, reprinted in *The Novelist as Innovator*, ed. Walter Allen (London, 1965).

When John Barth speaks of *Roderick Random* as a "healthy, hard-nosed counteragent to the cult of Love,"[21] his engaging truculence, supported by the example of his own later fiction, helps us to see how alien to Smollett is the novel's standard assumption that its moral and social norms can be generated purely out of the presentation of personal relationships. That particular assumption, of course, belongs to a very limited phase of historical development. It is primarily middle-class, leisured, and secular; it is also mainly adolescent and feminine; and one need not argue that Smollett's contemptuous mysogyny is typically Augustan to see the emphasis on feminine sensibility in Richardson, and later in Fanny Burney and the women novelists, as contrary to the predominant Augustan emphasis.

Of course the opposition isn't absolute. If we venture so far as the second part of *Pamela*, for instance, the novel's Augustan quality becomes much more obtrusive: it is an important part of Richardson's general ideological commitment that his servant girl should eventually develop into someone who speaks with the voice of a man, and a very grown-up one at that—an Addison or even a Locke.

The contradiction between Augustan values on the one hand, and feminine and youthful attitudes on the other, comes to the fore most revealingly in Jane Austen. As has often been observed, her young heroines finally marry older men—comprehensive epitomes of the Augustan norms such as Mr. Darcy and Mr. Knightley. Her novels in fact dramatize the process whereby feminine and adolescent values are painfully educated in the norms of the mature, rational and educated male world.

Here, no doubt, is the essence of some contemporary objections to the Augustan attitude and to eighteenth-century fiction: that it's conformist, cautious, cold; too much superego and too little id. Perhaps that's why today the most popular eighteenth-century novel is the one which is least committed to disciplined and adult values. *Fanny Hill* is the delicious exception that proves the rule; if there's anything more anomalous than a young Augustan, it's surely an ancient Venus.

---

[21] "Afterword," *Roderick Random* (New York: Signet Classics, 1964).

# III.
# Reappraisals

# The Contributions of Formalism and Structuralism to the Theory of Fiction

ROBERT SCHOLES

What follows here is both a discussion of a topic and a review of currently available books on that topic. The topic itself is important for two reasons: (a) because formalism and structuralism have indeed made significant contributions to the poetics of fiction, and (b) because these contributions have not been sufficiently recognized by American (and British) critics. The achievements of formalism have not been sufficiently appreciated because they have simply been unavailable until recently to readers who, like myself, are ignorant of the Slavic languages. Even now, we do not have in English all the formalist criticism I, for one, would like to see available. We have the excellent little anthology of Lee Lemon and Marion Reis (*Russian Formalist Criticism: Four Essays*, Bison Books, 1965—hereafter abbreviated to L & R) and a new volume, also well edited, by Ladislav Matejka and Krystyna Pomorska (*Readings in Russian Poetics*, M.I.T., 1971—abbreviated to *RRP*)—and that is all. Beyond these, there are some translations into French, Italian, and German. Thus the formalists have been only recently, and then scantily, available through their own writings. But I believe it is possible now to make a fair estimate of their achievements, even for a reader who, like myself, is confined to English and French.

The structuralists pose another problem. Where formalism is in some sense a completed literary movement, which can be treated historically (as it is in Victor Erlich's excellent *Russian Formalism: History-Doctrine*, Mouton, 1955), structuralism is very much in a state of becoming, with all the subdivisions and internecine struggles that we expect to find in a revolution in progress—especially one that shows signs of being successful. And where formalism was primarily a literary movement strongly influenced by linguistics, structuralism is a whole movement of mind, which no single discipline can claim to dominate. Thus Jean Piaget, in his superb survey of structuralist thinking (*Structuralism*, Basic Books, 1970), can treat his subject as it appears in mathematics, logic, physical science, biology, psychology, linguistics, anthropology, and philosophy. The study of language and other semiotic systems can make a strong claim to being at the center of all structuralist activity, but the study of literature has only a small piece of this intellectual action.

In addition to this, structuralist literary criticism is mainly untranslated from the French at the present time, and some of it appears to be equally impenetrable in either language. To understand it, a considerable investment of time and energy seems to be required—much of it to be expended in studying disciplines which do not appear to be immediately useful in the neatly compartmented world most academic literary critics inhabit. And then there is the possibility that structuralist literary criticism is presently what Boris Eichenbaum feared formalism might become in 1929: the work of academic "second-stringers" who "devote themselves to the business of devising terminology and displaying their erudition" (*RRP*, 57).

Certainly, some structuralist critics are engaged in taxonomic games of dubious value, but I am convinced that the whole enterprise is not only sound but essential, that useful work will be done and is currently being done under the structuralist aegis. It is not my intention here to survey the whole field of structuralist activity, though I hope on other occasions to consider other aspects of it. For the present, I must confine myself to a single line of development which leads directly from the formalists of the "Society for the Study of Poetic Language" in Petersburg (the *Opoyaz* group) and the "Moscow Linguistic Circle" through the Prague Circle to the French structuralists. The Russian formalists flourished in the twenties, and as early as 1934, Roman Jakobson, who had moved from the Moscow Circle to Prague, was calling for a change from formalism to a structuralism which could accommodate the dynamics of literature—the diachronic as well as the synchronic—and thus outgrow its mechanist heritage and develop a dialectical method ("Le Cercle du Prague," *Change*, 3, p. 59). Thus formalism evolved naturally into structuralism, partly through its awareness of new linguistic developments and partly as a response to Marxist criticisms of the formal method.

This literary structuralism which evolved out of formalism has been continued in French primarily by the young Bulgarian critic (or poetician as he would have it) Tzvetan Todorov. Because Todorov has himself emphasized the continuities between Russian Formalism and his own brand of structuralism, he is an appropriate figure to consider in this limited survey that I am about to present to you. He has, in fact, translated an excellent selection of Russian Formalist essays into French (*Théorie de la littérature*, Seuil, 1965—abbreviated to *TL*), and in his most recent book (*Poétique de la prose*, Seuil, 1971) he has, in his first essay, given us useful survey of "The Methodological Heritage of Formalism." I have elected to concentrate on Todorov in part because of his connections to formalism and his appreciation of the achievements of the formalists, but also because of his own preeminence as a structuralist critic. As a student of Roland Barthes, he became a contributor to the important journal of the École Pratique des Hautes Études in Paris: *Communications*. Subsequently, he has been a founder and editor of the journal *Poétique*, which has quickly become the leading international periodical devoted to literary theory—where one can find Michael Riffaterre and Hélène Cixous in the same issue with Paul de Man and Wayne Booth. Todorov has also been the secretary for an international group of semioticians interested in narrative structures, and the author of four books of literary criticism and poetics. I have chosen him, then, to exemplify the structuralist development of formalism, because he is, as Paul de Man has called him, "Mr. Structuralism," and because the major theme of all his work has been precisely the subject of this discussion: the theory of fiction.

And now, as I am getting ready to turn to my proper subject, I must pause just once more, to observe that not only have formalism and structuralism been largely ignored in this country—they have also, when considered at all, been misunderstood. As a "horrible" example of this I can cite an essay by Frederic Jameson, which was recently given pride of place in the most widely circulated (if not the best) periodical in our discipline: *PMLA*.[1] In the lead essay of the January 1971 *PMLA*, Mr. Jameson has offered us views of both formalism and structuralism, in an article appropriately titled "Metacommentary." (Since I intend to disagree extensively with some of the main points of this essay, I should like to preface my remarks by saying that it is one of the best things I have ever read in that dreary journal, and that the views of formalism and structuralism presented, though they are not mine, and are in fact "wrong," are nonetheless views which are both clever and well-informed.) In his essay Mr. Jameson observes that

> *Formalism is thus, as we have suggested, the basic mode of interpretation of those who refuse interpretation: at the same time, it is important to stress the fact that this method finds its privileged objects in the smaller forms, in short stories or folk tales, poems, anecdotes, in the decorative detail of larger works. For reasons to which we cannot do justice in the present context, the Formalistic model is essentially synchronic, and cannot adequately deal with diachrony, either in literary history or in the form of the individual work, which is to say that Formalism as a method stops short at the point where the novel as a problem begins.*

This statement, which is based partly on the assumption that formalism is mainly an attempt to substitute concern for form in the place of concern for content, seems to me wrong in a number of ways. It would be truer to say that formalism is more concerned with poetics than with interpretation, more concerned with producing useful generalizations about "literariness" than with ingenious readings of individual works—with the qualification that many formalists have produced excellent readings when this was their aim. But that formalist and structuralist criticism have proved unwilling or unable to deal with the temporal dimension of either particular works or literature in general is simply untrue. Though there was plenty of pressure in the direction of the synchronic from the model of Saussurien linguistics, it was counterbalanced very quickly by the linguistic influence of Jakobson and by the counterpressure of Hegelian and Marxist models, as found, for instance, in the literary criticism of Lukács. And finally, far from being helpless before the novel as a literary form, the formal method has given us virtually all the poetics of fiction we have. Though some of our theory seems to be home grown in English, there is hardly anything in current Anglo-American thinking about fictional form which has not been touched on by the formalists and their structuralist descendants. Even the special prob-

---

[1] Jameson's *The Prison-House of Language: A Critical Account of Structuralism and Russian Formalism*, however, a Hegelian critique of formalism and structuralism, will be essential reading for all those interested in the subject. Recently published by Princeton, it will be reviewed by Stanley Fish in the Spring 1973 NOVEL.

lem of point-of-view in fiction, which we think of as belonging to a line of Anglo-American critics that extends from Henry James to Wayne Booth, was treated, and treated intelligently, by the formalists. Other important concepts in our critical thinking about fiction have come to us directly from formalism through the mediation of such critics as René Wellek, who came to this country from the Prague Circle. But this introductory polemic has gone on long enough. It is time to begin documenting the achievements of Russian formalism with respect to the theory of literature and the theory of the novel in particular.

In reading the formalists an American must be struck by the fact that they were truly a critical "school." American critics, with a few notable exceptions, have been loners. But the formalists spoke to one another, read one another's work, refined and developed one another's ideas. In fact, the way they were able to build on one another's work suggests that they were actually achieving to some extent that "science of literature" which was their aim—for our discipline is a science to the extent that it is cumulative and an art to the extent that each critical work is unique. This interaction among the formalists makes it difficult to credit individuals with the development of particular concepts, but the two critics who wrote most extensively on fiction were Victor Shklovsky and Boris Eichenbaum, and it is their achievement primarily that I shall be examining here. Of these two, Shklovsky was the more innovative, but also the more extreme and hyperbolical. Eichenbaum is rather systematic and judicious. It was Shklovsky, for instance, who defended *Tristram Shandy* against the charge of not being a novel by insisting that it should be recognized as "the most typical novel in world literature" (L & R, 57). To the names of Shklovsky and Eichenbaum a third must be added, mainly on the strength of a single essay which summarizes and systematizes the whole formalist poetics of fiction. This is Boris Tomashevsky, whose essay "Thematics" is reprinted along with important pieces by Shklovsky and Eichenbaum, in the anthology of Lemon and Reis. But the appropriate place to begin this consideration of formalism is with a more general question—the relationship of formalism to literary history—which was treated by Eichenbaum in an essay on "Literary Environment," published in 1929 (*RRP*, 56–65).

Eichenbaum begins by pointing out that "without theory no historical system would be possible, because there would be no principle for selecting and conceptualizing facts." History, for Eichenbaum, is itself *in* history, and therefore must be continually revised:

> History is, in effect, a science of complex analogies, a science of double vision: the facts of the past have meanings for us that differentiate them and place them, invariably and inevitably, in a system under the sign of contemporary problems. Thus one set of problems supplants another, one set of facts overshadows another. History in this sense is a special method of studying the present with the aid of the facts of the past.
>
> The successive change of problems and conceptual signs leads to the reasortment of traditional material and the inclusion of new facts excluded from

*an earlier system because of the latter's innate limitations. The incorporation of a new set of facts (under the sign of some particular correlation) strikes us as being the discovery of those facts, since their existence outside a system (their "contingent" status) had been from a scientific point of view equivalent to their nonexistence.* (RRP, 56)

The passage will bear some analysis. It is typical of formal/structural thought in that it insists that truth is relative and that it is created rather than discovered. We should note that this view does not deny the reality of facts; it only maintains that there are too many to be apprehended unless they are limited and organized by a conceptual system. Content and form are inseparable, because one cannot exist without the other. Far from denying the temporal aspect of life, this view explicitly recognizes it. And it is closely related to a major aspect of the formalist theory of fictional construction. In their writings on fiction the formalists employ a distinction between two aspects of narrative: *story (fable)* and *plot (sujet)*. The *story* is the raw materials of the narrative, that is, the events in their chronological sequence. The *plot* is the narrative as actually shaped. We can think of story as being analogous to the facts of history itself, always running on at the same speed, in the same direction. In a *plot*, the speed may be changed, the direction reversed, at will. Actually, a *story* already represents items selected according to some elementary law of narrative logic which eliminates irrelevancies. And a *plot* is then a further refinement which organizes these items for maximum emotional effect and thematic interest. But it is fair to say that the facts of life are to history as the story is to the plot. History selects and arranges the events of existence, and plot selects and arranges the events of story. The art of fiction is, then, most apparent in the artificial re-arrangement of chronology which makes a story into a plot. Time is indeed crucial to fiction, and the formalists are aware not only of how crucial it is but of the ways in which it becomes crucial.

After establishing the necessity of theory for history in general, Eichenbaum turns to the specific problems of literary history. He begins by raising the question of the nature of the data. What, he asks, is a "literary-historical fact"? The answer, he suggests, depends on the solution to a theoretical problem: the nature of "the relationship between the facts of literary evolution and those of literary environment."

*The traditional literary-historical system was forged without regard to the fundamental distinction between the concepts of genesis and evolution, these having been taken instead for synonyms. Likewise, it made do without attempting to establish what was meant by a literary-historical fact. The consequence was a naive theory about "lineal descent" and "influence," and an equally naive psychological biographism.* (RRP, 59)

Pointing out that "it is not only literature that evolves; literary scholarship evolves with literature," Eichenbaum notes that naive influence-studies and naive psychologism have given way to an equally naive sociology of literature:

*Instead of utilizing under a new conceptual sign the earlier observations of the specific features of literary evolution (and those observations, after all, not only do not contradict but actually support an authentic sociological point of view), our literary "sociologists" have taken up the metaphysical quest for the prime principles of literary evolution and literary forms. They have had two possibilities at hand, both already applied and proved incapable of producing any literary-historical system: (1) the analysis of works of literature from the point of view of the writer's class ideology (a purely psychological approach, for which art is the least appropriate, the least characteristic material) and (2) the cause-and-effect derivation of literary forms and styles from the general socioeconomic and agricultural-industrial forms of the epoch.* (RRP, 60)

Eichenbaum rejects these positions on the following grounds:

*No genetic study, however far it may go, can lead us to the prime principle (assuming that the aims envisaged are scientific, not religious). Science in the long run does not explain phenomena but rather establishes only their properties and relationships. History is incapable of answering a single "why" question; it can only answer the question, "what does this mean?"*

*Literature, like any other specific order of things, is not generated from facts belonging to other orders and therefore cannot be reduced to such facts. The relations between the facts of the literary order and facts extrinsic to it cannot simply be causal relations but can only be the relations of correspondence, interaction, dependency, or conditionality.* (RRP, 61)

After explaining briefly the terminology of relationship that he has just employed, Eichenbaum makes the following crucial statement:

*Since literature is not reducible to any other order of things and cannot be the simple derivative of any other order, there is no reason to believe that all its constituent elements can be genetically conditioned. Literary-historical fact is a complex construct in which the fundamental role belongs to literariness— an element of such specificity that its study can be productive only in immanent-evolutionary terms.* (RRP, 62)

This statement is crucial because it sums up the formalist position in the face of Marxist pressure to abandon it. It compromises in a healthy way (which might properly be called dialectical) by accepting the notion that extra-literary facts condition the genesis of literary works. But it insists that the fundamental external conditioner of any work of literature is the literary tradition itself. This certainly does not end the debate between Marxists and formalists, but it clarifies the possibilities for further development. It asks of Marxist or sociological critics a comparable subtlety, such as we can find in the work of a contemporary Marxist/structuralist like Lucien Goldmann, whose *Pour une sociologie du roman* (Gallimard, 1964) has affinities with Lukács and with formalism as well. At any rate, it should be clear now that far from ignoring history, the formalists had an appropriately formal view of it. This view will be evident again when we come to examine the formalist approach to fictional genres. But before considering the problems of genre as such, we should consider some of the basic conceptual vocabulary of the formalist poetics of fiction.

One of the great problems in the theory of fiction from Aristotle to Auerbach has been the relationship between fictional art and life: the problem of *mimesis*. The formalist approach to this problem, far from being a lapse into pure aestheticism, or a denial of the mimetic component in fiction, is an attempt to discover exactly what verbal art does to life and for life. This is most apparent in Victor Shklovsky's concept of *defamiliarization*. (Shklovsky's concept is grounded in a theory of perception which is essentially Gestaltist, though apparently arrived at independently, without direct contact with the work of the German Gestalt psychologists. Shklovsky himself cites only the linguists Jakubinsky and Pogodin in this connection—but he lived in Berlin for some years and quite possibly knew of the Gestalt psychologists' work.) "As perception becomes habitual," Shklovsky notes, "it becomes automatic." And he adds, "We see the object as though it were enveloped in a sack. We know what it is by its configuration, but we see only its silhouette." In considering a passage from Tolstoy's *Diary*, Shklovsky reaches the following conclusion:

> *Habitualization devours objects, clothes, furniture, one's wife, and the fear of war. "If all the complex lives of many people go on unconsciously, then such lives are as if they had never been."*
>
> *Art exists to help us recover the sensation of life; it exists to make us feel things, to make the stone stony. The end of art is to give a sensation of the object as seen, not as recognized. The technique of art is to make things "unfamiliar," to make forms obscure, so as to increase the difficulty and the duration of perception. The act of perception in art is an end in itself and must be prolonged. In art, it is our experience of the process of construction that counts, not the finished product.*
>
> (In quoting this passage, I initially intended simply to use the Lemon and Reis version [p. 12]. But their treatment of the last sentence, in particular, seemed to me strange. Their version reads this way: "*Art is a way of experiencing the artfulness of an object; the object is not important.*" This reading is too open to a narrowly "aesthetic" or "art-for-art's-sake" interpretation, in my judgment. Todorov's French version is more satisfactory: "*l'art est un moyen d'éprouver le devenir de l'objet, ce qui est déjà 'devenu' n'importe pas pour l'art*" [p. 83]. With the aid of Professor Thomas Winner of Brown University, I consulted the Russian text, which reads as follows: "*iskusstvo jest sposob perezit' delan'e vesci, a sdelannoe v iskusstve ne vazno.*" A close, literal translation would be: art is the means for experiencing the making of the thing, but the thing made is not important in art.)

Shklovsky goes on to illustrate the technique of defamiliarization extensively from the works of Tolstoy, showing us how Tolstoy, by using the point of view of a peasant, or even an animal, can make the familiar seem strange, so that we see it again. Defamiliarization is not only a fundamental technique of mimetic art, it is its principal justification as well. In fiction, defamiliarization is achieved through point of view and through style, of course, but it is also accomplished by plotting itself. Plot, by rearranging the events of story, defamiliarizes them and opens them to perception. And because art itself exists in time, the specific devices of defamiliarization themselves succumb to habit and become conventions which finally obscure the very objects and events they were invented to display. Thus there can be no permanently "realistic" technique. Ultimately, the artist's reaction to the tyranny of fictional conventions of representation is a parodic one. He will, as Shklovsky says, "lay bare" the conventional techniques by exaggerating them. Thus Shklovsky analyzes *Tristram Shandy* as primarily a work of fiction *about* fictional technique. Because it focusses on the devices of fiction it is also about modes of perception—about the interpenetration of art and life. The laying bare of literary devices makes *them* seem strange and unfamiliar, too, so that we are especially aware of them. Defamiliarization applied to art itself results in the exposure of literary devices. Thus art in general and fiction in particular can be seen as a dialectic of defamiliarization in which new techniques of representation ultimately generate counter-techniques which expose them to ridicule. And this dialectic is at the center of the history of fiction.

The best summary of the formalist poetics of fiction can be found in Boris Toma-shevsky's essay on "Thematics" (which is included in Lemon and Reis). Toma-shevsky begins by asserting that the unifying principle in a fictional structure is a general thought, or a theme. In a work of fiction, thematic materials reflect the presence of two rather different forces, one from the immediate environment of the writer, the other from the literary tradition in which he writes. They also reflect the different concerns of the writer and the reader. "The writer tries to solve the problem of artistic tradition," while the reader may simply want to be entertained—or he may want "a combination of literary interests and general cultural concerns." This latter kind of reader demands "reality—that is, themes that are 'real' in the context of contemporary cultural thought." Tomashevsky postulates a continuum of thematic materials ranging from the most local and topical themes, which will not sustain interest for long, to themes of general human interest such as love and death. "The more significant and long-lasting the theme, the better the guarantee of the life of the work." But even the en-during themes must be presented through "some kind of specific material" which must be relevant to reality if the formulation of the problem is not to "prove 'uninteresting'."

In any given novel the major theme can be seen as composed of smaller the-matic units. The irreducible units of fiction are *motifs*. Thus *story* can be defined as the sum of the motifs in their causal-chronological order, *plot* as the sum of the same motifs ordered so as to engage the emotions and develop the theme: "The esthetic function of the plot is precisely this bringing of an arrangement of motifs to the attention of the reader. Tomashevsky calls the principle of ar-rangement *motivation*, and he notes that motivation is always "a compromise between objective reality and literary tradition." Because readers needs the illusion of lifelikeness, fiction must provide it. But, since "realistic material itself does not have artistic structure," then "the formation of an artistic structure requires that reality be reconstructed according to esthetic laws. Such laws are always, considered in relation to reality, conventional."

In connection with motivation Tomashevsky discusses various kinds of motifs (bound and free, static and dynamic), the different value of motifs with respect to plot and story, the different kinds of narrators (omniscient, limited, and mixed), the treatment of time and place, the varieties of character (static and dynamic, positive and negative), the various devices of the plot (conventional and free, obvious or imperceptible), and finally the relation of these devices to the two major fictional styles (natural and artificial). This material is too rich and too specific to be more than mentioned here, since Tomashevsky himself has presented it with close to the maximum possible compression and concentration. Despite the nearly fifty years since its publication, it can still function as a primer of fictional poetics. Tomashevsky has not been superseded; he has only been qualified and refined upon by later writers.

The refinement of formalist poetics was begun by the formalists themselves. We can see one aspect of this refinement by considering an important essay of Victor Shklovsky's in relation to certain modifications of the formalist position developed by the formalists themselves and their structuralist descendants. In his essay "On the Construction of the Short Story and the Novel" (TL, 170–196), Shklovsky uses these two forms of fiction to develop some common properties of all fiction and to distinguish some of the special qualities of these two distinct types. He begins by raising the basic question of what makes a story a story: "It is not enough for us to be presented with a simple image, nor a simple parallel, nor even a simple description of an event, for us to have the impression that we are confronted with a story." He concludes that the story is much more end-oriented than the novel; that is, that the story is carefully constructed so as to give us a feeling of completion at its conclusion, while the novel often concludes its main action before the end, or seems capable of indefinite extension. Thus certain kinds of novels resort to the epilogue, changing the scale of time so as to conclude matters briskly. (This is actually a notion developed by Eichenbaum, working with Shklovsky's ideas.) But in the short story, the plotting functions more neatly to lead to a conclusion that is a true dénouement. What kinds of motivation, Shklovsky then asks, give us this important sense of an ending? He distinguishes two basic types: that of opposition resolved, and that of similarity revealed. In the one case our sense of completion is more oriented to action, in the other to theme. But in both cases there is a common principle at work, a circular movement which links the end with the beginning, either by comparison or by constrast.

Shklovsky also notes that collections of linked tales existed long before the novel established itself as a form. He is careful not to insist that the novel was necessarily "caused" by these earlier forms (as Eichenbaum points out, the novel derives from history, travel narratives, and other marginally literary forms), but he implies that the principles of construction found in the ancient collections of tales anticipate those found in the novel. He distinguishes two types of construction: linking and framing. Construction by framing leads to such things as the *1001 Nights,* the *Decameron,* and the *Canterbury Tales.* Construction by linking is most frequently found in works which present the various deeds of a single hero. Such narratives as *The Golden Ass* use a combination of linking and framing. Both methods, Shklovsky points out, lead to a certain enriching of these forms with matters outside the action, which point in the direction of the novel. In the framed collection of tales, for instance, the tellers themselves and the characters in the tales are not really developed: "Our attention is concentrated on the action; the agent is only a playing card which permits the plot to be developed." This trend continues for a long time. Even in the eighteenth century we find agents like Gil Blas, who is "not a man; he is a thread which connects the episodes of the novel—and this thread is gray." On the other hand, development of character can be found in earlier literatures: "In the *Canterbury Tales,* the connection between the action and the agent is very strong." The method of tales strung together around a single personage, when this becomes a person travelling in search of employment, as in *Lazarillo de Tormes* or *Gil Blas,* can lead to the enrichment of fiction with materials of a sociological nature, as in Cervantes's exemplary story of the "Glass Licentiate" and, of course, in *Don Quixote.* And such enrichment does point the way toward the modern novel and short story.

The evolution of these forms was taken up by Boris Eichenbaum in some passages of critical writing brought together by Tzvetan Todorov (*TL,* 197–211) under the title "On the Theory of Prose." (The second part of this material can be found in English in *RRP,* 231–238, in Eichenbaum's essay on "O. Henry and the theory of the Short Story.") Eichenbaum begins by considering the relationship between the oral tale and the written story. He first points out the way in which the prose genres, unlike verse, are cut off from vocal performance and develop techniques peculiar to written language. Thus written fictions orient themselves toward epistolary form, memoirs, notes, descriptive studies, journalistic sketches, and so on. Oral speech reenters fiction, however, in the form of dialogue. Eichenbaum suggests that such tales as those in the *Decameron* have a fundamental connection with oral speech: that is, they are related to the oral tale and the gossip's anecdote, in which the narrator's voice subsumes all others. Early novels, growing out of such collections of tales, kept this elementary oral quality. But by the eighteenth century, a new kind of novel, derived from a bookish culture, established itself. The oral element persisted in such features as the oratorical narrative voice of Scott or the lyrical voice of Hugo—but even these were closer to rhetorical declamation than to simple oral story-telling. In the main, however, the European novel of the eighteenth and especially the nineteenth centuries was dominated by description, psychological portraiture, and scenic presentation. "In this manner," says Eichenbaum, "the novel broke with narrative form and became a combination of dialogues, scenes, and detailed presentations of decor, gestures, and intonations. For Eichenbaum, then, the novel is a "syncretic" form, which is made up of other "elementary" forms. And in this connection he cites with approval the presence of this notion in earlier Russian literary criticism—quoting from Shevirev, who in 1843 had called the novel a new mixture of all the genres, with variant sub-classes such as the epic novel (*Don Quixote*), the lyrical novel (*Werther*), and the dramatic novel (Scott).

In turning to the history of the novel as a form, Eichenbaum naturally confronted the problem of genres:

> *In the evolution of each genre, there are times when its use for entirely serious or elevated objectives degenerates and produces a comic or parodic form. The same phenomenon has happened to the epic poem, the adventure novel, the biographical novel, etc. Naturally, local and historical conditions create different variations, but the process itself exhibits this same pattern as an evolutionary law: the serious interpretation of a construction motivated with care and in detail gives way to irony, pleasantry, pastiche; the connections which serve to motivate a scene become weaker and more obvious; the author himself comes on stage and often destroys the illusion of authenticity and seriousness; the construction of a plot becomes a playing with the story which transforms itself into a puzzle or an anecdote. And thus is produced the regeneration of the genre: it finds new possibilities and new forms.* (TL, 208–9)   (RRP, 236)

This is certainly diachronic thinking, and very convincing thinking, as well. It is as if, in 1925, Eichenbaum could envision Borges and Barth and a host of contemporary writers. (Nabokov, of course, emerged from an intellectual milieu closely allied to formalism.) Eichenbaum's generic thinking represents an increasing sophistication within formalism, which leads directly to structuralism. This sophistication is especially apparent in the work of Roman Jakobson, as we find it, for instance, in a lecture he gave at Masaryk University in 1935 on the Russian formalists.

In this lecture, Jakobson emphasized the importance of the concept of "dominance" as a key to formalist poetics. ("The Dominant," *RRP*, 82–87.) He defined the dominant as "the focussing component of a work of art: it rules, determines, transforms the remaining components. It is the dominant which guarantees the integrity of the structure" (*RRP*, 82). And beyond the individual work, "we may seek a dominant not only in the poetic work of an individual artist and not only in the poetic canon, the set of norms of a given poetic school, but also in the art of a given epoch, viewed as a whole" (83). Plastic art dominated in the Renaissance, music in the Romantic period, verbal art in the esthetics of realism. Using the concept of dominance, Jakobson is able to criticize the early tendency of formalism to insist on the purity of artistic language. A poem, he observes, does not have a merely esthetic function: "Actually, the intentions of a poetic work are often closely related to philosophy, social dialectics, etc." And he points out that the converse is true as well—that "just as a poetic work is not exhausted by its esthetic function, similarly, esthetic function is not limited to the poetic work." In oratory, journalism, even in a scientific treatise we may expect to find words used in and for themselves, and not in a purely referential way. Thus a monistic estheticism would obscure aspects of poetry. But a mechanistic pluralism, which sees art works only as documents of cultural history, social relations, or biography, is equally limited. Rather,

> a poetic work must be defined as a verbal message whose esthetic function is its dominant. Of course, the marks disclosing the implementation of the esthetic function are not unchangeable or always uniform. Each concrete poetic canon, every set of temporal poetic norms, however, comprises indispensable, distinctive elements without which the work cannot be identified as poetic. (RRP, 84)

In this view, poetic evolution can be seen as a matter of changes in the elements of a poetic system which are a function of a "shifting dominant":

> Within a given complex of poetic norms in general, or especially within the set of poetic norms valid for a given poetic genre, elements which were originally secondary become essential and primary. On the other hand, the elements which were originally the dominant ones become subsidiary and optional. In the earlier works of Shklovsky, a poetic work was defined as a mere sum of its artistic devices, while poetic evolution appeared nothing more than a substitution of certain devices. With the further development of formalism, there arose the accurate conception of a poetic work as a structured system, a regularly ordered hierarchical set of artistic devices. Poetic evolution is a shift in this hierarchy. The hierarchy of artistic devices changes within the framework of a given poetic genre; the change, moreover, affects the hierarchy of poetic genres, and, simultaneously, the distribution of artistic devices among the individual genres. Genres which were originally secondary paths, subsidiary variants, now come to the fore, whereas the canonical genres are pushed toward the rear. (RRP, 85)

Armed with an awareness sharpened by the concept of dominance, the formalists rewrote Russian literary history in a way both richer and more ordered. This new awareness also directed attention to a fruitful area of investigation: the boundaries between literature and other kinds of verbal message:

> Of special interest for investigators are the transitional genres. In certain periods such genres are evaluated as extraliterary and extrapoetical, while in other periods they may fulfill an important literary function because they comprise those elements which are about to be emphasized by belles lettres, whereas the canonical forms are deprived of those elements. (RRP, 86)

In his concluding paragraph, Jakobson pointed out how formalism finally encouraged the linguistic study of shifts and transformations, thus giving back to linguistics something in return for all that it had borrowed:

> This aspect of formalist analysis in the field of poetic language had a pioneering significance for linguistic research in general, since it provided important impulses toward overcoming and bridging the gap between the diachronic historical method and the synchronic method of chronological cross section. It was

*formalist research which clearly demonstrated that shifting and change are not only historical statements (first there was A, and then A₁ arose in place of A) but that shift is also a directly experienced synchronic phenomenon, a relevant artistic value. The reader of a poem or the viewer of a painting has a vivid awareness of two orders: the traditional canon and the artistic novelty as a deviation from that canon. It is precisely against the background of that tradition that innovation is conceived. The formalist studies brought to light that this simultaneous preservation of tradition and breaking away from tradition form the essence of every new work of art.* (RRP, 87)

Thus formalism, by refusing to abandon the diachronic aspect of poetics, helped structural linguistics become transformational.

In turning now to the structuralist poetics of fiction, as exemplified in the writing of Tzvetan Todorov, I want to emphasize what I take to be the importance of his work for the theory of fiction. We have, and will no doubt continue to have, in our Anglo-Saxon critical tradition, excellent works of criticism, sensitive readings of individual works, illuminating studies of various writers, and even useful discussions of certain technical problems, such as point-of-view. But we do not have any body of work by a single critic of fiction which is as wide-ranging and as systematic as the work of this young man. We have critics like Northrop Frye, who pay lip service to the notion of a science of criticism and then proceed on their astonishingly idiosyncratic ways. But we have no English equivalent for this cool and comprehensive study of fiction, which also manages to be extremely perceptive about individual works. If there can be a science of literature, critics like Todorov, rather than Frye, will bring it into being.

In addition to his personal gifts, Todorov has had the great advantage of working from the heritage of Russian formalism toward his own fictional poetics. Thus he has behind him not only the rich conceptual apparatus developed by Shklovsky, Tomashevsky, and Eichenbaum, but also the remarkable structural study of folk narrative by Vladimir Propp (see *Morphology of the Folk Tale*, Texas, 1969; and "Fairy Tale Transformations" in *RRP*, 94–114), and the subtle and flexible linguistics of Roman Jakobson. Structuralist criticism in general has benefited immensely from its association with linguistics, but the nature of this relationship has not been fully understood—especially by those of us on the sidelines. It can be illustrated in a fairly vivid manner, by a verbal exchange which took place at Johns Hopkins University in October, 1966. At that time Hopkins was holding a conference, attended by most of the leading structuralist theoreticians and representatives of other modern schools of thought as well. The proceedings—which are fascinating—were published by the Johns Hopkins Press in 1970 under the title *The Languages of Criticism and the Sciences of Man: The Structuralist Controversy* (edited by Richard Macksey and Eugenio Donato— abbreviated to *LCSM*). The exchange I am referring to took place when Nicholas Ruwet (Belgian linguist and French translator of Roman Jakobson) confronted Roland Barthes and Tzvetan Todorov, accusing them of using a limited and somewhat dated linguistics. Todorov replied:

*Ruwet has correctly remarked that all of us who have spoken of linguistics here have drawn on a few articles by Benveniste and not on the latest acquisitions in linguistics. I think that the explanation for this fact goes further than simple lack of information. Linguistics since Saussure has become a more and more limited field, which might be called grammar and which is a very abstract code which engenders sentences. Literature, however, is a type of discourse, not a language. Benveniste, along with Jakobson, seems to be one of the rare linguists who has continued to be interested in the questions which serve to convert language into discourse. (LCSM, 315–16)*

Ruwet answered that linguistics was not narrowing but broadening. Barthes countered by saying that literary semiotics needs a linguistics which does not yet exist. Ruwet agreed, with the final warning that most attempts to convert linguistic knowledge into literary criticism are merely impressionistic, having no more validity than any other kind of impressionistic criticism.

The whole of Todorov's work suggests two answers to this position. First, that there are genuine analogies between certain fundamental linguistic categories and basic fictional structures (such as character/noun, attribute/adjective, and action/verb). And second, that there is another discipline already existing which mediates between linguistics and literary study: namely, rhetoric. Thus, we can find Todorov reexamining Shklovsky's typology of fictional forms from these two perspectives. First, he observes that Shklovsky's two basic types of fictional structure—linking and framing—correspond to two fundamental syntactic structures—coordination and subordination (or embedding). This second structure results in a return at the end of a story to a situation which resembles the initial situation or stands in a parallel relation to it, like the story of Oedipus, which begins with a prediction and ends with its realization.

*In the passage cited above, it was a question of parallelism; this process is only one of those designated by Shklovsky. In analysing* War and Peace, *he cites, for example, the* antithesis *formed by pairs of characters: "1. Napoleon-Kutuzov; 2. Pierre Bezukov-Andre Bolkonsky and at the same time Nicholas Rostov who serves as an axis of reference between them". We find also* gradation: *many members of a family present the same character traits but in different degrees. Thus in* Anna Karenina *"Stiva is placed on a lower level than his sister".*

*But parallelism, antithesis, gradation, and repetition are also figures of rhetoric. One can thus formulate the thesis underlying the remarks of Shklovsky: there are fictional figures which are projections of rhetorical figures. (LCSM, 127, not well translated)*

From here Todorov goes on to develop similar projections of other rhetorical figures. Thus both linguistics and its less reputable brother, rhetoric, enter into his study of fiction. But the point which must be emphasized here is that for critics like Barthes and Todorov, linguistics is something familiar, handy—a collection of useful conceptual tools, not an arcane science which the literary critic must approach with awe or flee in esthetic disdain. This view of linguistics has much to recommend it.

Now it is time to turn to Todorov's achievement as a poetician (to use his word) of fiction. This achievement rests primarily on work to be found in the following six volumes:

1. *Théorie de la littérature* (Seuil, '65), his translation of texts from the Russian formalists.
2. *Littérature et signification* (Larousse, '67), a study based on *Les Liaisons Dangereuses*.
3. *Qu'est-ce-que le structuralisme* (Seuil, '68), a collection of essays by five authors, edited by François Wahl, which includes chapters on linguistics, poetics (by Todorov), anthropology, psychoanalysis, and philosophy.
4. *Grammaire du Décameron* (Mouton, '69).
5. *Introduction a la littérature fantastique* (Seuil, '70) [abbreviated hereafter to *ILF*].[2]
6. *Poétique de la prose* (Seuil, '71).

The extent of this body of work makes it impossible to treat in a brief compass, but I believe I can at least sketch the nature of it as a whole and point to certain specific achievements within it. I will begin by describing the most important studies and conclude with a more detailed discussion of some specific items.

Setting aside the translations, and the essay on poetics in *Qu'est-ce-que le structuralisme*, which is a kind of manifesto, we have four books that deal directly with the poetics of fiction as it manifests itself in particular texts. The first of these takes as its particular subject a single epistolary novel and considers it from the perspective of its meaning or signification. The second takes a collection of tales by a single author and tries to abstract from them a basic grammar, a deep structure which is transformed as it manifests itself in the particular utterance of each separate tale. The third takes up the problem of fictional genres and treats it in terms of one specific genre. And the last is a collection of essays written over a period of four or five years, which includes all the preoccupations of the other volumes and adds some new ones. This last book, then, *Poétique de la prose*, can serve to illustrate the themes of Todorov's work as a whole. It includes theoretical essays on the heritage of formalism, on the relationship between literature and language, on the relationship between poetics and criticism, on the "*vraisemblable*," on narrative transformations, and on how to read. These theoretical essays, which of course have continual recourse to particular texts, serve to frame essays on certain works of literature which illustrate specific aspects of fictional poetics. The works studied include detective stories, the *Odyssey*, the *Thousand and One Nights*, the writings (fiction and journals) of Benjamin Constant, the *Decameron*, the *Quest of the Holy Grail*, some novellas of Henry James, the ghostly tales of James, and the prose of Klebnikov and Artaud. The range is

---

[2] This work is being translated by Richard Howard and will be published by the Case-Western Reserve Press.

impressive. And it is functional, because Todorov's experience with this variety of fictional texts enables him to write with authority about the nature of narrative literature as a whole—and the special qualities of particular texts. Thus, when he singles out a particular problem as being of special importance, we must take him seriously:

> *The problem which is the most complex, the least clear in all literary theory . . . is:* how to speak of that which literature itself speaks about.
>
> *In schematising this problem, one can say that two symmetrical dangers are to be feared. The first would reduce literature to a pure content. . . . It is an attitude which leads to the ignoring of literary specificity, which puts literature on the same level, for example, as philosophical discourse. . . . The second danger, inverse of the first, would lead to the reduction of literature to a pure "form" and deny the pertinence of themes in literary analysis.* (ILF, 100–101)

Here, precisely, is where he locates the need for a structuralist poetics:

> *If structuralism has taken a single step beyond formalism, it is precisely through having ceased to isolate a form as the only valuable quality of a work while remaining uninterested in content. A work of art is not a form and a content but a structure of significations whose interrelationships must be understood.* (Poétique de la Prose, 54)

It is in the context of this problem that the title of Todorov's book on *Les Liaisons Dangereuses, Littérature et signification,* must be understood. He has selected de Laclos' epistolary novel as the text for this study because the letter itself raises all the important questions about literary signification, and offers a means of approaching the answers. The fictional letter suggests the usefulness of linguistic and semiotic models of communication to the critic who wishes to regard a fictional work as a significant text. The meaning of a letter depends on all the elements in the process of *énonciation* enumerated by Roman Jakobson: sender, receiver, context, and contact. And so does the meaning of a literary work. The work implies its own sender and receiver, and it shapes the relationship between them. The actual author and the actual reader meet only through these shadowy implied figures, who must share a system of signification which includes the evaluation of the things discussed. Thus in literary criticism we have both the "sense" of the work and all the interpretations that can be based upon it:

> *One can, with Stendhal, find that Mlle de Tourvel is the most immoral person in* Les Liaisons Dangereuses; *one can, with Simone de Beauvoir, assert that Mme de Merteuil is the most engaging character in it; but these are interpretations exterior to the sense of the book. If we do not condemn Mme de Merteuil, if we do not side with the Présidente, the structure of the work would be altered. We must take into account at the outset that there are moral interpretations of two totally different kinds; one is from inside the book (or any work of imitative art) and the other is that produced by readers without considering the logic of the work; and this latter will vary noticeably in different periods or for readers of different temperaments.* (Littérature et signification, 88)

Todorov is close to E. D. Hirsch here. (Jameson points out that the affinity between Hirsch and the structuralists on this point can be traced to Frege and Carnap.) But he has somewhat more to offer us than Hirsch in several areas. First, his notion of the sense of a text is more sophisticated than Hirsch's, both linguistically and esthetically. Second, his notion of literary genres is more developed. And finally, he is not paralysed by the "hermeneutic circle," but believes that structuralist criticism can indeed reach a true understanding of literary texts —and he offers us extended, convincing demonstrations of this method. All this is apparent in his book on the fantastic, which I shall now consider in some detail.

This introduction to fantastic literature is an essay in generic criticism. Thus it begins with a discussion of the problems of generic criticism in general. Noting that the concept of genre is borrowed from zoology, Todorov points out that literary genres are different from those of natural science (and those of linguistics as well). In literature, each new work makes a change in the whole species. Only in the lower literary forms are works produced according to generic stereotypes. But all literary works belong to literature, and the literary genres represent the connections between each work and the entire world of literature. At this point Todorov pauses to consider the generic theories of Northrop Frye, which he criticizes calmly but devastatingly as illogical and inconsistent internally—and in actual violation of Frye's own stated aims. Frye is not a structuralist but a taxonomist.

Todorov's own generic theory begins with a method for distinguishing three aspects of any work of fiction: the *verbal*, the *syntactic*, and the *semantic*. The *verbal* includes the style, or the resonances of language in the work, and also the question of point of view—the narrator/reader relationship and the relationship of these two to the characters. The *syntactic* includes the relationships among the parts of a work: logical, temporal, and spatial. And the *semantic* includes the themes or subjects presented. In generic study one looks for patterns in the relationships among all of these three aspects of the work. A generic scheme will finally be the result of a continual working back and forth from an abstract structure of generic theory to the actual works that have constituted a genre in history.

In turning to the actual works of fantastic literature, Todorov bases his preliminary definition on a hesitation in the mind of the protagonist—and of the reader—as to whether an event that has occurred is real or imaginary, natural or supernatural. This hesitation, he says, is at the heart of the genre, and if it is resolved, the genre itself is altered. If an apparently supernatural event is given a natural explanation, we leave the fantastic and enter the strange. On the other hand, if the supernatural is accepted as a matter of course (as in fairy tales), we leave by the opposite gate and enter the world of the marvelous. The fantastic exists as a line of demarcation between its more stable neighbors—thus it is one of those interesting cases that Jakobson suggested would repay investigation. The fantastic is also threatened by allegory, which would reduce its problematic events to figures hiding another meaning; and by poetry, which would diminish the mimetic or representational quality of the work. The fantastic is a specifically narrative genre, a fiction.

Thematically, the fantastic offers us two major categories, the themes of "I" and the themes of "thou." The first category deals with relationships between the percipient and objects. The themes of "I" include distortions in perception that function in fantastic fiction: the crossing of limits between matter and spirit, the derangement of consciousness—all those things that relate fantastic fiction to madness, mysticism, narcotic vision, and infantile views of the world. The second category—themes of "thou"—concerns the interaction of the individual with others. In the fantastic, these themes are primarily sexual, and especially concern forbidden or perverse desires:

> We have seen that one can interpret the themes of "I" as bringing into the work the relationship between man and the world, the system of perception-consciousness. . . . If we wanted to interpret the themes of "thou" at the same level of generality, we would have to say that it is rather a question of the relationship of man to his desire, and thus to his unconscious. (ILF, 146)

Finally, Todorov looks at the fantastic as a historical phenomenon, a genre that flourished in the nineteenth century:

> The nineteenth century lived, it is true, in a metaphysic of the real and the imaginary, and fantastic literature is nothing other than the bad conscience of the nineteenth-century positivist. But today one can no longer believe in a reality which is fixed, external, nor in a literature which would merely be the transcription of his reality. (ILF, 176)

The decline of fantastic fiction coincided historically with the rise of psychoanalysis, so that "the themes of fantastic literature became, literally, the preoccupations of psychological research." Thus the fantastic, a timeless possibility of generic theory, had a rise and fall in the temporal movement of generic history. And Tzvetan Todorov, whose achievement I have so inadequately presented here, has used this generic phenomenon to demonstrate precisely how a properly structuralist criticism can do what its opponents maintain it cannot: how it can deal effectively with the meaning of fictional works and the movement of fictional history, as these relate to the meaning and the movement of life itself.

# *Lukacs'* Theory of the Novel

GRAHAM GOOD

We do not expect lyricism from our literary critics any more, especially from a famed Marxist one. So the opening of Lukács' *Theory of the Novel*[1] may come as a shock: "Happy are those ages when the starry sky is the map of all possible paths. . . ." The author, after this paean to the "integrated" civilization of classical Greece, goes on to confound our modern taste for being reassured every now and then, by means of dates, names of writers and books, quotations and so on, that we know where we are: long reaches of Lukács' essay go by without these comforting little markers. Its lyrical-abstract style is the product of its period (it was written in 1914–15 and first published in a periodical in 1916 and in book form in 1920), a decade which saw feverish cults of Hölderlin and Kleist, Kierkegaard and Dostoevsky, as well as much millenial talk about the "god-abandoned world." The intellectual tone of that decade in Germany is wonderfully recaptured in parts of Thomas Mann's *Doktor Faustus*, and Lukács' turns of phrase are often reminiscent of those passages. Indeed, both Lukács in his 1962 introduction and the publisher in his 1971 advertisement seem to stress historical and biographical interest as the book's major claim on our attention. It is, of course, a fascinating juncture in Lukács' intellectual career: as he informs us, he was "in process of turning from Kant to Hegel" before finally arriving at Marx in the wake of the Russian Revolution. Nevertheless it would be a mistake to dismiss the essay as simply a period piece: despite its remote style and its other shortcomings, its intellectual substance can make a valuable contribution to the current debate on the theory of the novel.

I

Lukács begins his argument from the concept (central to much of his later work also) of totality. By this he means, both in art and in life, a whole within which everything is complete and from which nothing is consciously excluded; there is no need of anything beyond it to explain it. In certain ages (such as Homer's or Dante's) this completeness is given to art, and does not have to be established by the art-work itself. This idea is the basis for Lukács' principal generic distinction: "Great epic writing gives form to the extensive totality of life, drama to the intensive totality of essence." But here we should pause to clear up a possible confusion of generic terminology. Like other aestheticians in the German tradition, Lukács treats the novel as a form of the epic. He subsumes the epic proper

---

[1] Trans. Anna Bostock (London: Merlin Press, and Cambridge, Mass.: M.I.T. Press, 1971), 160 pp.

(*die Epopöe*) and the novel (*der Roman*) under the general heading of *die grosse Epik*, which is here usually, though not consistently, rendered as "great epic literature" or "great epic writing." It is often important to know whether "epic" in the English is *Epik* or *Epopöe* in the German, and it is not always clear.

The epic and novel, then, taken together as *die grosse Epik*, are distinguished from drama (in practice Lukács seems to equate this with tragedy) as different forms of artistic totality. Tragedy posits an essence or meaning (these terms appear to be roughly interchangeable, or else they are used in tandem) which is embodied in the hero and which proves to be incompatible with life as it is in reality. The tragic hero's function is "to make transcendence visible" through his death. Thus the role of the sensuous presentation of life on the stage is simply to show life's inadequacy to a higher principle. This does not mean that drama is not a totality, since the transcendence, the death, is still closed within the work; tragedy forms a totality in which life still contains essential meaning but can only hold it for a brief and crucial period, that is, intensively. Because of this brevity, because it is an *intensive* totality, tragedy is able to survive as an artistic whole in periods which are not themselves totalities, that is, cultures in which essence and meaning are felt as divorced from real life. Tragedy can still shape itself around a glimpse of that meaning even as it transcends life. This faith in a higher principle becomes, in modern tragedy, a problematic faith in others, in whom the hero vainly hopes to find the same essence that is in himself.

Tragedy, then, Lukács writes, can survive more or less intact. But epic writing (*die grosse Epik*), when it is confronted by the same divorce between life and meaning, ceases to be the true epic (*Epopöe*) and turns into the novel. All epic writing is an "extensive totality of life," and as such can only be a harmonious whole in cultures which are totalities, in which meaning and essence are felt as everywhere present and immanent within real life. At these times epic writing "did not have to leave the empirical in order to represent transcendent reality." The Homeric gods were felt as freely penetrating the empirical world, transcendence was immanent, and meaning and essence were everywhere in life. Dante, who represents the transition from the true epic to the novel, is confronted by a meaning that is beyond life; yet his work is a totality because he brings that beyond to life. Where Homer finds meaning in life, Dante gives life to transcendent meaning.

After Dante, however, the gap can no longer be jumped in this way, and we enter the age of the novel (Lukács does not say much about medieval romance, but does refer parenthetically to the "novels" of Wolfram von Eschenbach and Gottfried von Strassburg). "The novel," he writes, "is the epic of an age in which the extensive totality of life is no longer directly given, in which the immanence of meaning in life has become a problem, and which yet still thinks in terms of totality." This key definition leads into a discussion of verse and prose: where tragic verse conveys the isolation of the hero, his "distance" or estrangement from everyday things, and epic verse gives a joyful "distance" or novelty to all the familiar things of life, prose is the only medium for the novel, for only prose can encompass both the struggle for essence and meaning in the midst of a spiritless reality, and the rare attainment of them. Epic writing can no longer be consistently poetic. The novel is looking for something in life which it cannot often find: "The epic (*Epopöe*) gives form to a totality that is rounded from within (*eine von sich aus geschlossene Lebenstotalität*), the novel seeks, by giving form, to uncover and construct the concealed totality of life." A totality of life and meaning is given to the epic, the novel has to make its own.

The structural differences between the two follow from this. The epic has an organic, not a constructed unity: since meaning and essence are immanent in every part of life, the epic can simply accumulate parts, each of which contains its own meaning within itself. The meaning of each part does not depend on its structural relationship to other parts. Lukács avers that "in the story of the Iliad, which has no beginning and no end, a rounded universe blossoms into all-embracing life." The novel, however, is not the presentation of a totality virtually present in every part, but is constructed around the search for such a totality. This search is embodied in the psychology of the novel's heroes: "they are seekers." This gives the novel what for Lukács is the abstract and imposed form of the biography, the life story of a single separated individual. The parts of the novel are meaningful not in themselves (as with Homer) but only in relation to the hero's quest for meaning; they are not self-justifying, but have to be justified architecturally as incomplete and unsatisfactory stages of the quest, or as thematic parallels to it. "Thus the novel, in contrast to other genres whose existence resides within the finished form, appears as something in process of becoming."

The novel's heroes are seekers, but not necessarily finders: there is no guarantee of the reality, worth, or attainability of their goals. Here, crime and madness can only tentatively be distinguished from heroism and wisdom. Lukács calls the novel the art form of "transcendental homelessness," and crime and madness objectify respectively the homelessness of action and value in the world. Of course these things may appear in epic or tragedy; but there, vengeance tends to follow crime, and death to follow madness without the protracted moral lostness of the novel.

Society is of little help in this search for value. The hero encounters society and its laws as something no longer absolutely binding upon him. In fact, it is something alien, and confronts him as what Lukács calls a "second nature," not dumb and sensuous like the first nature, but "a complex of senses—meanings—which has become rigid and strange, and which no longer awakens interiority; it is a charnel house of long-dead interiorities. . . ." Lukács derives the Romantic and post-Romantic feeling for nature from this sense of the fossilization of society: "Estrangement from nature (the first nature), the modern sentimental attitude to nature, is only a projection of man's experience of his self-made environment as a prison instead of as a parental home." The "great moment" of lyric poetry can still affirm "the meaningful unity of nature and soul or their meaningful divorce," but "second nature" remains stubbornly unpoetic and demands detached or "essayistic" treatment.

Society, then, has become something rigid and external: the novel hero no longer takes part in its values and rituals, accepting their meaning as his meaning, as the epic hero did. Social customs and laws are no longer a living part of his reality. This is reflected in his different social status. The tragic hero has to be a king to symbolize his significant isolation and elevation above his community; the epic hero also has to be a king, but for him this position is a significant link to his community: the epic joins "an individual destiny to a totality." The first is an intensive connection (soon to be broken in death), the second an extensive one (enduring through many vicissitudes); but the novel hero has neither. The value system of his society, no longer organic, but fossilized into convention, allows a part of itself (the novel hero) to become self-enclosed and to find itself as a separate interiority, that is, a personality consciously distinct from others; the rounded totality of the epic cosmos never allows this.

The novelist's reality no longer presents him with the organic wholeness of life and meaning complete alike in characters, communities and objects. Instead, he has to make an abstract systematization "which emphasizes the conventionality of the objective world and the interiority of the subjective one." There are now two types of reality instead of one. They can only be related artistically by making the subject to whom meaning is present as an unrealized ideal, go on the impossible search for an object adequate to it. The search can only end in despair, compromise or resignation; yet it can be illuminated by a momentary vision of the totality of life and meaning, which, however, cannot be extensively incorporated into daily life. "The immanence of meaning which the form of the novel requires lies in the hero's finding out through experience that a mere glimpse of meaning is the highest that life has to offer." Lyrical meaning remains an isolated "great moment" or epiphany; it can never become extensively immanent in the real world, to whose laws the novelist must remain equally faithful. He has to hold the balance between subjective mood and objective, essayistic reflection. This accounts for the German Romantics' demand that the novel should include both pure thought and pure lyric poetry, thus representing both poles of the experience of reality.

Such, then, is the plight of the novel. "Der Roman ist die Epopöe der gottverlassenen Welt," Lukács writes. "The novel is the epic of a world that has been abandoned by God. The novel hero's psychology is demonic; the objectivity of the novel is the mature man's knowledge that meaning can never quite penetrate reality, but that, without meaning, reality would disintegrate into the nothingness of inessentiality." The epic hero, whatever his tribulations, is god-guided; but the novel hero has only a demon (*Dämon* is a term Lukács has borrowed from Goethe to signify a spiritual force that, enclosed within the individual, is no longer part of a cosmic order like the Olympiad). This demonism confronts the spiritless and God-abandoned world as an interiority seeking to know itself and prove itself through adventures. The epic hero does not have quite this moral isolation in his adventures; whatever his sufferings and doubts, he fundamentally trusts that what happens to him is in some way meaningful, is meant to happen. Though he may have to wait for enlightenment, he does not bear the sole onus of interpreting events.

Irony, the incongruous interplay between the demonic spirit of the seeker and the dispirited, inertly self-perpetuating world he wanders in, is the formal principle of the novel. Lukács calls irony "an attitude of *docta ignorantia* towards meaning," "a negative mysticism to be found in times without a god." The idealism of the seeker, though it must be balanced and checked against an objective account of reality, is no mere aberration, but presents a metaphysical absence whose implications extend far beyond his own personal sufferings. Irony "apprehends the demon that is within the subject as a metasubjective essentiality, and therefore, when it speaks of the adventures of errant souls in an inessential, empty reality, it intuitively speaks of past gods and gods that are to come...." The demons who drive the heroes of the novel are lost and displaced gods, no longer integrated with a cosmic order. Here, and again with his mysterious hints at the end of the book that Dostoevsky already "belongs to the new world" either as its forerunner or as its Homer or Dante, Lukács reveals the millenial hopes that form a persistent undercurrent in the book. A new age, a new integrated totality, is coming. In a conclusion reminiscent of Heidegger's valuation of Hölderlin and Rilke as poets "in a destitute time," Lukács defines the novel as that form of the *grosse Epik* whose structure corresponds to the time of waiting for the return of the gods. In our present literary context, this is certainly a fresh way of looking at the novel.

## II

Lukács' "Attempt at a typology of the novel form" (the sub-title of the second part) derives two principal types of novel from these theoretical presuppositions: "The abandonment of the world by God manifests itself in the incommensurability of soul and work, of interiority and adventure... either the soul is narrower or it is broader than the outside world." Lukács calls the narrowing of the soul "abstract idealism;" it is demonic, obsessively blind to reality, and it assumes that because the ideal *should* be that it *must* be. The hero of this type of novel has to be an adventurer: since he refuses to acknowledge the meaninglessness of reality, he can only try to impose his ideals in action. Here the archetype is of course Don Quixote: "a maximum of inwardly attained meaning becomes a maximum of senselessness, and the sublime turns to madness, to monomania." For Lukács "*Don Quixote* is the first great battle of interiority against the prosaic vulgarity of outward life;" but afterwards, as the world becomes progressively more and more prosaic and conventional, the demonically narrowed soul becomes merely a grotesque; no longer idealistically defying the inessentiality of the life around him, he simply flouts and negates the bourgeois concept of decent behavior. Lukács, in an unfortunately very sketchy way, outlines this development of the quixotic pattern through Sterne to Dickens, Gogol and Balzac.

The second type of incommensurability, where the soul is wider than its life-world, comes to the fore in the nineteenth-century novel (this transition too is inadequately accounted for). Where abstract idealism had to translate itself into defiant and active conflict with the outside world, here the tendency is towards passivity and the avoidance of conflict. Any struggle to realize the soul amid the conventions and meaningless laws of society is abandoned as hopeless. The despairing lyricism which renders the hero's experience is informed by the mood of "disillusioned romanticism": a Utopia is projected in the certain knowledge of its defeat. Where in the novel of narrow-minded idealism "subjectivity gave rise to the heroism of militant interiority," here the central character only demands sufficient material from the world to form himself as if he were a work of art. Lukács gives Jacobsen's Niels Lyhne and Goncharov's Oblomov as examples; he might well have added Huysmans' Des Esseintes or Wilde's Dorian Gray, and we might add the artist-philosopher heroes of Proust, Joyce, Mann and Musil. However, this subjectively created world apart is doomed to decay from within into dreary pessimism by the passage of time.

Here Lukács enters on the discussion of time in the novel which has often been singled out as the book's most impressive feature. Alone among literary forms, he says, the novel contains time among its constitutive principles. (Lukács, however, seems to apply the idea only to his second novel type.) In tragedy "the unity of time signifies a state of being lifted out of the duration of time." The time of the epic, such as the years of the Trojan war or of Odysseus' wanderings, is part of the magnitude of events, but "men and destinies remain untouched by it." Age is assimilated into character: "Nestor is old just as Helen is beautiful or Agamemnon mighty." "In the epic the life-immanence of meaning is so strong that it abolishes time," but in the novel "meaning is separated from life, and hence the essential from the temporal." In the novel of romantic disillusionment "poetry, the essential, must die, and time is ultimately responsible for its passing." Lukács now picks up his idea of the novel as the art form of the waiting period between two integrated civilizations. Time flows through the events of the novel, and implies that "all this had to come from somewhere, must be going somewhere; even if the direction betrays no meaning it is a direction none the less." Meaning, like God, is past and future: thus within the stream of time hope and memory "are experiences in which we come as near as we can, in a world forsaken by God, to the essence of things." There is comfort in the fact that however empty the present may be, something must have preceded it, and something must follow. Much of this is relevant to Proust, whose work Lukács did not know at the time of writing, but his points are adequately anchored in a discussion of L'Education sentimentale.

Two satisfying chapters on Goethe's Wilhelm Meister and on Tolstoy conclude the book. Lukács places Goethe's novel "aesthetically and historico-philosophically" between the novel of abstract idealism and that of romantic disillusionment (this point is stretched a little, at any rate in the historical aspect: Dickens, who is associated with the first novel type, died more than seventy years after Wilhelm Meister was published). "Its theme is the reconciliation of the problematic individual, guided by his lived experience of the ideal, with concrete. social reality." Goethe includes both the heroic activity of abstract idealism (Meister's "mission" to regenerate society through a national theater) and romantic passiveness, which interiorizes action and reduces it to contemplation (as in the example of the schöne Seele); the synthesis lies in "the possibility of human and interior community among men, of understanding and common action" (the Society of the Tower). The social world is therefore shown as "a world of convention, which is partially open to penetration by living meaning."

The idea of community is also present in Tolstoy, "whose great and truly epic mentality . . . aspires to a life based on a community of feeling among simple human beings closely bound to nature" (this ideal is somewhat different from Goethe's enlightened élite). But Tolstoy is unable to unite the three layers of his work, which correspond to three separate conceptions of time. The world of social convention is timeless, "an eternally recurring, self-repeating monotony." Beneath this is the great and continuous rhythm of nature, of the seasons, of birth, maturity and age, which invades each individual destiny in the same impersonal way. Thirdly, there are "the great moments which offer a glimpse of essential life," but which remain isolated from the other two. Yet these moments, if they could be spread out into an extensive totality, "would require a new form of artistic creation: the form of the renewed epic."

## III

Even from this outline it is clear that *The Theory of the Novel* is a flawed or incomplete work. Lukács acknowledges its datedness in his 1962 introduction, and points out the inadequacy of his twofold typology to cope with such novelists as Defoe, Fielding and Stendhal. From his later Marxist viewpoint he blames a lot of the book's faults on the inherent limitations of the *Geisteswissenschaft* method. From our own point of view, we can add other reproaches. "Architecture" is as overestimated in the novel as it is underestimated in the epic.[2] The notion of community as a synthesis of the estranged individual and the conventional world of society is hardly unique to Goethe or Tolstoy. Lukács' historical transitions are sometimes too sketchy to be convincing: for example, Goethe is the only novelist between Cervantes and Balzac to get more than a mention.

Despite all this, the theory is of major importance. It is still, as the author's introduction suggests, the best Hegelian treatment of the novel available to us. Lukács points to other intellectual debts (to Goethe for the idea of the demonic, to Friedrich Schlegel and Solger for irony as a modern structural principle), besides the methodological influences of Dilthey, Simmel and Max Weber. But the fundamental thrust of his thinking in this work is thoroughly Hegelian.

Hegel himself has only one or two substantial paragraphs on the novel in his *Aesthetics*. Not surprisingly in the 1820's, he did not anticipate the flowering of the novel into a major, if not *the* major, genre of nineteenth-century literature. He defines it as "the modern bourgeois epic" (*die moderne bürgerliche Epopöe*). It contains, he says, the richness and multiplicity of a total world and an epic presentation of reality. Yet what it lacks is the original poetic state of the world from which the true epic proceeds. The novel, in Hegel's view, sets out a reality already ordered into prose, and one can see here an affinity to Lukács' notion of "second

---

[2] *Cf.* the elaborate formal architecture and symmetry traced in the *Iliad* by Cedric H. Whitman in *Homer and the Heroic Tradition* (New York: Norton, 1965).

nature." In each case the wholeness of essence and life uncovered everywhere by poetic intuition, is said to have been dissipated by the systematization of social and scientific law, in which meaning is abstracted from life and exists in the system of relationships rather than in the individual phenomena themselves; poetic wholes are turned into parts in need of architectural support and outside elucidation. Yet poetry, for Hegel, is still present in the novel: one of the genre's most frequent conflicts is between the poetry of the heart and the prose of circumstances. This conflict can be resolved in two ways: either the character recognizes what is genuine and substantial in the society he has rebelled against, and reconciles himself to it in reality; or he rejects the prose of life and replaces it with a new reality related to beauty and art.[3] Here we can see the basis for Lukács account of *Wilhelm Meister* (which Hegel may also have had in mind), and for his second type of novel, where the disillusioned romantic retires into his own aesthetic world (the disillusionment is added by Lukács, whose examples are in any case post-Hegel; Hegel himself may have been thinking of Novalis' *Heinrich von Ofterdingen*). Lukács' first type, the novel of abstract idealism, seems to owe something to Hegel's comments on *Don Quixote*,[4] where, he says, we find the adventurousness of a noble nature, in which chivalry has become madness, in the midst of a reality that is precisely depicted in its outward relations. This produces the comic contradiction between a rational and self-ordered world, and the isolated mind of one who seeks to create this order and stability for himself simply through his own chivalric effort. Quixote is old, and dies; he is supplanted by the "youthful knights" of the novel, who run into conflict with bourgeois society out of idealism, ambition or love, but who end up settling for wife, children and job much like everyone else. Hegel takes a much more sarcastic view here of the "reconciliation" or "compromise" type of novel than he does in the previously discussed passage.

Yet for all these similarities, there is a fundamental reorientation of Hegel's perspective in Lukács. Hegel saw the "prosing" of the world essentially as a triumph, as the realization of thought in the consciously planned state. This made art problematic because it had been surpassed: the ideal was being realized in life, and its realization in art was no longer truly necessary. But the young Lukács does not accept this prose world with Hegel's apparent complacency: for him, nearly a century later, the prose world is a place and a time of waiting for a greening of Europe, for new gods, a new epic, a new Greece (a longing to which Hegel, for all his nostalgia for the Greek "art-period," never succumbed). What Hegel welcomed as the fusion of reason and reality has in our century more and more been assaulted as a despiritualized "technological rationality," under which art, far from being redundant, is a necessity for spiritual survival: this is Lukács' position here, and it finds many contemporary analogies.

But this reorientation is, I feel, more or less forced on any neo-Hegelian in one form or another by the actual course of history since Hegel's death, even more so

[3] I am paraphrasing the passage in Hegel, *Ästhetik*, ed. Friedrich Bassenge, intro. by Georg Lukács (Frankfurt: Europäische Verlagsanstalt, 1955), II, 452.

[4] Hegel, I, 566.

now than in 1914. However, one does not have to share the young Lukács' millenial hopes any more than Hegel's satisfaction with things in order to appreciate a perspective in which the novel is approached, not positively, as the rise of realism, but negatively, as the decline of the epic.

## IV

How does this Hegelian approach to the novel compare with theories of fiction current in the English-speaking world? These are usefully grouped and discussed in Bernard Paris's essay "Form, Theme and Imitation in Realistic Fiction."[5] Roughly speaking, Paris divides our classics of novel theory into two groups: those which emphasize imitation (which he himself prefers), and those which emphasize form and ethical theme. In the first category is Ian Watt's *The Rise of the Novel*. "Formal interests cannot be paramount in a 'genre' which, as Watt describes it, 'works by exhaustive presentation rather than by elegant concentration.' Like E. M. Forster, Watt sees 'the portrayal of "life by time" as the distinctive role which the novel has added to literature's more ancient preoccupation with "life by values." ' " In the same category Paris places Auerbach's *Mimesis*, which concerns "the contrast between the classical moralistic and the existential problematic ways of presenting reality. The distinction is basically between the representation of life in terms of fixed canons of style and of ethical categories which are *a priori* and static, and a stylistically mixed, ethically ambiguous portrayal which probes 'the social forces underlying the facts and conditions.' "[6]

Paris commends criticism based on this type of definition of the novel, as against that which seems to him to transfer techniques developed primarily for use on poetry and poetic drama, genres in which formal and ethical patterning is tighter. As examples of this he gives the dictum "No theme, no story" from *Understanding Fiction* by Cleanth Brooks and Robert Penn Warren, and the insistence he finds in Wayne Booth's *The Rhetoric of Fiction* on the necessity for moral intelligibility ("the clear thematic ordering of fictional materials"), and on the omnipresence of the author as moral interpreter, whether overt, as in earlier novels, or covert, as in the novel after Flaubert and James. Paris states that we go to the novel not for moral and formal definiteness, but for immersion in the inner and outer lives of the characters, and that critical method should reflect this.

Whichever of these two approaches is preferable, it is clear that Lukács is offering a third avenue. Both of the methods outlined by Paris define the novel primarily in relation to the drama: the "imitation" critics stress the differences between the two genres, whereas the "form and theme" critics implicitly stress the similarities by treating novels as if they were organized in much the same way as a Shakespeare play. Either way, drama vs. novel is the contrast which

[5] NOVEL, I, (Winter 1968), 140–49.

[6] Coming out of the Germanic tradition, Auerbach is often closer to Lukács. For example, his treatment of the story of Odysseus' scar contains the idea that, as meaning was present in every part of Homeric life, no part of the epic can be called a digression. The two authors give similar accounts of Dante. But genre definitions play hardly any role in *Mimesis*. The notion of genre seems almost an obstacle to realism, and Auerbach's method of reviewing excerpts rather than overall structures seems to reflect this.

underlies discussion. Ian Watt, in his chapter on "Fielding and the Epic Theory of the Novel," specifically rejects that theory by quoting Richardson's dismissive comments on the epic's bellicosity and superstitious paganism, and by treating Fielding's "epic" theory as an attempt to establish respectable neo-classical credentials for his work while using dramatic comedy as his generic point of departure. For Watt, the novel "rises" mainly away from the drama. Wayne Booth, though he several times mentions Homer as a provider of clear moral certitudes, also usually turns to drama for support in justifying authorial guidance. He concedes to Watt that the novel exists in a "more ambiguous, relativistic, and mobile world" than the classical genres, but suggests that, rather than yielding to the ambiguity, "the novelist must work harder at providing, *within his work*, the kind of definition of his elements that a good production gives to a play."[7]

Instead of these views of the novel as a modified drama or as a non-drama, created by a new historical situation which elicited a more internalized, extended, particularized and formally loosened picture of experience, Lukács presents us with the novel as modified epic or epic manqué, created by a new historical situation which deprived the epic of immanent spirituality, isolated its hero, and turned it from verse into prose. The extensiveness and the wealth of concrete particularity which appear to be new elements if you are looking mainly at seventeenth-century drama, are viewed by Lukács as common to all "great epic writing," and are thus constant in the transition from the epic to the novel: the "loss of totality" is the new element.

Among recent books, only Robert Scholes' and Robert Kellogg's *The Nature of Narrative* offers us a unitary approach of similar scope: their term "narrative," like Lukács' *Epik*, covers both the epic and the novel, as well as other types of fiction. Yet, as they imply in using "nature" rather than "history" in their title, their procedure is Aristotelian where Lukács' is Hegelian: after general chapters on the oral and classical heritages of narrative, the bulk of the book is made up of a synchronic treatment under the categories of Meaning, Character, Plot and Point of View.

More of Lukács' ideas in *The Theory of the Novel* are to be found in Northrop Frye's *Anatomy of Criticism* than in any other current English-language work on genre-theory. Frye's first section begins by outlining a historical progression from myth, through romance, high mimetic and low mimetic to ironic, all of which are defined as stages of the hero's declining power in relation to his human and natural environment. Epic and tragedy belong mostly to high mimetic, comedy and realistic fiction to low mimetic. Though the categories are more numerous, the general sweep of this perspective is close to Lukács'. But Frye is here classifying what he calls "modes"; "genres" he distinguishes by "radicals of presentation." "*Epos*" is defined by its medium of oral address, "fiction" is the "genre of the printed page." Here, and in his subdivision of "fiction" into novel confession, anatomy and romance, Frye says he is practicing "rhetorical" criticism, where the "modes" are established by "historical" criticism. Thus the types of

---

[7] *The Rhetoric of Fiction* (Chicago: Univ. of Chicago Press, 1961), pp. 387-88.

fiction are treated as available to any period, while the modes follow in historical succession. Lukács, however, is practicing what his introduction calls "an historicization of aesthetic categories:" within the overall genres (though Lukács' three —*Epik*, lyric and drama—seem to be as synchronic as Frye's four— epos, lyric, drama and fiction) the sub-genres follow a rough "historico-philosophical" progression. Frye produces both a historical and a generic perspective (as well as two others) which he wants to keep separate; Lukács wants to fuse the two into a description of the "inner form" of works (Frye's "radicals of presentation" are, in effect, "outer" form).

Though we can find scattered resemblances to the ideas of Lukács' book among our present pantheon of fiction theories, it still places the novel in what for us is an unusual light. We are accustomed to oppose the novel to "the classical genres," either to claim for it their aesthetic dignity as Flaubert and James first did, or to claim for it a vigorous multiplicity of life that bursts the restraints of classical form, to give us, as Ian Watt puts it, "exhaustive presentation" rather than "elegant concentration." But it is rare for the epic to figure in this notion of "classical form." By making his basic distinction (between epic writing's "extensive totality of life" and drama's "intensive totality of essence") philosophical as well as formal, and by contrasting the epic to the novel *within* the first category, Lukács reminds us that the classics are not all elegantly concentrated. Homer's extended presentation of human action and physical reality in all their crowded detail is the great precedent for these aspects of the novel, and is actually older than the severe shapeliness of Greek tragedy. The word "epic," which we instinctively want to use of certain novelists, such as Tolstoy, need not be banished from the vocabulary of novel criticism. There is a real continuity here, and within it, for Lukács, the novel is not the sudden product of eighteenth-century England's bustling middle class, but a historical mutation within the West's senior literary form. Cervantes is working in the same form as Homer, Vergil and Dante, but for Lukács he inaugurates a new version of it: the novel, the art-form of sadness. The search of its isolated heroes for meaning in life is only momentarily lit up by flashes of the old epic radiance, and its realism is the disenchantment of the world.

# From Imitation to Rhetoric:
## The Chicago Critics, Wayne C. Booth, and Tom Jones

JOHN ROSS BAKER

I

Toward the end of his NOVEL essay on the reception of *The Rhetoric of Fiction*, Wayne C. Booth raises the difficult question of whether he and various commentators on his book "belong as critics to a profession in which there is any chance whatever of cumulative discourse."[1] The praise accorded his book, he finds, is hardly more helpful than the blame, for both often spring from failures to grasp clearly not only the specific problem he has dealt with but also, more crucially, the specific assumptions about fiction and criticism underlying his approach to the problem. Since each critic approaches his own problem with his own assumptions, since indeed he is probably led to discover his problem *because of* his assumptions, these also come to govern his approach to the work of other critics. His praise of others' work, then, like the blame, turns out to be essentially irrelevant to it. Depending thus on fortuitous agreements and disagreements as to assumptions, problems, and even terms, discourse among critics breaks down, with critics "forever shout[ing] slogans at each other from distant armed camps." Booth does not set forth this pessimistic view merely as a way of suggesting that no one has really "understood" *The Rhetoric of Fiction;* he admits, in fact, similar failures of his own in dealing with other critics. Yet his argument has the effect of rendering *The Rhetoric of Fiction* somehow beyond critical appraisal, for the book becomes truly accessible only to those who happen to share its assumptions and are thus able to understand what the book attempts. The only way to break through this Struldbrugg-like isolation of one critic from others and achieve in critical discourse "progress of a limited kind," Booth urges, is to agree that "there are many legitimate questions based on differing assumptions and definitions and amenable to differing methods": then "those willing to share a mode, an interest, a language" will at least be able to communicate. But, it would seem, those unwilling—or unable—"to share a mode" must remain in "distant armed camps."

Is it possible to enter Booth's "camp" in order to understand his work without at the same time becoming a member of his army? The location of the camp is Chicago, and the governing principles are Neo-Aristotelian. In fact, an earlier Neo-Aristotelian has put very directly this matter of the confusions and mis-

[1] "*The Rhetoric of Fiction* and the Poetics of Fictions," NOVEL: *A Forum on Fiction*, 1 (1968), 105–17.

understandings resulting from attempts to assess from one particular critical point of view criticism written from a different point of view: "True interpretation is impossible when one system is examined in terms of another, as is true refutation when the refutative arguments are systematically different from those against which they are directed."[2] If we must become Chicago critics in order to arrive at a "true interpretation" or a "true refutation" of *The Rhetoric of Fiction*, then communication among critics becomes indeed impossible—a strange situation arising from the arguments of self-professed pluralists who recognize in theory the legitimacy of alternative approaches.

If nothing short of an examination of Booth from a strictly Neo-Aristotelian point of view—or nothing, in other words, short of an acceptance of the Neo-Aristotelian "mode," "interest," and "language"—would meet the methodological objection Booth and other Chicagoans raise, then even the "progress of a limited kind" in critical discourse Booth hopes for becomes impossible; for "to share a mode, an interest, a language" with the Neo-Aristotelians is to embrace Neo-Aristotelianism at the expense of any other "mode" one may have a commitment to. However, I believe we may go part way toward overcoming the methodological objection by making an effort to see Booth's work *in the context of* Chicago criticism. Although such a procedure will not of course "share" Booth's method in the way he would demand, it should at least constitute a provisional "sharing" to bring us as close to an understanding of Booth as anything short of a full "sharing" can.

In the past *The Rhetoric of Fiction* has been properly enough read mostly as a work about prose fiction, but the book's importance is such as to warrant an attempt at "placing" it according to its general critical and theoretical orientation. Although this procedure may seem to risk forcing Booth into a Neo-Aristotelian bed of Procrustes, it will actually turn out to provide a way of assessing his originality and independence. The late R. S. Crane has referred to *The Rhetoric of Fiction* as offering "a fuller development and more specific applications of the general approach to critical problems outlined" in his *The Languages of Criticism and the Structure of Poetry*, but Booth has in fact achieved a broadening of Neo-Aristotelian theory that amounts to wholesale revision.[3] Nevertheless, *The Rhetoric of Fiction* opens with the particular distinction among literary "kinds" most fundamental to the Neo-Aristotelians. The very first paragraph of the Preface, with its insistent differentiation of "didactic" from "non-didactic," employs Chicago terminology, even though for the orthodox "imitative" Booth substitutes "non-didactic"; the works he cites as "didactic" are among the handful cited in

---

[2] Elder Olson, "An Outline of Poetic Theory," in R. S. Crane *et al., Critics and Criticism, Ancient and Modern* (Chicago: Univ. of Chicago Press, 1952), p. 547. See also Richard McKeon's extensive development of this argument in "The Philosophic Bases of Art and Criticism," in *Critics and Criticism*, pp. 463–545, esp. p. 466.

[3] See Crane's note in *Modern Criticism: Theory and Practice*, ed. Walter Sutton and Richard Foster (New York: Odyssey Press, 1963), p. 267. Not recognizing that we order these matters differently in America, the *TLS* asserts that the Chicagoans are "no longer functioning," yet describes *The Rhetoric of Fiction* as "a book which has . . . become a major influence." The "influence" behind critics like Booth "interested in questions of rhetoric" is, for the *TLS*, W. K. Wimsatt ("Son of New Critic," September 25, 1965, pp. 1078-79).

earlier Chicago criticism as convenient examples of the "didactic."[4] Only by stressing at the outset Booth's affiliation with Neo-Aristotelian theory can I show the reorientation of this theory that he has effected and thus come close to an understanding of his work. Finally, I hope to provide a way of moving beyond the Neo-Aristotelian "mode" by moving through it. If I appear only to be building on ashes that result from the burning of Neo-Aristotelian straw men, then discourse among critics—and criticism of criticism—does indeed virtually break down.

## II

Booth's aim in *The Rhetoric of Fiction* was of course much more specific than I have indicated—he was working with the problem of "the author's voice" in fiction—and I cannot claim that he was consciously attempting the radical "broadening" of Neo-Aristotelianism I have stressed. Given his care to argue that his concept of "rhetoric" is merely an expansion of Aristotle's, that indeed "Aristotle never completely repudiates the rhetorical dimension of poetry" (p. 92), Booth obviously sees his own work as the sort of extension and refinement of Aristotle's method that Crane has urged and has asserted *The Rhetoric of Fiction* has helped to supply. What I am concerned with, however, is the actual effect this work has on Chicago theory. The problem of "the author's voice" that Booth grapples with provides the most convenient way not only into his conscious aim but also into the actual reorientation of Chicago theory he brings about, for although he appears to be reacting to fiction criticism deriving from James, he is in reality challenging what for Crane is central, "the imitative principle itself."[5]

Let me risk oversimplification and continue treating Booth for the moment in terms of the awkward appearance-reality contrast I have used thus far. *The Rhetoric of Fiction* easily takes on the appearance of fitting into the general Chicago enterprise somewhat as follows. Just as Crane and Elder Olson, in particular, challenged the New Critics in several of the essays collected in *Critics and Criticism*, so Booth is attacking what by the time of *The Rhetoric of Fiction* could be called a "new criticism" of fiction: a criticism originating in the Prefaces and Notebooks of James, elaborated and partially codified in Percy Lubbock's *The Craft of Fiction*, and in our own time assuming the weight and authority of dogma even in textbooks such as the Allen Tate-Caroline Gordon *House of Fiction.* Many tenets of this criticism are alluded to in the titles of Booth's early chapters —"True Novels Must Be Realistic," "All Authors Should Be Objective," and "True Art Ignores the Audience." Focusing plausibly enough on point of view as central in fiction, the principal tenet—and Booth's first chapter is appropriately titled "Telling and Showing"—sets up a hierarchy of possible points of view, with

---

[4] *The Rhetoric of Fiction* (Chicago: Univ. of Chicago Press, 1961), Preface; Crane, *The Languages of Criticism and the Structure of Poetry* (Toronto: Univ. of Toronto Press, 1953), p. 157; *Critics and Criticism*, pp. 66, 136.

[5] "The Concept of Plot and the Plot of 'Tom Jones,' " in *Critics and Criticism*, p. 623.

the Jamesian "Central Intelligence" superior to the others. Tate and Gordon put the matter bluntly:

> *This fourth method [that of the Central Intelligence] gains most of the immediacy of the First Person Narrative, yet allows the Narrator to evade our natural impulse to judge his capacities. In fact, this method combines the advantages of the three others and involves the artist in fewer of their disadvantages. But it requires* the greatest possible maturity of judgment, the greatest mastery of life, and the highest technical skill to control it.[6]

Thus pre-Jamesian fiction, especially that employing the convention of the "intrusive" omniscient author who may on occasion "tell" rather than "show," "assert" rather than "dramatize" or "render," becomes inferior to the extent that its "method" allows less "realism," is less able to sustain a "convincing" illusion. Booth undertakes to argue—and, given his premises, usually does so ably—that there may be room in fiction for "the author's voice," that "impersonal narration" is only one of several alternatives for the novelist. He even goes so far as to raise questions about what he takes to be the high "price of impersonal narration" and "unreliable narrators." His efforts, then, particularly since Tate is a prominent spokesman for the Jamesian view, might appear to parallel one of Crane's or Olson's efforts against the sort of "monistic reduction of critical concepts" the Chicagoans find in the New Critics: in fact, Crane mentions Tate's own theory of "tension" as such a "reduction."[7] So Booth seems to be doing for the criticism of fiction what the original Chicagoans in their dispute with the New Critics did for the criticism of lyric poetry. When René Wellek speaks of *The Rhetoric of Fiction* as "the best practical application of the [Neo-Aristotelian] principles,"[8] he may be entertaining such a view.

Yet such a view of Booth's place among the Chicagoans, though certainly plausible, is somewhat oversimplified and misleading as well. The fact of the matter is that Tate's ideas on "rendering" as opposed to "telling" are very close to those of Crane. Booth could have launched his attack specifically against the Crane of the essay on *Tom Jones*, which states in straightforward Neo-Aristotelian terms the very notions about fiction that Booth seeks to correct. A case can easily be made that the James-Lubbock-Tate view of fiction with its emphasis on *mimesis* or realism which Booth reacts against is a largely Aristotelian affair.

Although the bulk of the essay on *Tom Jones* is devoted to an analysis of "plot," that "part" of the whole "which most sharply distinguishes works of imitation from all other kinds of literary productions," Crane does deal briefly with "other relevant principles . . . in artistic imitations." The first of these other "principles"

---

[6] *The House of Fiction: An Anthology of the Short Story with Commentary,* 2nd ed. (New York: Charles Scribner's Sons, 1960), p. 444 (emphasis added).
[7] "The Critical Monism of Cleanth Brooks," in *Critics and Criticism,* p. 84. Crane says that he deals with Brooks rather than with Tate or Ransom or Warren because Brooks has expounded the position most fully.
[8] *Concepts of Criticism,* ed. and with an intro. by Stephen G. Nichols, Jr. (New Haven: Yale Univ. Press, 1963), p. 322.

is "the imitative principle itself, the principle that we are in general more convinced and moved when things are 'rendered' for us through probable signs than when they are given merely in 'statement,' without illusion, after the fashion of a scenario" (pp. 622–23). "Rendering," as opposed to "statement," is for Crane thus "the imitative principle itself," that which separates from the "didactic" the enormous kind embracing most poems, plays, and novels. If the "force and meaning" of the explanation of the "principle" are not sufficiently clear, Crane directs his reader, in a footnote, to compare *The Ambassadors* with James's "preliminary synopsis" in the Notebooks or to see "the excellent remarks of Allen Tate . . . in his 'Techniques of Fiction.' " If "Techniques of Fiction" illuminates "the imitative principle itself," Tate in turn seems to agree with Crane about the primacy of plot in certain species of the "imitative" kind: Aristotle's "definition of a play as an imitation of an action of a certain magnitude will serve as well for the short story or novel."[9]

Crane's comments on Fielding's "intrusive" narrator are of a piece with his view of the "imitative principle." Despite the occasional intrusions of the narrator, some justified, some not, "the author of *Tom Jones* had moved a long way in the direction of the imitative and dramatic." The omission of the article before "dramatic," in fact, serves to equate "imitative" and "dramatic." In what ways are the "intrusions" of the narrator not justified? The introductory essays—"while we should not like to lose them from the canon of Fielding's writings"—serve mostly as "embellishment," and as such provide only diminishing "returns" before the novel is over. The essay, in other words, is not an "imitative" kind, and can be, for the whole-parts critic like Crane, only imperfectly assimilated into a work of the "imitative" kind. Furthermore, "in many chapters where [the narrator] might better have 'rendered' he merely 'states' and . . . even in the most successful of the scenes in which action and dialogue predominate he leaves far less to inference than we are disposed to like" (p. 639). May we conclude that for Crane and for Neo-Aristotelianism in general, as for Lubbock, there is a progress in the history of fiction toward pure "rendering" and the "disappearance of the author"? Neo-Aristotelianism is not quite so inflexible as that, for Crane is able to justify some of the "intrusiveness," some of the "statement" in terms of the specific kind of "imitative" work he finds *Tom Jones* to be. Although the introductory essays seem to be mostly beyond defense because they go directly against the "imitative principle itself," this "principle" Crane sees as subordinate to the "formal demands" of the specific kind of artistic whole in which it is employed—or so he leads us to infer at certain points. The idea, in other words, is not that everything in a novel or other "imitative" work must be "rendered," that fiction should aspire to the condition of "drama," but that in fact *some* matters, in *some* situations, are best left "stated" instead of "rendered." If *Tom Jones* is "comic" as a whole, the "noncomic elements" must be "minimized." If the "comic" quality of the whole is to be maintained, then it is appropriate that certain "painful" matters not be "imitated" or "rendered" directly but merely

[9] *The House of Fiction*, p. 449.

"stated." So with the important but "painful" scene in which Allworthy condemns and banishes Jones: Fielding's "device consists in slurring over a painful scene by generalized narration" (p. 642).

The "imitative principle" for Crane, we might sum up, although it does move in the direction of "drama" ("action and dialogue"), perhaps even pure "rendering" in the manner of the later James, is nevertheless flexible enough to allow, in appropriate circumstances, mere "statement" or "generalized narration." The "appropriateness" of the circumstances is of course determined by the nature of the artistic whole.[10] What the "imitative principle" cannot allow is the sort of "intrusion" found in the introductory essays, where the "intrusion" has nothing to do with the primary "part" of the "whole," the "plot" and its effects. Whether a formalistic criticism which did not find "plot" or some other "part" primary would regard the essays as "intrusive" or unassimilated need not detain us at this point.[11]

Now it is just this sort of "intrusiveness," among other sorts, that Booth attempts to find a place for in fiction, a place denied not only by Jamesians like Tate and Gordon but by Crane as well. Since Booth, like Crane, deals with the *Tom Jones* narrator and even adapts to his purpose Crane's key phrase "comic analogue of fear" without taking note of the relation of the Neo-Aristotelian "imitative principle" to the "telling"-vs.-"showing" issue, it is fitting to approach Booth through his analysis of Fielding's narrator (pp. 215–18). If we can accept his account of the essentially "rhetorical" function of this narrator, he obviously succeeds better than Crane in finding *Tom Jones* a unified whole, for Crane is unable to see the narrator as always properly subordinate to the plot. Yet—and the point is crucial—Booth must see the novel finally as a *different kind* of whole. Although he speaks of a "subplot" involving the narrator and the reader, his focus subtly shifts from the "imitative" to the "didactic." Despite his prefatory statement that he is "not primarily interested in didactic fiction," in the end he sees most fiction as what the earlier Chicagoans call "didactic."

---

[10] This is also the position of the Neo-Aristotelian Norman Friedman, who even more than Crane regards limited and "dramatic" points of view as superior: an author "gives up certain privileges [like 'Editorial Omniscience'] and imposes certain limits in order the more effectively to render his story-illusion, which constitutes artistic truth in fiction" ("Point of View in Fiction: The Development of a Critical Concept," *PMLA*, 70 (1955), 1160–84).

[11] Since I am pressing Crane perhaps too hard for systematic consistency in what is after all only a subordinate theme in his essay, I must point out what is possibly an equivocation in one of the remarks I have based my analysis on: "The narrator, for one thing, though it is well that he should intrude, perhaps intrudes too much in a purely ornamental way; the introductory essays, thus, while we should not like to lose them from the canon of Fielding's writings, serve only occasionally the function of chorus, and the returns from them, even as embellishment, begin to diminish before the end" (p. 639). In what way is it "well that he should intrude"? Not, it would seem, as he does in the introductory essays. I have taken the acceptable intrusion to be exemplified in the "generalized narration" of Jones's banishment, even though Crane brings that matter up several pages later. But is this sort of "generalized narration" an "intrusion"? In the chapter in question (VI, xi) the narrator—who mentions the feelings of the reader—appears in his customary guise of historian, appropriately for the "imitative" *History of Tom Jones*.

A good part of the difficulty may lie in the terms critics of fiction sometimes use: to say that an intrusion is "justified" is to deny that it is an intrusion; to say that an intrusion is not "justified" may be to utter a redundancy.

## III

Before examining in detail Booth's argument about Fielding's narrator, let us see how his particular version of "rhetoric," together with certain other key interests, is able to effect this radical shift in Neo-Aristotelianism from the "imitative" to the "didactic." To begin with, Booth expands the concept of "rhetoric" beyond its classical (and, it may be added, Neo-Aristotelian) role in persuasion to embrace the fictional techniques used by an author "to impose his fictional world upon the reader" (Preface). His main interest is thus apparently hermeneutic—how the novel is "communicated" to the reader, by what devices and features of the work the reader is able to grasp the novel. Hence anything and everything in a novel—but especially point of view—may become a "rhetorical" element in Booth's expanded sense of the term. But this hermeneutic interest—because of the prevalence of "impersonal" and "unreliable" narration since James, and before James, too[12]—quickly comes to rest in what is for Booth the problem of discerning the novelist's "norms." Although these "norms" resemble what for a hermeneutic theorist like E. D. Hirsch, Jr. would be the sense of the "whole" into which the particulars fit,[13] they are for Booth much more specific than merely "what the work means": they involve "the reader's need to know where, in the world of values, he stands—that is, to know where the author *wants* him to stand" (p. 73). There is of course little problem when the author "tells" him where to stand, but in fiction which "shows" the action—in fiction which adheres closely to Crane's "imitative principle itself"—and does not "tell" him where to stand, the problem may become acute. The problem is compounded, too, because as a Neo-Aristotelian and a sensitive reader Booth must see the work as an artistic whole somehow detached from its author: how can the author tell the reader where to stand when the author should not be in the work in the first place? Booth's way out—the invention of the "implied author"—is difficult to regard as anything more than a verbal evasion of a problem that remains insoluble in Neo-Aristotelian terms, and perhaps in other terms, too.

I must speak of the "implied author" as an invention and an evasion because despite Booth's protests to the contrary the distinction between "real" and "implied" author remains unearned and finally tends to evaporate. Thus occasional assertions to the effect that "signs of the real author's untransformed loves and hates are almost always fatal," and that, indeed, "the weaker the novel . . . , the more likely we are to be able to make simple and accurate inferences about the real author's problems" (p. 86), depend upon a distinction that elsewhere is not really made. The "implied author" is of course largely an inference from the work, but it is also for Booth much more than that, too: "however impersonal [an author] may try to be, his reader will inevitably construct a picture of the [author] who writes in this manner—and of course that [inferred author] will

---

[12] Booth discusses "unreliable" narration in Sterne, Defoe, Swift, and others.

[13] *Validity in Interpretation* (New Haven: Yale Univ. Press, 1967), p. 76.

never be neutral toward all values."[14] In fact, in the individual work the author as he writes "creates . . . an implied version of 'himself' that is different from the implied authors we meet in other works" (p. 70). But in speaking of the "picture" the reader "constructs" Booth is doing nothing more than acknowledging (and providing a label for) the sort of linguistic convention we ordinarily employ when we use "Darwin" to refer to the complex of ideas about natural selection to be found in *The Origin of Species*. When we speak thus of "Darwin" we clearly are referring not simply to the *man* who lived at a certain time, but to the man *as responsible for the ideas*. When in these pages I mention "Booth" I suppose I am referring to a professor at the University of Chicago, but primarily, though giving the man at Chicago credit, I am referring to the *ideas* I find in *The Rhetoric of Fiction*. Surely in any book, in any utterance, there is such an "implied author"— *if* we agree with Booth about the "inevitability" of our inferring such an author or "construct[ing] a picture" of such an author. How, then, is this "implied author" different from the real one, the man who happened to write the book—the man who is not *in* the book as "implied author" but is, as it were, *behind* the book, the "real" author—especially if the "real" one *creates* the other, the "implied version of 'himself' "? Surely the "implied author" in *A Tale of a Tub*—who is of course not the hack who serves as narrator—is impossible to distinguish, in Booth's commentary, from Jonathan Swift, the "real" author: "Though careful reading reveals Swift's genius at work everywhere, it would not be hard to find fairly extensive quotations which, if read straight, would be . . . dull. . . . The narrator here is a dull and foolish man, but the book he 'writes' is a great one partly because of the contrast between his role and that of the implied author" (pp. 234–35). What is the difference between the Swift whose "genius [is] at work everywhere" and the "implied author"? That from which the "genius" may be inferred must be the same as that from which the "implied author" may be inferred: the work. Whether we speak of the real or the "implied" author, our interest would seem to be in the work.

This distinction between "real" and "implied" authors is similar to those Elder Olson makes among the "dramatic conception" of the author, the work, and the "effect" of the work,[15] but there is nevertheless a crucial difference: Booth's "implied author" is the vehicle of those "norms" the reader must grasp in order "to know where, in the world of values, he stands—that is, to know where the author *wants* him to stand." Whereas the intentionalism causing the other Chicago critics at times to speak of authorial "conceptions" is mostly circular and hypothetical, Booth's intentionalism is an altogether different affair. It is as if Booth, like Crane,[16] accepted the Wimsatt-Beardsley view about "intention"— that authorial and other prior or genetic concerns are not strictly relevant to judgment and interpretation—yet still needed, unlike Crane and Olson, to be able to refer important parts of his arguments to the author rather than to the work. The

---

[14] I have substituted the bracketed terms for "official scribe," which like "second self" Booth here regards as synonyms for "implied author." These alternative terms, simply as terms, are even closer to the actual author than "implied author" is.

[15] *Tragedy and the Theory of Drama* (Detroit: Wayne State Univ. Press, 1961), pp. 159–60, 168.

[16] *The Languages of Criticism and the Structure of Poetry*, p. 182.

concept of the "implied author," with its air of being an inference from the work and thus as it were, like plot, an objective feature of the work, enables Booth to talk about the author under the guise of still appearing to talk about the work. Besides, to return to Booth's emphasis on "rhetoric," when the critic begins to search into the novel for the means by which it is communicated to the reader, he is in fact looking for what the *author* has done—"rhetorically"—to communicate with the reader. To the "rhetorical" critic "communication" must be a three-way affair involving an author, a work, and a reader, even though to the Neo-Aristotelian interested in "imitative" artistic wholes for their own sakes (or for the "pleasures" appropriate to them) questions of "rhetoric" are largely irrelevant. Thus when Olson theorizes about "dramatic conceptions" of authors in order to write about tragedy, it is only to account for the "cause" of the "plot," the primary "part" of tragedy, which produces the tragic "effect." But when Booth invents the "implied author," it is to be able to write about the "norms" of this "implied author," which—though nothing more than inferences from the work —become the "norms" of the *real* author. Like many things we think of as objects of our experience, the "real author" as well as the "implied author" is of course a construct, and such constructs may be heuristic: if we are interested in "rhetoric" and "communication" yet still have scruples about intentionalism, what better way out of the dilemma than to invent an "implied author" as a feature of the work, especially if this construct can perform the same function as a construct of a different order—the "real author" demanded by a naively realistic theory of rhetoric?

Booth's "norms" begin merely as a means of "communication." If for some reason they are not clearly discernible within the work, the "communication" Booth seeks between author and reader breaks down. So Part II of *The Rhetoric of Fiction* is devoted largely to the help "the author's voice in fiction" provides the reader in discerning the "norms," Part III to the obstacles that "impersonal narration" sometimes puts between the reader and the "norms." But, because they will finally contribute to the shift Booth effects in Neo-Aristotelianism from an aesthetic to a frankly moral interest, what is important for our present purposes is the sort of thing they involve. Quite simply, they are the beliefs of the author that the reader must grasp if he is to grasp the novel or if "communication" is to take place. But even though Booth has expanded "rhetoric" to encompass this sort of "communication," he has not altogether abandoned its older sense of *persuasion*, for not only must the reader grasp the norms but he must share them as well. In fact, Booth speaks of "some great works" of Shakespeare as able "to *win* readers of all camps," as if Shakespeare were a classical rhetorician (p. 141). The "norms" turn out to be standards of moral judgment whereby the reader knows whether to condemn or sympathize with a character and his attitudes.

Should one condemn the governess in *The Turn of the Screw* as a hallucinating neurotic, or sympathize with her as the victim of real ghosts? Though "all of the glamor is on the other side," Booth inclines to sympathy but questions James's "impersonal" method which leaves the tale—and its "norms"—a "puzzle" (pp.

311–15). The question of the governess and her ghosts, I need hardly emphasize, would be important for any Neo-Aristotelian: if the plot is primary, then surely one must know whether the governess's antagonists are internal or external. But Booth's troubles with the tale are not those of a critic trying to see just what action is "imitated," they are those of a moralist who does not know what to approve, what to disapprove. If James had been more obvious in his "rhetoric," if he had been more conscientious about what he needed to *persuade* his reader of, Booth could be less hesitant about the sympathy he extends to the governess.

He is of course far from condemning all "impersonal narration" or "authorial silence." When the author is "silent" yet still able through his "rhetoric" to make the "norms" accessible—as in the Jason section of *The Sound and the Fury*—a remarkable kind of "communication" takes place between author and reader: because of the author's "silence" the "communication" becomes "secret communion." The reader requires no explicit commentary from the author to judge accurately Jason's "vicious" attitudes and conduct:

> [O]ur path through Jason's perverted moral world . . . is built out of secret jokes passing between ourselves and the author. . . . We take delight in communion, and even in deep collusion, with the author behind Jason's back. Most of Jason's faults and crimes are so glaring that there would be no fun in talking about them openly. . . . To call Jason a bigot, a braggart, a thief, and a sadist offers none of the comic delight that his vicious behavior offers. But to commune with Faulkner behind Jason's back is a different matter. . . . The technique enables us to skirt the thrilling regions of melodrama without embarrassment.
> (pp. 306–7)

If the "silent" accessibility of the "norms" enables the reader to respond with pleasure, then Booth's "rhetorical" interests might not after all be taking him too far from the Neo-Aristotelian view of the work of art: perhaps the "secret jokes," the "fun," the "delight" are after all only the "pleasure" appropriate to the specific kind of work to which *The Sound and the Fury* belongs. But even if the emphasis here on "pleasure" might seem to align Booth with the earlier Neo-Aristotelians, the primary emphasis on "norms" subordinates "pleasure" to something altogether different: "What all this [secret communion] amounts to is that on this moral level we discover a kind of collaboration which can be one of the most rewarding of all reading experiences. To collaborate with the author by providing the source of an allusion or by deciphering a pun is one thing. But to collaborate with him by providing mature moral judgment is a far more exhilarating sport" (p. 307).

Although near the beginning of *The Rhetoric of Fiction* (pp. 33–34) Booth mentions the Horatian "instruction and delight" formula as a general criterion of an earlier age, he demonstrates with startling clarity elsewhere—but perhaps nowhere more forcefully than here in his discussion of *The Sound and the Fury* —just what a long time that formula has taken in dying. If we might find slightly embarrassing in the original Neo-Aristotelians the emphasis on pleasure (even though it is the pleasure appropriate to particular kinds of art), the pleasure is here tamed by collocation with an end no moralist could object to: "mature moral judgment." But just as the "pleasure" appropriate to *The Sound and the Fury* is coarsened into "secret jokes" and "fun," so the "mature moral judgment" itself turns out to be a simplistic affair. The "norms" on which this "mature moral judgment" depends might be summed up as follows: it is wrong to be a bigot, it is wrong to be a thief, it is wrong to be a braggart, and so forth. Nor am I wrenching Booth's argument to reduce it to absurdity, for the *King Lear* "norms" that he spells out earlier are "self-evident, even commonplace"—similar, though he does not note the fact, to those "simplistic" "meanings" that W. R. Keast sees Robert Heilman as finding in *Lear*.[17] Booth says:

> *Shakespeare requires us to believe that it is right to honor our fathers, and that it is wrong to kill off old men like Lear or grind out the eyes of old men like Gloucester. He insists that it is always wrong to use other people as instruments to one's own ends, whether by murder or slander, that it is good to love, but wrong to love selfishly, that helpless old age is pitiable, and that blind egotism deserves punishment.... Certainly, to work in accordance with such universals is not enough to make an author great. But to accept them in the works where they are pertinent is a fundamental step before greatness can be experienced.* (pp. 141–42)

And so it is actually only a short step to the end of *The Rhetoric of Fiction* and what Wellek calls the "distressingly Philistine plea for a sound and sane morality, to be clearly and publicly announced by the novelist."[18] Given Booth's notion of "rhetoric," the announcement need not be too public, but it must be clear: presumably he would have no objection to experiencing "intensely the sensations and emotions of a homicidal maniac" in *Le Voyeur* if Robbe-Grillet had provided explicit commentary or some other sort of "rhetoric" to enable himself and Booth to experience the open "communication" or "secret communion" that would allow Booth to make the appropriate "mature moral judgment" on the "homicidal maniac" (p. 384). This "communication" of "norms," this "secret communion," finally takes precedence, for Booth, over the "imitative" demands of the earlier Neo-Aristotelians. The writer is to be less concerned with making a well-wrought "imitation" of an action than with supplying the right sort of "norms." If Booth thus seems a reactionary in morals, the trouble surely stems from the concern with "norms" forced on him by his interest in "rhetoric"; whatever Philistinism there may be in Booth is a result of his approach to fiction: as long as the "norms" are to be public, no one can demand less than that they be admirable. Booth's advice to the novelist is explicit: "the writer should worry less about whether his *narrators* are realistic than about whether the *image he creates of himself*, his implied author, is one that his most intelligent and perceptive readers can admire" (p. 395). The Neo-Aristotelian aesthetic "ought" has become moral.

---

[17] "The 'New Criticism' and 'King Lear,' " in *Critics and Criticism*, pp. 123–27.

[18] *Concepts of Criticism*, p. 322.

We have witnessed in Booth's "rhetorical" criticism a change not only in critical approach but—more importantly—in *the object the critic studies*. The original Neo-Aristotelians discern two large *kinds* of poetic wholes, the "imitative" and the "didactic." In the "imitative" kind the completeness and the unity of the artistic whole depend on the action "imitated." In the "didactic" kind, however, although it may use certain devices of the "imitative," the completeness and the unity of the whole depend not on the action but on the "doctrine" to be inculcated.[19] Booth of course recognizes this basic distinction when he finds that the indecipherability of the "norms" in the fourth book of *Gulliver's Travels* is "paid for by a loss of satiric force" (p. 321), for satire is a "didactic" species in which "doctrine" is central.[20] But what are the "norms" in presumably "imitative" fiction if they are not the same as the "doctrine" that Booth and the other Chicagoans find in the "didactic"? The "imitative" part of fiction remains important for Booth, but it gives way before the "norms"—the "doctrine." If "doctrine" is to be inculcated, "norms" are to be "communicated." In short, what had formerly been the "imitative" kind has now become the "didactic" kind. As if he were a latter-day Horace, Booth finds the "pleasure" afforded by "imitation" combining with the moral utility of "doctrine" to provide a new—or a very old—view of literature.

Such to Neo-Aristotelianism is the cost of its recent interest in "rhetoric"—it has lost the poetic kind to which most of its attentions were directed. Crane observed that if Aristotle had dealt with "didactic" works he would probably have treated them in terms of "rhetoric."[21] He might have observed, too, that to treat "imitative" poems in terms of "rhetoric" would be to make them "didactic." Is our literature, in some sense, only what we make of it?

Perhaps Booth makes fiction "didactic" in order to defend it. The concluding paragraph of *The Rhetoric of Fiction* sees the work by which author and reader "communicate" as an object whose function would be far more defensible than the provision of "pleasure":

> *The author makes his readers. If he makes them badly—that is, if he simply waits, in all purity, for the occasional reader whose perceptions and norms happen to match his own, then his conception must be lofty indeed if we are to forgive him for his bad craftsmanship. But if he makes them well—that is, makes them see what they have never seen before, moves them into a new order of perception and experience altogether—he finds his reward in the peers he has created.*

[19] This account of the Neo-Aristotelian distinction between "imitative" and "didactic" is based on Olson, "A Dialogue on Symbolism," in *Critics and Criticism*, p. 589.

[20] Crane's 1955 essay on "The Rationale of the Fourth Voyage" (first published in the 1961 Norton Critical Edition of *Gulliver*) focuses on, among other things, the "form and purpose of [the] unifying argument" of the "satirical thought"—clearly a matter of "doctrine."

[21] *The Languages of Criticism and the Structure of Poetry*, p. 197. See Olson's similar point in "William Empson, Contemporary Criticism, and Poetic Diction," in *Critics and Criticism*, p. 66.

This is of course an impressive defense of fiction, but are the "norms" enabling one to sympathize or to condemn in the same fashion as the author—real or "implied"—actually the sort of "norms" which might enable readers to "see what they have never seen before," to move "into a new order of perception and experience altogether"? Since the "norms" Booth worries about in *The Rhetoric of Fiction* are so much a matter of commonplaces, even when they are the "norms" in *King Lear*, the defense is hardly earned. Probably such a defense, even if more systematically pursued than Booth's other interests seem to permit, could not be launched from a position which focuses on "rhetoric" and "communication." Booth, at any rate, often gives the impression of wanting the author's "norms" to be cut down to manageable size, as when those in *Lear* turn out to be the eternal verities. Who needs the "norms" of *Lear*, no matter how intense the "pleasure," if they are platitudes? Undeniably many of the works Booth deals with move us "into a new order of perception and experience altogether," and Booth is a serious and sensitive enough man to know this, but with his approach to literature he is actually unable to argue the point. Although, like Booth, the earlier Neo-Aristotelians seem everywhere convinced of the value of literature, as far as I know they never try systematically to defend this value. Perhaps they do not feel the need. Crane, in fact, speaks of the New Critics' "morbid obsession . . . with the problem of justifying and preserving poetry."[22] And Olson, when he deduces "practical wisdom" in the reader as the potential end result of the "effect" of tragedy, refrains from making the Horatian defense he seems in a position to make.

Not only does Booth's emphasis on "rhetoric" cause the novel to shift from the "imitative" to the "didactic" kind, but along with this comes what is for Neo-Aristotelian formalism a surprisingly new view of the writer. Although he is still an "imitator" in his making of "plots," he is more importantly the source of the "norms" to be "communicated" to the reader. The "norms," the "rhetoric" tend to grow as the work, the "imitation," the form, diminishes. That last paragraph of *The Rhetoric of Fiction*—together with the concern throughout the book with the "author's voice" and the "secret communion" necessary when the demands of the "imitative principle" silence that voice—is enough to make us conclude that Booth has managed to give Neo-Aristotelianism a clearly expressionistic coloring. Booth himself reminds us that for Longinus "such distinctions as that between didactic and imaginative [i.e., 'imitative'] works were unimportant" (p. 33), and Olson persuades us that we should define Longinian "sublimity" "in terms of that communication of nobility which is made possible by the perfection of the human soul and of art, and which receives its answer in the wonder and admiration of all men."[23] Is this "communication" very far from that "communication" Booth envisions at the end of *The Rhetoric of Fiction* where the author "creates" in his readers "peers" who move with him "into a new order of perception and experience altogether"?

[22] "The Critical Monism of Cleanth Brooks," in *Critics and Criticism*, p. 105.

[23] "The Argument of Longinus' 'On the Sublime,' " in *Critics and Criticism*, p. 259.

## IV

But if Booth's theory has this strong didactic, even expressionistic emphasis, it still retains much of the appearance of Neo-Aristotelianism. If the work as "imitation" *is* diminished, Booth is still enough of a Neo-Aristotelian formalist to want to see it as "a unified work of art," even though the unity turns out to be dependent not so much on the action "imitated" as on the "doctrine," the "norms" expressed. Thus what Crane, with his purer formalism, must regard as the "intrusive," "ornamental" essays in *Tom Jones* can become for Booth, on the other hand, a "subplot" involving the "implied author" and the reader. Although like other admirers of the novel he wants to see it as "a unified work of art and not half-novel, half-essay," as Crane must in effect see it, the unity his theory leads him to see becomes the unity of a "didactic" work, an "essay" as it were with "imitative" embellishment. Booth asserts "a genuine harmony of the two dramatized elements," but the author-reader "subplot" comes close to dominating the main "plot" involving Jones. Or does the "subplot" not come to dominate the other altogether? "For the reader with his mind on the main business, . . . the narrator becomes a rich and provocative chorus. It is his wisdom and learning and benevolence that permeate the world of the book, set its comic tone between the extremes of sentimental indulgence and scornful indignation, and in a sense redeem Tom's world of hypocrites and fools." "Tom's world," judged by the "norms" of the narrator, "offers no single character who is both wise and good," yet "the author is always there on his platform to remind us, through his wisdom and benevolence, of what human life *ought to be and might be*" (italics added). So successful is the communication achieved by Booth's author-reader "subplot" that as we read the novel the author's "world . . . is ours."

To revert to the phrasing at the end of *The Rhetoric of Fiction*, if the author "creates" in his readers his "peers" in "wisdom and learning and benevolence," we have no longer the "imitative" work Crane has taught us to appreciate but instead a "didactic" work of first rank, made persuasive by this moving "subplot," embellished—is it too much to say?—with "Tom's world of hypocrites and fools." We have also, it would seem, the "expression" of the great soul, a kind of Longinian "sublimity," in Olson's words the "communication of nobility which is made possible by the perfection of the human soul and of art, and which receives its answer in the wonder and admiration of all men." If this interpretation of Booth's argument about Fielding's narrator appears extravagant and unfair—his special interest here is after all in defending the presence of the narrator —it is nevertheless consistent with what we have seen the focus on "rhetoric" and "norms" and "communication" making of fiction. Booth himself makes the author the book, and the book the author: "The gift [the narrator] leaves—his book —is himself, precisely himself. The author has created this self as he has written the book. . . . It is not Fielding we care about, but the narrator created to speak in his name." So, here as elsewhere, the "implied author"—who in *Tom Jones* happens to be the same as the narrator—may as well be the man who wrote the book.

Perhaps most striking of all is the specific quality of the "belief" induced in the reader by the "subplot": "our growing intimacy with Fielding's dramatic version of himself produces a kind of comic analogue of the true believer's reliance on a benign providence in real life."

Here, after seeing what Booth has made of *Tom Jones*, we may return to what Crane makes of it. Let us note that Crane sees the character of the narrator somewhat as Booth does, but to a different purpose; the narrator for Crane is subordinate to the "imitative" whole and so helps to produce the specific "comic" quality of that whole: "the clearly evident attitude of Fielding's narrator" is a "determinant of our frame of mind." "He is," Crane continues,

> a man we can trust, who knows the whole story and still is not deeply concerned; one who understands the difference between good men and bad and who can yet speak with amused indulgence of the first, knowing how prone they are to weakness of intellect, and with urbane scorn, rather than indignation, of the second, knowing that most of them, too, are fools. This combination of sympathetic moral feeling with ironical detachment is bound to influence our expectations from the first, and to the extent that it does so, we tend to anticipate the coming troubles with no more than comic fear. (pp. 641–42)

Although like the other Chicagoans Crane speaks here of the effect of the novel on the reader—"our frame of mind," "our expectations," "no more than comic fear," and so forth—his concern with the reader is utterly different from Booth's. Whereas Booth is interested mainly, as we have seen, in a sharing of "norms" between author and reader, Crane's concern is merely a hypothetical matter. His mode of analysis begins with the "tentative" hypothesis that a work is designed to produce an effect appropriate to a specific kind of poetic whole; then it continues with an analysis of the technical "causes" that contribute to this "effect." Since for Crane *Tom Jones* is an "imitative" work, much of his analysis is devoted to an exploration of the "expectations" and "probabilities" of the "plot," the primary "part" of an "imitative" work. Even the "imitative" lyric, for Crane and Olson, has "choice" as a "plot"-like primary "part."[24] Other "parts," like "character," are subordinate to "plot." Consequently, the introductory "essays" are at best often only "embellishment" for Crane, and in the main they constitute a blemish. It is, I believe, altogether inconceivable that Crane should see the "essays" as forming a "subplot"—especially if, like Booth, he were to acknowledge that "the 'plot' of our relationship with Fielding-as-narrator has no similarity to the story of Tom"—unless, again like Booth, he thought of *Tom Jones* for some reason as "didactic." In that case, of course, the "doctrine" would serve as the unifying "part," and the story of Tom could properly be regarded as subordinate! Crane—with *his* theory, or his conviction that *Tom Jones* is "imitative" —has no alternative to seeing the "essays" as intrusive, and the work as flawed. He says, though not specifically of the intrusion of the "essays," "There are no perfect works of art, and, though many of the faults that have been found in

---

[24] "An Outline of Poetic Theory," in *Critics and Criticism*, pp. 563–64.

*Tom Jones* are faults only on the supposition that it should have been another kind of novel, still enough real shortcomings remain to keep one's enthusiasm for Fielding's achievement within reasonable bounds" (p. 638).

If one accepts Booth's argument about the "genuine harmony of the two dramatized elements," one has no need "to keep one's enthusiasm for Fielding's achievement within reasonable bounds," for the "essays" now are truly an integral "part" of the novel. Booth, then, makes a better case for the novel than Crane, although—or because—he sees it as a different *kind* of novel. It would appear that the critic's initial "hypothesis" about the kind of work it is serves in large part to determine what he will find in it. Crane begins with the assumption —a reasonable assumption, no doubt—that *Tom Jones* is an "imitative" work, and finds it flawed, but not seriously so. Booth begins with the assumption that it is a "didactic" work—though of course the "assumption," running counter to his statement that he is dealing with "non-didactic" fiction, is discoverable only through the sort of analysis of "rhetoric" and "norms" I have engaged in—and finds it virtually perfect. Since both procedures, illustrating what Hirsch has called the "hermeneutic circle,"[25] find what their initial assumptions determine they shall find, choice between them may appear difficult. If the work is more important than the criticism—as surely it must be—then Booth's sort of criticism would seem superior to Crane's. But as soon as we grant the superiority of Booth's "rhetorical" criticism and preserve *Tom Jones* as unflawed, we may have to sacrifice at the least, say, many works of James, and many of the works thus saved we will value for such "norms" as we have seen. But surely we will question the enormous amount of "imitative" embellishment in the essentially "didactic" *Tom Jones*.

Hence Crane's sort of criticism, looking for "imitative" rather than "didactic" wholes, may after all be preferable to Booth's: even if we must see *Tom Jones* as flawed—we can, like Crane, apparently read the essays as essays, wishing they were not in the novel but also not wishing them away either—we need not sacrifice works in which the author's "norms" are not perfectly clear. Yet we may be disposed to quarrel with Crane's casual statement, "There are no perfect works of art": although we cannot prove the contrary, neither can we prove the statement itself, for the work of art may actually test the critical system that would find it deficient. Perhaps—and ironically, since *Tom Jones* with its classic plot might seem a work predestined for Crane's sort of study—this novel does serve to reveal some of the limits of Neo-Aristotelian "whole-part" analysis; perhaps not even in a work like *Tom Jones* is everything really subordinate to what Crane regards in all "imitative" works as the primary "part." And this does not necessarily take us back to Booth as the only alternative. Although his "rhetorical" criticism might seem an advance in that his "norms" at least try to relate the work more closely to our concerns as human beings than Crane's (and the other Neo-Aristotelians') emphasis on "pleasures" and "effects" does—this advance is largely illusory. Since they let us know when to sympathize and when to condemn, the "norms" are linked to that "effect" which indicates to Crane the kind of

[25] *Validity in Interpretation*, pp. 75–76.

"imitative" whole he is dealing with; only when pursued as Booth pursues them with his interest in "rhetoric" and "communication" do they become the sort of "doctrine" which we have seen turning "imitative" art into "didactic."


V


If, as I believe, Neo-Aristotelianism reaches here a point of exhaustion, an insoluble dilemma, possibly we may find a way out in a suggestion of Geoffrey Hartman: "the faults of . . . formalists are due not to their formalism as such but rather to their not being formalistic enough."[26] Booth and Crane, like the other Neo-Aristotelians, are formalists enough to want to see *Tom Jones* as a unified whole, yet in various ways neither succeeds: perhaps in each case the "form" of *Tom Jones* eludes the critic because the idea of "form" he starts with, either "imitative" or "didactic," does not quite fit the novel. Although Crane's statement, "There are no perfect works of art," may sober us, it may also hide from us our own ignorance, our own all too evident lack of perfection: it may simply provide us with a way of keeping our critical systems intact. Under the circumstances, we had better assume, until we can be surer of ourselves, that Fielding's work *is* a unified whole.[27] If we remember some of Tate's "excellent remarks" in "Techniques of Fiction" about the difficulty of knowing novels as wholes, we had better try, in the beginning at least, not to have too narrow a hypothesis about the kind of form *Tom Jones* is: although this may not really get us out of Hirsch's "hermeneutic circle," it may prevent that initial hypothesis from determining what we finally make of the novel. We must, in other words, be prepared to have our hypotheses bend and break under the pressures we allow the work to exert on them, hoping that in the process the work will somehow determine what we make of it.

Let us explore cautiously the possibility of being more "formalistic" than Booth and Crane by making use of whatever their hypotheses lead them to see in the novel, recognizing at the outset that their hypotheses do not take them far enough toward the "form" of the novel. We may thus use what we can in both Booth and Crane, not hoping to reconcile the "imitative"-"didactic" differences between them, but simply seeking whatever hints we may find helpful. If this

---

[26] *Beyond Formalism: Literary Essays 1958–1970* (New Haven: Yale Univ. Press, 1970), p. 42. The formalists Hartman is concerned with are those of Yale, not Chicago; in addition, his way of becoming more "formalistic" differs from mine.

[27] In *Shakespearean Meanings* (Princeton: Princeton Univ. Press, 1968) and *The Drama of Language: Essays on Goethe and Kleist* (Baltimore: The Johns Hopkins Press, 1970), Sigurd Burckhardt often proceeds on the hypothesis of the perfection or "infallibility" of the work: seeming inconsistencies or "discrepancies" may serve as clues enabling the interpreter to discover the "law" of a work. In an appendix to the Shakespeare volume, "Notes on the Theory of Intrinsic Interpretation," he offers a theoretical justification of the procedure. His strategies, however, are meant to resist codification into the rigidity of method, for there is no rule by which one can uncover the "discrepancy" that leads to the discovery of the deeper unity, the more comprehensive "law." With less imaginative, less rigorous minds than Burckhardt's the hypothesis of perfection could of course produce the worst excesses of belletristic criticism.

procedure, which Olson might reject as "syncretism," implies that all critical or philosophical positions are partially false,[28] I see no viable alternative at the moment. "Pluralism" may allow everyone to tend his own garden, but the positions of Booth and Crane—however internally consistent each may be—reach sufficiently different conclusions about *Tom Jones* to make us suspect that neither critic can be more than partially right. But surely Booth is right—or properly "formalistic"—in looking for some *relationship* between Crane's "imitative" main "plot" and what he takes to be the "subplot," and surely Crane himself is convincing in his argument about the "comic" structure of the incidents and characters in the story of Tom. Perhaps both are wrong, however, in reducing one or the other "part" to embellishment.

At one point Crane, in trying to differentiate the "comic" quality of the "plot" from that in certain other "comedies," makes a statement that appears to clash with one of Booth's about the "subplot": if there is "a genuine harmony of the two dramatized elements," that "harmony" is something other than concord. Crane says, "We are not disposed to feel, when we are done laughing at Tom, that all is right with the world or that we can count on Fortune always intervening, in the same gratifying way, on behalf of the good" (p. 638). Yet, in an important statement already cited, Booth says, "our growing intimacy with Fielding's dramatic version of himself produces a kind of comic analogue of the true believer's reliance on a benign providence in real life"—just the sort of thing that with Crane "We are *not* disposed to feel."[29] And just the sort of "doctrine" Fielding's narrator does not *ever* feel, at least when he addresses us in his "essays":

> There are a set of religious, or rather moral writers, who teach that virtue is the certain road to happiness, and vice to misery, in this world. A very wholesome and comfortable doctrine, and to which we have but one objection, namely, that it is not true. (XV, i)

Is there, then, a conflict between the "imitative," "dramatic" plot convincingly analyzed by Crane and what the narrator "tells" us? In any event, the narrator and Crane caution us about what we see of a "benign providence" in the novel. The narrator invites us, for the moment here as on some other occasions, to look away from the beautifully wrought action in Tom's world—where Fortune does indeed act (or is *made* to act?) as a "benign providence" protecting and rewarding Tom—to our own world, where this "comfortable doctrine . . . is not true." He invites us to acknowledge that Tom's world is a fiction, an "imitation" made for its own sake, to view it with the sort of detachment Mr. Partridge is unable to summon up before the "imitated" ghost in *Hamlet*. Although it does not in any sense "imitate" our own world, although it is not a mirror held up to any nature we may know—which is to claim that Fielding's narrator is a good enough Neo-

---

[28] "An Outline of Poetic Theory," in *Critics and Criticism*, p. 547.

[29] What can epitomize more clearly the differences between their positions than Booth's ingenious modification of Crane's phrase "comic analogue of fear" (p. 637) into "comic analogue of the true believer's reliance on a benign providence"?

Aristotelian to imply that Tom's world "imitates" only itself—this "imitation" may nevertheless not be made entirely for its own sake. For this "imitation" may enable many of us to see how far our own world falls short of the perfection of Tom's providential world. Nor does it, despite Booth's suggestions, offer us models of what "human life ought to be, and might be," certainly not of course in the "fools and hypocrites" of Tom's world, and not even in the "wisdom and learning and benevolence" of the narrator. Must we not say that the narrator is able to maintain these qualities, to keep his equilibrium "between the extremes of sentimental indulgence and scornful indignation," precisely because he creates not readers who are his "peers" but characters toward whom he can have such attitudes? Must we not say, further, that the narrator thus creates the characters in order to be able to have such attitudes, and that he has such attitudes in order to be able to create the characters? If I seem to be arguing for a circularity in the relationship between the narrator and Tom's world, do I not after all acknowledge, but from a different direction, the "form" of the whole to be the sort of "genuine harmony" Booth sought to demonstrate? Not really, because whereas Booth's "harmony" resolves itself in the direction of "doctrine," I am suggesting a "harmony" that maintains itself only by virtue of the unresolved tensions between the "imitative" structure of Tom's providential world and the narrator's denial that this world, for all its attractiveness, is anything more—or, for that matter, less—than "imitation." The novel, in other words, presents a tension between Tom's world with its elaborate workings of a beneficent Fortune and the narrator's presence, which reminds us that he has constructed this world: such is the "form" of *Tom Jones*, with the narrator inside the "form" yet outside the "imitation," the story of Tom.[30]

In arguing thus for "unresolved tensions" among "parts" of *Tom Jones*, I am in effect arguing against the *primacy* of any one "part" and the consequent relegation of any "part" to mere "embellishment," hoping to discern in the qualifications one "part" urges on another the unique form of this novel. If that form is less consistently "comic" than the one Crane so persuasively discerns for us, if indeed that form with its "unresolved tensions" seems to push *Tom Jones* away from the "comic" toward the "tragic," I do not wish to suggest that generations of readers have been wrong in regarding the novel as a comedy. Fielding's urbane narrator—and, I believe, any "author" one might find "implied" in the novel—is

---

[30] In exploiting the ambiguity of "imitation" in order to stress how *Tom Jones* convinces us of the reality of its world at the same time that the presence of the narrator makes us acknowledge that world as mere illusion, my procedure may seem to echo the general approach of Murray Krieger in his important recent book, *The Classic Vision: The Retreat from Extremity in Modern Literature* (Baltimore: The Johns Hopkins Press, 1971). If I may simplify, Krieger finds the sustaining power of each of the "classic" poems and novels he studies to reside in its capacity to work for us as a "reductive metaphor"—an "elaborate contextual system" that creates for us a world with nothing left out even as we retain "the steadfast common sense" to see that "*everything* is left out" (p. 365): total inclusion and total exclusion. Thus we should be able to regard successful metaphors or successful imitations as fully earned, as capturing for us the fullness of the world, and yet at the same time to recognize that the metaphors are after all "reductive," that the imitations of reality are after all still only *imitation*; otherwise, we are not entirely justified in smiling at that arch-literalist, Mr. Partridge.

Since I read *The Classic Vision* after this essay was completed, the parallel here is very likely the result of my close familiarity with Krieger's earlier works.

too far removed from anything approaching a tragic consciousness, even though he does enable us to see obliquely through the perfect workings of his creation the flaws in our own world. I do suggest, however, that attempts at more "formalistic" approaches may lead us at least to question the ease with which we may be disposed to pigeonhole some of our works into convenient classes, even as I must admit that if we did not put them into classes to begin with we would not see how they sometimes transcend these classes.

I believe Booth might respond to my altogether too brief suggestions here by observing that I have objected to his "didactic" approach only to substitute a "didactic" approach of my own that finds Fielding's "rhetoric" operating to reveal simply a different sort of "doctrine" from those his approach leads him to find. Crane—in addition to pointing out obvious ways in which I have been influenced by Cleanth Brooks's poetics of tension and especially the remark that in tragedy the "clash" of elements "is at its sharpest"[31]—might observe that I have played fast and loose with the concept of "imitation," detaching from it its basic analogy to human action. To which the only reply can be that although Crane may convince us that a "plot" is an "imitation" in this analogical sense, the "whole" of which the "plot" is a "part" must be something altogether different once we abandon the idea that one "part" has primacy over the others. Can we even say that the "whole" is an "imitation" in any sense other than that basic Aristotelian sense of being a product of human art rather than nature? This position we have ended with is close to the assumption Crane elsewhere says the critic should begin with when the "task" is to make "formal sense out of any poetic work": "the assumption that it may in fact be a work for whose peculiar principles of structure there are nowhere any usable parallels either in literary theory or in our experience of other works."[32] We can arrive at this most "formalistic" sort of formalism which Crane recommends, I submit, only by beginning with a hypothesis—perhaps like Crane's, for example, about "imitation" or Booth's about "rhetoric"—and then trying to allow the work to teach us in just what sense that hypothesis can be nothing more than "tentative." Certainly we should, like Booth, hope for others "to share" with us "a mode, an interest, a language"; but we should also recognize—and try to overcome—the limitations that our modes, our interests, and even our languages impose on us and on the works we study.

Hence, in fairness to Crane and Booth, I must admit that my own "mode" may appear just one more circular critical procedure in which the initial assumptions, though here disguised as a probing into Neo-Aristotelian "imitation" and "rhetorical" theory, determine what the work shall become. I may as well acknowledge, too, that my reading of *Tom Jones*, which depends so heavily on the

---

[31] *The Well Wrought Urn: Studies in the Structure of Poetry* (New York: Reynal & Hitchcock, 1947), pp. 229–30. Whereas Tate's "tension," mentioned in section II of this essay, is derived from the logical terms "extension" and "intension" and applies in a special way to the language of lyric poetry, Brooks's "tension" is closer to the ordinary senses of the term and refers to relations among larger as well as smaller elements in a work.

[32] *The Languages of Criticism and the Structure of Poetry*, pp. 167–68.

tension between the narrator and the "imitation" he creates, might easily be used as a *formula* for dealing with other novels with "intrusive" omniscient narrators. In fact, Crane's own care to explain how the "probabilities" in *Tom Jones* prevent our becoming too fearful for the hero might point the way to a "tensional" reading of the novel similar to the one I have suggested: the very inevitability of the providential workings of Fortune invites the suspicion of parody. But this would be again to open up the questions of the "intrusiveness" of the narrator and of the unity of the whole.

# The Basic Concepts and Criteria of
# F. R. Leavis's Novel Criticism

R. P. BILAN

F. R. Leavis's work on the English novel seems to me his most distinctive and original contribution to modern literary criticism. I do not mean to slight Leavis's achievement as a critic of poetry, but much of his writing on poetry is deeply indebted to T. S. Eliot and does not have the decisive independence of his fiction criticism. The view of Leavis's criticism taken by George Steiner in *Language and Silence* strikes me as being fundamentally sound: "Undoubtedly, Leavis's principal achievement is his critique of the English novel. *The Great Tradition* is one of those very rare books of literary comment (one thinks of Johnson's *Lives of the Poets* or Arnold's *Essays in Criticism*) that have re-shaped the inner landscape of taste." [1] Steiner is right to single out *The Great Tradition* (1948) both for its merits and for the great impact it has had, but I believe that *D. H. Lawrence, Novelist* (1955) is of almost equal importance. It is a pioneering book that established Lawrence as a major writer and it further develops and clarifies Leavis's thinking about the novel. Both of Leavis's later books dealing primarily with the novel—*Anna Karenina and Other Essays* (1967) and, in collaboration with Q. D. Leavis, *Dickens the Novelist* (1970)—add considerably to his achievement as a critic of fiction. His essay on Dickens's *Little Dorrit*, in fact, may be the most ambitious and impressive single piece of criticism Leavis has ever written.

It is his specific judgments on novelists that have provoked the widest response and received the most attention, but perhaps just as deserving of close scrutiny are the concepts about the nature of fiction and the criteria he advances in making those judgments. While Leavis does not give an explicit or theoretical definition of his concept of the novel, nor of his criteria, implicit in nearly all of his fiction criticism are two firmly held ideas: first, that there is a particularly close relation between the novel and morality; second, that great novels present an affirmation of life. Leavis's thinking about the moral dimension of fiction is especially complex and revolves around a number of closely related ideas: a definite concept of form in fiction, the concepts of the novel as moral fable and dramatic poem, and a notion of moral enactment and moral exploration.

One of Leavis's central contentions is that great novelists show an intense moral interest in life and that this moral interest determines and conditions the

---

[1] George Steiner, "F. R. Leavis," in *Language and Silence* (New York: Atheneum, 1967), p. 229.

nature of their preoccupation with form in fiction. In the opening chapter of *The Great Tradition* Leavis attempts to set out what he considers to be the proper relation between form (or "composition") and moral interest, or art and life. He contends that:

> *Jane Austen's plots, and her novels in general, were put together very 'deliberately and calculatedly.'* . . . *But her interest in 'composition' is not something to be put over against her interest in life; nor does she offer an 'aesthetic' value that is separable from moral significance. The principle of organization, and the principle of development, in her work is an intense moral interest of her own in life that is in the first place a preoccupation with certain problems that life compels on her as personal ones.*[2]

Leavis refuses to separate art from life, the aesthetic or formal from the moral. He insists:

> *When we examine the formal perfection of Emma, we find that it can be appreciated only in terms of the moral preoccupations that characterize the novelist's peculiar interest in life. Those who suppose it to be an 'aesthetic matter', a beauty of 'composition' that is combined, miraculously, with 'truth to life', can give no adequate reason for the view that Emma is a great novel, and no intelligent account of its perfection of form.*[3]

Leavis's view of the proper relation of form and moral interest in fiction has proven to be as contentious an issue as certain of his evaluations; the statement above is frequently quoted and argued with. David Lodge, for instance, in *Language of Fiction*, reverses Leavis's terms and suggests that the "moral preoccupations" of *Emma* can be appreciated only in terms of "the formal perfection" of the novel.[4] It is a dogma of modern criticism that the moral and the formal in a successful work of art are one—what Eliseo Vivas calls "informed substance"— and it is a tenet that Leavis would subscribe to. But Leavis's formulation *seems* to bring the two apart by regarding the moral as prior to the formal, and certainly as the more important. (This may not be quite fair to Leavis; his insistence is that the preoccupation with form is inseparable from moral concern, not that it is less important.) We should nonetheless consider whether Leavis does not give us a proper understanding of the nature of form in major works of fiction, as opposed to the more rigid, stylized kind of form found in the use of, say, the sonnet.

We can further consider Leavis's position by examining the criticisms he makes of Henry James's notion of form. James's position is a more formalist one than Leavis's, and the word 'composition' or 'form' is often used as an important criterion in his criticism. For example, James complains that for George Eliot the

---

[2] *The Great Tradition* (1948, rpt. Harmondsworth: Penguin Books, 1966), p. 15.
[3] *Ibid.*, p. 17.
[4] David Lodge, *Language of Fiction* (New York: Columbia University Press, 1966), p. 68.

novel was "not primarily a picture of life, capable of deriving a high value from its form, but a moralized fable, the last word of a philosophy endeavouring to teach by example." [5] Leavis objects strenuously to what he calls the "misleading antithesis" of James's position: "What, we ask, is the 'form' from which a 'picture of life' derives its value?" [6] And he insists that a great novelist's preoccupation with form is a matter of his responsibility towards a rich moral interest. Leavis is not denying that there are works of art with a limited formal concern, but his point is that they are not the greatest kind of fiction. This point is made most clearly, perhaps, in his essay on Tolstoy's *Anna Karenina*. In this essay Leavis attempts to "confute" James's critical censures and to show the nature of the composition that makes *Anna Karenina* a great work of art. James found Tolstoy's novel lacking in composition and architecture, and Leavis answers that whereas a limited and clearly concerned interest determined the "composition" of a Jamesian novel,

> the relation of art to life in Tolstoy is such as to preclude this kind of narrowly provident economy. It is an immensely fuller and profounder involvement in life on the part of the artist, whose concern for significance in his art is the intense and focused expression of the questing after significance that characterizes him in his daily living. . . . Tolstoy might very well have answered as Lawrence did when asked, not long before his death, what was the drive behind his creating: 'One writes out of one's moral sense; for the race, as it were.' [7]

Leavis makes almost the same point in explaining, in *The Great Tradition*, why Conrad is a greater novelist than Flaubert. Leavis's statement offers a further elaboration of his view of the proper relation between form and moral interest, and it serves to introduce the topic of the moral fable. He claims:

> James would have testified to [Conrad's] intense and triumphant preoccupation with 'form'. He went to school to the French masters, and is in the tradition of Flaubert. But he is a greater novelist than Flaubert because of the greater range and depth of his interest in humanity and the greater intensity of his moral preoccupation: he is not open to the kind of criticism that James brings against Madame Bovary. Nostromo is a masterpiece of 'form' in senses of the term congenial to the discussion of Flaubert's art, but to appreciate Conrad's 'form' is to take stock of a process of relative valuation conducted by him in the face of life: what do men live by?—what can men live by?—these are the questions that animate his theme. His organization is devoted to exhibiting in the concrete a representative set of radical attitudes, so ordered as to bring out the significance of each in relation to a total sense of human life. The dramatic imagination at work is an intensely moral imagination, the vivid-

[5] Henry James, quoted in *The Great Tradition*, p. 40.
[6] *The Great Tradition*, p. 40.
[7] F. R. Leavis, *Anna Karenina and Other Essays* (London: Chatto & Windus, 1967), pp. 11–12.

*ness of which is inalienably a judging and a valuing. With such economy has each 'figure' and 'situation' its significance in a taut inclusive scheme that* Nostromo *might more reasonably than any of George Eliot's fictions except* Silas Marner . . . *be called a 'moralized fable'.*[8]

There can be no significant form apart from this kind of radical moral inquiry into life, and the organization that results—the inclusive scheme—is that of the moral fable or moral pattern.

It is *Hard Times* which perhaps is best known as the example of what Leavis means by the novel as moral fable, but in fact most of the novels he praises in *The Great Tradition*—*The Secret Agent* as well as *Nostromo, The Europeans* and *The Portrait of a Lady, Silas Marner*—are described as being, essentially, "moral fables." Under this heading Leavis attempts to define a distinct concept of the novel and to reject the conventional view. In discussing *Hard Times* he criticizes the traditional approach to "the English novel":

> *The business of the novelist, you gather, is to 'create a world', and the mark of the master is external abundance—he gives you lots of 'life'. The test of life in his characters (he must above all create 'living' characters) is that they go on living outside the book. Expectations as unexacting as these are not, when they encounter significance, grateful for it, and when it meets them in that insistent form where nothing is very engaging as 'life' unless its relevance is fully taken, miss it altogether. This is the only way in which I can account for the neglect suffered by Henry James's* The Europeans *which may be classed with* Hard Times *as a moral fable. . . . Fashion, however, has not recommended his [James's] earlier work, and this . . . still suffers from the prevailing expectation of redundant and irrelevant 'life'.*
>
> *I need say no more by way of defining the moral fable than that in it the intention is peculiarly insistent, so that the representative significance of everything in the fable—character, episode, and so on—is immediately apparent as we read . . . [an] inclusive significance that informs and organizes a coherent whole.*[9]

It may seem paradoxical to find Leavis speaking of "redundant and irrelevant life" in a novel, but, as this passage reveals, the "life" that he values in a novel must be controlled art. One obvious problem which arises with the conception of the novel as moral fable is that of deciding how much "irrelevant life" can be sacrificed to the inclusive significance. A. J. Waldock, writing about Leavis's analysis of *Hard Times*, objects that it "remains a highly questionable point whether a novelist is entitled to secure his 'significance' at the cost of jettisoning his life." [10]

We get a fuller understanding of what Leavis means by "moral fable" by con-

[8] *The Great Tradition*, pp. 41–42.
[9] *Ibid.*, pp. 249–50.
[10] A. J. Waldock, "The Status of *Hard Times*," *Southerly*, 9 (1948), 33.

sidering his remarks on James's novel *The Europeans*. Leavis writes: "In fact, all
the figures in the book play their parts in this business of discriminating attitudes
and values, which is performed with remarkable precision and economy. . . .
*The Europeans* (as the very names of the characters suggest) is a moral fable." [11]
Leavis again insists on the concentrated, or inclusive, significance as the distinguishing feature, and the characters in the novel are limited to their place in
this scheme. It seems to me that the difficulty with this concept is that it is too
centered on the scheme of values and slights the novelist's achievement in creating character. The desire to present and explore the full complexity of the individual character may not be fully compatible with the intent to create a work
of art where the representative significance is "immediately apparent." In discussing James's novel, Leavis argues that the two Europeans "stand for different
things: they have, in their symbolic capacities, different—even conflicting—
values." [12] This is typically the way in which Leavis deals with character in fiction,
by referring to the values they "stand for" or "represent." James perhaps achieves
a satisfactory balance between character and value in *The Europeans*, but in
Dickens's *Hard Times* the emphasis is too heavily on the values represented.
Leavis contends that in this novel Dickens is for once possessed by a comprehensive vision in which the inhumanities of Victorian civilization are seen as fostered
by the hard philosophy of utilitarianism. The philosophy, Leavis claims, is represented in the novel by Gradgrind, who "stands for" one aspect of it, and Bounderby, who *is* "Victorian rugged individualism." Surely to be able to say that
Gradgrind "stands for" and Bounderby "is" an aspect of a philosophy or ethos
indicates that the characters are simplified, almost conceptual. They are perhaps
suitable for fulfilling their part in a moral fable, but not for embodying the full
creation and complexity of art. We finally value novels for their exploration of
character as well as values, and both must be given their due.

Both *Hard Times* and *The Europeans* are short novels and Leavis's praise of
them alone might raise questions about the possibility of extending the concept
of the moral fable to longer, more complex works; but he insists that the major
novels of James and Conrad have a similar organization. He writes of *The Portrait
of a Lady*:

> Though Pansy serves obvious functions as machinery . . . her presence in
> the book has, in addition, some point. As a representative figure . . . she brings
> us, in fact, to the general observation that almost all the characters can be seen
> to have, in the same way, their values and significances in a total scheme. For
> though The Portrait of a Lady *is on so much larger a scale than* The Europeans,
> *and because of its complexity doesn't invite the description of 'moral fable', it
> is similarly organized: it is all intensely significant. It offers no largesse of irrele-
> vant 'life'; its vitality is wholly that of art.*[13]

[11] *The Great Tradition*, p. 157.
[12] *Anna Karenina and Other Essays*, p. 60.
[13] *The Great Tradition*, p. 169.

Again we have the clear—if surprising—distinction between art and life: the organization and total significance is one of art. It is true that, because of its greater complexity, Leavis does not actually classify *The Portrait of a Lady* as a moral fable, but his praise of the novel depends on its presentation of a "total scheme" of values.

A similar term to moral fable is moral pattern and in describing Conrad's greatest works Leavis singles out this aspect of the novels. His high praise of *Nostromo* is based on the claim that the whole book forms a rich and subtle but highly organized pattern of moral significances. And of *The Secret Agent* he claims: "The theme develops itself in a complex organic structure. The effect depends upon an interplay of contrasting moral perspectives, and the rich economy of the pattern they make relates *The Secret Agent* to *Nostromo*: the two works, for all the great differences between them in range and temper, are triumphs of the same art." [14] The essays on Conrad in *The Great Tradition* were written before Leavis advanced the phrase "moral fable," but it is apparent that "moral pattern" involves the same concept of the novel. It is the presence of the controlling moral pattern that constitutes the greatness of a novel for Leavis. Graham Hough, however, asserts that the "moral" approach Leavis takes "can only throw a limited illumination on the art of the novel, for no novel worth the name can be pared down to a structure of moral significances." [15] Hough seems to imply—"pared down"—that "a structure of moral significances" excludes "life," but in fact one of Leavis's central criteria for a novel is its adequacy to the complexities of the real, or to life. For example, he praises George Eliot over Henry James for the greater specificity—the fuller reality—of her art. Nonetheless there probably is a certain difficulty in thinking of a novel in this way, and it does suggest at least the possibility that a clearly presented pattern of moral concepts may be too readily granted the status of fully achieved art.

Whatever the difficulties with the concept of the novel as moral fable, we should be careful not to misconstrue Leavis's critical procedure, nor his view of how a novel presents its moral significances. Hough objects to what he considers the standard method of Leavis—and other "moral" critics—in dealing with the novel: "His procedure is to extract a moral essence—with our traditional novelists not a very arduous task—and then to seal it with his approval." [16] I want to show that Hough misrepresents Leavis's normal procedure, but first to consider an instance where the description is applicable. One of the few places where Leavis approves of the "moral" of the work is in his essay on *Hard Times*. He writes: "And there follows the solemn moral of the whole fable, put with the rightness of genius into Mr. Sleary's asthmatic mouth," [17] and on the following page asserts: "Here is the formal moral." Here Leavis is, in effect, extracting a moral which he approves of and his treatment of the entire novel comes very close to reducing it to a battle of conflicting values, one which he approves and the other

[14] *Ibid.*, p. 231.
[15] Graham Hough, *The Dream and the Task* (London: Gerald Duckworth & Co., Ltd., 1963), p. 50.
[16] *Ibid.*, p. 48.
[17] *The Great Tradition*, p. 268.

rejects. There are other instances where we find Leavis discussing the conflicting values within the novel in such a way as to indicate not only that he is writing as a moral critic in the manner Hough deprecates, but also that he is considering the novelist primarily as a moralist. Yet this is not characteristic of Leavis's thinking; he usually insists that the moral value of a work depends on its being art. In discussing *Felix Holt* he makes the point that "to speak of George Eliot here as a moralist would, one feels, be to misplace a stress. She is simply a great artist—a great novelist, with a great novelist's psychological insight and fineness of human valuation." [18] And in a further description of that novel he insists: "There is no touch of the homiletic about this; it is dramatic constatation, poignant and utterly convincing, and the implied moral, which is a matter of the enacted inevitability, is that perceived by a psychological realist." [19] That is, Leavis thinks of a novelist primarily as a novelist, not as a moralist, and in his criticism does not treat novels like moral tracts. Hough, in fact, is trying to make it appear that Leavis approaches the novel much as Samuel Johnson approaches Shakespeare, and this is not so—as an examination of Leavis's use of the concept "the novel as dramatic poem" will clarify.

If we look at Leavis's discussion of James's *The Europeans* and Conrad's *The Shadow-Line*—both essays are in *Anna Karenina and Other Essays*—we shall see how little he "extracts" a moral essence from the novels. The essay on *The Europeans* is one of Leavis's finest and most convincing; it is also of great importance in being the second essay he wrote under the headings moral fable and dramatic poem. Leavis interprets the novel as a comparative enquiry, enacted in "dramatic and poetic terms," into the criteria of civilization and its possibilities. The two Europeans—Felix Young and the Baroness—he explains, stand for conflicting values, but these values are brought out dramatically and poetically; that is, these values are not simply stated, but we determine what they are from the whole novel. In explaining how these values are established Leavis writes:

> *But perhaps it would be better not to refer, in this way, to James himself. When we elicit judgments and valuations from the fable—which is perfectly dramatic and perfectly a work of art—we don't think of them as coming from the author. It is a drawback to the present kind of commentary that it tends in some ways to slight this quality of art, this creative perfection; it doesn't suggest the concrete richness and self-sufficiency of the drama, or the poetic subtlety of the means by which the discriminations are established. No instancing can convey the variety and flexibility of these means.*[20]

What Leavis is approving of is not a "moral essence" but the enacted moral quality expressed by the whole novel.

This point is made more explicitly in Leavis's essay on *The Shadow-Line*—

---

[18] *Ibid.*, p. 69.
[19] *Ibid.*, p. 72.
[20] *Anna Karenina and Other Essays*, p. 70.

which is also one of his finest studies of a single novel. Leavis asks about *The Shadow-Line:*

> Is the moral of the tale that one must achieve a maturity for which the 'boredom' of the jaded, adult, settled-down routine of life must be accepted. . . . Nothing so simple, I think. In fact, I don't think the tale is a simple enough kind of thing to have what can be called a 'moral', or the ordeal a simple enough kind of thing to have an easily summarizable outcome or significance. What one can do is to point to some of the major elements, themes, and insistences that work together in the delicate complexity of the total effect; the tale, as I suppose I've by now virtually said, being a kind of dramatic poem that communicates a meaning such as couldn't have been communicated in any other way.[21]

I want to emphasize the last observation, that the meaning "couldn't have been communicated in any other way." Much of modern poetry criticism, particularly the New Criticism of the 1930's, was concerned with the problem of explaining how poetry communicates what cannot be expressed in any other way; one of Leavis's many distinctions is to have provided a comparable explanation of how a novel functions. The work as a whole, he insists, conveys the moral quality:

> You may say that the moral is given in the final 'There's no rest for me till she's out in the Indian Ocean and not much of it even then'. . . . The point I have to make is that the significance of the kind of creative work ('dramatic poem', I have called it) we have in The Shadow-Line is such that it can't be represented by any moral. I have spoken of 'symbolism': I have not meant to suggest that The Shadow-Line is symbolic in such a way as to admit of a neat and definitive interpretation.[22]

Leavis explains that even Conrad couldn't have provided a summing up of the tale's significance, and that the critic's procedure is not to abstract a message but to balance one suggestion against another until one's sense of the tale has settled into an inclusive poise.

It should be clear from this that for Leavis the whole work is moral, and that as a critic he assesses the entire work, and not its moral essence. A reference here to Leavis's essay on Samuel Johnson may help to clarify the point I am making. Johnson's criticism is also known for its uncompromising association of literature and morality, but Leavis's objection to Johnson's central position brings out their clear difference on this matter. Leavis argues:

> Johnson was representative in his inability to appreciate the most profoundly creative uses of language. He cannot appreciate the life-principle of drama as

---

[21] *Ibid.,* pp. 101–02.
[22] *Ibid.,* pp. 108–09.

*we have it in the poetic-creative use of language—the use by which the stuff of*
*experience is presented to speak and act for itself.*

*This disability has its obvious correlative in Johnson's bondage . . . to*
*moralistic fallacy. . . . Johnson cannot understand that works of art enact*
*their moral valuations. It is not enough that Shakespeare, on the evidence of his*
*works, 'thinks' (and feels), morally; for Johnson a moral judgement that isn't*
*stated isn't there. Further, he demands that the whole play shall be conceived*
*and composed as statement. The dramatist must start with a conscious and*
*abstractly formulated moral and proceed to manipulate his puppets so as to*
*demonstrate and enforce it.*[23]

For Johnson, then, literature is moral by being didactic—it enforces values that
exist prior to the work; but Leavis does not hold a didactic view at all, for he
thinks of the creative use of language as involved in the exploration and creation
of values—not their enforcement. We should recall that his recent harsh criticism
of *Lady Chatterley's Lover* is based on the view that it is a didactic novel, one
where Lawrence writes with a willed purpose to enforce his moral. In a successful
work, Leavis insists, values are not stated but *enacted* by the whole work; the
concept of "enactment" is at the center of Leavis's thinking about morality and
the novel. He praises, for instance, *Women in Love* because "an experimental
process of exploring, testing, and defining does seem really to be enacted, dramatically, in the 'tale'; so little are we affected as by any doctrine formulated in
advance, and coming directly from Lawrence." [24] The morality of a novel is
inseparable from its integrity as art.

Leavis's concept of "enactment" is closely related to his insistence that literature is an "exploration" of values. At times he seems to prize literature primarily
for the search for values it embodies, for creative questioning and exploration.
One of the clearest examples of this is in his lecture on C. P. Snow, "Two Cultures," where Leavis writes: "what for—what ultimately for? What, ultimately,
do men live by? These questions are in and of the creative drive that produces
great art in Conrad and Lawrence." He praises the "urgent creative exploring"
represented by their works and then declares:

*Of course, to such questions there can't be, in any ordinary sense of the word,*
*'answers', and the effect of total 'answer' differs as between Conrad and*
*Lawrence, or as between any two great writers. But life in the civilization of an*
*age for which creative questioning is not done and is not influential on general*
*sensibility tends characteristically to lack a dimension: it tends to have no*
*depth.*[25]

The notion of "creative exploring" or "creative questioning" should make it com-

---

[23] F. R. Leavis, "Johnson And Augustanism," in *The Common Pursuit* (1952; rpt. Harmondsworth: Penguin
Books, 1966), pp. 110–11.
[24] F. R. Leavis, *D. H. Lawrence, Novelist* (1955; rpt. Harmondsworth: Penguin Books, 1968), p. 187.
[25] F. R. Leavis, *Nor Shall My Sword* (London: Chatto & Windus, 1972), p. 56.

pletely obvious that Leavis's view of literature is the antithesis of a didactic one.

Leavis, of course, does not describe literature just as an exploration of life or values, but more characteristically as an affirmation of the possibilities of life, and I now want to examine this aspect of his criticism. It is, however, essential to remember that for Leavis literature is an affirmation only by first being an exploration; this is the central point he makes in discussing Tolstoy's novel, *Anna Karenina*: "While what makes itself felt as we read *Anna Karenina* is decidedly a positive or creative nisus, it affects us as an exploratory effort towards the definition of a norm." [26]

Perhaps Leavis's best-known statement about the writer's affirmation of life is that given at the opening of *The Great Tradition*, where he outlines his criteria, for selecting the great novelists:

> *It is necessary to insist, then, that there are important distinctions to be made, and that far from all of the names in the literary histories really belong to the realm of significant creative achievement. And as a recall to a due sense of differences it is well to start by distinguishing the few really great—the major novelists who count in the same way as the major poets, in the sense that they not only change the possibilities of the art for practitioners and readers, but that they are significant in terms of that human awareness they promote; awareness of the possibilities of life.*[27]

The influence of D. H. Lawrence's criticism is apparent here in examining literature in terms of the "possibilities of life," but there are in fact two criteria annunciated—possibilities of art, as well as life—and it is frequently remarked that Leavis really only considers the latter. In a way this is true, yet as a criticism it is misleading. For example, both Joyce's *Finnegans Wake* and the later novels of James are obvious examples of works which appear to extend the possibilities of art, and Leavis judges both harshly. In fact, what those works exemplify, to Leavis, is an innovation and extension only of "technique," involving a separation between life and art, that does not enhance the possibilities of art. In effect, in Leavis's thinking, to extend the possibilities of art and the possibilities of life are almost the same thing; art cannot be reduced to technique.

Leavis provides a completer statement of his demand that great novelists promote awareness of the possibilities of life in his essay "James As Critic":

> *. . . art is a manifestation of life or it is nothing. The creative writer's concern to render life is a concern for significance, a preoccupation with expressing his sense of what most matters. The creative drive in his art is a drive to clarify and convey his perception of relative importances. The work that commands the reader's most deeply engaged, the critic's most serious, attention asks at a deep level: "What, at bottom, do men live for?" And in work that strikes us as great art we are aware of a potent normative suggestion: "These are the possibilities*

[26] *Anna Karenina and Other Essays*, p. 12.
[27] *The Great Tradition*, p. 10.

*and inevitablenesses, and in the face of them, this is the valid and wise (or the sane) attitude.*[28]

Thus, only affirmative art, or, as he calls it here, normative art, can be considered great. It is worth emphasizing at this point that Leavis's concept of affirmation is much more explicit in his writings on the novel than in his poetry criticism. While he does judge poets by their attitudes to life—and criticizes Eliot for his negative, life-rejecting attitudes—he is more concerned with the question of a poet's "sincerity." The notion of literature as an affirmation of life can be worked out more fully in the novel where characters can represent aspects of life that the novelist—and Leavis—value. Also we should note that while the affirmation of the possibilities of life is announced as the central criterion in the introductory chapter of *The Great Tradition*, Leavis's discussion in that book is not carried out simply, or even primarily, in those terms. Much of his discussion of George Eliot, for instance, is taken up with examining the maturity and specificity of her art. It is in *D. H. Lawrence, Novelist* that Leavis really makes a full and extensive use of the concept of the novel as an affirmation of life, and this approach has dominated his later writings on the novel. Further, in *D. H. Lawrence, Novelist* Leavis introduces the concept of the "normative," a term which he does not use at all in *The Great Tradition*. Much of his discussion of Lawrence is focused on the question of the normative bearings of Lawrence's work and, again, in his later novel criticism Leavis has largely dealt with the normative implications of the work examined. Clearly, the discussion of a novel in terms of its normative bearings is closely allied to the view of literature as an affirmation of life.

Lawrence, of course, has his pre-eminence for Leavis because of the affirmative nature of his fiction, but also in Leavis's writings on the novel collected in *Anna Karenina and Other Essays* it is particularly apparent that his praise for a novel is tied to his sense of the affirmation the work is making. In discussing Tolstoy's novel he emphasizes "that Kitty and Levin have . . . a clear normative significance —that they represent . . . the especially clear affirming presence of the normative spirit that informs the whole work." [29] And in both of the essays on James it is clearly the affirmative nature of the art that wins Leavis's admiration. Of *The Europeans* he writes: "The informing spirit of the drama is positive and constructive: James is unmistakably feeling towards an ideal possibility that is neither Europe nor America." [30] He is even more explicit in praising *What Maisie Knew* for the affirmation he insists it makes: "The strength of the pathos, as of the comedy in which it finds its felicitous definition, is the strength of the affirmation of positive values that it conveys. We have it here, the affirmation; the normative concern with a concept of an essential human goodness." [31]

The difficulty with this position is obvious: Leavis can praise only those writers

---

[28] F. R. Leavis, "James As Critic," Introduction to Henry James, *Selected Literary Criticism*, ed. Morris Shapira (London: Heinemann, 1963), p. xviii.

[29] *Anna Karenina and Other Essays*, p. 14.

[30] *Ibid.*, p. 59.

[31] *Ibid.*, p. 84.

whose response to life is unquestionably positive, and who affirm—even if in an exploratory manner—positive values. This would seem to rule out, almost automatically, such a writer as Samuel Beckett, makes it very difficult to be fair to Thomas Hardy, and I'm not sure how Melville can be saved. Melville and Hardy, it is true, both affirm certain values, but their affirmation is qualified. Melville's paradisal vision of the grand armada is offset by his sense of the constant presence of the sharks; his response to life is balanced between affirmation and rejection. In Hardy's vision of life the positive forces of life are almost inevitably destroyed; one can't describe his response as essentially affirmative. I don't want to give a distorted view of Leavis's position: by affirmative he does not mean simply "with a happy ending." He insists that *The Portrait of a Lady* is tragic, but that nonetheless certain possibilities of life are convincingly affirmed by James —and Leavis generally focuses his attention on the affirmation contained in the work.

Leavis's dealings with both Conrad and Mark Twain are instructive on this issue. One of the things that makes Leavis's writings on Conrad in *The Great Tradition* so interesting is the difficulty he has in convincing us (and possibly himself) that Conrad is an affirmative—and therefore, great—writer. Conrad is frequently thought of as being as much of a pessimist as Hardy, and there would seem to be some grounds for regarding his response to life as despairing and bleak, at moments almost nihilistic. D. H. Lawrence's judgment of Conrad is interesting and representative in this matter: "The Conrad, after months of Europe, makes me furious—and the stories are *so* good. But why this giving in before you start, that pervades all Conrad and such folks—the Writers among the Ruins. I can't forgive Conrad for being so sad and for giving in." [32] This is an interesting evaluation, for while Lawrence rejects Conrad's lack of affirmation, he still praises his work; I do not think Leavis ever gives us a similar kind of response. In writing on Conrad in *The Great Tradition* Leavis struggles to present him as an affirmer of life, but it is an unconvincing argument. Leavis regards *Nostromo* as Conrad's masterpiece but is hard put to interpret it as an affirmation, or to find *any* positive values in it. Leavis writes of the novel: "It will probably be expected, after so much insistence on the moral pattern of *Nostromo*, that something will be said about the total significance. What, as the upshot of this exhibition of human motive and attitude, do we feel Conrad himself to endorse? What are his positives? It is easier to say what he rejects or criticizes." [33] In *Nostromo* there are not any clear positives Leavis can point to, as there are in so many of the other novels he praises. This presents a distinct difference from James's *The Portrait of a Lady*, where James clearly endorses the fineness represented by Isabel Archer. Whatever spiritual values are presented in *Nostromo* are submitted to a severely ironic testing, and the background of the mountain and gulf dwarfs the lives of the characters and their supposed values. Leavis observes that this negative sense of life corresponds to something radical

---

[32] *The Letters of D. H. Lawrence*, ed. Aldous Huxley (London: William Heinemann, 1932), p. 68.
[33] *The Great Tradition*, p. 219.

in Conrad, then leaves the case for *Nostromo* up in the air; we can only assume that on the evidence of his "greatest" work Conrad is not an affirmative writer. The question here, of course, is whether, supposing that *Nostromo* is a totally ironic novel, this means it can not be considered a great novel.

Leavis makes Conrad appear to be more of an affirmative writer than he actually is only by leaving his questions about *Nostromo* unanswered and shifting his discussion to *Victory*. This novel, he argues, presents a "victory over scepticism, a victory of life," although, he notes, Conrad is no simple yea-sayer and Heyst's irony merges into the author's own. Despite the ambiguity in the irony of the book, it is clear that the novel advocates an acceptance of life: much as Gradgrind's utilitarian philosophy is proven inadequate in the face of life, so is Heyst's scepticism. The difficulty is that Leavis has put this discussion of *Victory* at the center of his study of Conrad and it doesn't belong there. The novel is a late work of Conrad's and is not his major work (the thinness of texture and the schematic quality of the book—the use of almost allegorical figures—weaken it); the presence of a more positive attitude that we find in this work can not be taken to represent the attitude to life that Conrad conveys in those novels—*Nostromo* and *The Secret Agent*—which Leavis takes to be his greatest works. *The Secret Agent* in particular seems to present a negative view of life—it is after all a story of despair and suicide; Leavis has praised this novel, but it doesn't seem to accord with his basic criteria. (It may be possible to argue that *The Secret Agent* is actually about the futility of the nay-sayers, but this doesn't leave us with much more of a direct presentation of a positive sense of life.)

I should point out that in his two later essays on Conrad, Leavis makes a very convincing case for him as a positive writer, affirming certain potentialities of human experience. Writing about *The Secret Sharer*, Leavis praises the "insistence on the inescapable need for individual moral judgment, and for moral conviction that is strong and courageous enough to forget codes and to defy law and codified morality and justice." [34] Further, he insists that the captain of the ship, in aiding the swimmer, "acts on his full human judgment. A man's supreme obligation is to recognize his own moral responsibility—to have the courage to recognize it and to act on it." [35] The tale definitely centers on the need for moral responsibility, but I get the impression that Leavis is using the story, and his essay, to make his own assertion of the necessity of moral responsibility. In *The Shadow-Line* it is not the presentation of a specific moral quality that Leavis praises, but the affirmative sense of life Conrad conveys: "You have the added life-dimension Captain MacWhirr can never have known, that which is given in the young captain's response to the ship's beauty: it is good to be alive in a world in which such things exist. The beautiful ship, of course, is representative and symbolic in this matter." [36]

Mark Twain provides another revealing test case of Leavis's critical procedure,

---

[34] *Anna Karenina and Other Essays,* p. 114.
[35] *Ibid.,* p. 119.
[36] *Ibid.,* p. 120.

and further, the essay on *Pudd'nhead Wilson* indicates quite clearly his negative response to satire. Twain is occasionally regarded as a pessimistic, even cynical or misanthropic writer—that is, anything but affirmative. D. H. Lawrence, for example, holds this view of Twain, regarding him essentially as a satirist. In the preface to *Max Havelaar* Lawrence writes: "The book isn't really a tract, it is a satire. Multatuli isn't really a preacher, he's a satirical humorist. Straight on in the life of Jean Paul Richter the same bitter, almost mad-dog aversion from humanity that appeared in Jean Paul appears again in Multatuli, as it appears in the later Mark Twain." [37] Further, Lawrence insists that the "great dynamic force" in Multatuli and Mark Twain is "hate, a passionate honourable hate." This diverges considerably from Leavis's position, for Lawrence is not asking for any clear positives in the work, any affirmation; he is quite willing to praise satire and literature whose main purpose is to repudiate all that has gone dead.

Leavis's response towards Mark Twain and satire is quite different. Leavis insists that the attitude conveyed in *Pudd'nhead Wilson* is remote from cynicism or pessimism, and that the book shows neither contempt for human nature nor a rejection of civilization; that is, it does not reveal an attitude of "passionate hate." Leavis seems to regard satire—or the satiric attitude—as a rather straightforward rejection of life and thus he insists: "Astringent as is the irony of *Pudd'nhead Wilson,* the attitude here has nothing of the satiric in it (the distinctively satiric plays no great part in the work as a whole)." [38] Leavis takes great pains to insist that those writers he considers great are not satiric—part of his discussion of George Eliot's *Middlemarch* is centered on demonstrating that she is not a satirist because she treats mankind with compassion rather than contempt; conversely, Leavis gives vent to his own contempt in dismissing a writer like Samuel Butler who is primarily satiric. Twain's novel earns Leavis's praise—not as it might earn Lawrence's for its repudiatory force—but for its affirmation; Leavis typically focuses his praise on a character who, he claims, represents "life":

> *We are not, by way of dismissing the suggestion of any general contempt, confined to adducing Wilson himself. . . . Most impressively, there is Roxy. . . . We feel her dominating the book as a triumphant vindication of life. Without being in the least sentimentalized, or anything but dramatically right, she plainly bodies forth the qualities that Mark Twain, in his whole being, most values—qualities that, as Roxy bears witness, he profoundly believes in as observable in humanity, having known them in experience.*[39]

Here Leavis very plainly praises the qualities of a character in a novel just as he would praise a person in life; he also gives a further explanation of the nature of the life that Roxy embodies: "She is the presence in the book of a free and generous vitality, in which the warmly and physically human manifests itself

[37] D. H. Lawrence, *Phoenix*, ed. Edward D. McDonald (1936; rpt. London: Heinemann, 1970), p. 238.
[38] *Anna Karenina and Other Essays*, p. 130.
[39] *Ibid.*, p. 132.

also as intelligence and spiritual strength. It is this far-reaching associative way in which, so dominating a presence, she stands for—she *is*—triumphant life that gives the book, for all its astringency and for all the chilling irony of the close, its genial quality." [40] It is essentially this positive assertion of life that earns Leavis's praise. But despite this description of Roxy, to speak of "affirmation of life" is still vague, and leaves the sense of "life," and of the positive values associated with it, undefined. We get a better idea of the sense of life and of the positive qualities Leavis approves of by examining his writings on D. H. Lawrence and Charles Dickens.

It is Lawrence who, of all writers in the modern period, most fully affirms "life" in a manner Leavis endorses, and in his discussion of *St. Mawr* Leavis most forcefully argues his case that Lawrence's work represents an affirmation of life. Leavis contends that St. Mawr embodies forces of life the modern world frustrates, that he stands for "the deep springs of life." Further, he describes the attempt to geld St. Mawr as a hatred of the really living, as "a determination to eliminate every element of danger and wildness from life." [41] This quality of wildness, openness, along with vital instinct, is partly what Leavis means by "life." This sense of life is very close to Lawrence's own, and not at all easily accommodated to the image of Leavis as a traditional moralist. But the main point he makes about the story is that there is nothing of the merely postulated about the positives Lawrence affirms:

> The power of the affirmation lies, not in any insistence or assertion or argument, but in the creative fact, his art; it is that which bears irrefutable witness. What his art does is beyond argument or doubt. . . . Great art, something created and there, is what Lawrence gives us. And there we undeniably have a world of wonder and reverence, where life wells up from mysterious springs. It is no merely imagined world; what creative imagination of the artist makes us contemplate bears an unanswerable testimony.[42]

It is the "wonder" and "reverence" of Lawrence's fiction which primarily define the qualities that Leavis values in life. And it is essential that the positive qualities, "life," not simply be asserted or "merely imagined," but be fully realized, given concrete embodiment in art.

By examining Leavis's writings on Dickens we can see, first, how Leavis extends his criterion of "affirmation," second, his completest explanation of how a novel *presents* its affirmation of life, and finally, a further definition of his use of "life." While Leavis generally speaks of literature as an affirmation of life, he occasionally refers to it, like Arnold, as a criticism of life. (To be more exact, Leavis's phrase is usually "a criticism of civilization.") For example, Leavis praises *Hard Times* for its comprehensive criticism of Victorian civilization, and

[40] *Ibid.,* p. 133.
[41] *D. H. Lawrence, Novelist,* p. 252.
[42] *Ibid.,* p. 246.

much of his analysis is devoted to the criticism of Gradgrind's philosophy that the novel is making. But literature for Leavis is a criticism of life only by also being an affirmation; he writes of Dickens's presentation of positive values: "The virtues and qualities that Dickens prizes do indeed exist, and it is necessary for his critique of Utilitarianism and industrialism, and for (what is the same thing) his creative purpose, to evoke them vividly." [43] And in discussing *Hard Times* Leavis isolates for praise the characters who represent positive qualities—Sissy Jupe and Sleary's Horse-Riding Circus. He comments on Sissy:

> *What may, perhaps, be emphasized is that Sissy stands for vitality as well as goodness—they are seen, in fact, as one; she is generous, impulsive life, finding self-fulfilment in self-forgetfulness—all that is the antithesis of calculating self-interest. There is an essentially Lawrentian suggestion about the way in which the 'dark-eyed and dark-haired' girl, contrasting with Bitzer, seemed to receive a 'deeper and more lustrous colour from the sun', so opposing the life that is lived freely and richly from the deep instinctive and emotional springs to the thin-blooded, quasi-mechanical product of Gradgrindery.*[44]

It is instructive that here, where Leavis is giving what is perhaps his most explicit statement of "life" as a value term in *The Great Tradition*, he invokes Lawrence. He praises the life that is lived from the deeper "springs," and we should also note the equation of impulsive life-vitality-goodness, an equation Leavis frequently makes. The presentation of these positive qualities gives the criticism in the novel its force.

There is, however, a question that arises with regard to Leavis's praise of art as a "creative criticism of civilization," and that is whether this describes what all great literature does. J. R. Harvey raises this point in his review of *Dickens the Novelist*, and suggests that it does not apply to Shakespeare. He then asks, "If *Lear* can be superior to *Little Dorrit* while being so inferior to it as a criticism of civilization, what relative importance does belong to the criticism of civilization in the total economy of criteria." [45] The problem here is partly that Harvey is comparing a Renaissance play with a Victorian novel, and there is no doubt that the nineteenth-century novel is more involved with presenting a critical reaction to society—to the new society created by industrialism—and in this sense Leavis's criterion seems more applicable to the novel than to Shakespeare's play. The kind of enquiry being made in *King Lear* is not only, or primarily, about man's relation to society, but about man's relation to his fate, the universe, God; there is a metaphysical concern in the play that is not encompassed by Leavis's criteria. While this reveals a certain limitation in his criteria for approaching literature as a whole, the novel as a genre, with only a few exceptions (*Moby Dick* would be an obvious one), does not centrally express a metaphysical concern, but

---

[43] *The Great Tradition*, p. 257.
[44] *Ibid.*, pp. 253–54.
[45] J. R. Harvey, "The Leavis's Dickens," rev. of *Dickens the Novelist*, by F. R. Leavis and Q. D. Leavis, *Cambridge Quarterly*, 6 (1972), 89.

examines man in society; and for dealing with this, Leavis's criteria are entirely satisfactory.

Leavis's study of *Little Dorrit,* as well as being his latest essay on the novel, is also a *locus classicus* for a discussion of his view of the novel as an affirmation of life. In the essay Leavis pellucidly explains the nature of the artist's exploration and definition of values and criteria. He begins by praising the novel as a criticism of Victorian civilization: "He conveyed his criticism of Victorian civilization in a creative masterpiece. . . . What, at a religious depth, Dickens hated about the ethos figured by the Clennam house was the offense against life, the spontaneous, the real, the creative, and, at this moment preceding the collapse of the symbolic house, he represents the creative spirit of life by art." [46] While showing us how Dickens intimates his own sense of life, Leavis is, in effect, giving us his own creative definition of "life"—"the spontaneous, the real, the creative." He continues his explanation of the novel as a criticism of life:

> For Arthur Clennam the ethos is that which oppressed his childhood. . . . It is the beginning of the sustained criticism of English life that the book enacts. For Clennam himself it is the beginning of an urgently personal criticism of life in Arnold's sense—that entailed in the inescapable and unrelenting questions: 'What shall I do? What can I do? What are the possibilities of life—for me, and, more generally, in the very nature of life? What are the conditions of happiness? What is life for? . . . he can't but find himself with such a criticism of life as his insistent preoccupation.[47]

This is perhaps the best statement of how Leavis adapts Arnold's description of literature as a criticism of life; but, as I've argued, what finally gives literature its importance to Leavis is not just this criticism or questioning, but the presentation of norms or "answers." He explains the kind of "answer" the novel gives:

> Clennam . . . opens, out of a particular situation and the pressure of a personal history, the critique of Victorian civilization. The questioning, so largely for him a matter of self-interrogation that implicitly bears on the criteria for judgment and value-perception, starts in that reverse of theoretical way, but—or so—with great felicity. The answer implicit in Little Dorrit is given creatively by the book, and it is not one that could have been given by Clennam himself. Not only is it something that can't be stated; the Clennam evoked for us is obviously not adequate to its depth and range and fullness, his deficiency being among the characteristics that qualify him for his part in the process by which the inclusive communication of the book is generated. Each of the other characters also plays a contributory part, inviting us to make notes on his or her distinctive 'value' in relation to the whole.[48]

That is, literature does provide an "answer" to this questioning, though it is not

---

[46] F. R. Leavis and Q. D. Leavis, *Dickens the Novelist* (Harmondsworth: Penguin Books, 1972), p. 285.

[47] *Ibid.*, pp. 285–86.

[48] *Ibid.*, p. 287.

a simple, abstractable—one might say paraphrasable—answer. The entire book presents the answer and each character stands for certain aspects of life. Particularly in this novel Leavis thinks of the inquiry, or criticism of life, as demanding an answer because of the challenging presence of Henry Gowan, who represents not just irresponsibility but a negation of life. The full answer to Gowan the book gives involves an explanation of basic criteria and values—in fact, an evaluative definition of life.

Leavis gives one of his most important explanations of how Dickens—or any novelist—provides a creative definition of "life," and concurrently gives a lucid statement of his own use of the word "life":

> 'Life', it may be commented, is a large word. Certainly it is a word we can't do without and unquestionably an important one, and the importance is of a nature that makes it obviously futile to try to define abstractly, by way of achieving precision, the force or value it has as I have just used it. We feel the futility the more intensely in that, as we consider Dickens's art in Little Dorrit, we see very potently at work a process that it seems proper to call definition by creative means.[49]

It is this kind of creative defining of life in the concrete that gives literature its importance, and Leavis emphasizes that the process of definition the artist provides is a very real form of thought (if not the *only* real form)—anti-theoretical. He insists that Dickens's capacity for effective thought about life is indistinguishable from his genius as a novelist. Leavis then explains:

> There are other important words, so clearly associated—as, prompted by Little Dorrit, we find we have to evoke them—with 'life' that we judge them to be equally unsusceptible of what is ordinarily meant by definition; and these we unquestionably see getting a potent definition in the concrete. . . . what the prompted words in association portend gets its definition as the creative work builds up. Dickens's essential 'social criticism', his inquest into Victorian civilization is inseparable from this process.[50]

The affirmation of life is largely a matter of bringing out the significance of these other words, or criteria, as Leavis goes on to explain:

> My obvious next move is to record some of the notes that one finds oneself jotting down, as one reads, regarding the criteria implicit in Dickens's critique of civilized England. When one has noted the set of indicative, or focal, words one is prompted to seize on, the words to which I have just referred, and made the essential commentary on them, one has at the same time done a lot to explain the force of calling Little Dorrit an 'affirmation of life'. But to say that is to

[49] *Ibid.*, p. 296.
[50] *Ibid.*, pp. 296–97.

*point to the difficulty; the words are focal, and the aboundingness . . . was not redundant. So I must make it plain at once that there can be no neat and systematic exposition.*[51]

This is possibly the clearest explanation Leavis gives of how the critic goes about explaining a novel as an affirmation of life. While the explanation of "life" given can not be systematic, it can, nonetheless, have its own precision.

In elaborating the focal words associated with "life" Leavis concentrates on the qualities that each character embodies. He particularly focuses on Little Dorrit and the normative human possibility she represents. He compares her to James's Maisie and contends that the affinity between them is that they both prompt the characterizing notes "ego-free love," "disinterestedness," and "innocence"; these are the qualities that Dickens, and Leavis, mean by "life." But what Leavis finds in Little Dorrit and Maisie is not all that is involved in his understanding of life, and he points to the importance of Daniel Doyce, who represents an indefeasible "responsibility towards something other than himself." It is the impersonality of Doyce's response to life that Leavis praises. Further, Leavis insists on the essentially creative nature of life, and on the importance of art as the highest manifestation of that creativity. He emphasizes the affinity of Dickens and Blake on these grounds:

*I have in mind, of course, the way in which the irrelevance of the Benthamite calculus is exposed; the insistence that life is spontaneous and creative, so that the appeal to self-interest as the essential motive is life-defeating; the vindication, in terms of childhood, of spontaneity, disinterestedness, love and wonder; and the significant place given to Art—a place entailing a conception of Art that is pure Blake.*[52]

Leavis convincingly shows how—through Doyce, Flora Casby, and Pancks—Dickens makes the creativity of the artist and the creativity of life present in *Little Dorrit*. When Leavis concludes that "reality, courage, disinterestedness, truth, spontaneity, creativeness—and, summing them, life: these words, further charged with definitive value, make the appropriate marginal comment," [53] he has succeeded in fully showing us the presence of these values in Dickens's novel and has clearly explained the way in which a novel enacts an affirmation of life.

In the course of elucidating Dickens's novel, Leavis's own criticism has been a process of exploration and definition of values. That is, what Leavis offers us is a creative exploration of its own—a radical enquiry into values and criteria. When he states that "life always has to be defended, vindicated and asserted against Government, bureaucracy and organization—against society in that sense. The defence and assertion are above all the business of the artist," [54] we know quite

---

[51] *Ibid.*, p. 297.
[52] *Ibid.*, p. 301.
[53] *Ibid.*, p. 334.
[54] *Ibid.*, p. 342.

vividly, by this time, what Leavis means by "life." René Wellek's central objection to Leavis's criticism is the use he makes of the term "life": "I am, I fear, too much of a theorist not to feel strongly the ambiguity, shiftiness, and vagueness of Leavis's ultimate value criterion, Life." [55] It seems to me that, particularly in the light of such an example as Leavis's essay on *Little Dorrit*, Wellek's complaint is unfounded. As we have seen, Leavis does not use the term vaguely; he practices a form of criticism that allows him to use the term and to bring it to a fairly precise and concrete "definition." Wellek wants a theoretical definition, but Leavis demonstrates that critics, as well as artists, can convincingly offer other kinds of explanations.

Leavis is not what we consider a theoretical critic, but nonetheless he has presented in his work an extremely cogent and full conception of the novel. In his thinking on the very central issues of the relation of the novel and morality and in his conception of the novel as an affirmation and criticism of life, Leavis has decisively influenced modern views of fiction as a major art. As George Steiner argues, "our sense of the novel as form, of its responsibility to moral perception and 'vivid essential record,' is that defined by Leavis' treatment." [56] Among other critics of the novel only Henry James and D. H. Lawrence can be considered to have done so much to help us understand the nature and the possibilities of prose fiction—to say which is a way of indicating the importance of Leavis's achievement.

[55] René Wellek, "The Literary Criticism of Frank Raymond Leavis, in *Literary Views: Critical and Historical Essays*, ed. Carrol Camden (Chicago: The University of Chicago Press, 1964), p. 190.
[56] *Language and Silence*, p. 230.

# IV.

# Biography and Theory

# The Whole Contention Between Mr. Bennett and Mrs. Woolf

SAMUEL HYNES

For most of the readers of this journal, Arnold Bennett's literary criticism probably exists—if it exists at all—only as a reflection in his enemy's eye. Virginia Woolf's "Mr. Bennett and Mrs. Brown" has become the standard example of her kind of impressionism; it is included in anthologies of modern criticism, and is mentioned in histories of modern literature. But who attends to Bennett's criticism? Not one of his eight critical books is in print either in the United States or in England, and his hundreds of articles have simply disappeared. The colorful, opinionated, influential artist that was Arnold Bennett has faded into the author of one Edwardian novel, and the defeated antagonist of a fierce bluestocking.

A consequence of this state of affairs is that Mrs. Woolf's essay has come loose from its context, and is read as though it were a complete, objective statement of the differences between two writing generations. But in fact it is neither complete nor objective: it is simply one blow struck in a quarrel that ran for more than ten years, and was far more personal than generational. Reading "Mr. Bennett and Mrs. Brown" as a separate critical document is like watching the third round of a fifteen-round fight. We will understand both the essay and the combatants better if we understand the whole of their quarrel.

In 1919, when the quarrel began, Bennett was 52, successful, and astonishingly prolific. He had been writing novels at the rate of one a year for twenty years; he had had eight plays produced; and in his spare time he had turned out a vast amount of lively popular journalism. He wrote rapidly and easily, budgeted his time, and counted his words—that is to say, he was a professional. He was probably the best-known English novelist of the time; as he noted with satisfaction, his name on a poster sold newspapers, and strangers recognized him on the street. His evident pleasure in this sort of fame helped to establish what is still the dominant image of Bennett, as the self-satisfied provincial philistine who would write on any subject for two shillings a word, and who kept a yacht and a mistress on the proceeds.

But if there is truth in this version of Bennett, it is not the whole truth. There was another and more important side to him as a writer. One can see the other Bennett most clearly in the earlier critical writings, and especially in the columns that he contributed to the *New Age* under the pseudonym of Jacob Tonson (he collected some of the best in *Books and Persons*). These casual weekly pieces, which Bennett wrote for nothing, did much to make Edwardian England conscious of the twentieth century. Bennett was one of the few Englishmen in that insular time modern enough to be aware of what was happening in Europe, and he used his column to spread the news. He was the first English critic to testify to the greatness of *The Brothers Karamazov* (he had read it in French before Constance Garnett's translation appeared); he praised *The Cherry Orchard* when it was first performed in London, and scolded the audience for walking out; and he recognized the significance of the first Post-Impressionist show in London, not only for painters, but for all artists, including himself. He was a shrewd judge of his fellow novelists, and most of his judgments of writers like James, Conrad and Galsworthy will stand without revision. In all these matters he had what one might call *modern* intuitions.

When Bennett wrote about the novel, he was likely to make two main points: one, that the novelist should consider his audience; and two, that the novel is a serious art form. In the popular image of Bennett the first point has been stressed and the second ignored; consequently he appears as at best a skillful hack (this is the point of Ezra Pound's portrait of Bennett as "Mr. Nixon" in *Hugh Selwyn Mauberley*). But the essence of Bennett's theory of the novel was that both these points should be made:

> there is a theory [*he wrote in 1901*] that the great public can appreciate a great novel, that the highest modern expression of literary art need not appeal in vain to the average reader. And I believe this to be true—provided that such a novel is written with intent, and with a full knowledge of the peculiar conditions to be satisfied; I believe that a novel could be written which would unite in a mild ecstasy of praise the two extremes—the most inclusive majority and the most exclusive minority.[1]

Here Bennett is testifying to his belief in what he called "the democratization of art"; but it is important to note that the critical standards that the passage imposes remain those of *literary* art. A few years later, reviewing a book by Sturge Moore, Bennett wrote:

> His value is that he would make the English artist a conscious artist. He does, without once stating it, bring out in the most startling way the contrast between, for example, the English artist and the Continental artist. Read the correspondence of Dickens and Thackeray, and then read the correspondence of Flaubert, and you will see. The latter was continually preoccupied with his craft, the two former scarcely ever—and never in an intelligent fashion. I have been preaching on this theme for years, but I am not aware that anybody has been listening. I was going to say that I was sick of preaching about it, but I am not. I shall continue....[2]

The striking thing about this passage is the number of ways in which it echoes the views, and even the phrases, of Edwardian writers with whom Bennett is not usually connected—James, for example, and Conrad and Ford. One can find the idea of the "conscious artist," the comparison of English and Continental attitudes, the admiration for Flaubert's dedication and the contempt for Thackeray, all in Ford's *The English Novel,* and similar remarks are scattered through the essays and intro-

---

[1] *Fame and Fiction* (New York, 1901), p. 16.

[2] "Books and Persons," *New Age,* VI (March 24, 1910), 494.

ductions of James and Conrad. The best of Bennett's novels—*Clayhanger, The Old Wives' Tale, Riceyman Steps*—are built on these critical principles, and the best of his criticism unambiguously proclaims his serious commitment to art. If one considers Bennett in these terms—in terms, that is, of his *best* work and his most thoughtful critical statements, then one must conclude that his place among Edwardian novelists is with the Conscious Artists, and not with Galsworthy and Wells. If this is true, then ironically he belongs among the literary ancestors of Virginia Woolf.

In 1919 Mrs. Woolf was younger, less known, and less productive than Bennett. In eleven years she had written three novels, none of which had sold well. She also wrote reviews and articles, as Bennett did, but she shunned the publicity that might have attended literary journalism; much of her reviewing was anonymous in the *TLS*, and other pieces were signed with initials. To all her writing, whether a novel or a short review, she gave the same meticulous attention; a single paragraph of an unimportant review might go through a dozen drafts before it pleased her. She worked slowly and painfully and at great emotional expense, and she was excessively sensitive to criticism of what she had written. And what was true of her art was also true of her life: she was a reserved, fastidious, aristocratic woman who found human relationships difficult, and who stayed within the familiar and protective limits of her Bloomsbury circle.

Clearly Bennett and Mrs. Woolf were antithetical in all the important particulars of their personalities. It is equally obvious, I think, that they were *not* antithetical in their views of their common art. Their quarrel, when it came, rose out of their personal differences, and not out of their aesthetic convictions; but it soon lost definition, and became an untidy and bitter wrangle that marred both their lives for more than a decade.

The first document in the case is perhaps not, strictly speaking, the beginning of the quarrel: it is an unsigned essay by Mrs. Woolf, titled "Modern Novels," and published in the *TLS* in April, 1919 (a revised version called "Modern Fiction" was included in *The Common Reader* in 1925). The essay is a sketch of the criticism of Bennett, Wells, and Galsworthy that was later elaborated in "Mr. Bennett and Mrs. Brown": it attacks the three writers for their "materialism," calls Bennett the worst culprit of the three, and—in a figure that recurs in later essays—compares Bennett's novels to well-built houses in which nobody lives. It is worth noting that at this stage, Mrs. Woolf was willing to concede (though with qualifications) Bennett's skill at characterization:

> *His characters live abundantly* [she wrote], *even unexpectedly, but it still remains to ask how do they live, and what do they live for? More and more they seem to us, deserting even the well-built villa in the Five Towns, to spend their time in some softly padded first-class railway carriage, fitted with bells and buttons innumerable; and the destiny to which they travel so luxuriously becomes more and more unquestionably an eternity of bliss spent in the very best hotel in Brighton.*[3]

[3] "Modern Novels," *TLS* (April 10, 1919), 189.

As so often in Mrs. Woolf's criticism, the point is blurred by fancy, but there is surely a note of class-conscious disapproval in the well-built villa and the Brighton hotel.

While there is no evidence that Bennett read this essay, or guessed the identity of its author, it seems unlikely that a man so conscious of his status would have missed a front-page notice in the *TLS*; and London literary life being what it is, it is equally unlikely that he would not have known who his critic was. But if Bennett did know, he cannot have been much upset, for he took four years to retaliate. It was not until March, 1923, that he referred to Mrs. Woolf in print. Then, in an article called "Is the Novel Decaying?", he cited *Jacob's Room* as an example of the sort of thing the new novelists were doing. "I have seldom read a cleverer book," he wrote. "It is packed and bursting with originality, and it is exquisitely written." But, he added, the novel had one flaw: "the characters do not vitally survive in the mind, because the author has been obsessed by details of originality and cleverness."[4] The point is not one that most readers of Mrs. Woolf would dispute—even her friend E. M. Forster agreed that she was not much good at characterization— but Mrs. Woolf disputed it. By choosing characterization as a critical issue, Bennett had inadvertently chosen the battlefield for the quarrel that followed.

Two months after Bennett's article appeared, Mrs. Woolf was still brooding over his offense. In her diary for June 19 she wrote:

> People, like Arnold Bennett, say I can't create, or didn't in Jacob's Room, *characters that survive. My answer is—but I leave that to the* Nation: *it's only the old argument that character is dissipated into shreds now; the old post-Dostoevsky argument. I daresay it's true, however, that I haven't that 'reality' gift. I insubstantize, willfully to some extent, distrusting reality—its cheapness.*[5]

The *Nation and Athenaeum* was the instrument through which Mrs. Woolf had decided to strike back—quite naturally, since her husband was its Literary Editor. On December 1, 1923, an article by Mrs. Woolf appeared in its pages, titled "Mr. Bennett and Mrs. Brown." This is not the much-anthologized essay of the same title, however; it is a shorter and very different first draft. The differences are worth pausing over.

In this first rebuttal, Mrs. Woolf moved directly, if a little clumsily, to the attack. "The other day," the essay begins,

> Mr. Arnold Bennett, *himself one of the most famous of the Edwardians, surveyed the younger generation and said: "I admit that for myself I cannot yet descry any coming big novelist."*[6]

This quotation from "Is the Novel Decaying?" is followed by two paragraphs of further summary and quotation (or rather, of *misquotation*, for Mrs. Woolf was not over-scrupulous in controversy, and revised and rearranged Bennett's words

---

4 *Cassell's Weekly*, II (March 28, 1923), 47. The essay is reprinted in *Things That Have Interested Me*, Third Series (New York, 1926), pp. 160–163.

5 *Writer's Diary* (New York, 1954), p. 56.

6 *Nation and Athenaeum*, XXXIV (Dec. 1, 1923), 342.

to suit her needs), which prepare the ground for a vigorous counterattack. As the basis for her defense, Mrs. Woolf chose the point on which Bennett had criticized *Jacob's Room*—the point of characterization. Yes, she agreed, the novel *is* a remarkable machine for the creation of human character, and yes, vivid characterization *has* disappeared from English fiction. But the culprits were not of her generation. During the Edwardian years, two things had happened: first, sensitive men had become aware of the iniquities of the Victorian social system; and second, Mrs. Garnett's translations of Dostoevsky had appeared. Social awareness turned novelists into reformers; Dostoevsky destroyed their conventional notions of what a "character" was. Together these two influences altered writers' minds and, Mrs. Woolf suggests, the effect was to make them better men, but worse artists.

> *The Edwardian novelists therefore give us a vast sense of things in general; but a very vague one of things in particular. Mr. Galsworthy gives us a sense of compassion; Mr. Wells fills us with generous enthusiasm; Mr. Bennett (in his early work) gave us a sense of time. But their books are already a little chill, and must steadily grow more distant, for "the foundation of good fiction is character-creating, and nothing else," as Mr. Bennett says: and in none of them are we given a man or woman whom we know.*[7]

One must admire the skill of the in-fighting here—the use of Bennett to abuse Bennett, and the parenthetical dismissal of all his later work—but it scarcely amounts to a theory of fiction.

Mrs. Brown, the illustrative figure in the second version of the essay, appears in the first only at the end, and confusedly there, as though she were an afterthought. She has no identity, no distinct appearance, no mysterious story; she is simply a name. What does the young novelist do, Mrs. Woolf asks, when he finds himself disagreeing with Wells, Galsworthy, and Bennett concerning the character of Mrs. Brown?

> *... it is useless to defer to their superior genius. It is useless to mumble the polite agreements of the drawing-room. He must set about to remake the woman after his own idea. And that, in the circumstances, is a very perilous pursuit.*
>
> *For what, after all, is character—the way that Mrs. Brown, for instance, reacts to her surroundings—when we cease to believe what we are told about her, and begin to search out her real meaning for ourselves? In the first place, her solidity disappears; her features crumble; the house in which she has lived so long (and a very substantial house it was) topples to the ground. She becomes a will-o'-the-wisp, a dancing light, an illumination gliding up the wall and out of the window, lighting now in freakish malice upon the nose of an archbishop, now in sudden splendor upon the mahogany of the wardrobe. The most solemn sights she turns to ridicule; the most ordinary she invests with beauty. She changes the shape, shifts the accent, of every scene in which she plays her part. And it is from the ruins and splinters of this tumbled mansion that the Georgian writer must somehow reconstruct a habitable dwelling-place; it is from the gleams and*

---

[7] *Ibid.*, 343.

*flashes of this flying spirit that he must create solid, living, flesh-and-blood Mrs. Brown. Sadly he must allow that the lady still escapes him. Dismally he must admit bruises received in the pursuit. But it is because the Georgians, poets and novelists, biographers and dramatists, are so hotly engaged each in the pursuit of his own Mrs. Brown that theirs is at once the least successful, and the most interesting, hundred years. Moreover, let us prophesy: Mrs. Brown will not always escape. One of these days Mrs. Brown will be caught. The capture of Mrs. Brown is the title of the next chapter in the history of literature; and, let us prophesy again, that chapter will be one of the most important, the most illustrious, the most epoch-making of them all.*

That is the whole of Mrs. Brown in her first appearance; she simply flits through the conclusion of the essay, like a Georgian Ariel, wooing novelists away from Caliban-Bennett. It is not a happy fancy.

But then, the first version of "Mr. Bennett and Mrs. Brown" is not very impressive in other respects, either. It has few virtues and many faults, and those of kinds that are not often found in Mrs. Woolf's critical writing—faults of clumsiness, of ill-temper, of failure of imagination. The essay seems hastily done; and yet her diary shows that Mrs. Woolf was at work on it six months before it appeared. And apparently Mrs. Woolf did not find the piece unsatisfactory; she published it in three places in three months—once in England and twice in the United States. Then she set about to re-write it, for delivery as a lecture at Cambridge, where she read it to the girls of Girton College in May, 1924.

The argument of this, the familiar second version of the essay, is essentially that of the first, but the strategy is very different. Most noticeably, Mrs. Brown's part in the show has been expanded from her brief appearance as Ariel to a starring role in a dramatic vignette about a clean old lady in a Waterloo train. The scene takes up a good deal of space, and one may wonder why an imaginary character should so dominate an essay concerned with the art of the novel. The ostensible answer is that Mrs. Woolf is demonstrating by example how human character has changed, and the inadequacy of the old methods of characterization to deal with the new task. But Mrs. Brown quickly expands beyond this function, and one may conclude that her real role in the essay is simply to *be* an imagined character; Mrs. Woolf, still brooding over her lack of "that 'reality' gift," is demonstrating that she has it, by creating a character right before our eyes. It is a demonstration designed not only to prove that she can create character, but to show the superiority of her method to Bennett's (which is ridiculed in a lengthy and somewhat misleading analysis of a passage from *Hilda Lessways*[8]). But in fact, if we examine Mrs. Brown carefully, we will find that she is put together in pretty much the same way that Hilda is, out of physical description and details of a characteristic environment; "I thought of her in a seaside house, among queer ornaments" is not unlike Bennett's account of Hilda's house.

The tone of the second version is also remarkably changed. Perhaps Mrs. Woolf

---

[8] For an excellent analysis of Mrs. Woolf's methods, see Irving Kreutz, "Mr. Bennett and Mrs. Woolf," *Modern Fiction Studies*, VIII (Summer, 1962), 103–115.

had recovered her temper; or perhaps she realized that cheerfulness and charm were better weapons in a lady's hands than abuse. In any case, she managed in her revised version to ridicule, patronize, and actually distort Bennett's writing without raising her voice. Like the first version, this essay was published and republished: first in T. S. Eliot's *Criterion* (where it was called "Character in Fiction"), then as the first pamphlet in the Hogarth Essays series, and again the following summer in the *New York Herald Tribune*. For one paragraph of mixed praise and criticism of *Jacob's Room*, Bennett had reaped six separate published attacks and one lecture.

In the summer of 1924, Bennett and Mrs. Woolf appeared together in a symposium, "What is a Good Novel?", published in *The Highway*, a Socialist journal of adult education. Each took the occasion to reaffirm and harden previously stated critical views. Bennett repeated his opinion that good fiction depends on character-drawing, plotting, and "an effect of beauty"; Mrs. Woolf argued that "a good novel need not have a plot; need not have a happy ending; need not be about nice or respectable people; need not be in the least like life as we know it," and renewed her attack on the use of exhausted conventions. Neither writer mentioned the other, but one can sense a critical drawing apart; for the first time, the critical attitudes they take are orthogonal. It is at this point, I think, that the two become self-consciously representatives of opposed schools; and it seems clear that it was Mrs. Woolf who had forced the breach.

Bennett was aware of both Mrs. Woolf's replies, but he did nothing to extend the quarrel, even though Eliot proposed in September, 1924, that Bennett reply to "Character in Fiction" in *The Criterion*. In May, 1925, Mrs. Woolf provided a new target in *Mrs. Dalloway*, but Bennett did not comment on the book for more than a year. Then, in November, 1927, Leonard Woolf reviewed Bennett's *Lord Raingo* unfavorably in the *Nation*. The Woolfs and Bennett met shortly after at a dinner at H. G. Wells'. According to Woolf, Bennett contributed nothing to the conversation except to stutter, at frequent intervals, "W-w-woolf d-d-does not l-l-like my novels." Bennett's own note on meeting the Woolfs was: "Both gloomy, these two last. But I liked both of them in spite of their naughty treatment of me in the press."[9] And he regretted that he had not been seated where he could "have a scrap with Virginia Woolf."

He found his opportunity later the same month, when he began a new series of weekly "Books and Persons" articles for the London *Evening Standard*. His second and third articles were addressed to young writers, and the latter of these focussed particularly on Virginia Woolf, and on the Woolf-Bennett quarrel.

*The real champion of the younger school [he wrote] is Mrs. Virginia Woolf. She is almost a senior; but she was the inventor, years ago, of a half-new technique, and she alone, so far as I know, came forward and attacked the old. She has written a small book about me, which through a culpable neglect I have not read. I do, however, remember an article of hers in which she asserted that I and my kind could not create character. This was in answer to an article of mine in which I said that the sound drawing of character was the foundation of good fiction,*

[9] Woolf, *Beginning Again* (London, 1964), p. 124; Bennett, *Journal* (New York, 1933), p. 910.

*and in which incidentally I gave my opinion that Mrs. Woolf and her kind could not create character.*[10]

This is a fairly accurate account of the origins of the controversy, though one may doubt whether Bennett was in fact guilty of "culpable neglect"; certainly he had read both versions of "Mr. Bennett and Mrs. Brown" in the periodicals in which they first appeared.

Bennett then moved on to a more direct criticism of Mrs. Woolf's books:

*I have read two and a half of Mrs. Woolf's books. First, 'The Common Reader,' which is an agreeable collection of elegant essays on literary subjects. Second, 'Jacob's Room,' which I achieved with great difficulty. Third, 'Mrs. Dalloway,' which beat me. I could not finish it, because I could not discover what it was really about, what was its direction and what Mrs. Woolf intended to demonstrate by it.*

*To express myself differently, I failed to discern what was its moral basis. As regards character-drawing, Mrs. Woolf (in my opinion) told us ten thousand things about Mrs. Dalloway, but did not show us Mrs. Dalloway.*[11]

The reader familiar with "Mr. Bennett and Mrs. Brown" will recognize that final charge: it is simply a paraphrase of Mrs. Woolf's judgment of *Hilda Lessways*.

From this point on, the public side of the argument was all Bennett's. The weekly column in the *Standard* provided him with a platform, and an appropriate stance. For as Bennett proceeded in his anti-Woolf campaign, he saw it more and more as a quarrel between popular art and coterie art, and for the champion of the popular a popular evening paper was an ideal medium. He was addressing the People—the tube-riders and commuters—and he addressed them as one of themselves, an ordinary bloke who wrote novels, and who knew what he liked.

Between 1927 and 1930 Bennett reviewed three books by Mrs. Woolf, and disliked them all. He liked *To the Lighthouse* the best—thought it her best book—but having said that, he withdrew his praise in a series of slurring qualifications: Mrs. Ramsay *almost* amounts to a complete person, the story is wilful and seemingly designed to exhibit virtuosity, the middle part doesn't work, the style is tryingly monotonous.[12] The following year he was more aggressively hostile to *Orlando*: the book was "fanciful embroidery, wordy, and naught else," it lacked imaginative power, and it was even ungrammatical.[13]

That same year (1928) Bennett had another opportunity to advance his cause; he was asked to write on "The Progress of the Novel" for *The Realist*, a journal on which he was a member of the editorial board.[14] The essay that he wrote is a recapitulation of his later views of the novel, but the form that his views took seems keyed to Mrs. Woolf's criticisms of his own work. What he was writing was one more—and as it turned out, the last—refutation of "Mr. Bennett and Mrs. Brown."

---

[10] *Evening Standard* (Dec. 2, 1926), 5.

[11] *Ibid.*

[12] *Evening Standard* (June 23, 1927), 5.

[13] *Evening Standard* (Nov. 8, 1928), 5.

[14] *The Realist*, I (April, 1929), 3–11.

He therefore began his essay with a defense of social criticism: "The chief mark of the serious novelist, after fundamental creative power, is that he has a definite critical attitude towards life." (Mrs. Woolf had complained that the Edwardian novelists' books were incomplete: "in order to complete them it seems necessary to do something—to join a society, or, more desperately, to write a cheque.") Bennett countered by praising novelists who were critics of life: Balzac, Wells, and Galsworthy (Mrs. Woolf's two other Edwardian victims, linked to an unquestioned master). But, Bennett continued, "Simply to ask whether they are image-breakers or image-makers would be too simple and too crude." (Mrs. Woolf had described Joyce as "a desperate man who feels that in order to breathe he must break the windows.") He looked for examples of "the constructive spirit" in modern fiction, and found it in the novels of Galsworthy and Wells.

Bennett had always admired Wells, but his praise of Galsworthy seems pretty clearly a reaction to Mrs. Woolf, for in earlier essays his judgments had been on the whole unfavorable (and more in line with his own high standards). He wrote of *The Man of Property* and *The Country House*, for example, "personally I do not consider that either of Mr. Galsworthy's novels comes within the four-mile radius of the first-rate," and he objected to Galsworthy's treating oppressors with less sympathy than the oppressed—i.e., he disliked his social criticism; but those opinions were uttered in the days before Mrs. Woolf, when Bennett was in his own eyes an artist, and not a *popular* artist.

At the end of "The Progress of the Novel," having defended Edwardianism, Bennett turned to the young. And there, between R. H. Mottram and Henry Williamson, he found room for a few words on Mrs. Woolf.

> *Virginia Woolf has passionate praisers, who maintain that she is a discoverer in psychology and in form. Disagreeing, I regard her alleged form as the absence of form, and her psychology as an unco-ordinated mass of interesting details, none of which is truly original. All that I can urge in her favor is that she is authentically feminine, and that her style is admirable. Both these qualities are beside my point.*

This would seem to be the definitive and final dismissal of his antagonist, but one further opportunity presented itself, and Bennett took it. In October, 1929, Mrs. Woolf published *A Room of One's Own*, and Bennett commented on it, and on her, in the *Standard*. "If her mind were not what it is," he wrote, "I should accuse her of wholesale padding. This would be unjust. She is not consciously guilty of padding. She is merely the victim of her extraordinary gift of fancy (not imagination)."[15] This distinction is a new one in Bennett's criticism; what it seems to distinguish is the kind of mind that could create Mrs. Brown (fancy) from the kind of mind that had created Hilda Lessways. A more significant, and unfortunate, distinction is the one Bennett makes between himself and Mrs. Woolf:

> *She is the queen of the high-brows; and I am a low-brow. But it takes all sorts of brows to make a world, and without a large admixture of low-brows even Bloomsbury would be uninhabitable.*

[15] *Evening Standard* (Nov. 28, 1929), 5.

Here the class bias that had been implicit in the quarrel from the beginning nearly reached the surface. This is sad, because Bennett was not a lowbrow, either socially or artistically. But he had been despised in public by a lady, and voluntary vulgarity was one defense against her; and so he abdicated his place among serious artists, and widened the gap between two excellent kinds of fiction.

Even after such severe words, the two combatants met socially, and apparently amiably. In December, 1930, they were together at dinner; Bennett's journal-note was "Virginia is all right; other guests held their breath to listen to us." In her diary, Mrs. Woolf was less generous: "This meeting I am convinced was engineered by B. to 'get on good terms with Mrs. Woolf'—when Heaven knows I don't care a rap if I'm on terms with B. or not." She ridiculed his stutter, his vanity, his art. "I like the old creature," she noted. "I do my best, as a writer, to detect signs of genius in his smoky brown eye. . . ." But she concluded that she did not feel him to be a creative artist. The whole entry makes unpleasant reading—most unpleasant because it is gratuitous cruelty and aggressiveness recorded for the private eye alone.

Three months later Bennett was dead. Mrs. Woolf recorded the event in her diary:

> *Arnold Bennett died last night; which leaves me sadder than I should have supposed. A lovable genuine man; impeded, somehow a little awkward in life; well meaning; ponderous; kindly; coarse; knowing he was coarse; dimly floundering and feeling for something else; glutted with success; wounded in his feelings; avid; thicklipped; prosaic intolerably; rather dignified; set upon writing; yet always taken in; deluded by splendor and success; but naive; an old bore; an egotist; much at the mercy of life for all his competence; a shopkeeper's view of literature; yet with the rudiments, covered over with fat and prosperity and the desire for hideous Empire furniture; of sensibility. Some real understanding power, as well as a gigantic absorbing power. These are the sort of things that I think by fits and starts this morning, as I sit journalising; I remember his determination to write 1,000 words daily; and how he trotted off to do it that night, and feel some sorrow that now he will never sit down and begin methodically covering his regulation number of pages in his workmanlike beautiful but dull hand. Queer how one regrets the dispersal of anybody who seemed—as I say— genuine: who had direct contact with life—for he abused me; and I yet rather wished him to go on abusing me; and me abusing him. An element in life—even in mine that was so remote—taken away. This is what one minds.*[16]

A curious, exposed comment. Mrs. Woolf twice says that Bennett was *genuine*—a quality which she associated with grossness, coarseness, and appetite. He had "direct contact with life," and that gave him, perhaps, the "reality gift" that Mrs. Woolf doubted in herself, the gift that she despised and envied. But Bennett was also the critic who had abused her, and even at his death she had to go on abusing him back, sneering in private at his "shopkeeper's view of literature" and his vulgar taste in furniture.

16 *Writer's Diary*, pp. 165–166.

There is one further comment in the diary, and it is a revealing one. In May, 1933—two years after Bennett's death—Mrs. Woolf was preparing to write *The Pargiters*, the book that eventually became *The Years*.

> *I think I have now got to the point where I can write for four months straight ahead at* The Pargiters. *Oh the relief—the physical relief! I feel as if I could hardly any longer keep back—that my brain is being tortured by always butting against a blank wall—I mean Flush, Goldsmith, motoring through Italy. Now, tomorrow, I mean to run it off. And suppose only nonsense comes? The thing is to be venturous, bold, to take every possible fence. One might introduce plays, poems, letters, dialogues: must get the round, not only the flat. Not the theory only. And conversation: argument. How to do that will be one of the problems. I mean intellectual argument in the form of art: I mean how give ordinary waking Arnold Bennett life the form of art?*[17]

The whole of the contention is in that final phrase: for Mrs. Woolf, Arnold Bennett represented Life—ordinary, waking life. For Bennett, Mrs. Woolf represented Art—highbrow, bloodless, supercilious art. These are the poles of a quarrel that has little to do with generations, or Edwardians vs. Georgians, though it has a lot to do with the history of the novel in the twentieth century. The quarrel between Bennett and Mrs. Woolf publicized the divorce of art from ordinariness in the novel, and thus helped to create a coterie audience for Mrs. Woolf (which was certainly bad for her reputation). It also speeded the decline of Bennett's reputation as a novelist, and this is even worse for Bennett, who deserves the place that Mrs. Woolf denied him, among the conscious artists.

[17] *Ibid.*, p. 201.

# Henry James and Walter Besant:
# "The Art of Fiction" Controversy

MARK SPILKA

On April 25, 1884, the popular novelist and antiquarian Walter Besant delivered a lecture called "The Art of Fiction" at the Royal Institution in London. On the following day the *Pall Mall Gazette* devoted a short paragraph to the lecture in its "Occasional Notes"; and on April 30 it printed a longer response—also called "The Art of Fiction"—from the critic Andrew Lang. In May, Chatto and Windus published the lecture with the author's notes and additions. The *Spectator* for May 24 carried an unsigned review of this edition, "Mr. Besant on the Art of Fiction," by its editor, R. H. Hutton; and passing references appeared that year and next in other journals.[1] Henry James joined the debate in *Longman's Magazine* in the fall with his own version of "The Art of Fiction"; to which Robert Louis Stevenson rejoined in the winter *Longman's* with "A Humble Remonstrance." In 1891 the *New Review* revived the debate through two symposia, "The Science of Fiction," featuring Besant, Paul Bourget, and Thomas Hardy, and "The Science of Criticism," featuring James, Lang, and Edmund Gosse. In 1895 James's erstwhile friend, the young novelist Vernon Lee, added some relevant ideas "On Literary Construction" in the *Contemporary Review*. These are the chief British contributions to that "era of discussion," as James called it, through which the novel in England and America acquired its first modern credo. The American contribution was more noncommittal: it consisted of brief reviews of Besant's lecture in the *Nation* (July 3, 1884), the *New York Times* (August 31, 1884), and the *New York Tribune* (August 29, 1884); of copious quotations from James's essay by his friend Grace Norton in the *Nation* (September 25, 1884); and of pirate editions coupling Besant's lecture with James's response as central items in the great debate.[2]

Technically the "era of discussion" had begun in 1882 with William Dean Howells' controversial essay, "Henry James, Jr.," in *Century Magazine*, and Stevenson's "A Gossip on Romance" in *Longman's*. A small uproar over the role of character and incident in fiction had been set off by these entries which re-

[1] See, for example, Mrs. Margaret Oliphant's unsigned review, "Three Young Novelists," *Blackwood's Edinburgh Magazine*, CXXVI (1884), 296–297, 306; and James Purves on "Mr. Thomas Hardy's Rustics," *Time*, I, new series (1885), 715–716.

[2] An edition of Besant's lecture was published in America by Cupples, Upham & Co. in 1884. The lecture was then bracketed with James's reply in a single volume called *The Art of Fiction* published in the same year by the same company. A second edition of this version, published by Cupples & Hurd, appeared either in 1887 or 1888. In 1899 a Boston Journal, *The Writer*, reprinted the essays serially in its August and September issues (XII).

echoed through the main debate. James had responded to it in his own "Art of Fiction," but the immediate stimulus for his manifesto was Besant's cheerful, garrulous, sometimes shrewd, more often foolish lecture.

## I

That an amiable fool should have set James going is not without its Jamesian ironies. Besant has been called an "efficient and good-natured hack" by one modern critic and a "not very bright" Victorian moralist by another.[3] Mark Twain, who considered him a friend, refused to review his later tract for writers, *The Pen and the Book* (1898), because there wasn't "a rational page in it" and only "a sworn enemy" would assay its lunacies.[4] Besant's lecture tends to space its lunacies more loosely than the tract. He calls fiction "the most religious of all the Arts" on one page, for instance, finds on another that religious subjects are beyond the powers of fiction, and dismisses them on a third with a blithe comparison:

> *What picture, let us ask, what picture ever painted of angels and blessed souls, even if they are mounting the hill on which stands the Four Square City of the jasper wall, is able to command our interest and sympathy more profoundly than the simple and faithful story, truly and faithfully told, of a lover and his mistress?*

On still another page Besant urges the young writer to "examine the construction" of works "acknowledged to be of the first rank in fiction," such as George Eliot's *Silas Marner* and Nathaniel Hawthorne's *Scarlet Letter;* then he chooses James Payn's *Confidential Agent*, the story of a diamond robbery—"a work showing, if I may be permitted to say so, constructive power of the very highest order"— for his own "lesson in construction and machinery." Or waxing expansive toward the end, he advises "that in story-telling, as in almsgiving, a cheerful countenance works wonders, and a hearty manner greatly helps the teller and pleases the listener." As these examples indicate, Besant was an incorrigible enthusiast with a flair for unplanned incongruities. The flair was promoted by his "easy, flaccid style" for the lecture, which even his recent apologist, Frederick Boege, finds "more suitable for telling . . . how to finish a piece of furniture than how to write good fiction."[5] Why then did James endorse such mindless babble?

One answer is that Besant held in half-baked solution the whole swirl of received ideas about fiction, including some dear to James's heart. Another is that James badly wanted an audience for his own ideas and would have used almost any pretext to reach one. He was writing a novel then, *The Bostonians*, which

[3] See Leon Edel, *Henry James: The Middle Years, 1882-1895* (Philadelphia and New York: Lippincott, 1962), p. 124; and Maxwell Geismar, *Henry James and the Jacobites* (Boston: Houghton Mifflin, 1963), p. 99n.

[4] As cited by Frederick Boege in "Sir Walter Besant: Novelist," *Nineteenth-Century Fiction*, XI (June 1956), 36.

[5] Boege, 38.

featured a popular feminist lecturer, the lovely Verena Tarrant, whose name rhymes with Besant and whose inspirational style resembles his in its pleasing delivery—through a hazy amalgam of current ideas—of her own attractive personality. Besant's lovable and extremely public self may be refracted through Verena and her circle. He was probably the most popular author of his day in England, partly for his shallow romances but more notably for his East End novels which roused considerable sympathy for the poor. The People's Palace, a recreation hall in the East End, was built by subscription in 1887 as a direct result of his novel, *All Sorts and Conditions of Men*, which in 1882 had first projected it. He was also an association man, a charter member with James of the Rabelais Club in the 1870s, a founder of the Society of Authors in 1884 and later editor of its journal, the secretary of the Palestine Exploration Fund for 18 years, and a lifelong advocate of closer Anglo-American ties through institutes like the Atlantic Union. A self-effacing busybody, a selfless philanthropist who loved controversy, publicity, and important people, Besant was everyone's public saint and private fool. His lecture on "The Art of Fiction" may well have prefigured Verena's style in *The Bostonians*, as defined by her skeptical admirer, Basil Ransom, who plainly speaks for James:

> He had taken her measure as a public speaker, judged her importance in the field of discussion, the cause of reform. Her speech, in itself, had about the value of a pretty essay, committed to memory and delivered by a bright girl at an 'academy': it was vague, thin, rambling, a tissue of generalities that glittered agreeably enough in Mrs. Burrage's veiled lamplight. From any serious point of view it was neither worth answering nor worth considering, and Basil Ransom made his reflections on the crazy character of the age in which such a performance was treated as an intellectual effort, a contribution to a question. . . . (Chap. 28)

James's reflections on Besant's lecture must have been similar, if not so harsh. Like Ransom he could admire the speaker and deplore his speechification; but unlike Ransom he could also indulge the speaker's "generalities" with a public tenderness and a straight face because—from his own "serious point of view"— that was all "the age" could offer. Besant was a kind of parody of public seriousness about art; as Boege has shown, he was anything but a serious thinker and could not even follow his own good advice. But James was "the real thing," a serious theorist much in need of the audience Besant had set up for him. And so he bows to Besant, as his essay opens, for giving him a "pretext" for his comprehensive subject, and for showing that an audience for his own remarks exists; and he admits to being "anxious not to lose the benefit of this favourable association, and to edge in a few words under cover of the attention which Mr. Besant is sure to have excited"; he finds "something very encouraging in his having put into form certain of his ideas on the mystery of story-telling."

The connection here between a receptive audience and the expression of "certain ideas" is worth pursuing. James had long felt that the English were not an aesthetic people, but a moral one; that the artistic point of view was the last they would naturally take, and only then with apology or defiance for taking it. In writing about one of Besant's respondents, the popular critic R. H. Hutton, George Saintsbury would similarly complain of "the general distaste for pure criticism" in England, where readers seemed relieved when artistic issues were "alloyed and sweetened by sentimental, or political, or religious, or philosophical, or anthropological, or pantopragmatic adulteration."[6] Yet here was a popular speaker, the amiable Besant, asking the British public to take fiction seriously as an art, putting it on a plane with "Painting, Sculpture, Music, and Poetry," calling it their "sister and equal." Later Besant would revert to moral type: he would congratulate himself and his audience that "the modern English novel . . . almost always starts with a conscious moral purpose": but chiefly he would insist that fiction was as fine an art as any, and that novelists—like musicians, painters, poets— should be seen as artists. He had begun by saying that these propositions were "not new," which was true enough—they had been in circulation since mid-century; he said also that they were "not likely to be disputed," which proved false when everyone except James disputed them: "and yet," he tellingly concluded, "they have never been so generally received as to form a part, so to speak, of the national mind." This for a moment was exactly right: the "desire to consider Fiction as one of the Fine Arts" was not then a national sentiment. Yet it became one the moment he spoke, for Besant himself was a register for the national mind, and what he had just recorded was the arrival of a newly-received idea, the joining of a new commonplace to the old ones by which his adversaries would dispute it. Here, I think, is the chief source of James's encouragement from Besant's lecture. If only he could press strongly and intelligently enough in favor of this newly-arrived commonplace, he could affect the English and American climate for his own kind of fiction; he could educate and enlarge his own limited audience and so insure his own artistic freedom.

As Leon Edel has shown, James in the early 1880s had turned away from the upper classes and had begun "to form friendships . . . with the members of his own class, the writers and artists of London: to involve himself with their family life; to become godfather to their children and a genial visitor at their board." With the recent death of both parents his own family life had more or less ended; but he could still take his ease "with men whose accomplishments were analogous to his own." At the same time he was becoming more professional. While visiting America he had appeared unexpectedly before the American Copyright League in New York and for ten or fifteen minutes had addressed "the men of his own guild in his own country."[7] In 1884 Besant had founded a similar group in England, the Society of Authors, which he mentions in his lecture, and to which James now alludes as he writes of "the brotherhood of novelists" whose "life and curiosity" have been proven by Besant's remarks. It was not impossible,

[6] George Saintsbury, *A History of Criticism and Literary Taste in Europe*, III (Edinburgh and London: William Blackwood, 1917), p. 543.

[7] Edel, pp. 81, 71–72.

apparently, to accept Besant as the spokesman, the organizer, even the publicist for that community of fellow artists James was seeking. He had found such friendly groups in France during his several visits there. He had recently spent a memorable evening at Daudet's, discussing how the worn French language had to be refined by modern writers. That evening must have been vividly in his mind as he responded now—so gently and so generously—to Besant's crude ideas. It is within this comparative context, at any rate, that he continues, in his second paragraph, with his superb remarks on the history and value of discussion:

> Only a short time ago it might have been supposed that the English novel was not what the French call discutable. It had no air of having a theory, a conviction, a consciousness of itself behind it—of being the expression of an artistic faith, the result of choice and comparison. I do not say it was necessarily the worse for that: it would take much more courage than I possess to intimate that the form of the novel, as Dickens and Thackeray (for instance) saw it had any taint of incompleteness. It was, however, naif (if I may help myself out with another French word); . . .

James was helping himself out with more than French words. He was quietly invoking a novel more discussible than the English, a theory more sophisticated, as he knew from his visits with Flaubert and Daudet and from his friendship with Turgenev. The reference to Thackeray and Dickens is no idle instance here. James's close friend and fellow novelist, William Dean Howells, had courageously roused these spectres in his controversial essay of 1882. "The art of fiction," he had then asserted, has "become a finer art in our day than it was with Dickens and Thackeray. . . . These great men are of the past. . ."; whereas the "new school . . . which is so largely of the future as well as the present, finds its chief exemplar in Mr. James; it is he who is shaping and directing American fiction at least." In a letter to Howells James noted the storm these claims had roused in England: "articles about you and me are thick as blackberries—we are daily immolated on the altar of Thackeray and Dickens."[8] To allay these national gods, and to dissociate himself from Howells' temerity in offending them, James makes his nice distinction between completeness and *naivete*—and subtly shifts attention from American upstarts to French sophisticates. The fineness of Howells' analysis of his work had pleased him, however, and he now alludes more directly to the discussion which that essay—along with Stevenson's offsetting case for romance —had roused, as well as to Besant's essay and its rejoinders (I include in brackets hereafter his emendations for the 1888 version of the essay in *Partial Portraits*):

> During the period I have alluded to there was a comfortable, good-humored feeling abroad that a novel is a novel, as a pudding is a pudding, and that this was an end to it [and that our only business with it could be to swallow it]. But within a year or two, for some reason or other, there have been signs of returning animation—the era of discussion would appear to have been to a certain

8 Edel, p. 71.

*extent opened. Art lives upon discussion, upon experiment, upon curiosity, upon variety of attempt, upon the exchange of views and the comparison of standpoints; and there is a presumption that those times when no one has anything particular to say about it, and has no reason to give for practice or preference, though they may be times of genius [honor], are not times of development, are times, possibly even, a little, of dulness. The successful application of any art is a delightful spectacle, but the theory, too, is interesting; and though there is a great deal of the latter without the former, I suspect there has never been a genuine success that has not had a latent core of conviction.*

Scholars have since demonstrated that the period to which James first refers was lively enough to generate most of his own ideas, and was scarcely content with puddings.[9] But its novelists were not intellectually conjoined, whether in public or in private, and what James seems to stress is the lack of mutual stimulation, of public exchange and private community, of intellectual fellowship of the kind he now invokes:

*Discussion, suggestion, formulation, these things are fertilizing when they are frank and sincere. Mr. Besant has set an excellent example in saying what he thinks, for his part, about the way in which fiction should be written.... Other labourers in the same field will doubtless take up the argument, they will give it the light of their experience, and the effect will surely be to make our interest in the novel a little more what it had for some time threatened to fail to be—a serious, active inquiring interest....*
*It must take itself seriously for the public to take it so.*

Here Besant is granted frankness and sincerity, then bypassed as James asks others as serious as himself to "take up the argument," to help out, as it were, in rousing serious public interest. His distress when no one immediately did so was severe. To the one friend who wrote him in appreciation of the essay he replied that it had "not attracted the smallest attention here," not even an allusion, and went on to lament: "There is almost no care for literary discussion here,—questions of form, of principle, the 'serious' idea of the novel appeals apparently to no one, & they don't understand you when you speak to them."[10] But that winter Stevenson's reply heartened him so much that he wrote a warm letter of thanks, from which began exactly the kind of literary friendship he wanted. Later he was to enjoy for a time a similar friendship with H. G. Wells; and with increasing frequency he became the writer's writer, the "Master" for younger novelists like Paul Bourget, Vernon Lee (Violet Paget), Constance Fenimore Woolson, Howard Sturgis. When Turgenev died Woolson had touchingly written to James: "You are our Turgenev." To this extent he realized his hope for literary friendship and exchange; but he would not reach the wide audience he wanted until the

[9] See the introductions to Richard Stang's *The Theory of the Novel in England: 1850–1870* (New York: Columbia, 1959; and London: Routledge and Kegan Paul, 1959) and Kenneth Graham's *English Criticism of the Novel: 1865-1900* (London: Oxford, 1965).

[10] See Roger Gard, ed. *Henry James: The Critical Heritage* (London: Routledge and Kegan Paul, 1968; New York: Barnes and Noble, 1968), p. 149.

New Criticism turned to fiction in the late 1940s and took James and his disciple Percy Lubbock as exemplars. Then his fiction and the theory which espoused it would indeed work together for his greater glory.

Were there hints of such glory for him in Besant's lecture? When, on his second page, Besant asserted "that the great Masters of Fiction must be placed on the same level as the great Masters of the other Arts," did those barren capitals quicken James's heart? Certainly when Besant argued that regard for novelists could be proven low by the absence of public honors for them, James pointedly agreed. "I suppose it is the demon of envy," he had written to a friend at this time, "but I can't help contrasting the greater reward of a successful painter, here, and his glory and honour generally, with the so much more modest emoluments of the men of letters."[11] Thus, where others raised prickly objections, James insisted with Besant that novelists deserve "all the honours and emoluments that have hitherto been reserved for the successful profession of music, poetry, painting, architecture." He even credited Besant with the richness of his own case for fiction, saying "It is of all this evidently that Mr. Besant is full," etc., when all too evidently Besant was full of bombast. Besant's sociological point, that public honors are a sign of public standing, was shrewdly taken; but ironically it was Besant himself who would be knighted in 1895, chiefly for his antiquarian and humanitarian labors, but also for his fiction, whereas James would lose much of his audience and would even endure public abuse.[12]

As if to temper such reversals Besant spoke out in his lecture against another kind of public irony: the "bad fashion" of measuring a novelist's success by the "large sale of his works." Contending that "the Art of a great writer . . . may never become widely popular," he cited a case familiar to his audience, "of a man whose books are filled with wisdom, experience, and epigram: whose characters are most admirably studied from the life, whose plots are ingenious, situations fresh, and dialogues extraordinarily clever," but who had never been widely popular and whose market value was considerably less than "many another whose genius is not half so great. . . ." Whether the man in question is Meredith or James, this clumsy tribute from the most popular novelist of the day, whose books sold in the hundreds of thousands while theirs sold in the hundreds, must have seemed endearing. James was only too mindful of the economic hazards of his craft, and he could forgive much for this kind of self-effacing sympathy.

With Besant's chief concern in the lecture, the teaching of fiction to young people with a talent for it, James was only superficially engaged. Yet Besant's remarks were aimed, with an originality for which he is seldom given credit, at young

[11]See Edel, p. 111.

[12] See Boege, 33–34. To Frank Harris's contention that Besant had been undeservedly knighted as "the representative of literature," Boege replies: "Besant was not knighted for his literary achievement but for the philanthropy and effectiveness of his writings on the East End—specifically for his part in the People's Palace." But since these writings included novels about the East End, in one of which the idea for the palace originated, Boege partly contradicts himself. One kind of literary achievement was certainly being rewarded. Another kind, his multi-volume "History of London" on which he had only recently embarked, was probably also being recognized. Meanwhile James had undergone failure and public abuse as a dramatist.

writers for whom no school or mode of training existed. His plea, in effect, for creative writing courses in fiction was one of the first public arguments of its kind.[13] In pointing out that fiction was the only fine art which had "no school or college or Academy, no recognised rules, no text-books," and was "not taught in any University," he made the question of its teachability a public issue, a matter for debate and experiment, and eventually for public action. By this point in the nineteenth century the novel had a definite history, a distinct variety of forms, and a large body of important work behind it: it could now be taken seriously as an academic subject. Yet as Besant nicely observed, "Even the German Universities, which teach everything else, do not have Professors of Fiction, and not one single novelist, so far as I know, has ever pretended to teach his mystery, or spoken of it as a thing which may be taught." It would take some time before fiction would be taught as literature in English and American schools, and creative writing would follow, at least in American universities, only after the first great war. Meanwhile Besant had planted the idea of a teachable craft; and by the early 1900s he had apparently moved James himself to "teach his mystery" through a series of prefaces for the New York edition of his works.

"My pages, in *Longman*, were simply a plea for liberty: they were only half of what I had to say, and some day I shall try and express the remainder." So James had written to Stevenson in warm response to his "Humble Remonstrance" to "The Art of Fiction." Stevenson wrote back urging him on to a sequel, "for my own education and the public's," to which he would then fashion a second rejoinder so as to "woo or drive" James from his "threatened silence."[14] But these promised exchanges took place only through conversations and letters, and the public's education had to wait till Stevenson was dead, and James had spread "the remainder" through his prefaces. By then the public was indifferent and the edition sold poorly; but its editor, Percy Lubbock, would so profit from his labors as to produce *The Craft of Fiction* in 1921, a book which would affect the teaching of fiction as literature and art for the next three decades; and the prefaces themselves would be collected and prefaced by R. P. Blackmur as *The Art of the Novel* in 1934, a document which would figure strongly in the New Critical shift to fiction after World War II. So the prefaces did become the promised rejoinder, the missing half of James's manifesto; and they became also his attempt to "teach his mystery" to young writers after Besant's dubious example.

## II

What seemed so dubious to James, in Besant's example, were the "general laws" by which he proposed to teach the mystery. In *The Bostonians* James had gently satirized Olive Chancellor for being "exceedingly fond of illustrations of laws"

[13] A writer for the *Saturday Review* had called for "an Institute of Novel-Writing" in 1874 (XXXVII, 415–416); and Trollope and others had affirmed the need for training and for following "rules for the writing of novels."

[14] See *Henry James and Robert Louis Stevenson: A Record of Friendship and Criticism,* ed. Janet Adam Smith (London: Rupert Hart-Davis, 1948), pp. 102–103.

(Chap. 19). Besant was similarly fond of laws, rules, principles, and their illustrations. In his addled view powers and faculties could be acquired by simple rules and methods; prescriptions and prevailing practices had the force of laws. He put special stress on "the simple method adopted by Robert Houdin, the French conjuror," of taking notes in a commonplace book to improve his memory. This method might prove embarrassing, "say—at a dinner party, or a street fight"; but the observant man could learn to jot things down afterwards "so that nothing is lost." No mean conjuror himself, James would magically transform that final phrase in his famous maxim, "Try to be one of the people on whom nothing is lost!" in which retention is subsumed by imaginative apprehension. He was particularly troubled by Besant's initial rule, "never to go beyond your own experience," because it denied the ranges of imagination; and he would redefine experience in his essay as in fact more consonant with apprehension than event. Besant's distance from imaginative apprehension, not to say logic, may be instanced by his remarkable summary of his long battery of laws in a single sentence:

> The Art of fiction requires first of all the power of description, truth, and fidelity, observation, selection, clearness of conception and of outline, dramatic grouping, directness of purpose, a profound belief on the part of the story-teller in the reality of his story, and beauty of workmanship.

What the art required "secondly" Besant did not say. To this list of injunctions, so jumbled and inadequate (or as James would generously say, "so beautiful and so vague") that no one could follow it, he simply added five new homilies in quick succession and a coda on "the most important point of all—the story," which he had somehow forgotten to discuss. But here, he wisely concluded, "teaching and theory can go no further."

For James they had already gone far enough. In what must be one of the mildest (and most devastating) reproofs in literary history, he said he would "take the liberty of making but a single criticism of Mr. Besant, whose tone is so full of the love of his art":

> He seems to me to mistake in attempting to say so definitely beforehand what sort of an affair the good novel will be. To indicate the danger of such an error as that has been the purpose of these few pages; to suggest that certain traditions on the subject, applied a priori, have already had much to answer for, and that the good health of an art which undertakes so immediately to reproduce life must demand that it be perfectly free. It lives upon exercise, and the very meaning of exercise is freedom.

In other words, James would simply throw out Besant's rules. It was "impossible not to sympathize" with most of them and "difficult to dissent from" all but one (that a writer from the lower middle-class "should . . . avoid introducing his characters into Society"); but it was also "difficult positively to assent" to any except the injunction to take notes. If these recommendations were suggestive, even inspiring, they were "not exact"; their value lay "wholly in the meaning one attache[d] to them." And for the rest of his essay James would expand upon the artist's freedom to attach meanings to his own categories.

As Roger Gard contends, James was replying to his reviewers as well as to Besant throughout the essay. This was obvious enough when he took up Andrew Lang's snide allusion to one of his stories, "An International Episode," in the *Pall Mall Gazette*. While responding to Besant's lecture, Lang had voiced his own preference for a fashionable romance, *Margot La Balafree*, "to all the Bostonian nymphs who ever rejected English dukes for psychological reasons." He had named neither James nor his story, and James pointedly failed to name him in his reply. A few years later he would name him bluntly enough in a letter to Stevenson: "Lang, in the D.N. [Daily News], every morning, and I believe in a hundred other places, uses his beautiful thin facility to write everything down to the lowest level of Philistine twaddle—the view of the old lady round the corner or the clever person at the dinner party."[15] This is in fact an excellent description of Lang's treatment of Besant's lecture. After systematically discrediting Besant's view of fiction's pedigree and his penchant for generalities, he takes up the question of story versus character, passes it off as one of taste, denies the value of debating it, saying that "one might argue any point either way in the metaphysic of fiction," and concludes benignly: "All sorts of fictions . . . are good if they amuse us, and waken, as Mr. Besant said, our sympathy with men, and take us out of ourselves and away from this world of trouble." He is safe, clever, escapist, and more than a little smug about serious writers from abroad—Zola, Howells, James, Edmund de Goncourt. It was against a hundred Langs, then, that James fashioned his own mild rebuffs of critics who prefer happy endings, incident and movement, sympathetic characters, and wholesome subjects, and who meet the question of artistic form with "positive indifference."

These were the "traditions" which, applied *a priori*, "had much to answer for." Their pressure upon James had become all too evident since Howells had written them off in 1882, and roused a critical storm in their defense. In his essay on James, Howells had defined his fiction as eschewing incident, or story, for the analysis of character; as eschewing commentary and the sympathetic depiction of character for impartial presentation; and as favoring open endings over closed ones. "In one manner or other the stories were all told long ago," said Howells in his provocative conclusion; now readers wanted analytic studies and might well relinquish the "childish" demand for "finished" tales. Both Lang and Besant were reacting, then, to Howells' essay in seeing "story," "adventure," or "romance" as the essence of good fiction. And James, in replying to these and a score of critics like them, was advancing the battle for his own kind of fiction which Howells had bumptiously, if courageously, begun. His argument for the value of "psychological adventures," like those involving "the development of the moral consciousness of a child," was generous in its bow to romantic childhood adventures, such as the "delightful story" of *Treasure Island* by Robert Louis Stevenson; but Stevenson too had come out in favor of romance in 1882, as part of the *a priori*

[15] See Gard, p. 184.

opposition; and James wanted to show now that his own adventures were as valid as those preferred by all these critics. "We must grant the artist his subject, his idea, his *donnée*," he argued; "our criticism is applied only to what he makes of it." But this plea for artistic freedom was, in effect, a plea for the acceptance of a new kind of fiction—the kind he was writing himself—along with the old.

James's argument for the organic nature of fiction must be seen in the light of this controversy. He begins by objecting to the use of terms like character, description, dialogue, and incident "as if they had a kind of internecine distinctness" instead of being melded "parts of one general effort of expression":

> *I cannot imagine composition existing in a series of blocks* [he continues], *nor conceive, in any novel worth discussing at all, of a passage of description that is not in its intention narrative, a passage of dialogue that is not in its intention descriptive, a touch of truth of any sort that does not partake of the nature of incident, or an incident that derives its interest from any other source than the general and only source of the success of a work of art—that of being illustrative. A novel is a living thing, all one and continuous, like any other organism, and in proportion as it lives will it be found, I think, that in each of the parts there is something of each of the other parts.*

James next dismisses generic categories such as "novel of character" and "novel of incident," or "novel" and "romance," as artificial and unreal and of little value to the producer. Later he objects to the existence of a "school," to which both Lang and Besant allude in their reactions to Howells, "which urges that a novel should be all treatment and no subject." Every school is conscious, he asserts, that there must be "something to treat," a subject or a story, and in this sense only can a story be considered "as something different from its organic whole." As such arguments confirm, James was defending his own new school of fiction by artfully disowning it. His plea for freedom, his invocation of the organic theory, are important precisely as they allay critical prejudices roused by Howells, yet still allow for his own impartial, open-ended, character-centered novels, which Howells had accurately defined. The organic theory would provide an important point of continuity, moreover, with the defense of this kind of fiction in the late 1940s by those arch-organicists and professional defenders of modern poetry, the New Critics, who had by then begun to expand their generic empire. Some scholars argue that the organic approach to fiction did not originate with James, and that other writers of his time would present such concepts with greater ingenuity and force;[16] but the history of missed connections is less important to novel theory than the history of battles fought and won. It was Henry James who began the successful defense of the modern novel, and of the art novel from which it sprang, by putting inherited concepts to intelligent use in that worthy and barely heralded cause. He had some embarrassing help in this task from his far-sighted friend

---

[16] See Richard Stang, pp. 134–135; and Kenneth Graham, pp. 135–139, in which he calls Vernon Lee's article "On Literary Construction" (1895) "more comprehensive and more sympathetic than James's" and ranks it "beside any single similar piece of writing by James for its qualities of originality, reasonableness, and devotion to the craft of novel-writing," p. 138.

Howells, who foresaw the novel's future; and he received an unwitting boost, a covering "pretext" for his efforts, from the amiable Besant, who registered the novel's present disarray: but the main job begins with his own admirable and brilliantly tactical essay on "The Art of Fiction."

### III

James's redefinition of the terms of experience is an unconscious instance of his futuristic aims. In his preface to *The Princess Casamassima*, a novel written shortly after "The Art of Fiction," James would make a curious equation between feeling and doing: "What a man thinks and what he feels are the history and character of what he does." This equation seems plausible enough until we remember that, in James's fiction, thoughts and feelings are the history and character of what a man *doesn't* do, or fails to do, or renounces doing. James's preoccupation with mental drama has somehow nullified, in his mind, more active kinds of drama, more engaged forms of emotion and relationship. This nullification begins with his striking definition of Experience, in "The Art of Fiction," as "an immense sensibility, a kind of huge spider-web of the finest silken threads suspended in the chamber of consciousness, and catching every air-borne particle in its tissue. It is the very atmosphere of the mind. . . ." Jamesian apprehension is really more aggressive than this passive image allows; but even granting the vigor of his mental probing, the definition is still peculiar. Most of us live with an emotional and sensual immediacy which includes apprehension without being reduced to it. Our emotional and sensual relations are not the same, after all, as our comprehension of them. If experience is *only* the apprehension of experience, then James is proposing that withdrawal and isolation into the realm of consciousness which finds its formal expression in the point of view and stream of consciousness techniques of much modern fiction. His aesthetic principle points to a particular condition of the modern novel in some of its major forms; and he is not himself aware of what he helps us to see, that the condition doesn't apply to older forms of the novel, where people are still able to relate to one another with some success, or where their failures are failures of engagement, not renunciations and withdrawals. James's definition of experience speaks to the modern predicament, then, of alienation and isolation, in a way he did not fully comprehend.

His defiance of conventional morality was more conscious. Simply by granting the artist his *donnée* he had broken with the community of shared assumptions to which Trollope, for example, still belonged. If writers could choose their own subjects, they were no longer bound to choose agreeable ones. In the 1870s James had put "the importance of subject" above all else while dealing with French writers, and had even criticized Baudelaire for making "fine verses on ignoble subjects." It was the subject, seen as "the essential richness of inspiration," that determined the moral quality of works of art; by which test a writer like Turgenev, with "a sound philosophy of life" to inspire him, was preferable to equally artistic writers like Flaubert and Balzac, who lacked such inspiration.[17] By 1884,

---

[17] See Morris Roberts, *Henry James's Criticism* (Cambridge, Mass.: Harvard, 1929), pp. 44–45.

however, James had apparently changed his mind. Probably his experience of misjudgment at the hands of English critics had made him see his inconsistency with French writers. He had imposed upon them a prescription like those he now opposed. So it is himself he corrects, as well as his prescriptive critics, when he tests Flaubert and Turgenev by execution and defends them equally for choosing subjects which "fly in the face of presumptions." Earlier that year, in a letter to Howells from Paris, he had even embraced "unclean" subjects. Of a popular success in America he writes: "I would rather have produced the basest experiment in the 'naturalism' that is being practised here than such a piece of sixpenny humbug." And of Daudet, Goncourt, and Zola:

> there is nothing more interesting to me now than the effort and experiment of this little group, with its truly infernal intelligence of art, form, manner—its intense artistic life. They do the only kind of work, today, that I respect; and in spite of their ferocious pessimism and their handling of unclean things, they are at least serious and honest. The floods of tepid soap and water which under the name of novels are being vomited forth in England, seem to me, by contrast, to do little honour to our race.[18]

Base, infernal, pessimistic, unclean, the French group is nonetheless "serious and honest" about art; this "least" point of the letter becomes the salient point of the essay; and the humbug of English moralism, the preference for tepid cleanliness, becomes inimical to art. Early in the essay, for instance, James singles out the old superstition about fiction being "wicked," which has "doubtless died out," but which still lingers in the public suspicion of its artfulness:

> 'Art,' in our Protestant communities, where so many things have got so strangely twisted about, is supposed, in certain circles, to have some vaguely injurious effect upon those who make it an important consideration, who let it weigh in the balance. It is assumed to be opposed in some mysterious manner to morality, to amusement, to instruction. When it is embodied in the work of the painter . . . you know what it is . . . and you can be on your guard. But when it is introduced into literature it becomes more insidious—there is danger of its hurting you before you know it. Literature should be either instructive or amusing, and there is in many minds an impression that these artistic preoccupations, the search for form, contribute to neither end, interfere indeed with both. They are too frivolous to be edifying, and too serious to be diverting; and they are, moreover, priggish and paradoxical and superfluous. That, I think, represents the manner in which the latent thought of many people who read novels as an exercise in skipping would explain itself if it were to become articulate.

Here James confronts two popular assumptions which undermine the novel's status as an art form. He was not really troubled by the demand for entertainment; he believed himself that a novel must "be interesting" and was fairly confident of his own power to amuse (his reviewers had only just begun to call him "boring"). But the demand for moral seriousness, as *opposed to* artistic seri-

<hr>

[18] See Gard, p. 142.

ousness, troubled him considerably. He seems to have sensed that English moralism was responsible for his own low estimation even with non-skipping readers, and for the general misjudgment of his work. As Roger Gard has shown, James was consistently *understood* by the best reviewers, and yet just as consistently misjudged. This was chiefly because of the demand for "clear-cut moral and social credentials." James's contemporaries could respond to edifying subjects like the religious problems dramatized in J. H. Shorthouse's popular novel, *John Inglesant.* By contrast James's subjects seemed thin and elusive; they were "not *manifestly* serious and worth the application of serious men," and accordingly his books fell short of greatness.[19] Thus James was victimized by the same English standard he had applied to French deficiencies. His reviewers considered *him* more French than English or American, and he was now about to prove their case. To defend himself against the crudities of English moralism he had to speak out radically for complete artistic freedom.

Late in the essay James takes up "the question of the morality of the novel." He sees it as "a question surrounded with difficulties" and uses Besant's brief and easy certainties as his point of departure. Unlike Besant, he argues, most people will find "moral timidity" rather than moral purpose in the English novel; they will remark upon its diffidence before the great range of moral subjects, its failure to survey the field, its deference to the young, its *lack* of moral energy and passion. The negativeness of English moral purpose is what strikes him, and by citing it he scores a negative blow for his "unclean" friends, Daudet, Goncourt, Zola. In his closing lines he censures Zola's vitiating pessimism; but he grants the darkness of his subject and objects only to his lightless treatment; and he immediately plays off Zola's pessimism against the "shallow optimism" of English fiction—of which Besant's shallow romances were so representative, incidentally, especially in their tepid cleanliness, that the adjective "Besantine" was coined to describe the type.

James's positive moral argument was even more radically French in its challenge to English readers:

> There is one point at which the moral sense and the artistic sense lie very near together; that is, in the light of the very obvious truth that the deepest quality of a work of art will always be the quality of the mind of the producer. In proportion as that mind is rich and noble [as that intelligence is fine] will the novel, the picture, the statue, partake of the substance of beauty and truth. To be constituted of such elements is, to my vision, to have purpose enough. No good novel will ever proceed from a superficial mind; that seems to me an axiom which, for the artist in fiction, will cover all needful moral ground; if the youthful aspirant take it to heart it will illuminate for him many of the mysteries of 'purpose.'

This bold coupling of the moral and artistic senses, with its mock-Besantine axiom and its interesting emendation in the direction of finer sensibility, introduced modern moral consciousness into the Victorian arena. It was less a new

---

[19] Gard, p. 8.

idea than a new juxtaposition of ideas, a new insistence upon the moral complexity of experience, upon the need for fineness of discrimination in place of moral certainties and edifying subjects. Gard's argument, that a change of sensibility must be posited to account for the delay in James's reception as a great novelist, is certainly *a propos:* but it was a change *to* sensibility, a shift from easy moral abstractions to fine moral consciousness, which James was calling for, and which his own age was unready to accept. He would hedge his proposition by making *taste* the ultimate arbiter, by which some subjects prove mysteriously more rewarding than others. But to relate edification to taste was to make conventional morality seem willful; and to incorporate morality into sensibility was, in any case, to make apprehension the only true form of edification, at least for those honest enough to confront the complexities and uncertainties of experience. To "grant the artist . . . his *donnée*," then, was to break through the "Victorian frame of mind" to a new state of consciousness, a new awareness of those "difficulties with which on every side the treatment of reality bristles." For James the breakthrough would lead, in the late 1890s and after, to an exploration of the full range of precocious sexual awareness, as in *The Turn of the Screw, What Maisie Knew,* and *The Awkward Age;* and to what seems to have been his own painful discovery, in *The Ambassadors,* that the *sexual* and artistic senses "lie very near together"—as if "unclean things" had all the while inspired his own richly moral sensibility. Joyce, Mann, Yeats and other modern writers would similarly come to accept "squalor" as the medium for art, the "foul rag and boneshop of the heart" from which it necessarily rises. James's essay prepared for that characteristically modern acceptance, and for his own belated discovery that sex is— if not the mother of beauty—at least its secret lover.

## IV

The breakthrough of modern sensibility took other forms in the essay. James's fascination with the painting analogy is a case in point. Besant had repeatedly compared fiction with painting and had borrowed its terminology to advance his arguments. James would do likewise. But where Besant pressed for an exact correspondence between "the laws of harmony, perspective, and proportion" which governed both arts, James pressed for a common purpose: the "attempt to represent life." Originally James had called it an attempt to "compete with life," a phrase which Stevenson found "daring," but which he criticized so severely in "A Humble Remonstrance" that James made the above revision for the 1888 version in *Partial Portraits.* Stevenson took "competition" to mean that fiction can be as inclusive and as vivid as experience. Finding that claim ridiculous, he called instead for differentiation from life through selection, arrangement, design. The only kind of "imitation" he would allow was that of speech, "the emphasis and the suppressions with which the human actor" tells a story. "Truth," he argued, was "a word of very debateable propriety . . . for the labours of the novelist"; he should occupy himself "not so much in making stories true as in making them typical; not so much in capturing the lineaments of each fact, as in marshalling all of them towards a common end." With much of this James would agree, and said so in his appreciative letter. He had even said in the essay that "Art is essentially . . . a selection whose main care is to be typical, to be inclusive." And he had made his own plea for "marshalling" lineaments by stressing the organic nature of fiction. But he did stress "inclusive" along with "typical," and he did attack the artificiality of design, taken as the last word on fiction. For James "the supreme virtue of a novel" was to create an "air of reality" through "solidity of specification," an "illusion of life" through "truth of detail." To cultivate this process was "the beginning and the end of the art of the novelist":

> It is here, in very truth, that he competes with life; it is here that he competes with his brother the painter, in his attempt to render the look of things, the look that conveys their meaning, to catch the colour, the relief, the expression, the surface, the substance of the human spectacle. . . . . . . . . . . . Catching the very note and trick, the strange irregular rhythm of life, that is the attempt whose strenuous force keeps Fiction upon her feet.

One way in which fiction "competes with life," then, is by conveying the feel or illusion of reality. James wanted this meaning to stick, and so kept the phrase intact in the passage quoted above. But he revised its three appearances in the long third paragraph of the essay, where the painting analogy begins, so as to avoid the implication of gargantuan totality and vivacity which Stevenson had found there.

What James had originally meant by "competition," in that paragraph, was what we generally mean by "representation": that fiction re-presents, or bodies forth, a version of reality which commands our interest as life commands it. It was an artist's version, his personal impression, his *donnée*, but James had failed to make that distinction clear until the fifth paragraph, where he states emphatically: "A novel is in its broadest definition a personal impression of life; that, to begin with, constitutes its value, which is greater or less according to the intensity of the impression." Apparently he felt that this distinction should have come earlier, and in a more explicit fashion, again as a result of Stevenson's strictures against the totality of his claims. So, in the *Partial Portraits* version, he inserted in the third paragraph the parenthesis which I have italicized below. It comes in the course of his famous criticism of Trollope for his aside to the reader that "he and this trusting friend are only 'making believe' . . . and that he can give his narrative any turn the reader may like best":

> Such a betrayal of a sacred office seems to me, I confess, a terrible crime; it is what I mean by the attitude of apology, and it shocks me every whit as much in Trollope as it would have shocked me in Gibbon or Macaulay. It implies that the novelist is less occupied in looking for the truth (the truth, of course I mean, that he assumes, the premises that we grant him, whatever they may be) *than the historian, and in doing so it deprives him at a stroke of all his standing room.*

At first glance the emendation seems to reduce the search for truth to the novelist's sincerity about his own assumptions—as Besant had said, he must believe in his own story—and to our willingness to grant them. But this allusion to his *donnée* makes for a more complicated view of the creative process than James altogether realized. The emendation changes the meaning of the passage and indeed of the long paragraph in which it appears. The novelist is no longer merely looking for the truth *out there,* in whatever evidence life affords him; he has developed a hypothesis about it, a set of assumptions, an intention which can only be realized through his treatment, his execution of his vision of how things are. But this is to shift the question of truth from subject to treatment, and to anticipate modern versions of this problem like Mark Schorer's theory of "technique as discovery," or like Eliseo Vivas's theory of the constitutive symbol, through which we view the world. James himself misses these implications and seems more concerned with preliminaries than with provings; his eye is on the novelist's sensibility, his "capacity for receiving straight impressions," and though he later claims that a fine intelligence will produce novels which "partake of the substance of beauty and truth," he does not talk about the realization of truth through treatment. He *quarrels* with Zola over the truth of his treatment, calls him an "ignorant" man "working in the dark," albeit with magnificent energy; but this is as close as he comes to discussing how treatment might substantiate those intense straight impressions that he prizes.

The sophistication of his ideas is nonetheless striking. Like some of the later New Critics, he asks us to take seriously the novelist's *interpretation* of experience, his attitudes toward it, his "givens," as a form of hypothetical truth; and he almost asks us to test that truth against its realization through form. He also develops Besant's painting analogy (which begins as early as Bulwer-Lytton) into a complex epistemology, a "magnificent heritage" involving history and philosophy as well as painting. When it comes to verisimilitude, moreover, he makes no easy equation, but finds instead that "the measure of reality is very difficult to fix":

> The reality of Don Quixote or of Mr. Micawber is a very delicate shade; it is a reality so coloured by the author's vision that, vivid as it may be, one would hesitate to propose it as a model: one would expose one's self to some very embarrassing questions on the part of a pupil. It goes without saying that you will not write a good novel unless you possess the sense of reality; but it will be difficult to give you a recipe for calling that sense into being. Humanity is immense and reality has a myriad forms; the most one can affirm is that some of the flowers of fiction have the odour of it, and others have not. . . .

James's pliant view of verisimilitude was at odds at this point with his practice. In *The Bostonians,* which he was then writing, and in *The Princess Casamassima* which followed, he was dealing for the first time with public issues—feminism and revolution—and was attempting a "solidity of specification" which ran against his grain. His admiration for the naturalists had led to a kind of forced emulation, especially in *The Bostonians,* in which the "air of reality" thickens into heavy coastal fog. Oddly, Stevenson had to fight his natural penchant *for* solidity of detail through what now seems like an attempt to "compete with life" through form. He sounds more Jamesian than James as he propounds an "emasculate" realm for art where people rise clear from "material circumstance" and conversation departs from how men actually talk. James himself would draw closer to this kind of competition with life in his later work. As Leo Bersani observes, James's later fiction tends toward the compositional hermeticism of his prefaces; characters are seen in terms of compositional appeal, conflict becomes "the conflicting implications of designs," and morality becomes a matter of "structural coherence."[20] Yet James himself did not consider this development hermetic. To the accusation put forth by H. G. Wells, that he made literature an end in itself "like painting," he replied emphatically: "It is art that *makes* life, makes interest, makes importance, for our consideration and application of these things, and I know of no substitute whatever for the force and beauty of its process." Here the terms of dependency are reversed: in the competition with life art finally triumphs; it becomes the shaping experience by which life itself acquires meaning and value. Its mimetic function continues: "I live intense and am fed by life," said James, "and my value . . . is in my own kind of expression of that." But the "extension of life," the making of life's "interest" and "importance," had become "the novel's best gift."[21] To "compete with life," then, was to interpret and express its fullness and intensity, to convey its rhythm and texture, and to create ostensibly hermetic forms *through which* its interest and importance come into being as matters for contemplation and use. Ironically James would discard this all too pregnant phrase, "compete with life," before its final meaning had become apparent. But its troublesome presence in 1884 already signalled the direction which his own thought would take, and much modern theory after him.

One final point worth mentioning is James's distance from his audience as compared with Trollope's, Stevenson's, or Besant's. By stressing treatment over subject James was trying to bridge that distance. In *The Moral and the Story* Ian Gregor argues that nineteenth-century novelists shared conventions with their readers and found techniques to convey them, whereas modern novelists have had to invent techniques so as to create conventions for their readers: "For the former the problem was to keep an audience; for the latter it is to find one."[22] By this formula Besant, Stevenson, and Trollope, in their different ways, shared conventional expectations with their readers; but James had to sweep those expectations aside in order to create new ones. Thus, by asking readers to grant the artist's subject, and to concentrate instead upon its treatment, he was being more "daring" than either he or Stevenson or even Howells had supposed: he was opening the way for himself and later novelists to create that broad audience of

[20] Leo Bersani, "The Jamesian Lie," *Partisan Review*, XXXVI (Winter 1969), 53–79.

[21] *Henry James and H. G. Wells: A Record of their Friendship, their Debate on the Art of Fiction, and their Quarrel*, ed. Leon Edel and Gordon N. Ray (Urbana, Ill.: University of Illinois Press, 1958), pp. 264, 266–267.

[22] Ian Gregor and Brian Nicholas, *The Moral and the Story* (London: Faber and Faber, 1962), pp. 253–254.

uncommon readers by whom the modern novel and its conventions have in fact been assimilated. Late in his essay James had written: "It is an adventure—an immense one—for me to write this little article." Through his honest belief in the vitality of ideas, in the value of discussion, experiment, exchange of views, and through his generous response to near- and far-sighted friends, amiable fools, and facile Philistines, he had indeed begun an adventure of immense importance to the novel's history.

# V.

## History and Culture

# Tolstoy and the Ways of History

JOHN HENRY RALEIGH

Tolstoy on the idea of history has been discussed so often and so well—as in Isaiah Berlin's *The Hedgehog and the Fox*—that it would seem supererogatory to review it again. Nevertheless, so much attention has been paid to Tolstoy's explicit and abstract discussions that it is often overlooked that in *War and Peace* itself there are several divergent ways of looking at history. In *Anna Karenina, What is Art?* and other works there are views expressed on history quite at odds with some of those expressed in parts of *War and Peace*.

In *War and Peace* Tolstoy sees history as having several dimensions, the most important of which is the vertical, the total chain of circumstances extending from the present back into the past and, inferentially, into the future. This sequence of cause-and-effect includes the sum total of all human actions since the beginning of time. Though such a conception deals with vast stretches of history, it is not really a temporal process. Time and its Augustinian mysteries and paradoxes are not really involved, and in this respect, although in this respect only—for Tolstoy detested Hegel—the conception is analogous to Hegel's in *The Philosophy of History*, which is really about the presumed logic of history and not about the passage of time. Sydney Hook has described Hegel's system as an historical evolution with time left out, or as an abstract scheme of what had actually evolved in the course of national and human history translated into logic and shifted to an ontological plane. There is in Tolstoy's outlook no hint of evolution; quite the contrary. But there is a logic to history—the logic of cause-and-effect—and there is an ontology, namely, that reality is human bodies in continuous movement. Consciously, Tolstoy denied that there was any ontology to history. What I am maintaining is that from *War and Peace* can be inferred a kind of Hobbesian minimal ontology which maintains that only material bodies exist. To put it another way, if the definition of time is movement, then Tolstoy's system has a temporal aspect, but what is stressed by Tolstoy is not the temporal side of the equation but the motional.

Having said this much, one still has the problem of defining the nature and the source of the power that moves history. According to Tolstoy, human reason cannot solve this problem—but, as he also said, reason is not completely helpless. It can, for example, refute other theories about power in history: the "great man" theory, or the progressive theory, or the various ideological theories, or the Hegelian Idea. More important, reason can guess at what power in history is. Although Tolstoy asserts in the Second Epilogue that the actual workings of this force are a mystery, we can have no doubt as to its ultimate source: it is finally located in the actions of the human body. All the historical theories that Tolstoy dismisses have one thing in common: they are all, so to speak, "history in the head"—the ideas expressed by writers and ideologues; the will of a great man imposed upon his people, or conversely, the collective will of the people embodied in the head of a state; history as a great unfolding idea, Hegelian or otherwise, which nations and civilizations progressively realize. For what history in *War and Peace* finally comes down to is great masses of men moving back and forth over continental landscapes, and, more importantly, these same men killing one another. Thus it is that war, mass movement and mass murder, become the perfect metaphor for history since war concentrates the power of human action as no other activity can and its object and eventuation is the ultimate physical act: the destruction of one man by another. An army thus is the mightiest historical force, and in *War and Peace* during the review of the troops before the Battle of Austerlitz (bk. III, chap. VIII), Tolstoy remarks that all soldiers, from highest to lowest, feel their insignificance in this vast array of troops, but also a sense of the power they share as a part, however insignificant, of that great whole. Thus, also, the reiterated statements throughout the novel that in the battle itself strategies, tactical maneuvers, chains of command, orders, all the verbal and intelligential apparatus of war are meaningless—what counts is physical exertion and destruction. Thus, too, there is always a fundamental ratio at work: the farther away from a human event, as with a statesman or a ruler or a general, the less an individual has to do with its outcome; the closer and more direct one's physical engagement, the more one's impress upon the event and upon history itself. History then is the labors and exertions of the billions of human bodies that have had a terrestrial existence. Moreover, this sense of moving human bodies as constituting the basic force in the human drama is not limited to the high historical discussions in the book; it is implicit in the most private and "unhistorical" sections, and is the water-wheel that works the plot. For the male characters are always on the move, coming and going, leaving and returning, never remaining long in the same place. The cowed women at Bald Hills listening to the sound of the walk of old Prince Bolkonsky—if he is walking on his heels then he is in a bad mood and they are in trouble—may be taken as an emblem of the human condition of the time: stationary women and moving men. Women are the receptors; men the projectors who will come to rest only when they die.

If man did not move or act, history would come to a halt. And since history is the history of human unhappiness, non-action is precisely the answer to the social ills of man. To be sure, Tolstoy can usually be found to be on both sides of every primary question of human life. Thus as he is the apostle of work or labor in some contexts, in others he takes as his text the Biblical injunction of neither spinning nor toiling. In "Non-Acting," an essay written in 1893 expressly to contradict a speech made by Emile Zola to an association of young people and propounding work as the only answer to the pangs, disasters, and sorrows of life, Tolstoy denounced work. In this essay he asserted that in the modern world labor was usually in the services of something pernicious and that it was generally used or pursued because, like a drug, it stopped thought and stifled conscience.

Two forces, said Tolstoy, rule mankind: the force of routine, of keeping on the same path, and the force of reason and love drawing men to the light, but work was all in the services of routine. Noting that the cruelest of men, Nero or Peter the Great, were always *busy* about something, Tolstoy quoted Lao Tsze and the Tao:

> If men would, as he says, but practice non-acting *they would be relieved not merely from their personal calamities but also those inherent in all forms of government.* ("Non-Acting," I, Maude trans.)

As an admirer of the *Pensées*, he was certainly aware of Pascal's dictum that a great part of the unhappiness of men arises from the fact that they cannot stay quietly in their own chambers. This conception lies at the root of Tolstoy's doctrine of passive resistance and non-violence. For the power of the state rests ultimately in the physical power—the very hands and feet—of its myrmidons. Tolstoy meant this quite literally, and in the concluding autobiographical outburst (chap. 12) of *The Kingdom of God Is Within You*, after describing the flogging of peasants by a contingent of soldiers, he concludes:

> *All power therefore depends on those who with their own hands, execute the deeds of violence—that is, on the soldiers and police,* . . . (Maude trans., chap. XII, sec. 2)

But the ultimate paradox of the physical view of history is that despite the fact that everything finally depends on the human body and despite the simplicity of the doctrine of physical passivity, the last thing that men can do is to cease what they are doing. For they are bound, body and soul, to the wheel of Necessity right from the beginning. And the bondage, while initiated by the circumstances of birth (". . . that elemental force against which man is powerless—" VIII, I) and thus beginning with the local and the idiosyncratic, successively broadens out as the individual life goes on. It comes under the aegis of the state and finally under the dominion of history itself. At each stage each individual is thrust into an ongoing mechanism, each time entering into a web of events over which he has no control and can only react in a stimulus-response fashion.

Moreover, in this devolutionary process the individual becomes successively less autonomous until under the historical perspective he is an ant. And his puniness and slavery are underlined by the spatial and logical grandeur of the historical scene itself, which is continental or larger in space, and endless in its cause-and-effect sequence. Though *War and Peace* is thus indubitably about nations and their conflicts, the high historical view is supra-national, with Tolstoy viewing the polyglot army of Napoleon generically as the men of the West who in the first part of the nineteenth century burst into eastern Europe, rebounded, and flowed back into the west pursued by the counter-surging men of the East. And in the Second Epilogue he minimizes even this mighty drama as being, after all, only a European affair, for Europe, after all, is but a small corner of the world. Moreover, in *War and Peace* itself the grandiosity of events is often undercut by the metaphors and similes that are used to analogize them. There are, for example, two elaborate similes describing Moscow near the end of the book: the captured and deserted Moscow as a dying bee-hive (XI, XX), and the freed, resurgent Moscow as a ruined ant-hill being rebuilt by the indefatigable energy of its inhabitants (XV, XIV).

If the full spatial panorama reduces the size and importance of the events of 1812, the full temporal dimension reduces them still further by showing them to be an infinitesimal part of an almost incomprehensibly vast chain of circumstances. For if history is continuous motion, then no event can be said to have a definable beginning in time. Thus everything and everybody is on the moving-belt of the world, and everybody and everything is connected by an infinity of causes to what had preceded them in the historical sequence and thus an infinite causal regress opens out to the rear.

In the vertical dimension then of history in *War and Peace,* history is movement and force caused by the moving and acting bodies of men, governed by cause-and-effect or by action and counter action, and unaffected by temporal evolution. Any great event or collision, such as the War of 1812, is the force engendered by the sum of all the exertions of all the participants in it, but the precise way in which all these actions conjoin to produce the results that they do is a mystery because of its complexity. Equally mysterious is the precise manner in which such a multifarious event takes its place in, and fits into, the great historical chain of causation that had preceded and led up to it. Anyway one looks at it, individual man is a puny creature and mankind itself, for all its power and force, can only make things happen within the framework which the past has bequeathed.

It is important to stress the magnitude of this conception: not a sparrow falls but that, not a Deity, an historical necessity is at work. The necessity is not only contemporary and immediate; it is also total and cosmic, emanating from the depths of time and reaching out to enmesh all of human history, past, present, and to be. In its impersonality it is reminiscent of Oriental cosmologies wherein eons of time slowly revolve through their preordained patterns and individual volition is unthinkable and a universal fatalism obliterates human character. It was just this aspect of Tolstoy's philosophy of history that Lenin, who so much admired him as a writer, dismissed and stigmatized as Oriental fatalism:

> It is precisely the ideology of the Oriental order, the Asian order, that is the real historical content of Tolstoyism. Hence, asceticism, non-violent resistance to evil, that deep note of pessimism, and the conviction that 'everything is nothing, all that is material is nothing' ('On the Meaning of Life'), and belief in 'Spirit,' 'the beginning of everything,' in relation to which man is merely a 'laborer,' 'appointed for the work of saving his soul,' and so forth.[1]

Yet Tolstoy does not assert this historical fatalism in religious or mystical terms, whatever may have been its correlative in his ethical outlook. It is put with great lucidity and some force as a simple affair of logic: every effect has an antecedent cause.

There is a certain grandeur to such a conception, and a certain fascination as well.

[1] V. I. Lenin, *Tolstoy and His Time* (New York, 1952), pp. 27–28.

It constitutes one of the most powerful and comprehensive statements of the idea of human un-freedom. Of all the forms of slavery the slavery to history is the most seductive and to one like Tolstoy, who all his life worried about the enigmas of fate and free will, it was practically irresistible. Merely to think of it, in all its unanswerable logic, is to succumb. In the words of Nicholas Berdyaev:

> The greatest of all forms of the seduction and slavery of man is connected with history. The solidity of history and the apparent magnificence of the processes which go on in history impose upon man and overawe him to an unusual degree. He is crushed by history and consents to be a tool for the accomplishment of history, to be made use of by the artfulness of reason.

Berdyaev continues:

> ... in actual fact history takes no notice of personality, of its individual irrepeatability, its uniqueness and irreplaceability. It is interested in the 'common' even at such times as it turns its attention to the individual. History is made for the average man and the masses but for history the average man is an abstract unit and not a concrete being.[2]

Thus just what Tolstoy most prized, the unique configuration of a single personality, disappears into the faceless anonymity of mass-history.

At the same time it is true that given his premises, his conclusions are inescapable. History as a chain of actions is in fact a chain, and it is salutary to recognize this un-freedom, especially in the context of nineteenth-century Europe which, among the educated classes anyway, tended to think of itself as having escaped the thralldom of the past. Thus it is also bracing and stimulating to shred and shed an illusion—and Tolstoy, among others, may be said to have helped to do for the study of history, what Marx, on his critical-historical side, did for the history of society, Darwin for biology, and Freud for psychology, although it should be added that Tolstoy and Freud were the real pessimists. Like each of the other three, he represented that peculiarly nineteenth-century phenomenon of a combination of astringent honesty, moral fearlessness, large aims, and intellectual precision, all lodged in a man who, though a supreme individualist and a humanist, is yet intent upon uncovering and pointing out the mass character of human experience, the mass bondage of the human race, and the fallacy of the illusions that man has devised to mask the abjectness of his condition—slave alike to his body, to his unconscious, to his environment, and to his history. Each locates a prime center of power in the human drama lying outside the conscious wills and intelligences of men. Taking nineteenth-century European man in the pitch of his pride and, supposedly, at the frontier of the whole historical process, they strip him of his specious present, place him back in an almost endless historical process, and demonstrate his essential sameness, and his un-freedom, in all ages. As sermons in the illusions of human pride, the work of these men constitutes a kind of supreme

---

[2] Nicholas Berdyaev, *Slavery and Freedom* (New York, 1944), p. 255.

assertion of the human intelligence, no matter what the cost to human pride. Taken in this sense *War and Peace* is a sermon on the historical pride of European man.

The vertical dimension, however, is not the only historical perspective in the novel. Several different kinds of horizontal impulses and forces are at work, cutting across and complicating the vertical chain. The sense of an outside power or force moving men is just as pervasive, but it does not seem to emanate from the depths of time and in its workings there can be seen the power of the irrational, the local, the contingent, and even the moral. Moreover, these powers are not explicitly connected to the vertical chain, although Tolstoy has gone to some lengths in his discussion of history to prove that nothing in history can exist in isolation: everything is connected to everything else. There would seem to be an inconsistency here, but, in actual fact, there is not, if the totality of Tolstoy's historical scale is considered.

In the first place there is a kind of break between the abstract discussions of history in which the vertical succession of cause-and-effect is insisted on, and the dramatic parts of the novel wherein the actual workings of history or historical forces are often described or referred to in a more limited or circumscribed fashion, and where these workings and forces are either explicitly characterized as—or indirectly intimated to be—something other than the result of the sum total of the human actions that had preceded them. Thus, for example, the battle of what Tolstoy called "Schön Graben" is described, during its continuance, as having a problematical conclusion. Though the battle took place in 1805, Tolstoy set his perspective at the level of a contemporary eyewitness and made the outcome depend on the question of which side had the more powerful morale. Further, he located the precise moment in the struggle when a delicate poise between the respective morales of the two opposing armies was disturbed in the disfavor of the army, the Russian, that was to lose: "That moment of moral hesitation which decided the fate of battles was evidently culminating in panic" (bk. II, chap. XX). In other words the outcome had not been decided in advance by destiny, though a retrospective historical glance would make it appear to be so, but was an affair of the moment. And the infinity of vertically organized causes that led to this effect, the battle of Schön Graben, did not inevitably lead to a victory by one side or the other but to a seesaw condition at the climax of the battle and to a precise moment in time when one flew up and the other plunged down and victory was awarded to the staunchest of the contenders. All battles seen close-up are affairs of freedom:

*A countless number of free forces (for nowhere is man freer than during a battle, where it is a question of life and death) influence the course taken by the fight, and that course never can be known in advance and never coincides with the direction of any one force. (XIII, VII)*

Here then Tolstoy suspended what he himself had denominated the "law of retrospectiveness," whereby all events of the past are seen as a preparation for the present.

Thus the historical point of view in *War and Peace* is not a constant but a variable, and a kind of perspectivism is woven into the narrative. The gradations of this perspectivism cannot be delineated exactly, but for purposes of discussion three different vantage points can be described: first, how an event would look from an Archimedean vantage point (the vertical chain); second, how an event would look in retrospect to an informed and intelligent observer such as an historian; and third, how an event looks to a participant or to a novelist attempting to describe the feelings of a participant. It should be added that the first vantage point is impossible of complete attainment; the second, while possible, is grievously limited; and the third is purely fictitious or imaginary.

From the second perspective, that of the historian, history is a collocation of powerful forces moving men, and these forces sometimes have an inception that can be located in space and time. Further, their make-up can be described or guessed at. Unlike the great vertical chain of cause-and-effect, the forces are often, although not always, pictured in horizontal terms, and they are not ruled by logic. Some are fundamental irrationalities of human life, hypostasized as almost palpable forces which like whirlwinds sweep across landscape and disappear into the silence of history; others erupt from below among masses of men. Still others are single instances of an arbitrary stroke of fate, sometimes seen as chance, a factor in history which is expressly ruled out of the operations of the vertical chain, but which works with great profusion in the novel itself. In the historical or fictional or novelistic renderings of the workings of force or chance or fate, the perspective is non-Archimedean; history is what it is as seen by an intelligent observer.

The great horizontal image and metaphor is of contemporary Europe as a vast sea, never quiet in its totality but during times of peace seething with activity only in its depths and with a placid surface; while in times of war its surface is galvanized and swept by torrents and gales. Thus the first Epilogue, in the year 1820, opens with this metaphor, for which the whole of the book with its sense of great space and turbulent, yet rhythmical, movement underlines and prepares:

> *The sea of history was not driven spasmodically from shore to shore as previously. It was seething in its depths.*

Historic figures were no longer borne by the waves from coast to coast. Rather each revolved on his own point in small eddies. But the human energy and thus the collective force of mankind had neither ceased nor slackened; it was temporarily deflected into diplomatic and other channels, the inference being that it will soon break out again to the surface and galvanize the sea or ocean of Europe once more. The First Epilogue looks forward to the next convulsion, in Russia itself, the rebellion of the nobles in December of 1825. At the very end, young Prince Andrew, like his father before him, is looking forward to a critical, fluid, tumultuous moment when history will present him with the Toulon denied his father. The unspoken assumption in the horizontal-sea metaphor is that history works by pulsation, by wave and counter-wave, and that in these tidal movements it toys with men, none more than in the case of the greatest, tossing them from wave to wave and from shore to shore in its state of frenzy and chaining them to a still, small point, a backwater, in times of surface quiescence. In this metaphor history is not an affair of logic, as is the case in the vertical view, but an affair of rhythm, more akin to breathing. In such a perspective history and individual human lives are analogues, the macrocosm and the microcosm respectively. The pulsation or rhythmical movement of the life of the characters often runs parallel to the larger rhythms of history itself: thus as the Battle of Borodino is a mighty disturbance and turning point of history, it also serves the same function for the principal characters, it being a moral turning point for the two chief male characters, Pierre and Prince Andrew. In terms of the plot, the mortal wounding of Andrew and the renewal of Pierre make possible the marriages at the end of the novel and the domestic ménage described in the First Epilogue. Indeed this pulsation, this recurrent throb of history, has a formal analogue in the lives of the characters who expand and contract; wax and wane and wax; soar to unity and belief and sink to disorderliness and cynicism, only to rise again; go back and forth; change from place to place; as if the huge pulsations of history had imposed their rhythmical order on the private lives of single individuals.

This habit of analogizing single lives and the rhythms of history was endemic, and often unconscious, in Tolstoy's world. For example, the fundamental rhythm in the life of many of his male protagonists is a secular equivalent to the basic, human "V-shaped" myth of a Golden Age—a Fall—and a Promise of Redemption. This kind of movement is the archetype in both *Boyhood, Childhood, and Youth,* his first big work, and in *Resurrection,* his last, besides providing the outlines for the life of Pierre Bezukhov in *War and Peace.* Now, the same archetype appears as history in *What Is Art?,* which unlike *War and Peace* is a progressivist document. For it asserts that history is intelligible and evolutionary and that knowledge about it is cumulative and transmissable, from one generation to another. Furthermore, just as in Hegel, human consciousness expands with the passage of time. But history, like man, is also sinful and does not move in an unbroken line from lucidity to lucidity. The Catholic Church or the upper classes of Europe represent patent retrogressive forces. They can and do invent and sustain successfully for centuries historical perversions, which is what the upper classes have done with their kind of art, which in turn has become the "Art" of Western man. It is such distortions as these that warp the course of progress and hold back Western man from the millenarian destiny, with all men become brothers, that his natural desires and gifts destine him for. Briefly, *What Is Art?* holds that there was once a Golden Age or innocent childhood for art, the Bible story of Joseph being a classic example. The Fall occurred in the Renaissance. As the adolescent male individual is corrupted by lust, pride, and cynicism, so too when Art fell in the Renaissance, it began to cater to three allied sins: pride, weariness with life, and sexual desire. But the hour—Tolstoy labored over *What Is Art?* for fifteen years—of Redemption may be at hand.

As Pierre and the protagonist of *Resurrection* have finally a glimpse of the Promised Land, so at the end of *What Is Art?* Tolstoy professes to see manifestations all over Europe of the coming redemption of art. Modern art, the prostitute, or the ill-conceived spawn of the Renaissance, will disappear and a great, simple, unadorned, elemental, moral, and democratic art will take its place and resume its real function as the chief promoter of the brotherhood of man. Thus would Western history finally trace out the basic myth of *Paradise Lost* and *Paradise Regained* that so many of Tolstoy's heroes act out in their private lives, and thus the basic pulsation of human life, micro- or macro-cosm, was surge and counter-surge between beatitude and damnation, although, of course, in *War and Peace* this pattern applies only to life, not to history.

The metaphor of the sea, with its notion of surface and depths, and its continually seething depths, suggests of course the human unconscious with the almost irresistible inference that the real power in history emanates from the collective Id of mankind. And this is precisely the notion that Tolstoy invokes in his description of other forces at work in his world. There is, for example, what might be called the eruption from below, a feeling or purpose of some kind, that gets quickly transmitted through a large group of men almost sub-verbally and incites or inflames them to mass action of some kind. At times it is merely the irrationality of a mob, such as the one that murders a man, probably innocent, just before the French enter Moscow, and who are excited, even exalted, by the fire of Moscow. Again, it can be the "spirit of the troops," that mysterious manifestation of morale, or lack of it, in an army that spreads like wildfire among a large group of men and seems to be transmitted by telepathy:

> How such a consciousness is communicated is very difficult to define, but it certainly is communicated very surely, and flows rapidly, imperceptibly, and irrepressibly, as water does in a creek. (III, XIV)

Or it can be mass feeling of inhumanity that can course through a group of soldiers. When orders are given to the French soldiers to evacuate Moscow, it is as if some brutal power had seized on all these men and turned them into cold beasts:

> ... that mysterious, callous force which compelled people against their will to kill their fellow-men—that force the effect of which [Pierre] had witnessed during the execution.

With the Russian peasantry it is as if there were in fact some kind of collective unconscious, below the verbal, even below history itself, in whose depths are generated powerful, mysterious, and irresistible forces, which taking the form of mass-movements, set in motion an entire community in the same way, though on a smaller scale, as the French Revolution and the Napoleonic wars set in motion the sea of Europe. The uprising of the peasants at Bugocharovo described in Book X of *War and Peace* is just such an occurrence, and is cited by Tolstoy as a manifestation of

> *. . . the mysterious undercurrents in the life of the Russian people, the causes and meaning of which are so baffling to contemporaries, . . .* (X, IX)

Finally, among the dispositions of history in *War and Peace*, there is what might be called the dispensation from above, some order or coherence or tendency or set of laws promulgated and upheld by a Deity. As history has its laws, although we do not know what they are, so God or Providence has His laws as well, not incomprehensible, but difficult to ascertain and only to be grasped or seen or intuited by a few superior individuals who are able to apprehend them and be guided by them. Their reward for this perspicuity is the contempt of their fellow men:

> *Such is the fate, not of great men* (grands hommes) *whom the Russian mind does not acknowledge, but of those rare and always solitary individuals who discerning the will of Providence submit their personal will to it. The hatred and contempt of the crowd punishes such men for discerning the higher laws.* (XV, V)

"The will of Providence" is no less than the sum of human wisdom, as described and paraphrased by Isaiah Berlin in *The Hedgehog and the Fox*. Here is the "true" nature of things, of which only Kutuzov and Karatev, of the major characters in the novel, are aware although Pierre comes close to it near the end of the novel. The assumption here is that God is—using Einstein's phrase—subtle but not malevolent, and that there is some sense (not a logic) to the grand course of human affairs in the respect that a single, superior individual can learn to live equably in the present and can hazard a very good guess as to what is going to happen in the future. In short, it is possible, for a very few people, to be at home in the universe and to go with the tide of history, while the bulk of mankind are either unknowingly or indifferently borne along or unwittingly try to swim against the historical tide. The concept of the exceptional person is analogous to Hegel's, of the Virtuous Consciousness, the ethical person, the transcender, who is not subordinate to history or destiny but is absolute and divine in himself. Further, according to Hegel also, it *was* possible not to be a victim of history, as most people were, but to stand outside of it, like a Wordsworthian or a Tolstoyan peasant (I take Walter Kaufmann's translation of a passage from *Die Vernunst in der Geschichte*):

> *The religiosity, the* Sittlichkeit *of a limited life of a shepherd, a peasant—in its concentrated inwardness and its limitation to a few and wholly simple conditions of life has infinite value, and the same value as the religiosity and* Sittlichkeit *of well-developed knowledge and an existence rich in the scope of relations and actions. This internal center, this simple region of the right of subjective freedom, the hearth of willing, deciding, doing, the abstract content of conscience, that in which guilt and value of the individual, his eternal judgment, is enclosed, remains untouched and outside the loud noise of world history—outside not only external and temporal changes but even those which are involved in the absolute necessity of the concept of freedom.*

This is no less than a description of Tolstoy's *beau ideal*, Platon Karataev. No one escapes history, and Karataev is killed by an historic event, the French retreat. But he had lived, in so far as he could, outside of history and its loud noise, and is thus, in the perspective of the novel as a whole, the polar opposite of Napoleon who is not only history itself but history's greatest victim as well. Historically considered, what Karataev represents is Tolstoy's version of the ancient idea of salvation from below, which, as Friedrich Heer shows in *The Intellectual History of Europe*, erupted all over Europe in the nineteenth century.

Having said all this we have still not arrived at a final meaning of history in Tolstoy's world, for in the last analysis—or at the outermost reaches of human thought—history remains a mystery. And it is a mystery precisely because the instrument, human reason, by which it is apprehended is equivocal in its operations. Reason finally fails in its task of comprehending history for two reasons: first, because it cannot assimilate an infinity of facts; and, second, because it is limited in what it can see, being restricted to perceiving only the necessities of history and never the freedom. Thus the rational mind is limited in some areas and blind in others. As for its limitations: if an action or event in history is the result of the force exerted by *all* its participants, then it is manifestly impossible for one human mind to grasp, much less sort out, classify, and reach conclusions about, such a multiplicity of factors (although Tolstoy ventures the opinion—foreseeing perhaps, the advent of computers—that someday the human mind will have devised ways of dealing more efficiently with such phenomena). A second—but correlative—limitation arises from the fact that history is absolute motion, making it so that no event has any marked-off or definable beginning—since all events are predetermined from eternity—and thus giving the mind no way of entering into the endless succession of causes-and-effects so as to establish just where the specific causes for an event, such as the War of 1812, could be justly considered to have had their inception. A third correlative resides in the fact that while the human mind is finite, space, time, and causality, the ultimate constituents of all historical actions or events, are infinite. And the two categories, the finite and the infinite, cannot touch. The gap between the two constitutes the primary dilemma of man, and in a religious document, like *A Confession*, it is asserted as the basic dilemma of religious belief as well: "What am I?—A part of the infinite. In those few words lies the whole problem" (*A Confession*, VIII, Maude trans.). All of man's intellectual activities split on this primary dilemma and must finally turn back on themselves or eventuate in a circle:

> In the last analysis we reach the circle of infinity—that final limit to which in every domain of thought man's reason arrives if it is not playing with the subject. Electricity produces heat, heat produces electricity. Atoms attract each other and atoms repel one another. (Second Epilogue, chap. VII)

But the real mystery to history poses a problem that is totally obscure to the rational mind. To see the force of this part of the argument, one must first accept one of Tolstoy's basic distinctions, that between form and content:

> Among the innumerable categories applicable to the phenomena of human life one may discriminate between those in which substance prevails and those in which form prevails. (X, VI)

In its context Tolstoy asserts the above distinction in order to make an invidious contrast between the social world of St. Petersburg (the world of form) and the social world of Moscow (the world of content), but it applies to the study of history as well. In the Second Epilogue Tolstoy makes an analogous distinction. There are, he says, two sources of cognition: reason and consciousness; by reason we observe ourselves; by consciousness we know ourselves; thus reason gives expression to the laws of necessity, while consciousness gives expression to the reality of free will.

> Freedom is the thing examined. Inevitability is what examines. Freedom is the content. Inevitability is the form.
> Only by separating the two sources of cognition, related to one another as form to content, do we get the mutually exclusive and separately incomprehensible conceptions of freedom and inevitability.
> Only by uniting them do we get a clear conception of man's life.
> Apart from these two concepts which in their union mutually define one another as form and content, no conception of life is possible.
> All that we know of the life of man is merely a certain relation of freedom to inevitability, that is, consciousness to the laws of reason. (Second Epilogue, chap. X)

There is thus an element of freedom in human history, but we do not know what it is. What we know we call the laws of necessity or inevitability; what we do not know we call free will.

Reason then is paradoxical: it begins its operations as a liberator and light-bringer: it destroys superstitions, saps unjust authority, makes religion tenable, tells us what is what and what goes with what and what does not. Reason says that man is naturally what Rousseau said he was: happy and free; it is his institutions that are corrupt and corrupting. Tolstoy's two watch-words were the great watch-words of the great century, the eighteenth: Reason and Nature. He was, said Isaiah Berlin:

> . . . a martyr and a hero—perhaps the most richly gifted of them all—in the tradition of European enlightenment.[3]

Yet reason is equivocal and, like the letter of the law, it killeth "life": "If we admit that human life can be ruled by reason, the possibility of life is destroyed" (First Epilogue, chap. I). Applied to history, reason, like a creeping paralysis, successively obscured the possibilities of the exercise of human freedom in the past and

---

[3] "Tolstoy and Enlightenment," *Encounter*, XVI (February, 1961), 40.

left mankind a victim of necessitarianism. Moreover, as knowledge of the past accumulated and as the past itself receded, the area left open for the supposed exercise of autonomy by single men or aggregates of men successively narrowed—specifically in relation to three factors: first, to time, that is, the further back in history an event, the more the sense of inevitability about it; second, to context, that is, the more that is known about the aggregate of circumstances enclosing a past event, the less does it appear that any single individual involved in it had any autonomy; and, third, to the web of antecedent causes, that is, once the event is considered in the light of the vertical chain of historical cause-and-effect, free will or human freedom entirely disappears. Thus reason, the tyrant, possesses all we know of history.

Reason then was really triply equivocal when applied to human history, past, present, and to-be. As regards the past, it was helpless in the face of the multiplicity of factors with which it must deal. At the same time it was overpowering, in so far as it could deal with these factors, in its claims for human un-freedom. However, for the present and the future it still remained the herald of freedom and the dissolver of the tyrannies and irrationalities of human life. In *A Confession* Tolstoy said, "I was now ready to accept any faith if only it did not demand of me a direct denial of reason" (X, Maude trans.). Reason thus was simultaneously the blessing and the bane of human existence. If, on the one hand, it delivered man from present tyrannies and advanced him into a freer future, at the same time it constructed out of the past a vast and universal prison house, and history itself became the jailor of mankind.

The only freedom then for man lies in his own single, individual consciousness, although this is a mystery as well. All his life Tolstoy marveled at, and worshipped at, the shrine of the Ego, at the miracle of personality, of "I-ness." In his eighty-first year in his diary, he wrote,

> I remember very vividly that I am conscious of myself in exactly the same way now, at eighty-one, as I was conscious of myself, my "I" at five or six years of age.[4]

Again:

> ... And consciousness is everything. (This is good.)[5]

So in some sense a single ego could cancel or revoke that miasmic mass of the past that weighed or loomed, in Marx's phrase, like an alp or a succubus in the brain of the living. And there is another whole side to Tolstoy's world that I have barely touched on here. For he always insisted that despite the tyranny of history there was such a thing as private life, which he often called "real life," and that this world had its freedoms. This two-sidedness of Tolstoy's world comes down in some senses to a discrepancy between an orientation in space and an orientation in time: in a rough way space is the realm of human felicity, that is, individual freedom and

[4] *Last Diaries*, trans. Lydia Weston-Kesich (New York, 1960), p. 43.

[5] *Ibid.*, p. 88.

timelessness; whereas time is the province of mass-man and of the slavery of history. At one pole is a single instant of individual experience or awareness or consciousness; at the other is the totality of events of which human history is composed. The unique instant is immanent and transcendent; the totality of events is configurational and phenomenal. The one is the realm of human freedom and is apprehended by human consciousness; the other is the domain of human slavery and is apprehended by human reason. The one embodies the content of human life; the other constitutes its form. The one observes the world; the other observes the observer. All this, however, is another story, best told by Tolstoy in his descriptions of the private lives of his vast gallery of fictional characters.

What are we to make of Tolstoy? A man is often best defined by what he does not like. Tolstoy disliked foreigners generally and, on an international basis, Russians included, he detested "great men," generals, statesmen, rulers, doctors, professors, writers, historians, the ruling, professional, and middle classes, and cities. With all this in his favor, he cannot then be said to have been a wholly bad man. More subtly, a man is defined by what he worries about, and Tolstoy all his life worried at four problems: the problem of God; the problem of sex; the problem of death; and the problem of history, which for him came down to the enigma of fate and free will. He learned to live with God (although uneasily, like two bears in the same den, said Gorky); his powerful sexual impulse, in many ways the bane of his life, finally left him in his extreme old age; he must finally at the last, at the railroad station at Astopovo, have come to terms with death, like another mad old man, King Lear, who was the character in literature he most detested—*and* most resembled—and, like Lear, learned, in Freud's splendid phrase, to bow to that eternal wisdom which bids the old man to renounce love, choose death and make friends with the necessity of dying. But we may imagine his shade in eternity forever pondering the enigmas of human freedom.

# The Knowable Community in George Eliot's Novels

RAYMOND WILLIAMS

There is always change in the village,[1] but we can only understand its bearings on literature if we first understand what is happening to the literature itself. Just as the difference between Jonson and Crabbe is not the historical arrival of the "poor laborious natives" but a change in literary bearings which allows them suddenly to be seen, so the difference between Jane Austen and George Eliot and Hardy is not the sudden disintegration of a settled, traditional order but a change in literary bearings which brings into focus a persistent rural disturbance hitherto unrepresented in fiction. Thus we can say that the traditional novel, by which is meant very often the traditional novel of country and provincial life, depends essentially on a knowable community. This is a point to consider with Dickens, who, responding to the scale and complication of the city, had to remake the novel in a quite different direction. But a real continuity from Jane Austen to George Eliot, and then on to Thomas Hardy, can focus our attention on the problem of the knowable community within country life.

I

It is so often taken for granted that a country community, most typically a village, is an epitome of direct relationships: of face-to-face contacts within which the novelist can find the substance of a fiction of personal relationships. Certainly this aspect of its difference from the city and the suburb is important, but a knowable community, within country life, is still a matter of consciousness as well as evident fact. Indeed it is in just this problem of knowing a community—of finding a standpoint from which community can be known—that the essential history and development of this kind of novel has to be seen.

Take simply, to start with, the knowable community of Jane Austen. It is outstandingly face-to-face; its crises, physically and spiritually, are in just these terms: a look, a gesture, a stare, a confrontation; and behind these, all the time, the novelist is watching, observing, physically recording and reflecting. That is the whole stance—the grammar of her morality. Yet while it is a community wholly known, within the essential terms of the novel, it is as an actual community very precisely selective. Neighbors in Jane Austen are not the people actually living nearby; they are the people living a little less nearby who, in social recognition, can be visited.

---

[1] This essay will appear in slightly different form in Mr. Williams' forthcoming book, *The Country and the City*.

What she sees across the land is a network of propertied houses and families, and through the holes of this tightly drawn mesh most actual people are simply not seen. To be face-to-face in this world is already to belong to a class. No other community, in physical presence or in social reality, is by any means knowable. And it is not only most of the people who have disappeared, in a stylized convention as precise as Ben Jonson's. It is also most of the country, which becomes real only as it relates to the houses which are the real nodes; for the rest, the country is weather or a place for a walk.

It is proper to trace the continuity of moral analysis from Jane Austen to George Eliot, but we can do this intelligently only if we recognize what else is happening in this literary development: a recognition of other kinds of people, other kinds of country, other kinds of action on which a moral emphasis must be brought to bear.

Thus *Adam Bede* is set by George Eliot in Jane Austen's period: at the turn of the eighteenth into the nineteenth century. What she sees is of course very different: not primarily because the country has changed, but because she has available to her a different social tradition.

> *The germ of* Adam Bede *was an anecdote told me by my Methodist Aunt Samuel . . . an anecdote from her own experience. . . . I afterwards began to think of blending this and some other recollections of my aunt in one story, with some points in my father's early life and character.*

Thus the propertied house is still there, in the possession of the Donnithornes. But they are now seen at work on their income, dealing with their tenants:

> *"What a fine old kitchen this is!" said Mr Donnithorne, looking round admiringly. He always spoke in the same deliberate, well-chiselled, polite way, whether his words were sugary or venomous. "And you keep it so exquisitely clean, Mrs Poyser. I like these premises, do you know, beyond any on the estate."*

We have encountered this "deliberate, well-chiselled, polite" way of speaking before, but it is not now among relative equals, just as the old Squire's way of looking is not now simply an aspect of character but of character in a precise and dominating social relationship. As Mrs. Poyser says, it seems "as if you was an insect, and he was going to dab his finger-nail on you."

The proposition that is put, through the politeness, is in fact a reorganization of the tenancy, for the estate's convenience, which will take away the Poyser's corn land; it is accompanied by a threat that the proposed new neighbor, "who is a man of some capital, would be glad to take both the farms, as they could be worked so well together. But I don't want to part with an old tenant like you."

It is not a particularly dramatic event, but it is a crucial admission of everyday experience which had been there all the time, and which is now seen from an altered point of view. The politeness of improvement is then necessarily counterpointed by the crude facts of economic power, and a different moral emphasis has become inevitable. This is then extended. The young squire is anxious to improve the estate—as the tenants saw it, "there was to be a millennial abundance of new gates, allowances of lime, and returns of ten per cent"—and he takes up Adam Bede as the manager of his woods. But in what is essentially the same spirit he takes up Hetty Sorrel as his girl and succeeds in ruining her. A way of using people for convenience is an aspect of personal character—this emphasis is not relaxed—but is also an aspect of particular social and economic relationships. And then, as George Eliot observes ironically:

> It would be ridiculous to be prying and analytic in such cases, as if one was inquiring into the character of a confidential clerk. We use round, general, gentlemanly epithets about a young man of birth and fortune.

Jane Austen, precisely, had been prying and analytic, but into a limited group of people in their relations with each other. The analysis is now brought to bear without the class limitation; the social and economic relationships, necessarily, are seen as elements, often determining elements, of conduct.

It is more important to stress this aspect of George Eliot's development of the novel than her inclusion of new social experience in a documentary sense. Certainly it is good to see the farmers and the craftsmen, and almost the laborers, as people present in the action in their own right. But there are difficulties here of a significant kind. It is often said about the Poysers in *Adam Bede*, as about the Gleggs and the Dodsons in *The Mill on the Floss*, that they are marvellously (or warmly, richly, charmingly) done. But what this points to is a recurring problem in the social consciousness of the writer. George Eliot's connections with the farmers and craftsmen—her connections as Mary Ann Evans—can be heard again and again in their language.

Characteristically, she presents them mainly through speech. But while they are present audibly as a community, they have only to emerge in significant action to change in quality. What Adam or Dinah or Hetty say, when they are acting as individuals, is not particularly convincing. Into a novel still predicated on the analysis of individual conduct, the farmers and craftsmen can be included as "country people" but much less significantly as the active bearers of personal experience. When Adam and Dinah and Hetty talk in what is supposed to be personal crisis—or later, in a more glaring case, when Felix Holt talks—we are shifted to the level of generalized attitudes or of declamation. Another way of putting this would be to say that though George Eliot restores the real inhabitants of rural England to their places in what had been a socially selective landscape, she does not get much further than restoring them *as a landscape*. They begin to talk, as it were collectively, as what middle-class critics still foolishly call a kind of chorus, a "ballad-element." But as themselves they are still only socially present, and can emerge into a higher consciousness only through externally formulated attitudes and ideas.

I would not make this point bitterly, for the difficulty is acute. It is a contradiction in the form of the novel, as George Eliot received and developed it, that the moral emphasis on conduct—and therefore the technical strategy of unified narrative and analytic tones—must be at odds with any society—the "knowable community" of the novel—in which moral bearings have been extended to substantial and conflicting social relationships. One would not willingly lose the Poysers, the Gleggs, and the Dodsons, but it is significant that we can talk of them in this way in the plural, while the emotional direction of the novel is towards separated individuals. A knowable community can be, as in Jane Austen, socially selected; what it then lacks in full social reference it gains in an available unity of language in all its main uses. But we have only to read a George Eliot novel to see the difficulty of the coexistence, within one form, of an analytically conscious observer of conduct with a developed analytic vocabulary, and of people represented as living and speaking in mainly customary ways; for it is not the precision of detailed observation but the inclusive, socially appealing, loose and repetitive manner that predominates. There is a new kind of break in the texture of the novel, an evident failure of continuity between the necessary language of the novelist and the recorded language of many of the characters.

This is not, it must be emphasized, a problem of fact. The consciousness of actual farmers and tradesmen was as strong and developed as that of the established and maneuvering proprietors of Jane Austen's world; these people also are, and are shown as, inclusive, socially appealing, loose and repetitive; it is a common way of talking at any time. But whereas the idiom of the novelist, in Jane Austen, is connected with the idiom of her characters, in George Eliot a disconnection is the most evident fact and the novelist herself is most acutely aware of this. Speech and narrative and analysis, in Jane Austen, are connected by a *literary* convention: while the "deliberate, well-chiselled, polite" idiom is the product of a particular education and of the leisured, dominating relationships which the education served, it is also idealized, conventionalized; the novelist's powers of effect and precision are given without hesitation to her characters, because, for all the individual moral discrimination, they are felt to belong in the same world. At points of emotional crisis and confrontation this is especially so, and it is the novelist who articulates a personal experience, in a way for the sake of her group, and to give it an idiom. But then it is clear that George Eliot is not *with* anyone in quite this way: the very recognition of conflict, of the existence of classes, of divisions and contrasts of feeling and speaking, makes a unity of idiom impossible. George Eliot gives her own consciousness, often disguised as a personal dialect, to the characters with whom she does really feel; but the strain of the impersonation is usually evident—in Adam, Daniel, Maggie, or Felix Holt. For the rest she gives forth a kind of generalizing affection which can be extended to a generalizing sharpness (compare the Poysers with the Gleggs and Dodsons), but which cannot extend to a recognition of lives individually made from a common source; rather, as is said in a foolish mode of praise, the characters are "done." There is a point often reached in George Eliot when the novelist is conscious that the characters she is describing are "different" from her probable readers; she then offers to know them, and to make them "knowable," in a deeply inauthentic but socially successful way. Taking the tip from her own difficulty, she works the formula which has been so complacently powerful in English novel-writing: the "fine old," "dear old," quaint-talking, honest-living country characters. Observing very promptly the patronage of economic power—"deliberate, well-chiselled, polite" in the exercise of its crude controls—she still slips against her will into another patronage: since the people she respects in general (and of course for good reasons) she cannot respect enough in particular unless she gives them, by surrogate, parts of her own consciousness. There are then three idioms uneasily combined: the full analytic, often ironic power; the compromise between this and either disturbed, intense feeling or a position of moral strength; and the self-consciously generalizing, honest rustic background.

I can feel enough connection with the problems George Eliot was facing to believe I could make these points in her presence; that I am, in a sense, making them in her presence, since her particular intelligence, in a particular structure of feeling, persists and connects. Some years ago a British Council critic described George Eliot, Hardy, and Lawrence as "our three great autodidacts." It was one of the sharp revealing moments of English cultural history. For all three writers were actively interested in learning, and while they read a good deal for themselves, were not without formal education. Their fathers were a bailiff, a builder, and a miner. George Eliot was at school till sixteen and left only because her mother died. Hardy was at Dorchester High School till the same age and then completed his professional training as an architect. Lawrence went into the sixth form at Nottingham High School and after a gap went on to Nottingham University College. It is not only that by their contemporary standards these levels of formal education are high; it is also that they are higher, absolutely, than those of four out of five people in contemporary Britain.

So the flat patronage of "autodidact" can be related to only one fact: that none of the three was in the pattern of boarding school and Oxbridge which by the end of the century was being regarded not simply as a kind of education but as education itself: to have missed that circuit was to have missed being "educated" at all. In other words, a "standard" education was that received by one or two per cent of the population; all the rest were seen as "uneducated" or as "autodidacts"; seen also, of course, as either comically ignorant or, when they pretended to learning, as awkward, over-earnest, fanatical. The effects of this on the English imagination have been deep.

To many of us now, George Eliot, Hardy, and Lawrence are important because they connect directly with our own kind of upbringing and education. They belong to a cultural tradition much older and more central in England than the comparatively modern and deliberately exclusive circuit of what are called the public schools. And the point is that they continue to connect in this way into a later period in which some of us have gone to Oxford or Cambridge; to myself, for instance, who went to Cambridge and now teach there. For it is not the education, the developed intelligence, that is really in question; how many people, if it came to it, on the British Council or anywhere else, could survive a strictly intellectual comparison with George Eliot? It is a question of the relation between education—not the marks or degrees but the substance of a developed intelligence—and the actual lives of a continuing majority of our people: people who are not, by any formula, objects of record or study or concern, but who are specifically, literally, our own families. George Eliot is the first major novelist in whom this question is active. That is why we speak of her now with a connecting respect, and with a hardness— a sort of family plainness—that we have learned from our own and common experience.

II

The problem of the knowable community is thus, in a new way, a problem of language.

> In writing the history of unfashionable families, one is apt to fall into a tone of emphasis which is very far from being the tone of good society, where principles and beliefs are not only of an extremely moderate kind, but are always presupposed, no subjects being eligible but such as can be touched with a light and graceful irony. But then, good society has its claret and its velvet carpets, its dinner-engagements six weeks deep, its opera and its fairy ballrooms; rides off its ennui on thoroughbred horses, lounges at the club, has to keep clear of crinoline vortices, gets its science done by Faraday, and its religion by the superior clergy who are to be met in the best houses: how should it have time or need for belief and emphasis? But good society, floated on gossamer wings of light irony, is of very expensive production; requiring nothing less than a wide and arduous national life condensed in unfragrant, deafening factories, cramping itself in mines, sweating at furnaces, grinding, hammering, weaving under more or less oppression of carbonic acid—or else, spread over sheepwalks, and scattered in lonely houses and huts on the clayey or chalky corn-lands, where the rainy days look dreary. This wide national life is based entirely on emphasis—the emphasis of want, which urges it into all the activities necessary for the maintenance of good society and light irony. . . .

This striking paragraph from *The Mill on the Floss* is at once the problem and the response. The emphasis of want is undoubtedly central in George Eliot, and she sees work here as it is, without any sentimental contrast between the town and the village laborer. Emphasis, as a class feeling: this is what she acknowledges and accepts. But then it has to be noticed that she writes of it with her own brand of irony; she is defensive and self-conscious in the very demonstration of emphasis, so that in this structure of communication the very poor become the "unfashionable." Her central seriousness, and yet her acute consciousness of other and often congenial tones, is at once a paradox of language and of community. We find this again in two characteristic passages in *Adam Bede*:

> Paint us an angel, if you can, with a flowing violet robe, and a face paled by the celestial light; paint us yet oftener a Madonna, turning her mild face upward and opening her arms to welcome the divine glory; but do not impose on us any

*aesthetic rules which shall banish from the region of Art those old women scraping carrots with their work-worn hands, those heavy clowns taking holiday in a dingy pot-house, those rounded backs and stupid weather-beaten faces that have bent over the spade and done the rough work of the world—those homes with their tin pans, their brown pitchers, their rough curs, and their clusters of onions. In this world there are so many of these common coarse people, who have no picturesque sentimental wretchedness. It is so needful we should remember their existence....*

*I am not ashamed of commemorating old Kester: you and I are indebted to the hard hands of such men—hands that have long ago mingled with the soil they tilled so faithfully, thriftily making the best they could of the earth's fruits, and receiving the smallest share as their own wages.*

The declaration is again serious, but who is being spoken to in the anxious plea: "do not impose on us any aesthetic rules which shall banish . . . "? Who made the compact of "you and I," who must be shown as indebted? Who, finally, provoked the consciousness which requires the acknowledgment "I am not ashamed" and its associated language of "clowns" and "stupid weather-beaten faces," mixing as it so strangely does with the warmth of memory of the kitchens and with the truth about wages, the firm rejection of "picturesque sentimental wretchedness"?

In passages like these, and in the novels from which they are taken, George Eliot has gone further than Crabbe in *The Village*, and yet is more self-conscious, more uneasily placating and appealing to what seems a dominant image of a particular kind of reader. The knowable community is this common life which she is pleased to record with a necessary emphasis; but the known community is something else again—an uneasy contract, in language, with another interest and another sensibility.

What is true of language will be true of action. George Eliot extends the plots of her novels to include the farmers and the craftsmen, and also the disinherited. But just as she finds it difficult to individuate working people—falling back on a choral mode, a generalizing description, or an endowment with her own awkwardly translated consciousness—so she finds it difficult to conceive whole actions which spring from the substance of these lives and which can be worked through in relation to their interests. *Adam Bede* is the nearest to this, but it is overridden, finally, by an external interest: Hetty is a subject to that last moment on the road before she abandons her baby; but from that point she is an object of confession and conversion—of *attitudes* towards suffering. This is the essential difference from Hardy's *Tess of the D'Urbervilles*, which has the strength to keep to the subject to the end. Adam Bede and Dinah Morris—as one might say the dignity of self-respecting labor and religious enthusiasm—are more important in the end. Even the changed, repentant Arthur is more important than the girl whom the novelist abandons in a moral action more decisive than Hetty's own confused and desperate leaving of her child.

Yet still the history is active: the finding of continuity in the stress of learned feelings. *The Mill on the Floss* is the crisis of this determining history. It is an action from within the emphasis of want: in the guarded, unattractive rituals of survival of the small farmers, the Dodsons; in the rash independence of Tulliver, broken by the complications of law and economic pressure that he does not understand. In neither of these ways can any fullness of life be achieved, and there is no way through; only the weak, unwilled, temporary escape of the trip on the river: the fantasy of comfort. What then finally happens is a return to childhood and the river; a return, releasing feeling, to a transcending death. From the social history, which had been determining, the curve of feeling moves to the exposed and separated individual in whom the only action of value is located. And then what had been an active, desperate isolation becomes, in a new tone, a sad resignation.

In the subsequent works, for all their evidence of growing maturity and control, the actions become more external to the common world where the emphasis of want was decisive. As if overcome by the dead weight of the interests of a separated and propertied class, the formal plots of the later works are in a different world. *Felix Holt* is made to turn on the inheritance of an estate, and this is a crucial surrender to the typical interest which preoccupied the nineteenth-century middle-class imagination. Of course, Esther rejects the inheritance in the end; George Eliot's moral emphasis is too genuinely of an improving kind, of a self-making and self-made life, to permit Esther to accept the inheritance and find the fashionable way out. The corruption of that inheriting world, in which the price of security is intrigue, is powerfully shown in Mrs. Transome and Jermyn. But the emphasis of want is now specialized to Felix Holt: to the exposed, separated, potentially mobile individual. It is part of a crucial history in the development of the novel, in which the knowable community—the extended and emphatic world of an actual rural and then industrial England—comes to be known primarily as a problem of relationship: of how the separated individual, with a divided consciousness of belonging and not belonging, makes his own moral history.

This is the source of the disturbance, the unease, the divided construction of the later George Eliot novels (the exception, as always, is *Middlemarch*). We have only to compare George Eliot with her contemporary, Anthony Trollope, to see the significance of this disturbance. Trollope, in his Barsetshire novels, is at ease with schemes of inheritance, with the interaction of classes and interests, with the lucky discovery and the successful propertied marriage. The interest is all in how it happens, how it is done. An even, easy narrative tone, with a minimum of searching analysis, can achieve all that is asked of it: a recorded observation, an explanation of that level of social mechanics. To read *Doctor Thorne* beside *Felix Holt* is not only to find ease in Trollope where there is disturbance in George Eliot; to find a level of interest corresponding with the plot instead of struggling to break free of a dutifully sustained external complication; to find the conventional happy ending where property and happiness can coexist and be celebrated instead of an awkward, stubborn, unappeased resignation. It is also, quite evidently, to see the source of these differences in a real social history.

Near the beginning of *Doctor Thorne*, Trollope announces with characteristic confidence the state of his rural England:

> Its green pastures, its waving wheat, its deep and shady and—let us add—dirty lanes, its paths and stiles, its tawny-coloured, well-built rural churches, its avenues of beeches, and frequent Tudor mansions, its constant county hunt, its social graces, and the air of clanship which pervades it, has made it to its own inhabitants a favoured land of Goshen. It is purely agricultural: agricultural in its produce, agricultural in its poor, and agricultural in its pleasures.

Here the extent of realism is the mannered concession that the lanes are dirty. For the rest, what is seen is a social structure with pastoral trimmings. The agricultural poor are placed easily between the produce and the pleasures. While this easy relationship holds, there is no moral problem of any consequence to disturb the smooth and recommending construction.

> England is not yet a commercial country in the sense in which that epithet is used for her; and let us hope that she will not soon become so. She might surely as well be called feudal England, or chivalrous England. If in western civilised Europe there does exist a nation among whom there are high signors, and with whom the owners of the land are the true aristocracy, the aristocracy that is trusted as being best and fitted to rule, that nation is the English.

As a description of mid-nineteenth-century England, this is ludicrous; but as a way of seeing it without extended question, it is perfect. It takes the values for granted, and can then study with a persistent accuracy the internal difficulties of the class, and especially the problem of the relation between the inheriting landed families and the connected and rising cadet and professional people. Trollope shares an interest in getting into that class, which is what the inheritance plot had always mainly served, and he can describe its processes without further illusion, once the basic illusion of describing the landowners as an aristocracy has been accepted. George Eliot, by contrast, questioning in a profoundly moral way the real and assumed relations between property and human quality, accepts the emphasis of inheritance as the central action, and then has to make it external, contradictory, and finally irrelevant, as her real interest transfers to the separated, exposed individual, who becomes sadly resigned or must go away. What happens to the Transomes' land in *Felix Holt*, or to Grandcourt's in *Daniel Deronda*, is no longer decisive; yet around the complications of that kind of interest a substantial part of each novel has been built. In this sense, George Eliot's novels are transitional between the form which had ended in a series of settlements, in which the social and economic solutions and the personal achievements were in a single dimension, and the form which, extending and complicating and then finally collapsing this dimension, ends with a single person going away on his own, having achieved his moral growth through distancing or extrication. It is a divided consciousness of belonging and not belonging; for the social solutions are still taken seriously up to the last point of personal crisis, and then what is achieved as a personal moral development has to express itself in some kind of physical or spiritual renewal—an emigration, at once resigned and hopeful, from what had been offered as a decisive social world.

The complications of the inheritance plot, with its underlying assumption of a definite relation between property and human quality, had in fact been used in one remarkable novel, significantly based on a whole action rather than on individual analysis. Emily Brontë's *Wuthering Heights* is remarkable because it takes the crisis of inheritance at its full human value, without displacement to the external and representative attitudes of disembodied classes. There is a formal contrast of values between the exposed and working Heights and the sheltered and renting Grange, and the complicated relations between their families are consistently resolved by the power and endurance of the Heights. Yet the creation is so total that the social mechanism of inheritance is transcended. It is class and property that divide Heathcliff and Cathy, and it is in the positive alteration of these relationships that a resolution is arrived at in the second generation. But it is not in social alteration that the human solution is at any point conceived. What is created and held to is a kind of human intensity and connection which is the ground of continuing life. Unaffected by settlements, it survives them and, in a familiar tragic emphasis, survives and is learned again through death. This tragic separation of human intensity and any available social settlement is accepted from the beginning in the whole design and idiom of the novel. The complication of its plot is sustained by a single feeling, which is the act of transcendence. George Eliot, by contrast, working in a more critically realist world, conceives and yet cannot conceive acceptable social solutions; it is then not transcendence but a sad resignation on which she finally comes to rest. As a creative history, each of these solutions has a decisive importance, for each is reworked by the significant successors of George Eliot and Emily Brontë: Thomas Hardy and D. H. Lawrence.

## III

The country action of George Eliot's *Daniel Deronda* takes place in Wessex. But whereas the Loamshire and Stonyshire of *Felix Holt* had been George Eliot's England, the Wessex of *Daniel Deronda* might be Jane Austen's Hampshire or Derbyshire: the great and the less great houses, and the selected "knowable community," as it is to be found again later in Henry James and in other "country-house novels" of our own century. *Daniel Deronda* was finished in 1876, but by that time there was a new Wessex in the novel: the country of Hardy. To move from one to the other is to repeat, ironically, the movement from the world around Chawton to the world of *Adam Bede:* a reappearance, a remaking of the general life, with its known community and its hard emphasis of want.

George Eliot, in writing her only novel set in her own time, had moved significantly away from the full and known world of her earlier works. She had her own clear reasons for this. If the decisive history was that of character and of the frustration of human impulse by an unacceptable and yet inevitable world, she needed to create no more than the conditions for this kind of moral, intellectual and ideal history. The social conditions for a more generally valuing history were in every real sense behind her.

This is the right way, I believe, to introduce the question of George Eliot's important attitudes to the past, and especially the rural past. In *Adam Bede*, for example, she looked back with a generalizing affection to the first years of the nineteenth century, "those old leisurely times," and concluded:

*Leisure is gone—gone where the spinning wheels are gone, and the pack-horses, and the slow waggons, and the pedlars, who brought bargains to the door on sunny afternoons. Ingenious philosophers tell you, perhaps, that the great work of the steam-engine is to create leisure for mankind. Do not believe them: it only creates a vacuum for eager thoughts to rush in. Even idleness is eager now—eager for amusement: prone to excursion-trains, art-museums, periodical literature, and exciting novels: prone even to scientific theorising, and cursory peeps through microscopes. Old Leisure was quite a different personage: he only read one newspaper, innocent of leaders, and was free from that periodicity of sensations which we call post-time. He was a contemplative, rather stout gentleman, of excellent digestion—of quiet perception, undiseased by hypothesis: happy in his inability to know the causes of things, preferring the things themselves. He lived chiefly in the country, among pleasant seats and homesteads, and was fond of sauntering by the fruit-tree wall, and scenting the apricots when they were warmed by the morning sunshine, or of sheltering himself under the orchard boughs at noon, when the summer pears were falling. He knew nothing of week-day services, and thought none the worse of the Sunday sermon if it allowed him to sleep from the text to the blessing—liking the afternoon service best, because the prayers were the shortest, and not ashamed to say so; for he had an easy, jolly conscience, broad-backed like himself, and able to carry a great deal of beer and port-wine—not being made squeamish by doubts and qualms and lofty aspirations. Life was not a task to him, but a sinecure; he fingered the guineas in his pocket, and ate his dinners, and slept the sleep of the irresponsible; for had he not kept up his charter by going to church on the Sunday afternoons!*

*Fine old Leisure! Do not be severe upon him, and judge him by our modern standard; he never went to Exeter Hall, or heard a popular preacher, or read* Tracts for the Times *or* Sartor Resartus.

This wretched piece is worth quoting at length only because it has been the cue for a hundred similar ruminations: a sleepy fantasy of the past which has been extended into a kind of history; a personification, using the simplest devices of fiction, which can be composed into a general lie. The terrible thing is that she seems to know what she is doing; she is careful to guard her retreat with such phrases as "eager thought" and "the sleep of the irresponsible." But this makes the idealization worse, for it reminds us that it comes from the novelist who had recognized the "emphasis of want." Old Leisure is history, is a time and a period; but with his apricots and his orchard, his single newspaper, his port-wine and his guineas in his pocket, he is a class figure who can afford to saunter, who has leisure then precisely in the sweat of other men's work. More clearly because more crudely than anywhere else in literature, this invocation announces the modern rural retrospect in which, as a matter of what must be policy, the lives of millions of men are made to count for nothing; their labor and their hunger, their sickness and the deaths of their children, smilingly faded out, as the comfortable writer composes an easy and comfortable past.

Fine old, dear old lies. It was not *Tracts for the Times* or *Sartor Resartus* or the newspapers or science which disturbed Old Leisure as he fingered his guineas. It was men who in just those years were being broken by endless work and by the want of bread; Old Leisure the roundsman, Old Leisure with the pauper's letter on his back, Old Leisure in the workhouse as a reward for fifty years in the fields. Mr. Leavis, writing of *Adam Bede*, says that "memory, with its emotional accompaniments, recalling over the long gap of time, can be recognised as telling essentially in the effect. But the effect is the product of a creative writer's art." He goes on to celebrate in much the same tones the "England of before the railway." But what needs to be emphasized, of both the memory and the creation, is the selective, glazing quality which both George Eliot and Mr. Leavis are responsible for in direct ways, because they are in a position to have access to literature and to history. Of the years of *Adam Bede* George Eliot had no memory; she was born in 1819. *The Mill on the Floss, Felix Holt,* and *Middlemarch* are set in the years of her childhood and adolescence; memory, of course, is at work there, but in an apparently inextricable mix of the country and of childhood. There is a leisure, a quiet, of some childhood days, and of a father asleep on a Sunday afternoon, which is suddenly, in inattention, a whole past and a historical scheme. And the key to this response is not the condition of England in 1799 or 1830; it is the condition of the writer in 1860 or in 1960.

George Eliot's most extended exercise in this manner—important because it is not a dream by the fire but a conscious piece of writing—is the introduction to *Felix Holt*. It is more persuasive and more substantial than the dream of Old Leisure, but in its whole organization shows even more clearly the structure of feeling which was being laid over the country. The description of the meadows and the hedgerows has the warmth of observation and of memory; it is the green language of Clare. But the passenger on the box of the stage-coach, through whose eyes we are directed to look, is more than a nature poet; he has, as it were naturally, combined with these perceptions a quite solid set of social presuppositions. When he sees the shepherd "with a slow and slouching walk," he knows by some alchemy that he feels "no bitterness except in the matter of pauper labourers and the bad luck that sent contrarious seasons and the sheep rot."

What bitterness about the "pauper labourers"? That he might become one of them, which was always possible? Or that they troubled the ratepayers? And in this moment of watching, when the quiet landscape has "an unchanging still-ness, as if Time itself were pausing," and when "it was easy for the traveller to conceive that town and country had no pulse in common," there is a sudden conflation of "rural Englishmen" whose "notion of Reform was a confused com-bination of rick-burners, trades-unions, Nottingham riots, and in general what-ever required the calling-out of the yeomanry."

Who then, the traveller might ask as Time pauses, were the yeomanry called out to face? Who, always somewhere else, was burning the ricks or combining under the threat of transportation? These others by the conflation of "rural Eng-lishmen" are in fact abolished; they are "not-people."

*The passenger on the box could see that this was the district of protuberant optimists, sure that old England was the best of all possible countries, and that if there were any facts which had not fallen under their own observation, they were facts not worth observing: the district of clean little market-towns with-out manufactures, of fat livings, an aristocratic clergy, and low poor-rates.*

He can see this from his box-seat because he wants to see it, because George Eliot wants to see it. The low poor-rates—are they an irony or a comfort? We re-member that Cobbett rode this country and saw very differently; and it is creation only in the sense of a willing and shared illusion, from the point of view of a sentimental middle class. Where actual evils are admitted they are at once modi-fied by tone: the poor, for example, are suddenly present, but as "a brawny and many-breeding pauperism"—that word, "breeding," that George Eliot so often uses where the poor are in question, as if they were animals; in any case, not men, but a condition, an "ism." And "brawny"?—getting strong and fat, no doubt, on the poor-rates, on "*our* money."

The point of this willing illusion is then suddenly seen: it is manufacturing and the railways which destroy the old England. The full modern myth comes quite sharply into focus.

*The breath of the manufacturing town, which made a cloudy day and a red gloom by night on the horizon, diffused itself over all the surrounding country, filling the air with eager unrest. Here was a population not convinced that old England was as good as possible.*

The unrest, that is to say, is a product of industrialization; in being placed in that way, after the country idyll, it can itself be placed and rejected. What is being bought from this view on the box-seat is a political comfort: a position admitting but limiting radicalism through uneasy contrast with the content of the old rural order. The social position is then quite clear: a whole reality is admitted in the industrial districts; a selected reality in the rural.

*After the coach had rattled over the pavement of a manufacturing town, the scene of riots and trades-union meetings, it would take him in another ten minutes into a rural region, where the neighbourhood of the town was only felt in the advantages of a near market for corn, cheese, and hay, and where men with a considerable banking account were accustomed to say that "they never meddled with politics themselves."*

Of course; because the visible unrest of the town, in a whole action, is compared not with the whole knowable community of the rural region, but with the condition and point of view of "men with a considerable banking account." The willing, lulling illusion of country life has paid its political dividends; a natural country ease has been contrasted with an unnatural urban unrest; the "modern world," in both its cruelty and its protest against cruelty, can be mediated by a reference to a human condition which is superior to both and which can place both: a condition imagined out of a landscape and a selective observation and memory.

This is the structure on which we must fix our attention, for it connects crucially with George Eliot's development. A valuing society, the common condition of a knowable community, belongs ideally in the past. It can be recreated there for a widely ranging moral action. But the real step that has been taken is the withdrawal from any full response to an existing society; value is in the past, as a general condition, and is in the present only as a particular and private sensibility, the individual moral action.

The combination of these two conclusions has been very powerful; it has shaped and trained a whole literary tradition. And this is the meaning of George Eliot's Wessex in the only novel set in her own actual period: a narrowing of range and people to those capable, in traditional terms, of an individual moral action; the fading-out of all others, as most country people had been faded out in that view from the box-seat; the recreation, after all the earlier emphasis of want, of a country-house England, a class England in which only certain histories matter, and to which the sensibility—the bitter and frank sensibility—of the isolated moral observer can be made appropriate. She is able to narrow her range because the wide-ranging community, the daily emphasis of want, is past and gone with old England; what is left now is a set of personal relationships and of intellectual and moral insights, in a history that for all valuing purposes has, disastrously, ended.

We can then see why Mr. Leavis, who is the most distinguished twentieth-century exponent of just this structure of feeling, should go on, in outlining the great tradition, from George Eliot to Henry James. It is from that final country-house England of *Daniel Deronda* (of course with Continental extensions and with ideas, like Deronda's Zionism, about everywhere) to the country-house England of James. But the development that matters in the English novel is not to James; it is within that same Wessex, in the return of a general history, to the novels of Hardy.

# Pastoralism as Culture and Counter-Culture In English Fiction, 1800–1928

## From a View to a Death

JULIAN MOYNAHAN

*"The pastoral process of putting the complex into the simple"*—William Empson

I

The British, who by and large invented the Industrial Revolution and urbanization as far back as the later eighteenth century and who are a large population inhabiting a relatively small, sea-locked land area, have not been a pastoral society strictly speaking for a very long time. But they have clung throughout their modern history to what Empson calls "the permanent tradition of the country," to an idea of themselves as indeed a people with immemorial rural roots and of a spiritual disposition that is at home among tall trees, clear streams, hunting fields and sheepfolds, ricks, roses and hedgerows. There is a pleasant, superficial side to this continuing illusion of the pastoral in Britain: seen in the persistent English cult of the domestic and the homely; in East End cockney families picnicking in Kew Gardens on a Sunday; in the tradition among the more prosperous classes of long weekends spent at country retreats; in the habit, among the less prosperous, of visiting great ducal estates made over by their enterprising owners into private zoos, fun fairs and tea houses; in the habit of vigorous love-making in broad daylight on the greensward of the London parks; in country sports, including the rather ferocious sports of fox hunting and greyhound coursing; in weekend gardening, which, according to a recent survey, is the only hobby of some 22,000,000 Britons.

There is also a less pleasant, though still superficial side to the illusion. The reactionary and xenophobic politics of the Little Englanders, most recently under the leadership of Enoch Powell, are often fueled by sentimental ideas about preservation of the English rural establishment and English nature. It is the same impulse that makes small suburban property owners mortar sharp pieces of broken glass into the top of a garden wall and write letters to the newspapers demanding that Britain stay out of the Common Market in order to protect the British farmer, who is at present down to 3% of the general population and produces at a level of daunting technical efficiency that needs little protection from competition by the peasant agriculturalists of the continent.

In a country with a population density ten times that of the United States and three times that of Holland there is of course a perfectly realistic basis for this diffuse and superficial culture of pastoralism: "This thou perceiv'st which makes thy love more strong / To love that well which thou must leave ere long." But I am concerned with something else: with a really profound culture of pastoralism, entailing a whole view of English life and of life generally that is expressed in some novels about people living away from the large towns, written in the course of the nineteenth century, that are among the principal glories of the English literary tradition. As the century goes on this whole and wholesome view becomes increasingly difficult to sustain, owing to just such developments in society as can be marked through the use of terms like industrialism, urbanization, the cash-nexus, technology, imperialism, and plutocracy. The essential development is from a view to a death: from a rich composition of feeling and valuing centered on the destinies of people living in the country to a decomposition, or a disconnecting, as between the "complex" life of society at large and the "simple" fictions of private rural life in terms of which the most humane ideals of society at large have formerly been articulated. With this decomposition emerges a kind of novelist whose attachment to the primary values associated with "the permanent tradition of the country" causes him to conceive his task as a sort of rescue operation of these values, and whose poignant sense of cleavage between the insensate aims of society and the permanent truths of life and nature lead him to compose pastoral fictions the themes and values of which run deliberately counter to the projects and values of society at large. It is in this sense that the sort of pastoralism I am concerned with moves from culture to counterculture during a single century.

In 1802, during the breathing-space afforded by the short-lived British-French Peace Treaty of Amiens, Wordsworth began to compose his "Sonnets dedicated to Liberty." These magnificent poems have as an ulterior aim that of heartening and unifying the English people against the threat posed by the aggressive new nation-state of France under Consul Napoleon Bonaparte, and their characteristic strategy is to link English love of country with the cherished and familiar objects of English country life. In the sonnet composed near Dover during August, 1802, after Wordsworth's return from France, good English air, crowing cocks, curling smoke, pealing church bells, boys in white-sleeved shirts playing on a meadow ground, even the roar of "English" waves breaking upon the chalky shore, elicit the outcry "Thou art free / My Country!" and the sonnets as a group develop a richly pastoral image of a community that is customary, wholesome, peaceful and rooted in the earth. The sonnet mistitled "1801" but actually composed in May, 1802, which begins "I grieved for Buonaparté," reveals that this ideal community has an ideal governor:

> The Governor who must be wise and good,
> And temper with the sternness of the brain
> Thoughts motherly, and meek as womanhood.
> Wisdom doth live with children round her knees:

*Books, leisure, perfect freedom, and the talk*
*Man holds with week-day man in the hourly walk*
*Of the mind's business: these are the degrees*
*By which true Sway doth mount; this is the stalk*
*True Power doth grow on; and her rights are these.*

This well-tempered governor, whose thoughts, wisdom and power are more than half womanly, who has time and fondness for children, books and the sauntering daily round of ordinary business but none at all for weapons and battles, is not of course to be identified with any actual arm of English power in the age of Napoleon. Rather, he is a transparent image of community itself, one with the intimacy of scale and domesticity of a well-conducted, prospering village or extended family. These sonnets, by tying the abstraction Liberty to images of non-urban community—to "fireside, hall and bower"—give the English people, even and particularly those many English people who had never seen a prosperous village or enjoyed a happy home life, an idea of "home" they can fight for.

Just a century later, during the Boer War, the Anglo-Irish novelist George Moore, who had fallen deeply in love with those he called "the dull-witted Saxon race" while he was writing *Esther Waters*, awoke one day in London to discover that he so loathed the British military role in South Africa that his affection for England itself was fast ebbing. London now appears monstrous and graceless to him. Determining that his "condition would welcome a pastoral country" he goes down to Sussex to visit old friends—"Some South Saxon folk that lived in an Italian house on the downs." Here he tries to stay off the subject of the war and to forget the jingoistic horrors he had witnessed in London on Mafeking Night. He spends much time on horseback, revisiting various farms and hamlets that he has formerly known and loved. Yet nothing pleases him: the downs have become "an ugly, rolling country" and the weald is a "dim blue expanse" lying before him like a map which he studies "with hatred." "And all the things that I used to love—a red tiled cottage at the end of a lane with a ponderous team coming through a gateway—I hated." It is very terrible, this experience of falling out of love with an entire countryside when one's idea of an entire nation has changed for the worse. But Moore shows the courage of his new convictions and pushes on to a desolate conclusion:

*A few minutes later I was on the crest above Anchor Hollow. . . . I remembered how the coast towns light up in the evening: garlands of light reaching from Worthing to Lancing, to Amberley, to Shoreham, to Southwick, and on to Brighton. There is no country in England; even the downs are circled with lights. . . .* (Hail and Farewell [New York: Appleton, 1925], I, 286)

On the one hand, we have Wordsworth developing his homely pastoral images to nerve a whole people in a great national undertaking. On the other, we have Moore, convinced that Britain's national effort in Africa is a squalid imperialistic adventure, remarking the death of rural England. Remembering how Lawrence saw the English land-mass when he took ship for Italy at the end of the Great War—as a ghastly grey coffin sinking slowly into the sea; remembering how Wells's George Ponderevo saw England at the end of *Tono-Bungay* (1908), while his experimental destroyer, the X-2, steamed slowly down the reaches of the Thames—as a proliferating heap of waste and decay—we should acknowledge that Moore's response is something other than mere Irish caprice. Of course there is still country left in England, in 1901 and 1908 and 1919. Moore is actually recording the death of a feeling, and of an idea. The idea is that there is an essential, reciprocal, nourishing relation between the Country and the country, between culture and agriculture if you will. And when this relation or pact appears to someone to be severely damaged, owing to corruption or blundering in the general society, then for him the country, that is the country of pastoral, dies, disappears, ceases to be imaginable. It is a strange idea. But then island nations are always strange in their self-imaginings; for their insulated condition leads them to view themselves in light of ideals of intactness and inviolability that few if any land-locked nations with readily invadable borders have ever been in a position to afford.

## II

My excuse for the foregoing broad and miscellaneous speculations is that, as Empson suggests, pastoral is a queer business—a queer English business I should say—and invites much mulling over once one cuts loose from Samuel Johnson's reasonable definitions (*Rambler Essays* 36, 37), steps into the labyrinthine nineteenth century, and begins to examine the "pastoral process" of some masterpieces of English fiction.

Not so much child-cult as maiden-cult best focuses the pastoral theme, as it reflects and incorporates a wholesome ideal of community, for much of the nineteenth-century English novel. Empson appears to have missed this point when he made his great swerve from *The Beggar's Opera* to the Alice Books in *Some Versions of Pastoral*. As Jane Austen's valetudinarian fusspot, Mr. Woodhouse, puts it, "My dear Miss Fairfax, young ladies are very sure to be cared for," and caring for young ladies is in large part what the nineteenth-century English novel of pastoralism is about. However, only a few pages after Mr. Woodhouse makes his fond fuss over Jane Fairfax's wet feet we get another side of the coin of caring, when Jane, who anticipates having to take a job as a governess, bitterly compares the "governess trade" to the "slave trade." Evidently, even in so sheltered and privileged a milieu—a milieu so removed from the systems of valuing that obtain in urban market places—as that depicted in *Emma*, young ladies may be cared for in sharply divergent ways: by being cherished for their self-evident value; by being sought after eagerly in the market when they are sold, or have to sell themselves, as governesses and sometimes as something less respectable, if no more enslaved, than governesses.

It happens that Jane is not sold, does not go out to do governess work. She is able to find accommodation in love and a good marriage—to "settle" and to "make an establishment" as Jane Austen likes to put it—within the peaceful, prosperous world of country houses, agricultural estates and gossipy villages of which Jane Austen is the chronicler. Jane is—both Janes are—fortunate in having been born at the right time. Because, if we follow the career of the English maiden through the century, from Jane Austen, through the Brontë sisters, to the heroines of George Eliot and Hardy, we see that these accommodations become fewer, are fraught with difficulty when they do occur, and often do not occur at all. The movement from Jane Austen's Emma Woodhouse to George Eliot's Gwendolen Harleth or Hardy's Tess is one from a type of high pastoral comedy to a type of tragedy, from the incorporation of a value to its alienation.

Nevertheless, it is not as if the value perceived in the figure of the maiden declines as the century goes on. Quite the contrary. The language in which a novelist like George Eliot expresses this value can only be described as extravagant in its idealization. Consider the following panegyric from an early chapter of *Daniel Deronda*:

> *Could there be a slenderer, more insignificant thread in human history than this consciousness of a girl, busy with her small inferences of the way in which she could make her life pleasant?—in a time too, when ideas were with fresh vigor making armies of themselves, and the universal kinship was declaring itself fiercely . . . a time when the soul of man was waking to pulses which had for centuries been beating in him unheard, until their full sum made a new life of terror or of joy.*
>
> *What in the midst of that mighty drama are girls and their blind vision? They are the Yea or Nay of that good for which men are enduring and fighting. In these delicate vessels is born onward through the ages the treasure of human affections.* (New York: Harper, 1966, pp. 89–90)

George Eliot speaks here from the standpoint of a universal consciousness, at the vanguard of her age, as champion of new ideas with the vigor of armies, engaged in the struggle for what she calls "universal kinship," *and* with a keen sense of the limited, blinkered powers of "this consciousness of a girl"; but she concludes in language that is worshipful and sacramental by laying the entire "mighty drama" at the feet of "girls and their blind vision." "In these delicate vessels is born onward through the ages the treasure of human affections."

A comparable idealization, though it is tinged with bafflement, appears a generation or so later in Henry James's preface to *A Portrait of a Lady* when he recounts how he set to work "organizing an ado" about Isabel Archer. He mentions "the wonder . . . as we look at the world [of] how absolutely, how inordinately the Isabel Archers, and even much smaller female fry, insist on mattering." And he acknowledges "the value recognized in the mere young thing" without attempting to explain it, except by setting down in slightly garbled form George Eliot's worshipful sentence about "delicate vessels."

Hardy must also be added to the list of maiden worshippers. I have in mind the chivalric devotion to Tess expressed in the subtitle of that novel, "A Pure Woman Faithfully Presented"; the maternal tenderness and solicitude of its affixed Shakespearean motto—"Poor wounded name! My bosom as a bed / Shall lodge thee"—and the sense we get from the novel itself that Hardy cared for Tess, with a kind of shy yet passionate regard, as he cared for no other character in all the books he was ever to write.

Yet spoiled Gwendolen and presumptuous Isabel and Tess the peasant girl with a pedigree do not find accommodation for themselves, do not "settle." The value recognized in the mere young thing goes higher and higher but all three of these girls come to ruin in terms of the hopes and illusions they started out with. As a matter of fact they come to ruin absolutely and inordinately. It seems that in the world which Eliot, James and Hardy look at there is an insufficiency of ground for an establishment, an insufficiency of felt community actually, where the perceived value can root itself and flourish. To fall back upon George Moore and Mr. Woodhouse simultaneously, there is no country left in England where young ladies are sure to be cared for.

What is a maiden that we should care for her? An answer from the approximate vantage point of Jane Austen's time might go roughly like this. She emerges, fresh and new, out of her nonage or awkward age, from the shelter of nursery and schoolroom, into the full gaze of an aging and decorous, but interested and tolerant community. She is a mixture of natural grace and vitality, because she is young and fresh, and of cultivation, because she has already been trained to be pleasing, attractive, and perhaps clever, by toiling governesses and modish dancing, drawing and music masters. She is rather like an arable field in spring— an enclosed field to be sure—that has been cultivated but is still unsown. However, the maiden, as she embarks upon her proper business of courtship, love and the making of an establishment in marriage, is freer, less passive than the image allows, although it is a poignantly limited freedom. She has the freedom to choose among the suitors who solicit her consent, although she is not permitted to do the courting herself and must choose according to proprieties of social rank, real property and cash income under the control of her elders. Furthermore, she may easily choose wrong because of inexperience of the world and, whereas she may refuse all suitors for a certain term of years, she will have to take what she can get in the end or else be written off as a back number and old maid. If she is lucky, self-controlled and clever she chooses well, getting love and marriage together. Her freshness and vitality in their cultivated, pleasing form are incorporated in a community that is always in danger of going dry and stiff; which is to say that as a happy wife and then a mother she graces the country district in which she is established, replenishes the human stock with healthy, cultivated offspring, lives and dies surrounded by, as well as transmitting to the generation after her, the treasure of human affections that George Eliot mentions as the only real sanction of human struggle and human history.

Samuel Johnson closely followed his *Rambler* papers on pastoral with a paper on the miseries of women, and one does not have to be Simone de Beauvoir or Kate Millett to see much pathos in the limited freedom, scant education and disabling ignorance of the real world from which the mere young thing carries out her fraught and perilous enterprise. She makes a figure of grace under pressure, simplicity under pressure, as the pretty, perfectly intelligent spinster and occasional governess, Jane Austen, deeply, ironically understood. And she is also the pastoral figure, the "piece of nature," the point of girlish simplicity upon which all the humane ideals and expectations of a whole society with agrarian roots, that is devoutly non-revolutionary and not at all liberated, comes to dwell or even dance.

*Emma* (1816) is Jane Austen's masterpiece because it offers her fullest, tenderest *and* most ironical treatment of the maiden theme, with much of the irony directed outside the novel, at the reader. Early on, she tricks us into mistaking Emma's "errors of imagination" for evidence of a spoiled, snobbish and artificial temperament, then schools us, step by step, into delighted recognition that Miss Woodhouse is truly "this sweetest and best of all creatures, faultless in spite of all her faults." Early on, she tricks us into half-suspecting that Mr. Knightley is a dried stick of an aging, sententious country gentleman, then schools us into a recognition that he is strong, vital, and good as well as a gentleman. She accomplishes this pedagogical miracle with an art so intricate it would take hours to analyze even clumsily; but one way of putting the general trick is that she works toward a vantage point where we see Emma and Mr. Knightley converging as cultivated, good-natured, inescapably compatible lovers in a prospect of cultivated nature that is the best, most enduring thing this agrarian society has to offer. From this prospect are banished, or set at a distance, the unfortunate gypsies of the lanes, dismal weather with its attendant colds and putrid sore throats, and the poor cottagers of Highbury. Now I should like to come on to this prospect by way of a Highbury scene—the grand ball organized by Frank Churchill to take place at the town inn.

There is only space for a glimpse. Ill-natured Mr. Elton pointedly snubs the girl born out of wedlock, Harriet Smith, who is sitting down, waiting to be asked to dance. Mr. Knightley, who  does not dance, notices this and immediately leads Harriet into the set. Emma, watching, is moved and amused. At the chapter's end Mr. Knightley approaches Emma and asks her to dance. She says, "Indeed I will. You have shown that  you can dance, and you know we are not really so much brother and sister as to make it all improper." He says, "Brother and sister! no, indeed!" It is all quite playful, is one of the best moments in the book, and gives the effect of a perfect chord of feeling, valuing and fun. The values are those, I do believe, that Jane Austen would go to the stake for.

Now to come on to the prospect. Mrs. Elton, succumbing to a mood of fake pastoralism, has organized a "gypsy party" for strawberry picking at Mr. Knightley's Donwell Abbey. After a half hour's exercise in the sun she collapses raving into the beds but still insists on having the luncheon served *al fresco* under shade trees: "Everything as natural and simple as possible. Is not that your idea?":

Mr. Knightley: "*Not quite. My idea of the simple and the natural will be to have the table spread in the dining room. The nature and simplicity of gentlemen and ladies, with their servants and furniture, I think is best observed by meals within doors. When you are tired of eating strawberries in the garden, there shall be cold meat in the house.*" (New York: Dolphin, n.d., p. 322)

Mr. Knightley, like the author, well understands the nature of society people and the limits set on "nature and simplicity" by the real dispositions of gentlemen and ladies "with their servants and furniture." The lunch is eaten in the house. At other times and with different persons and classes the master of Donwell will construe the right relations of the natural and the sociable quite differently. He spends at least five hours a day with his overseer supervising the enlargement and improved cultivation of substantial agricultural holdings, and he will do more than his duties require for his tenants, as is shown by his determined sponsorship of farmer Robert Martin's impeded courtship of Harriet Smith.

And now the prospect. After lunch the party breaks up into groups. Emma walks with Mr. Weston to an eminence from which she studies a view of Abbey-Hill Farm, "with meadows in front and the river making a close and handsome curve around it.":

> It was a sweet view—sweet to the eye and the mind. English verdure, English culture, English comfort, seen under a sun bright, without being oppressive. (p. 326)

Culture here means cultivation of arable acres but of course it means culture too. The "culture" includes the eye and mind of the beholder, Emma. We see her as part of the picture. Her vitality and cultivation are mirrored in the prospect and sweeten it. She is standing where the future mistress of Donwell will often stand and is the future mistress of Donwell without knowing it. Mr. Knightley comes up with Harriet. He always goes where Emma is unless he thinks she does not want him, and Emma always likes him to come. That is what I mean by the convergence of Emma and Mr. Knightley within a prospect of cultivated nature.

We could move from *Emma* to *Jane Eyre* by way of Jane Fairfax's and Harriet Smith's exposure to and escape from what Jane Austen calls "the danger of degradation," but I prefer moving to *Wuthering Heights* (1847), a work of Shakespearean scope and boundless genius which is for my purposes the pastoral of pastorals among nineteenth-century novels, the book which explores the essential themes most deeply, thereby setting a standard against which all the other pastoral novels must be measured.

Emile Brontë is not afraid of degradation. She uses it not only as the main weapon of Heathcliff's revenge against society but also as a brutal and, in the end, effective therapy. Heathcliff is degraded by Hindley and is turned away by the superior people of Thrushcross Grange as a degraded specimen of humanity. In time he gets Hindley into his clutches and degrades him. He degrades Isabella Linton after eloping with her and dragging her off to Wuthering Heights. He degrades the second Catherine after stealing her from Thrushcross Grange; and Hindley's son, Hareton Earnshaw, who should have been heir to Wuthering Heights, is degraded to the status of an illiterate field hand. At the end, as Heathcliff begins to break up, Hareton and Catherine are coming shyly together as lovers. She is teaching him to read, cleaning up his uncouth accent, and persuading him to plant some cultivated berry bushes that can be brought up from the Grange. Watching this, Heathcliff admits to Nelly Dean that it is an absurd conclusion to all his exertions. He could still crush them flat but has lost the motive to do it. After Heathcliff has hastened to his death, Hareton and Catherine marry and go to live at the Grange, while the ghosts of Heathcliff and the original Cathy hold sway upon the Heights.

Along with this extraordinary business of degradation there is a shattering of what can be called the normal class distinction-recognition system, so that Lockwood, with his bad, town-based genteel style and nervous nose bleeds, has trouble telling whether Hareton is a servant. His confusion is not helped by the extreme liberties which the servants, Nelly and Joseph, take with their "betters." Nelly is especially flagrant in this regard when, for example, she works to keep Heathcliff away from Cathy, and Edgar ignorant of Cathy's dangerous condition of mental frenzy, after the big fight scene between Heathcliff and Linton in the Grange living room. And she is ruthless in her contempt later for Linton Heathcliff as "a sickly slip" who will "drop off" by spring—which he does.

All this brutality and impropriety makes vitally good sense as we begin to grasp what *Wuthering Heights* is about. It is, like all the greatest English romantic art, about the renaturing of society without the destruction of society, or alternatively, about the realigning of society with the realm of wild nature. This process is rather appalling from society's ordinary point of view—say from the viewpoint of a Lockwood—but it is absolutely necessary to accomplish because it is of the nature of society, through its genius for abstracted forms, to withdraw from the matrix of nature into an etiolated condition of separateness. With the breaking or weakening of the bond between the social and the natural, between civilization and wilderness, society becomes enfeebled and sickly, until, through a violent and degrading confrontation, the necessary realignment is achieved. Human kind cannot flourish cut off from the energies of wild nature. By the same token, men cannot flourish in wild nature, which is the realm of inchoateness, barrenness, formlessness and merging.

*Wuthering Heights* may be thought of as a breeding experiment, conducted in a place where a faltering, sickly cultivation—the Linton tradition—links to the more robust, more agrarian but also faltering heritage of the Earnshaws, with Heathcliff, that "arid wilderness of furze and whinstone," put in as catalyst to make the mix come right. *Heathcliff and Cathy:* issueless of course. They can't even make love. All they can do is merge, flowing together, amoeba-like, from adjacent graves, or as spirits in the air. *Heathcliff and Isabella:* too far apart. He burns her out with his savage energy and she retaliates upon him by bearing Linton Heathcliff, that "sickly slip." *Cathy and Edgar Linton:* she is too spirited, after a childhood spent with Heathcliff, to live long with Edgar, and he is too cultivated to know how to fight Heathcliff off. But they breed well together and produce a new Catherine who lives to be spirited and cultivated at once. *Hindley and the mysterious Frances from Cornwall:* a drunk and a consumptive produce Hareton, who is robust, affectionate and ready for cultivation. *Hareton Earnshaw and the second Catherine:* almost literally, they have been made for each other. The breeding experiment is a triumph.

The obligatory entertainment for the wedding of Hareton and Catherine the second is provided by a scene in *The Winter's Tale* where Florizel, disguised in rural garb and having dressed up Perdita according to country notions of a princess (neither knowing that the other is of royal birth), dally together until they are joined by Florizel's father, King Polixenes, who is also disguised as a commoner. The talk is about propagating brilliant varieties of gillyflowers by the method of grafting:

> Perdita:              *For I have heard it said*
> *There is an art which in their piedness shares*
> *With great-creating nature.*
>
> Polixenes:                         *Say there be;*
> *Yet nature is made better by no mean*
> *But nature makes that mean: so, over that art,*
> *Which you say adds to nature, is an art*
> *That nature makes. You see, sweet maid, we marry*
> *A gentler scion to the wildest stock,*
> *And make conceive a bark of baser kind*
> *By bud of nobler race: this is an art*
> *Which does mend nature, change it rather, but*
> *The art itself is nature.* (IV, iii, 86–97)

*Wuthering Heights* provides a standard for the whole nineteenth century by which we can distinguish between deep pastoral and mere pastoral, between novels that vitally embody "the permanent tradition of the country" and those that fall into a second rank as pastorals because they have too little of the art of "great creating nature" in them. In light of this standard the charismatic child-maidens of Dickens, from little Nell to little Dorrit, by way of his little Florences, Esthers, Doras and Biddies, fail to measure up, although of course Dickens is a supremely great novelist in other terms. But what about George Eliot, with her immense, tender, brooding attachment to the permanence of the countryside and the elevated valuation, as we have already noted, that she places upon girls?

George Eliot *is* a problem. Part of the problem is that she has a fascination for deep or base nature and yet shrinks from it fearfully. Part of it lies in her moral conservatism—the full assent she gives, at least consciously, to Maggie Tulliver's rhetorical question, "if the past is not to bind us, where can duty lie?" And part of it arises in her working intellectual's understanding of the mature, infinitely various civilization of her century in the midst of which country concerns and maidenly concerns cut so very small a figure. Perhaps what I mean here is that with George Eliot—with the later Eliot surely—the complex can no longer be put into the simple in such a way as to give a complete truth about either. Each part of the problem can be touched upon by referring to a particular novel.

*Adam Bede* (1850). The most charged and energized writing in this novel comes in the account of Hetty Sorel's flight from the Poyser household in Hayslope, especially in the part where Hetty wanders from the highroad into waste nature, encounters the old shepherd at his primitive hut, ignores his gruff warning and moves on to the commission of her terrible, yet no doubt for those times commonplace, crime. There follows in conspicuously less energized writing: Hetty's apprehension; Adam's agony; sorrow and shame at the Poysers; distress at Donnithorne Hall; Hetty's trial; Dinah's apotheosis into a pastoral figure out of the New Testament in the night prison scene; Hetty's reprieve and departure from the community; and the nuptials of Adam and Dinah. Hetty's is not a rich nature and no doubt her exclusion from the final settlement is defensible, even if the young squire does get to come back. Yet Hetty is the instrument by which this community has been scandalously challenged from the side of base, unregenerate nature, and her exclusion suggests a sort of sealing off and backing away. Deep nature is in the book because George Eliot's powerful episode of "wilderness" writing has put it there, and it demands some permanent accommodation with the merely decent moral and workaday energies of life in Hayslope if the novel's pastoral burden is not to seem more picturesque than vital.

The Mill on the Floss (1860). Maggie Tulliver's large, rich nature is fearfully constricted within the narrow decorums and limited intellectual horizons of an ordinary provincial milieu, and she puts up with it by making a cult out of self-suppression and a religion out of nostalgia, out of all those things that "my past life has made dear to me"—including home, parents and a brother. Yet habituation and nostalgia are a treacherous foundation for the whole duty a young life owes to itself, as Philip Wakem points out when he warns her not to turn her career into a "long suicide," and it is obvious that when Maggie constantly subdues her will to the wishes of brother Tom, who represents a distinct hardening and further narrowing of the provincial tradition, she is courting misery, abjection and death. The river flood, which ends all, is life in a phase of largeness and force commensurate with Maggie's real capacities. It gives her for once a sphere in which to exercise powers her society had taught her to turn against herself. Yet it also carries her back, to the mill and to Tom, and down, with Tom, "living through again . . . the days when they had . . . roamed the daisied fields together" in a supremely nostalgic moment that is the moment of death.

A raging force of unregenerate nature, by clearing the river banks of human habitations, makes mockery of that cult of the binding power of the past to which Maggie bound her "passionate sensibility." Maggie's crippled suitor, Philip, has thanked her, rather ghoulishly, for initiating him "into that enlarged life which grows and grows by appropriating the life of others," and for "this gift of transferred life." But this is second best at best. As the community rebuilds, Maggie's large powers, which, apart from one supreme moment, have been confined and shackled like the river itself, are lost to the community, except as her memory will afford opportunities for a renewed cult of nostalgia among a few sensitive survivors, while the hard, self-interested provincial routines of money-making and the calculated struggle for property and social preferment continue as usual.

Daniel Deronda (1876). It has the distinction, rare among George Eliot's narratives, of taking place in the near-present, only ten years before its time of composition, and its heroine has the distinction of being far from faultless and far from a position of country security at the point of her starting out. Mrs. Davilow and her unportioned daughters are poor relations and hangers-on in a rural district where they have no roots. And Gwendolen, who is thoroughly spoiled, superficially educated, probably frigid and certainly a man-hater, is bound to wreck as she attempts to mount high in an urbane society that is deceptive and vicious, that uses its landed resources for idle amusement and as something to trade against cash income, that knows the going market price of maidens but their value not at all. By becoming the virtual slayer of Grandcourt at Genoa Gwendolen fulfills all those hints and prophecies sprinkled lavishly in early pastoral scenes where she walks about, talking about piercing human targets with her archery set. But if Gwendolen is the figure of the maiden under the aspect of *femme fatale,* as Maggie is perhaps the maiden as suicide, we may well wonder why George Eliot chose this particular book to celebrate girls as vessels of human affection and why, in the Deronda plot, so much language and sentiment are lavished upon a sentimental notion of maiden rescue which Deronda represents but never actually carries out.

There is no rescue. At the end Gwendolen, a widow and childless, is left alone in the country, dying to the world, in a full solitude very like what she always feared, praying abjectly that "she will be better," while Deronda and the author recede from her, both caught up in a mighty drama of human betterment whose outcome, one knows, the countryside will be the last to hear of or benefit from. It is a curious conclusion and suggests that we are coming close to the end of the line: to a place where the value in the mere young thing goes on being recognized but where attempts to actualize that value only result in the spoliation and ruin of maidens.

The line really ends in Hardy's *Tess of the D'Urbervilles* (1891), a novel where the view of country life and girlish life that had sustained, with increasing difficulty, a whole and wholesome view of English culture itself, terminates in a death of country and girl that closes the cultural view as well. It is of course only the death of an idea and a feeling, yet these intangibles are what literature and culture attend to in anything but intangible ways, and what we must attend to now.

Tess, who is a poor peasant, who has sex experiences and bears a child before marrying, who has not been trained for the ordeal of courtship, and who has the distinctly aristocratic habit, as Lawrence shrewdly pointed out, of taking people on the terms in which they present themselves, is not a person with whom Miss Emma Woodhouse could be on speaking terms. Nevertheless, she belongs to, enriches, and finally apotheosizes the whole line because she is seen and represented, through Hardy's characteristic method of over-determination or multiple-determination in narrative, so fully and faithfully: at the beginning, when moving in the hoary yet debased May ritual of the club walking, as essential maiden; when a "maiden no more," as a decent girl whose boarding school education isolates her in self-judgment from the apparently callous but mainly tolerant view of "ruined" women taken by the peasant community; throughout, and with immensely knowledgeable authority, as a marginal agricultural worker in a stricken rural economy undergoing a crisis induced by a new technology of steam, where entire villages are "farmed" by absentee landlords when life-hold leases fall in, where all the manor houses are closed up and the forms of feudal obligation they once represented abandoned, where the church indulges itself in an extravagant evangelicalism while actually ignoring the needs of distressed people.

Tess is further seen and represented, idyllically, as a veritable "Queen of curds and cream" in the oozy, feminized world of the dairy-lands; orphically, as when like a vegetation goddess, she walks in the rank, untended dairy garden while Angel's harp music is wafted from a high window; in terms of the pathetic fallacy, as when she hides from a brutal farmer in a covert full of wounded, dying pheasants and our compassion for her blurs with our concern for the pheasants; emblematically, as when she blends with the Pauline figure of Charity—"she who suffereth long and is kind"—that is ubiquitous in Hardy's poems and novels; sacrificially, as she sleeps out on the sun-warmed stones of nature's temple at Stonehenge, until the chill dawn brings capture, a death sentence and a final release.

There is no real confusion or contradiction among these various perspectives, nor do they prevent us from seeing Tess throughout the novel changing, maturing, growing into her own distinct and complicated form of individuality and selfhood, yet always facing a set of intolerable conditions in life that must inevitably have brought her down unless—unless what? Unless Tess had been able unashamedly to take the measure of her own magnificently vital nature, to look at what her society had to offer in the way of options and opportunities, and then to turn her back upon society, going counter to a system that was organized to entrap, despoil and kill her.

To be sure, the possibility of Tess's rescue only emerges if we read the novel against the grain of its overt tragic burden. Hardy's final preface speaks of "the great campaign of the heroine." Although there is nothing wrong in being a great loser, there are a couple of moments in the narrative, one arising perhaps too early and the other certainly too late, that suggest lines along which Tess might have mounted a campaign which, without being necessarily great, might have led elsewhere than to continued victimization and death. When Tess returns pregnant from Trantridge to her mother's cottage she keeps apart from people in her "degraded" condition and a definite habit of free, self-reliant thinking grows in her. Meeting the painter of religious texts she argues him and his hateful, vengeful creed into the ground. When the parson is prevented from coming she baptizes her own dying infant "with a touch of dignity which was almost regal" to the awestruck brothers and sisters called from their beds to look on. She becomes more than ever a night-prowler and loves the dusk because it leaves her an "absolute mental liberty," so that "in the gloom she did not mind speaking freely." At this time hers is a deeply wounded nature in obscure, crepuscular revolt against everything the daytime world stands for, but since she finds nothing out there in the obscurity to connect with, she begins to respond to "an invincible instinct toward self-delight," to "the appetite for joy which pervades all creation," and to a "pulse of hopeful life," that beckon her on to brief happiness, protracted misery and final ruin.

The second point comes after Tess has murdered Alec and she and Angel take to the roads, a pair of hunted criminals, traveling by night, going north toward Salisbury Plain. They break into a furnished house that is up for rent by its absentee owner, hide there behind drawn blinds, and consummate their marriage at last, during several days and nights of furtive, passionate love-making. Tess and Angel come finally, fully together then, at a point of darkness beyond society, actually in the commission of a petty crime against property; but Tess, who is now society's legitimate prey, has her death upon her and there is nothing left for Angel to do but play Peter during the last Gethsemane-night at Stonehenge, and then go tottering off with Liza-Lu when the black flag is run up swiftly over Wintoncester prison on a fine July morning.

III

These moments are not much to put up against a smoothly operating and punitive social system that could place sixteen policemen on Salisbury Plain to take an exhausted girl and her semi-invalid husband, but they help us to understand Lawrence's great complaint that Hardy's characters do not fight hard enough for their lives, that they permit themselves to be mangled in the social machinery when they might instead have turned aside into the gloom and mystery of base nature and lived.

Lawrence, who had the habit of reading literary works, including the Bible, against the grain of their overt intent, for the "passional inspiration" they might yield, temporarily preserved the English tradition of deep pastoral by transforming it. Sticking, at least in his greatest works, with maidens and with nature, he turned against society and abandoned the attempt, upon which Hardy and his Tess came to grief, to connect the deep and simple values of pastoral—growth, wholesomeness and vitality, deep feeling and sexuality—with general cultural aims and standards in a late industrial era marked by dehumanization and abstraction. Seeking what he called in his "Study of Thomas Hardy" (1914) a "richness of new being" that would flower in intense problematic relationships between an individual woman and man sturdily at odds with society, he hoped that a new, renatured society and culture might be generated from the strength and mystery of these individual encounters, and he sometimes employed a therapeutic method of deliberate degradation, like Emily Brontë before him, in saving his characters from society and from their own abstracted selves. Usually it is the woman who must climb down off her high horse to meet the baseborn groom, gypsy, gamekeeper or Italian where he darkly lurks; but of course the aim and result are not feminine abjection. Lawrence seems to have grasped as early as his first novel, The White Peacock (1911), that such idealization of the girlish image and nature as we noted in passages from George Eliot and Henry James, by relegating the maiden to a merely emblematic role in the life of society, contributes at once to the miseries of women and the devitalization of culture.

*The Lost Girl* (1917) shows the Midlands spinster, Alvina Houghton, saving her life and health by becoming the mistress of the ignorant Italian laborer and "underman," Cicio, first clinging in England to his "dark, despised foreign nature," then running away with him to his primitive home in the Abruzzi, where, at the end, she is beginning to find new uses for British backbone and grit in organizing him and his peasant affairs. Yet *The Lost Girl* is relatively minor as Laurentian pastoral because it sets the actual bristling complexity of modern society and of modern civilized consciousness too much at a remove. We must go to his two greatest novels, *The Rainbow* (1915) and *Women in Love* (1917), to sketch how he preserved essential pastoral values while fully accepting the burden of civilized consciousness which the developed society and culture of his time imposed.

These books emerged from the plan of a narrative to be called *The Wedding Ring* or *The Sisters* that would show woman engaged in her traditional project of courtship, love and marriage but, for the first time, taking her life in her own hands and struggling into that "individual-distinctive" form of being traditionally denied her. *The Rainbow* recapitulates "the permanent tradition of the country" during several generations of declining vigor and industrial encroachment, then separates the heroine, Ursula Brangwen, from that tradition (although not from its vital roots) and affords her access to the civilized and corrupted consciousness of her time through education, work, and various shattering ordeals with lovers of both sexes. *Women in Love* matches Ursula with Birkin, an equally conscious and corrupted lover who is equally incorruptible at bottom, slowly disengages them from a society they know to be in its death throes and from tastes and tendencies shared with that society, and carries them in flight away from England to a "world elsewhere" and an "unknown land" that is wholly constituted by the deep nature of the bond of love they share as developed individuals. What Ursula finally knows and feels intimately with Birkin is what she knew and felt as a child in the rich darkness of the great barn at the Marsh farm. And what Birkin finally knows and feels intimately with Ursula is what he knew and felt when he recovered his life lying out in the ferns at Breadalby, after Hermione tried to kill him. In short, the deep pastoral values, marked by the symbol of the rainbow and other beautiful symbolic and narrative inventions in both novels, have been wholly preserved by being wholly internalized by two complicated people now free to do anything with their lives except to put them at the service of a society in critical, vital breakdown.

To conclude and sum up, after Hardy and Lawrence we get no more English novels about country matters where the simple and the complex intertwine in the notion of a community that mediates between the inexhaustible, unregenerate energies of primary nature and the powerful, abstracted orders of general civilization, and where the health and prospects of the community can be satisfyingly dramatized by focusing upon the adventures and misadventures of maidens. It seems to me that the holocaust of the Great War, much more than the changes in English society and culture that were set going or accelerated by the war experience, actually burned out of the English literary imagination all those illusions of an ultimate harmony between the aims of simple private life and of general society upon which the rich tradition I have been tracing depended. *Lady Chatterley's Lover* (1928), wherein two war-devastated adulterers approaching middle-age cohabit secretly in a fragment of forest which has supplied timber for the English trenches in Flanders and France from 1914 onwards, is surely the essential post-war English pastoral novel. Looking backwards, from that diminished and pathetic perspective—to the several country districts and villages where Tess, and Emma, and all those other cherishable girls so vividly flourished or failed, and looking even farther back, to the idealized, feminized village of the Wordsworth sonnets—is a way of contemplating the pastness of the past, of recognizing that some changes in culture, even in English culture with its tolerance for quaint historical survivals and its passion for continuity, are irreversible.

# Early Fiction and the Frightened Male

PATRICIA MEYER SPACKS

In our literary era of anti-heroes we may yearn for the days before Portnoy, when men were men, when Tom Jones grandly conceals the fact that he's broken an arm in rescuing his beloved Sophia, whom he treats with flawless respect until it becomes legal, thus moral, to take her to bed. How clear it all is as we recall it, this classic fiction: Squire Allworthy can't tell the good people from the bad, but the reader has no trouble at all. Sometimes a hero (Peregrine Pickle, for example) or a heroine's consort (say Squire B. in *Pamela*) requires educating before he earns his happiness, but happiness is a foregone conclusion. The hero suffers his conflicts, internal and external, without agonies of introversion; moreover, we can expect him to end up with the money and the girl.

Do money and girl satisfy his needs, is that what the heroes (and for that matter the villains) of eighteenth-century novels truly want? In fact a certain murk lies beneath the clarity of many early English novels, buried in each hero the shadow, the anti-hero, within many a villain the hidden sufferer. There are surprising ambivalences in this fiction, ambivalences particularly of sexual feeling, partly concealed, structurally important in the shaping of story tensions. Eighteenth-century fiction appears to work with simple dichotomies— seducer versus upright citizen, good woman versus bad—and to find infinite excitement in the movement between opposite poles: will Lovelace reform before it's too late? will Tom be ruined by his lustfulness? But what exactly it means to be a seducer or a man of feeling is often strikingly complicated.

The complications most often derive from the diverse meanings of sexual interchange, which usually involves money (elaborate financial settlements sometimes seem the real substance of eighteenth-century marriage) and which always demands physicality (even the supernaturally chaste Clarissa comments often on the superiority of Lovelace's "person" to that of her other suitor). In an era when sex led almost inevitably to procreation, it is emphatically a social as well as an individual concern, containing dynastic possibilities or threatening the destruction of family stability. Sexual relationship implies emotion and raises loudly the century's question of how emotion should properly be expressed and controlled. Novels deal with all these matters—money, bodies, families, feelings. They also reveal the problem of power which underlies them.

"Both sexes," Clarissa's cousin Morden observes, "too much love to have each other in their power: yet he hardly ever knew man or woman who was very fond of power make a right use of it." Power is—as Chaucer and Boccaccio knew—the crucial issue between men and women. To understand how fierce-ly the sexes struggle for mastery challenges optimistic belief in the possibility of rational marital arrangements as well as romantically irrational consum-mations. Cousin Morden's explicit statement is unusual for the eighteenth century, not only in its awareness of the struggle but in its pessimism about the likelihood of a happy resolution. Without explicit commitment to this view, many of the period's novels support the observation's implications, demon-strating their authors' consciousness that love means conflict (with its inevi-table emotional concomitants), and suggesting the probability that the win-ner in the struggle of love will misuse his or her achieved control.

Everyone, therefore, fears losing. For women to be afraid is socially accepta-ble, can even be a social grace; not so for men. Yet the central male charac-ters in early novels, half-conscious of the struggle in which they are engaged, fear defeat by the secret controlling force of the female nature, not subject to rationalization by any assignment of "pin money" or dowry. The hero may get the money and the girl without being sure of having won the battle; or lose on all fronts while still proclaiming his triumphant masculinity; or even be defeated by refusing to engage. Anxiety about the possibility of losing is often in the foreground of twentieth-century fiction; in the eighteenth century it provides many surprising undertones.

Smollett's novels, for example, often seem straightforward accounts of a young man's adventures, a loose picaresque series of disconnected episodes, leading happily to the hero's discovery and acceptance of his place in soci-ety. Roderick Random and Peregrine Pickle for a time suffer or enjoy roles as "outsiders," but value at last the securities of wealth and status; Humphry Clinker progresses from being a bare-bottomed postillion to finding a father, a bride, and a gainful occupation. But Peregrine in particular also learns the costs and dangers of security and acceptance; and Smollett's novels contain more or less blatant expressions of sexual fear, which comment oddly on the sexual transports of their happy endings.

To put it bluntly, men fear women. Roderick Random has little reason to, since most of his career has kept him safely away from all but the readily compliant who offer sexual gratification, demand nothing, and receive neither description nor characterization from the author. After the venomous female cousins in his early youth, he encounters no other versions of the threatening woman until he decides that matrimony is the best road to wealth, thus de-claring implicitly his willingness to use himself as a sexual commodity. He thereupon encounters several ravenous women, of whom the most frighten-ing is a passionate seventy-year-old from whom he flees "as if the devil had me in pursuit." In *Humphry Clinker* we find middle-aged Tabitha Bramble, desperate for a man, desperate for control: no more ludicrous than terrify-ing. Her brother remarks that he thinks her "the devil incarnate come to torment me for my sins." During his travels through Great Britain Matt Bram-ble encounters a Yorkshire cousin who "truckles to [his wife's] domineering and dreads, like a school-boy, the lash of her tongue," and an old friend ruined by his wife and involved in an unbreakable "thaldrom equally shameful and pernicious." He also hears Lieutenant Lismahago's detailed story of how American Indian women torture and emasculate captive men. Object lessons all.

*Peregrine Pickle* examines the matter in more detail. The hero sees around him men terrified of women or totally unmanned by them. Seeking power, Peregrine uses sexual means, relying on his own attractiveness, taunting other men with the possibility of cuckoldry or castration. The comic tradition from which such cruel jokes derive of course reflects man's fear of woman, whose power to give or to withhold creates a potential of complete dominion over the male. One may recall the comic donnée of *Joseph Andrews*: behind the conceit of a young man driven to guard his chastity lies not only awareness of the pervasiveness of male lust, but also a vision, and a fear, of woman's desire for sexual control. Peregrine has a similar vision. He displaces his sexual fears and declares his power by putting other men in frightening situations, often using women as his instruments. Unlike the older men he knows who yield to female dominion, Peregrine resists it by redirecting it and by asserting his own sexual force: to attract, to manipulate. But such power can survive only in the absence of full emotional commitment. Peregrine is afraid of marriage—as well he might be, knowing what he knows—and incapable of real relationship; he must be humbled by his author in order to wed.

Peregrine's youth reveals to him his power, his maturity discloses its limits. He listens to the lengthy memoirs of Lady Vane, an account of a woman's victimization, but its narrative of social and personal treachery tells him nothing about himself. So he is forced to recapitulate in masculine terms her experience of narrowing possibility, learning firsthand the faithlessness of the rich, the undependability of politics, the helplessness of the relatively upright individual before the manipulations of men with large intents. Losing his money, that universal metaphor of capacity, he finds himself in prison, discovers who his true friends are but is unwilling to accept their help, recovers the opportunity to marry Emilia but cannot endure the prospect of marrying from a position of weakness. His growing up demands the contraction rather than the expansion of his nature: he must reject part of himself, part of the masculine arrogance which has been the center of his life, in order to earn stability. If he gives up sexual pride he will be rewarded with the girl; but the novel makes us conscious that the price, humility, is high. Indeed, the novelist cannot endure the dilemma he has created. He provides an unexpected inheritance to equalize man and woman; the marriage can now take place, and Peregrine returns, his self-explorations ended, to fill the role of country gentleman. But the tone of the conclusion is sufficiently ambiguous to suggest some doubt about the value of what has been achieved, and the novel's final image is of Emilia taking over the household management: assuming her proper sphere of power: one wonders how far it will extend.

Peregrine's visions of pleasure and power, through his young manhood, depend on his emotional isolation. He refuses to allow himself to need others;

he cannot face the consequences of closeness. His sequence of practical jokes on friends and enemies alike is an extended exercise in self-distancing. As a seducer and exploiter of women, a mocker of men, he can feel himself free, driven toward this perverse vision of freedom by what he has seen of intimacy: men terrorized by their women, or betrayed by them, or—at very best, in the Commodore's case—the happy patterns of their lives disrupted by women. Peregrine, at the novel's end, is in a state of sexual felicity so manifest and impressive that even his misogynistic friend Crabtree recognizes its value. He has successfully resisted attempts to make him impotent through drink on his wedding night, as he earlier evaded a cuckolded husband's plot to castrate him. But he seems to be disappearing in a cloud of friends, relatives, servants. The conventional resolution to a comic action here has disturbing undertones. Peregrine has dwindled into a husband; his maturity involves accepting the ramifications of the real, which deprive a man of the power of his dreams. The fear of women, in this book as in other Smollett novels, is a fear of powerlessness; and the resolution of the hero's fear of being thus "unmanned" is the assertion that relative powerlessness is a social necessity (even for men) attended with emotional and sexual compensations. Peregrine willingly accepts his own diminishment for the sake of such compensations, but there is sadness in the acceptance: fear of weakness is precariously held at bay.

Clarissa, like Pamela, is a novel without a hero. Its villain, Lovelace, consumed by sexual anxiety, confirms the implications of the struggle for power dramatized in Smollett. Lovelace too fears weakness, and with reason. In him we discover more fully the vulnerabilities of the dominant male.

Lovelace enjoys believing that Clarissa is afraid of him; "No one fears whom they value not," he observes. His fantasy of ultimate triumph has Clarissa perpetually trembling in her total subjection to his will; he is in this respect not unlike her detestable other suitor, Solmes, who remarks that "fear and terror . . . looked pretty in a bride as well as in a wife" and believes that "the man who made himself feared, fared best" in marriage. It is a raw statement of the doctrine that the issue, and titillation, in sex is power. But in fact Clarissa's fear of her lover is most often subordinated to other emotions—anxiety, conflict, confusion, defiance, depression, anger. As for Lovelace, dominated by an elaborate mythology of maleness, he precipitates his death by his unwillingness to allow anyone the faintest cause to think him afraid of a potential challenger. He is not afraid of challenges and duels, easy ways of asserting manhood. He is afraid, desperately, of being unmanned in subtler fashion. He describes himself as standing before Clarissa "trembling . . . like a hungry hound who sees a delicious morsel within his reach (the froth hanging about his vermilion jaws), yet dares not leap at it for his life." The bewilderment and self-contempt—at the animality of lust as well as the cravenness of a fearful discipline—in this self-revealing metaphor are Lovelace's characteristic response to his intermittent recognition of his own unaccountable terror in the contemplation of Clarissa.

Lovelace's need for effective power is more compelling, and even more elaborately realized, than Peregrine's. In his relations with other men he finds it necessary to be the leader, the "emperor" of a troop of rakes. If his friend Belford appears to forget Lovelace's sovereignty, the "prince" finds some opportunity to taunt his comrade as personally unattractive and therefore relatively powerless with women. The only role Lovelace can imagine with a woman is one of equally absolute dominion. When he tricks Clarissa into fleeing with him, his summary to Belford is, "And so I became her emperor," the duplication of metaphor suggesting the significant limitation of his capacity to imagine relationship. If power is the issue between men and women, he will yield nothing: he is far from learning the lesson that Peregrine learns. But only briefly can he feel himself Clarissa's "emperor": mastery of a woman is not securely achieved, he discovers, even by rape, since, as Clarissa repeatedly points out, her will remains inviolate although her body is no longer intact. "Such a triumph over the whole sex," Lovelace writes, "if I can subdue this lady!" But he can't; instead, she subdues him. "I fear her as much as I love her," he writes, roughly halfway through the novel. Despite his semi-erotic fantasies about her terror of him, this confession of his own fear (repeated later) reveals Clarissa's power and her lover's comparative weakness. He has to drug her into unconsciousness before he can possess her. Raped, dying, dead, Clarissa always wins: she realizes this, and Lovelace realizes it yet more acutely.

What Lovelace admits to being afraid of in Clarissa is her moral superiority. By raping her perhaps he can neutralize or destroy it; then he may be free. Smollett describes men afraid of women's exploitation of female sexuality, which can betray or unman a lover. *Clarissa* depicts a man afraid of woman's fantasized *a*sexuality. Through Lovelace's repeated seductions he attempts to dominate women specifically by reducing them to the sexual, then despising them for it. But Clarissa appears to him and to his friends as an "angel" rather than a woman; Belford finally observes that it is impossible to think of sex in her presence. As an angel she is of course a focus of fear; and equally of course an object of what passes for love in a Lovelace. Her angelic nature declares her superiority, her power actual and potential; Lovelace must acknowledge that she has won, though he is altogether unable to accept his defeat. His fear of her, both before and after his betrayal of her, feels intolerable; he is driven to ever more outrageous devices to exorcise this fear by degrading its object.

If Lovelace recognizes his obsessive relation with female purity, he has other problems of which he is less conscious. His terror of marriage, more than a rakish convention, is substantiated by his vacillations of tone whenever the subject occurs to him. Repeatedly he vows to make amends to the wronged Clarissa by marrying her; repeatedly he panics at the idea, comforting himself either by the reflection that he doesn't have to do anything of the sort quite yet, or—more often—by fantasies of continued sexual excursions on the side despite the nominal restrictions of marriage. He cannot bear the idea of giving up the pursuit of women which seems itself the object of his lust. Not the fulfillment but the chase reassures him of his manhood; living only with a woman who has accepted him, he would lose the sources of reassurance. Never can he endure for long an imagining of faithfulness. Like Peregrine, he fears intimacy, keeping men and women alike at a distance by his insistent concentration on his irresistible forcefulness. His fear of commitment, of closeness, of sexual sobriety echoes his fear—which he admits more openly—of epistolary seriousness. Even in the context of Clarissa's slow dying and exemplary death, Lovelace cannot for long sustain on paper a contemplative or self-reproachful tone. Self-reproach turns readily into posturing, contemplation gives way to mockery; he tells Belford that he laughs in order not to weep, but the laughter seems a tic, a mechanism declaring his psychic disorder while protecting its possessor against the horrors of relationship.

Committed as he is to his personal politics of power, Lovelace can hardly risk marriage: he knows this, in some sense, although he doesn't understand it. A traditional male view of marriage has it that a woman, given security and opportunity, will do her best to rule her spouse. Clarissa's uncles and her father articulate this notion clearly, and Lovelace explicitly shares it. He worries because Clarissa is "haughty," has already showed herself unforgiving, holds his very soul in suspense: what will she do, once married? Despite his history of seducing and abandoning women, Lovelace's experience has not reassured him: even degraded women seem always in search of dominance. His victims are eager to be his mistresses in more than a sexual sense. The whores and madam who contribute to Clarissa's ruin are exemplary: urging Lovelace on, they trap him in his own self-display, taunting him with failure of manhood if he momentarily relents in his treachery. Demanding of him consistent performance as a seducer, they reveal no sexual needs of their own. (In *Clarissa*, as in *Peregrine Pickle*, sexual assertion is often quite divorced from sexual desire.) The compulsive, truly terrifying elaboration of his plot against Clarissa is Lovelace's most spectacular performance, intended to show his capacities, for his own benefit, perhaps for Clarissa's, but more immediately to impress his fellow-rakes and his female instruments. It is necessary to his psychic economy that women be only his instruments, but even these vividly subordinated women make demands: that Lovelace be and do what they expect. His fantasy of marriage is of the loss of personal control; the danger of lost control looms everywhere in his relations with women.

Not the least perceptive element in Richardson's characterization of Lovelace is his suggestion of the seducer's bewilderment at himself. Why does a man behave this way? The man doesn't know. "Once more," he writes, "how could I be such a villain to so divine a creature! yet love her all the time as never man loved woman! Curse upon my *contriving genius!* Curse upon my *intriguing head,* and upon my *seconding heart!* To sport with the fame, with the honor, with the *life* of such an angel of a woman! Oh, my damned incredulity! that, believing her to *be* a woman, I must hope to *find* her a woman!" And then, after a bit more in the same vein: "The world never *saw* such a husband as I will make. I will have no will but hers." He temporarily resolves his conflict by imagining his total subordination as a final triumph. But since his "genius," his head, and his heart all seem to him mysteriously dissociated from his true self, he is not, now or ever, truly in control of his own actions.

Modern terminology provides a glib explanation: Lovelace is in the grip of neurotic fear and compulsion. Richardson, lacking the terminology, understood the fact. *Clarissa* ends with the seducer's death not only because convention demands this dénouement (nemesis must attend violation of the heroine) but because Lovelace is irreconcilable: there is no way for him to live in society. His need for isolation amounts to a need for self-destruction. Unlike Peregrine, he learns nothing from his experience. An irresistible force has confronted an immovable object, Clarissa's pride and Lovelace's have fought to a standstill; the moral, as far as Lovelace is concerned, is that he tragically entangled himself with the wrong woman. He cannot accept any obligation to relinquishment, compromise, reconciliation with the real. A man compelled by his terrors and his defenses against them, he is doomed to alienation. His friends reform or die, his human instruments meet dreadful fates, he wanders alone on the Continent, embracing the prospect of a duel as an opportunity for action despite his full consciousness of the guilt which his opponent wishes to punish. The arrogance with which he confronts his destiny—it never occurs to him that he can lose—reveals the defensiveness of his self-absorption, a protection against the recognition of possible inferiority to man or woman.

The sexual fear in *Peregrine Pickle*, supported by a long tradition of dirty jokes and by observable social reality, seems as much a social as a personal fact. Lovelace's fears are all his own; his sexual anxiety, however he finds facts to support it, even comrades to share it, issues manifestly from within, reflecting his compulsion toward power and his painful consciousness of the impossibility of ever getting enough of it.

Is sex the reality to which all other experience refers, or is it a representation of some larger truth? The question keeps recurring: it is not only *sexual* power that Lovelace and Peregrine fear to lose. "Man's recurrent fear that he will be found wanting," the psychoanalyst Leslie Farber writes, "makes him peculiarly vulnerable to challenge. And that fear, as life proceeds, becomes vague and amorphous in his experience, imposing its painful claim not only on sexual performance itself but also on intellectual, emotional, and even spiritual realms." The description applies quite precisely to Peregrine and to Lovelace. It also suggests an interpretation for the eagerness of almost every eighteenth-century fictional hero to engage in duels, where physical performance is publicly demanded and displayed and power vividly affirmed. But indeed the fear of inadequacy is everywhere, in fiction as in fact. It may emerge through those who—again like Peregrine and Lovelace—characteristically deny it, as well as those who, like more modern fictional figures, attest it until they incapacitate themselves. A novel about superficial success, *Peregrine Pickle*, with its hint that marriage, affirming sexuality, yet opposes male vitality, confirms the validity of masculine fears as much as the account of Lovelace's downfall. Pessimistic in a different way is the direct fictional portrayal of the incapacitated male in *Tristram Shandy*, a novel dominated by sexual fears which spread to every area of endeavor.

Tristram's endless masturbatory writing about himself constantly reveals the fear of impotence, a conceivable fate for any man, symbolized by the richly dramatized impossibility of bringing a narrative to completion, emblematic always of the final powerlessness of death, before which all men are inadequate. Since power in interpersonal relations is the crucial issue here as in the other two novels, impotence becomes a problem of a man's effect on others. A man with an enormous nose is the wonder of the whole city, women yearn to touch the protuberance, men insist it must be a fraud. A man lacking whiskers feels it necessary to leave the court. These allegorical accounts of male potency and impotence foreshadow the drama between Uncle Toby and the Widow Wadman. Here the woman is the pursuer, although she manipulates the situation to give the man an illusion of control. Almost her sole concern is the degree of Toby's sexual power, given his wound in the groin. After all, her husband had a sciatica long before he died, it's been years since she's received sexual satisfaction, the end of courtship is nothing else. Toby's actual degree of sexual force remains ambiguous, but not his response to the widow's interest. He has valued her humanitarian concern for his wound; when he learns that it's motivated by sexual self-interest, he is deeply disappointed. As a man who doesn't know one end of a woman from the other, he is not himself concerned with physical matters. Fearing that a woman wishes to use his manhood for her own sexual purposes, he will reject her.

If the late Mr. Wadman suffered a potency-destroying sciatica, so did Mr. Shandy in the months before Tristram's conception. That conception, as Tristram lengthily emphasizes, was a precarious matter—a demonstration of virtual impotence in the very act of procreation. A man's sexual power is at the mercy of the most trivial opposition. If his wife inquires about winding the clock, his effective force diminishes: the flow of "animal spirits" at his conception, Tristram explains, was not all that could be wished. Sexual matters are puzzling for Mr. Shandy, who suffers also from intellectual impotence. He retreats from his physical problems to a realm of sterile ideas, never issuing in significant action, never brought to fruition. When his son's sexual potential is threatened by the inopportune fall of a window sash, Mr. Shandy turns to his books. Theory is a substitute for practice. But knowledge, Tristram asserts directly, is the enemy of physical potency, the life of the mind existing in direct opposition to that of the body. "Alas!" Tristram warns his uncle, the pursuit of knowledge will "exasperate thy symptoms,—check thy perspirations,—evaporate thy spirits,—waste thy animal strength,— . . . impair thy health,—and hasten all the infirmities of thy old age."

Knowledge is more Mr. Shandy's obsession than Uncle Toby's. Toby's substitute for sexual activity is an imitation of military action—one degree further removed from reality than those duels which attest masculinity. By playing with unreal cannon and mock-fortifications, Toby and Corporal Trim satisfy their deepest needs. It is the corporal who calmly assumes that an erection is the only sure sign of love; if he doesn't have one, it follows that he cannot be in love. The erections he seems to enjoy most, though, are of bridges and sentry boxes, expressing aggression without painful consequence, producing power without struggle. Mr. Shandy gains an illusory sense of power by silencing all opponents through his sheer inconsequence of knowledge; Toby and Trim find equally illusory, equally satisfactory, emblems of potency. These characters have discovered brilliant compensations for a fear they refuse to recognize.

But, recognized or not, sexual fear is an active presence in this novel. Tristram himself suggests something of its operations. He is, of course, an anti-hero before his time: he can hardly manage even to be born. The anti-hero feels none of the hero's obligation to display his courage, and his modes of power are often devious, but he may share with the hero a desire for mastery. Tristram seeks control through language, though control eludes him. Toby imitates military action, Tristram tries in his role as author to imitate psychic action: but nothing can be achieved, nothing finished, his book will stop but not be completed at his death. His relationship with the ambiguous Jenny —wife, daughter, mistress?—is too shadowy to assert meaning; no other relationships outside his family exist for him. His very fluency declares the impossibility of meaningful assertion: it's possible to say anything, so no conceivable saying matters. Traveling through France, he flees Death. With frenetic gaiety he insists that he's winning, escaping the inescapable enemy, the sign of his victory his lively sexual interest in every pretty girl. But he knows that a man's potency is at the mercy of any hot chestnut that chances to fly into his codpiece, he knows that Death must win in the end, he knows that it's difficult even to maintain faith in the value of human vitality.

The relation of this near-despair to the male's pervasive anxiety "that he will be found wanting" is not far to seek. Tristram's experience continually confirms such fear. At every point he finds himself wanting. He fears the operations of the sexual imagination, which may lead his readers astray even as it distracts him: once he thinks of sticking his finger in a pie, his imagination becomes so overheated that he can't continue his story. He fears and suffers from literal sexual impotence, describing himself, after an abortive encounter, standing, garters in hand, "reflecting upon what had *not* pass'd"—an emblem for his book, with its constant awareness of failed possibility. Laying plans to publish two volumes a year for the rest of his life, he knows that he can never keep up with his own story. Resorting to diagrams, blank spaces, black pages and marbled ones, he testifies his awareness of the inadequacy of language to his purposes. His life, like his book, feels incomplete, but Death is at his heels. His sexual impulses never lead to fulfillment; his experience in every respect is of frustration.

Pity and fear are orthodox emotional reactions to tragedy; but what is the reader's reaction to this particular sort of comedy? The novel seems to demand some reduced version of the tragic emotions: pity converted to an amused and slightly patronizing imitation of itself, fear limited to diffuse anxiety somewhat controlled by the novel's comic distancing. The book ends with Mr. Shandy—who copulates only "on principle"—discoursing on the ignobility of physical passion, wishing that the race could be continued by other means. He suggests that the work of destruction which Toby imitates is nobler than that of procreation. Then we learn about the local bull, which turns out to be unable to impregnate a cow. Toby sums up the immediate and the larger story as concerning a cock and a bull: the emblems of masculine power have become symbols of ineffectuality and meaninglessness. A world in which bulls are not virile, in which men prefer false battles to real sexual connection, in which windows threaten the penises of small boys—such a world, however ludicrous, is also disturbing to contemplate. It consolidates the troubling sexual implications of other eighteenth-century novels. The jokes about bulls and windows and imitation battles reduce to the trivial some fundamental and pervasive and serious human concerns. But trivialization does not destroy them. As we encounter one instance after another of frustrated intent, incomplete performance, we must feel some anxiety over the possibility that experience may be so organized that a man must *always* be found wanting. Of course the life of the novel is not "real life;" the book announces itself repeatedly as only a verbal construct, its tone declares its comic intent. Yet its undeniable link to reality, and its enormous energy, depend partly on its constant implicit reference to, and to some extent its evocation of, a fundamental human fear. Referring constantly to the sexual, it insists on the connection between sexual matters and those traditionally considered more dignified. Dignity, it suggests, is only a way of concealing the painful truths at the heart of reality. Unlike Lovelace, Tristram seems fully aware of the nature of those universal truths; unlike Peregrine, he has gone beyond reconciliation: the universe he perceives allows no possibility for reconciliation. Heroism and villainy are equally inconceivable in a world where everything reduces itself to the ridiculousness of inadequacy.

The fear of women as sexual manipulators and as angels, the fear of marriage as a sphere of intimacy and lost control, the fear of sexual and of literary impotence—all alike affirm the male obsession with the attainment and preservation of power. In *Tristram Shandy*, where fear of impotence supplies a central theme rather than an undertone of the fictional action, it also challenges the very possibility of novelistic success, demanding intricate recognitions from the reader: even as he enjoys Tristram's story, he must share Tristram's anxiety over the impossibility of valid narrative. The fear of woman, then, as novelistic subject, expands the possibilities of sex as metaphor, providing devices for achieving novelistic complexity. Qualifying the optimism of social comedy in *Peregrine Pickle*, the pattern of Peregrine's unresolved fear reminds the reader that the novel's sense of completion belongs to literature rather than life. The terrifying female figures on the fringes of the action in oth-

er Smollett novels suggest that the social order, with its assumed male dominance, may be more precarious than we usually choose to believe. Clarissa
ascends from her initial personal desperation to the security of being (presumably) an angel in fact as well as in male fantasy; but Lovelace's counterpointed
drama keeps the reader aware of the continuing insecurities involved in persistent determination to get what one wants on earth rather than in heaven.
And Tristram's drama of impotence, a justification for all his anxieties, suggests
that male fear reflects the fundamental and necessary human insecurity which
novels, in their completed achievements, only temporarily deny.

# Austen and Alcott on Matriarchy: New Women or New Wives?

NINA AUERBACH

Toward the end of her eccentric life, when her crusades for dress reform and feminism had fizzled out, Dr. Mary Walker settled down to become a local character on the family farm in Oswego, New York. On October 19, 1895, the *Oswego Times* ran a facetious article about her desire to found a community of women on her land, to be called "the Adamless Eden": "It was to be a colony for young women who would pledge themselves to single blessedness. They would work and study, and eventually go forth as samples of the new womanhood." This report was followed by a chuckly burlesque by Bill Nye.

In December the *Metropolitan Magazine* ran a heavily respectful piece about the idea with quotes from Mary Walker:

> "*Every woman must do something to be somebody. Girls who intend to marry must learn what housekeeping and household duties mean. This is especially true of women who are to become farmers' wives. My intention is to make my place a sort of training school for these women, and when desired, practical instruction in actual fieldwork.*" She denied the report that bloomers were required. Girls might choose their own apparel. It would not be a "*new woman's colony, but a new wives' training school.*" [1]

So far as is known the Adamless Eden was never born. But the questions it raises about the collective purpose of groups of women together find their way into much of our literature, including two novels about families that have become different sorts of classics. Jane Austen's *Pride and Prejudice* (1813) is the English novel's paradigmatic courtship romance, celebrating "the positive advantages of maturity over childishness" [2] and allowing us, as a successful romance must do, to believe in marriage as an emblem of adulthood achieved. Louisa May Alcott's *Little Women* (1868–69) is one of America's most beloved celebrations of childhood, its rather perfunctory concluding marriages giving a twilight flavor to the enforced passage into womanhood proper. But the darting adult wit of the one and the contagious nostalgia of the other treat a similar process: the passage of a bevy of sisters from the collective colony of women presided over by their mother to the official authority of masculine protection.

---

[1] Quoted in Charles McCool Snyder, *Dr. Mary Walker: The Little Lady in Pants* (New York: Vantage Press, 1962), pp. 129–130.

[2] Patricia Meyer Spacks, *The Female Imagination* (New York: Alfred A. Knopf, 1975), p. 121.

The families in both novels are explicitly matriarchal, and in both, the mother is indefatigably committed to the administrative "business" of marrying her vividly alive but economically superfluous daughters; it is she who forges the family's liaison with the outside world of marriage, morals, and money that eligible men embody. While the mother forges connections, the father retreats from the business of marriage to his library, wrapping himself in attenuated privacy and remoteness like a traditional Victorian wife. But while each matriarchy is a school for wives, each—in its very strength of purpose—has the potential of being "a new woman's colony" as well. Like Mary Walker's visionary community, both are poised precariously between these two self-definitions, creating for Austen the tension of comedy, and for Alcott, that of pathos and loss. But the dominant female worlds out of which the concluding marriages are generated give us two nineteenth-century versions of the family as an (almost) Adamless Eden, in all its power to repel or retain.

## I. *Pride and Prejudice*

*Anxious and uneasy, the period which passed in the drawing-room, before the gentlemen came, was wearisome and dull to a degree, that almost made her uncivil. She looked forward to their entrance, as the point on which all her chance of pleasure for the evening must depend.*[3]

Since Elizabeth Bennet has passed her life in a world of waiting women, and we have passed it with her for much of the previous two volumes of the novel, this passage need describe such a world only as a temptation to lose one's temper. The story, the glow, will begin with the opening of the door.

In an earlier description of a similar situation, we are given a chance, not so much to hear what women say to each other during this excruciating period, as to share the distrust and emotional pressure that forbid their saying anything:

*Elizabeth soon saw that she was herself closely watched by Miss Bingley, and that she could not speak a word, especially to Miss Darcy, without calling her attention. This observation would not have prevented her from trying to talk to the latter, had they not been seated at an inconvenient distance; but she was not sorry to be spared the necessity of saying much. Her own thoughts were employing her. She expected every moment that some of the gentlemen would enter the room. She wished, she feared that the master of the house might be amongst them; and whether she wished or feared it most, she could scarcely determine.* (p. 268)

The unexpressed intensity of this collective waiting for the door to open and a Pygmalion to bring life into limbo defines the female world of *Pride and Prejudice*; its agonized restraint is reflected microcosmically in the smaller community of the Bennet family, and macrocosmically in the larger community of England

---

[3] Jane Austen, *Pride and Prejudice*, ed. R. W. Chapman (London: Oxford University Press, 1932), p. 341. All page references to Jane Austen's fiction included in the text will be to R. W. Chapman's editions of the novels and of *Minor Works* (London: Oxford University Press, 1963).

itself. With a nod to V. S. Pritchett, Jane Austen's most recent biographer allows her to touch British history in a manner that most admirers of her self-enclosed miniatures have forbidden: "In his *George Meredith and English Comedy*, V. S. Pritchett has a challenging aside in which he describes Jane Austen as a war novelist, pointing out that the facts of the long war are basic to all her books. She knew all about the shortage of men, the high cost of living, and . . . about the vital part played by the Navy." [4] In presenting to us these drawing rooms full of women watching the door and watching each other, Jane Austen tells us what an observant, genteel woman has to tell about the Napoleonic Wars: she writes novels about waiting.

As her England is in large part a country of women whose business it is to wait for the return of the men who have married them or may do so, so her heroine's family has occupied much of its history in waiting, with increasing hopelessness, for a male to enter it:

> When first Mr. Bennet had married, economy was held to be perfectly useless; for, of course, they were to have a son. This son was to join in cutting off the entail, as soon as he should be of age, and the widow and younger children would by that means be provided for. Five daughters successively entered the world, but yet the son was to come; and Mrs. Bennet, for many years after Lydia's birth, had been certain that he would. This event had at last been despaired of, but it was then too late to be saving. Mrs. Bennet had no turn for economy, and her husband's love of independence had alone prevented their exceeding their income. (p. 308)

In the family microcosm the male whom all await can alone bring substance: by inheriting the estate, he will insure the family the solidity and continuity of income and land. The quality of their life is determined by the Beckett-like realization that the period of protracted waiting is not a probationary interim before life begins: waiting for a male is life itself.

As its name indicates, the Bennet home is not an autonomous, self-sustaining entity: unlike Lucas Lodge, the home of their neighbors, Longbourn House bears the name of the village in which it is set, although a son might have changed its name to his own. This interchangeability between village and home suggests the primacy of "the neighborhood" in *Pride and Prejudice*, a primacy which nobody questions. The walls of the family are made of brittle glass: when Longbourn House receives a piece of news, its inhabitants do not gather together to savor it as the March family will do; they disperse it instantly to the neighborhood, which makes of it what malicious use it may. Elizabeth accepts this primacy, though like her father she makes conversational capital out of its absurdity: "If he means to be but little at Netherfield, it would be better for the neighborhood that he should give up the place entirely, for then we might possibly get a settled family there. But perhaps Mr. Bingley did not take the house so much for

⁴ Jane Aiken Hodge, *Only A Novel: The Double Life of Jane Austen* (Connecticut: Fawcett Publications, Inc., 1973), pp. 238–239.

the convenience of the neighborhood as for his own, and we must expect him to keep or quit it on the same principle" (p. 178). Clearly the family exists to feed the neighborhood and not the other way round. The *reductio ad absurdum* of this is Mr. Bennet's mordant: "For what do we live, but to make sport for our neighbors, and laugh at them in our turn?" (p. 364). This is an ethos far from Jo March's euphoric cry at the conclusion of *Little Women*: "I do think that families are the most beautiful things in all the world!" [5] In *Pride and Prejudice* they are the most beautiful things in all the world to leave: "There was novelty in the scheme [of Elizabeth's journey to Hunsford], and as, with such a mother and such uncompanionable sisters, home could not be faultless, a little change was not unwelcome for its own sake" (p. 151).

The two evasive double negatives that suggest Elizabeth's non-feeling for her non-family suggest also the most striking characteristic of the Bennet menage: its non-existence. Jane Austen boasted to Cassandra of the success with which she had "lop't and crop't" the manuscript of *Pride and Prejudice*, and I suspect it was the scenes among the Bennets that were lop't and crop't, for the version we have contains scarcely any fully-developed sequence in which the family are alone together. It is true that in the second chapter, "the girls" all flock around Mr. Bennet in rapture at his having paid a call on Bingley, but this is the last time they act in concert. After their first shared joy at this possible escape hatch— the March girls are equally joyful at a letter from their father admonishing them to conquer, not hypothetical suitors, but themselves—the unity between the sisters fractures, the two youngest raucously pursuing officers in Meryton and the two eldest more decorously pursuing gentility at Netherfield, while plain Mary remains at home mouthing platitudes. The groupings between the sisters are rigidly separate and hierarchical. During her brief infatuation with Wickham, Elizabeth steps across the wide gulf between Jane's camp and Lydia's, and, when her vision clears, shifts with mortification back into Jane's. There is none of the emotional fluidity that exists between the March sisters, with each older girl mothering a younger one and the one most different from herself: the passionate tomboy Jo appropriates saintly Beth, while gentle domestic Meg nurtures vain ambitious Amy. In *Pride and Prejudice* this cross-fertilization and balance of opposing temperaments would threaten to complete a circle that by definition can never be complete so long as a "single man in possession of a good fortune" exists who is (or "must be") "in want of a wife"—or is wanted by one. The replacement of "is" by "must be" in the mother-evolved dictum of the famous first sentence lifts us from the empirical to the absolute, locating us irrevocably in a world ruled by women but possessed by men.

We are not allowed to see Longbourn House until a man does; for the reader as for its inhabitants it is an insubstantial place that exists to be left. When the unregenerate Lydia returns to make everybody miserable as the family's first bride, and looks "eagerly around the room, [takes] notice of some little alteration in it, and observe[s], with a laugh, that it [is] a great while since she [has] been

---

[5] Louisa May Alcott, *Little Women* (New York: Grosset & Dunlap, 1947), p. 539. Future references to this edition will appear in the text.

there" (p. 315), it matters to nobody what the little alteration might be. Details at Longbourn are not "known, and *loved* because they are known": here and elsewhere notice of the house evokes the joy of absence from it, not presence in it. Lydia's wedding parties crystallize the role of the household in the novel as a whole: "These parties were acceptable to all; to avoid a family circle was even more desirable to such as did think, than such as did not" (p. 318). Meg, the eldest and so the natural first bride of the March household, will turn longingly back toward the circle immediately after her wedding ceremony, crying, "The first kiss for Marmee!" But Lydia, the youngest and her mother's favorite, leaves with never a backward glance a family we have never seen together, a house with wavering contours and rooms we cannot visualize.

Further erosion of Longbourn's solidity comes from its lack of a past. For Elizabeth, the only inhabitant with whom we are intimate, the house has none of the density and texture which a childhood in it would bring: though she scrupulously watches and analyzes and talks, she is beyond a certain point devoid of memory. "The *present* always occupies you in such scenes—does it?" says Darcy to her "with a look of doubt," and she answers half-consciously, "Yes, always" (p. 93). Later he tries to lead her back into her past by saying, "*You* cannot have a right to such very strong local attachment. *You* cannot have been always at Longbourn." We never know the answer: Elizabeth merely "look[s] surprised" and clams up (p. 179). This vagueness that seizes her is all the more surprising in that in Austen's other novels, no matter how distant family relationships may be, expulsion thence is in some sense a loss of Eden; the family is enriched for her by its traditional incarnation as a microcosm of society, endowing the life within it with weight and purpose if not with the intimacy later writers learned to want.[6] Thus Elizabeth Bennet stands out as the only heroine who is deprived of a childhood and a setting for her childhood: Marianne Dashwood's rhapsody to the "dear, dear Norland" she is forced out of would have some resonance for all the rest. Consider in this light Maggie Tulliver's later panic at childhood dislodged: "The end of our life will have nothing in it like the beginning." With her home a vacuum and her memory a blank, such an end can only be Elizabeth's dearest wish. If she shares nothing else with her mother, her faculty of non-remembrance confirms Mrs. Bennet's perception of the non-life they have had together.

Oddly, it is men who bring domestic substance into the representation of this world and endow female existence with palpability. Mrs. Bennet is perpetually begging any and all eligible males to come to a dinner we have never seen the family at Longbourn eat, as if only in their presence can nourishment present itself. The first male to grace their table is Mr. Collins, and in token of the reality of male appetite, Mrs. Bennet gives us the first domestic detail of Longbourn we have seen—a fish they do not have: "But—good lord! how unlucky! there is not a bit of fish to be got to-day. Lydia, my love, ring the bell. I must speak to Hill,

[6] For a definition of Jane Austen in relation to the tradition of the familial Eden, see R. F. Brissenden, "*Mansfield Park:* Freedom and the Family," in *Jane Austen: Bicentenary Essays,* ed. John Halperin (Cambridge: Cambridge University Press, 1975), pp. 156–171.

this moment" (p. 61). Mr. Collins himself brings a sense of domestic reality to Longbourn by his interminable descriptions of the lay-out and situation of Huns-ford; he even permits us to hear about "some shelves in the closets up stairs," which stand out vividly in a house that as far as we know has neither closets nor shelves. While the sonorous presentation of these details reminds us primarily of the weighty tedium of Mr. Collins' self-absorption, like Miss Bates' outpourings in *Emma* they also unobtrusively fill the world for us in a manner that looks forward to the opulently detailed presentation of Darcy's Pemberley.

Pemberley is Elizabeth's initiation into physicality, providing her with all the architectural solidity and domestic substance Longbourn lacks. It has real grounds, woods, paths, streams, rooms, furniture; real food is eaten there: "The next varia-tion which their visit afforded was produced by the entrance of servants with cold meat, cake, and a variety of all the finest fruits in season; . . . though they could not all talk, they could all eat; and the beautiful pyramids of grapes, nectarines, and peaches, soon collected them round the table" (p. 268). The "pyramids" of fruit suggest both architectural and natural power, neither of which is available in the blank space of her mother's house. Surely, to be mistress of Pemberley is "something," in view of the imprisoning nothing of being mistress at Longbourn. But when Bingley and Darcy appear there for dinner at last, in all the glory of prospective husband-ness, food seems to spring into abundance for the first time: "The dinner was as well dressed as any I ever saw. The venison was roasted to a turn—and everybody said, they never saw so fat a haunch. The soup was fifty times better than what we had at the Lucas's last week; and even Mr. Darcy acknowledged, that the partridges were remarkably well done; and I suppose he has two or three French cooks at least" (p. 342). For the first time, Mrs. Bennet applies the numbers with which she is obsessed not to abstract and invisible sums of money, but to the immediately edible and nourishing. Contrary to sentimental myth, it is not women but available men whose presence makes a house a home.

If men can bring what seems a cornucopian abundance to the scanty Bennet dinner table, it is also men who create whatever strength of sisterhood we see in the novel. If at times the fight for male approval prevents co-operation between women, the mysterious power of a man can also draw women together in its aegis. During the many confidences we see between Elizabeth and Jane, they talk of nothing but Bingley and Darcy, speculating over their motives and characters with the relish of two collaborators working on a novel. Moreover, Lydia is never so much their sister as when she disgraces herself with Wickham and seems to spoil their chances of marriage as well: unwanted family solidarity is created by sexual disgrace as it is celebrated in sexual triumph. The abandoned fragment, *The Watsons*, defines more baldly the law that a family of women is never so much a family as when one member finds a man to remove her from it: "We must not all expect to be individually lucky replied Emma. The Luck of one member of a Family is Luck to all.—" (*MW*, p. 321). It is not merely that the descriptive energy of the novel is reserved for the homes the girls marry into: it is solely the presence of suitors that brings substance to the families they leave. The law governing the technique of *Pride and Prejudice* is at one with Mrs. Bennet's economic obsession: marriage and marriage alone gives the world contour.

As Jane Austen presents a family of women, invisibility is its essence: economic invisibility seeps into the physical world. In *Sense and Sensibility* the four Dashwood women, dispossessed of their estate by another patriarchal entail, settle into cramped Barton Cottage, on which no descriptive detail is lavished until dashing Willoughby brings it to romantic life:

> *"To me it is faultless. Nay, more, I consider it as the only form of building in which happiness is attainable, and were I rich enough, I would instantly pull Combe down, and build it up again in the exact plan of this cottage."*
> *"With dark narrow stairs, and a kitchen that smokes, I suppose,"* said Elinor. (p. 72)

The oppressive becomes the idyllic only to a man who is to be mistrusted, and it is vaguely insulting when Willoughby goes on to rhapsodize about Barton's "dear parlour" and the desecration of any "improvements" on it. *Little Women* will create a world where Laurie's exuberant affection for the cramped cottage of the March women shows the soundness of his heart and values; but Willoughby's effusions about such straitened surroundings render him emotionally suspect and deflect from what Elizabeth Bennet terms "a proper way of thinking." There is a similar aura of hovering insult in *The Watsons* when Lord Osborne and Tom Musgrave abruptly deign to pay a formal call on the stinted family of sisters. But in this more assertive and self-aware ambience food does not obligingly spring into being upon the entrance of men; rather, the men are driven away by the family's preparations for its unfashionably early dinner. This unwelcoming imminence of food hints at the statement that a woman's primary hunger is the need to feed herself rather than a man, but the novel was never finished and the implications of this self-sustainment were never explored.

Throughout Jane Austen's completed novels women lead a purgatorial existence together. When Maria Bertram is banished to the ministrations of Mrs. Norris in *Mansfield Park* we feel that such a colony of two is a fate worse than the death or transportation that are the usual recourses of the fallen woman; and in *Emma* living with Miss Bates and her mother can only be a mortifying exacerbation of Jane Fairfax' refined nerves. In fact, Jane Fairfax uses the female collectivity of the convent as a metaphor for her life's utter, deprived negation: "She had long resolved that one-and-twenty should be the period. With the fortitude of a devoted noviciate, she had resolved at one-and-twenty to complete the sacrifice, and retire from all the pleasures of life, of rational intercourse, peace and hope, to penance and mortification for ever" (p. 165). The "penance and mortification" endured by women living together springs from lives presented—through an avoidance of detailed presentation—as unshaped, unreal, in limbo.

The lack of texture with which Jane Austen delineates a family of women is the more surprising in that, during her major creative period, she lived in one. The household at Chawton in which she lived between 1809 and her death in

1817 consisted of herself, her sister Cassandra, their widowed mother, their unmarried friend Martha Lloyd, and sometimes brother James' daughter Cassy. It lacked even the token non-authoritative male the novels provide to give the little community official identity; in fact, Mrs. Austen chose the cottage that was as far as possible from the parent estate of Godmersham, where her son and patron, Edward Austen Knight, resided. Just before the move Jane Austen wrote a jaunty doggerel poem whose conclusion is the foundation for something of a "Chawton myth" on the part of her biographers: "You'll find us very snug next year." [7]

And so commentators have, particularly with sundry nieces and nephews always coming to stay and be amused. One's usual impression of life at Chawton is expressed in the phrase Frank Churchill finds so oddly euphonious in *Emma*: "a crowd in a little room." Jane Aiken Hodge creates an almost Orwellian Chawton—"The two letters Jane Austen wrote to Fanny that autumn . . . give one a frightening picture of the total lack of privacy in her life"—on which Brigid Brophy elaborates: ". . . quite apart from servants, the regular comple- ment of the house was four adult females and one child. A visit to Chawton makes it clear in turn that that *must* have been cramped—not intolerably so, and not, indeed, in comparison with the living quarters of most English people at the time, but in comparison with the milieux of Jane Austen's novels and with what, it can be legitimately guessed, Jane Austen herself had originally expected of life. . . . item after item in Jane Austen's letters seems to anticipate [the] horror of a transposition from grandeur to poverty. . . ." [8] Brophy's essay creates a vivid enclave of "distressed aristocracy" among which the proud Jane lived as deposed queen.

Except in the independent and possibly defensive orbit between Jane and Cassandra, this community of four manless women is never depicted as intimate but always as encroaching and intruding. Yet the Jane Austen we still want to know about was born there; it was at Chawton that she finally outgrew the role of family court jester and came to see herself as a serious writer, her books as alive. It is suggestive that her first serious projects there were almost certainly the re-casting of *Sense and Sensibility* and *Pride and Prejudice*, both of which deal extensively with the vacuum that is the lives of "superfluous" women. If both novels were originally epistolary, as some critics suggest,[9] her re-casting from letters into dramatized narrative would throw the sisters into a proximity impossible in the old form, and may reflect the intimacy of the new female world in which she lived. Though she may have been inspired by a sense of her new life's vacuity, inspired she was, and the Chawton community, which is almost always deplored as an impediment, must be given credit for some of the same generative power that living with George Henry Lewes possessed for George Eliot. Some of the strength of Chawton's productive impetus may have come from

[7] 26 July, 1809. *Jane Austen's Letters to her sister Cassandra and Others*, ed. R. W. Chapman (London: Oxford University Press, 1952), p. 68. Future references to this edition will appear by date in the text.

[8] Hodge, p. 207; Brigid Brophy, "Jane Austen and the Stuarts," in *Critical Essays on Jane Austen*, ed. B. C. Southam (New York: Barnes & Noble, Inc., 1969), p. 28.

[9] See B. C. Southam, *Jane Austen's Literary Manuscripts* (Oxford: Clarendon Press, 1964), pp. 55–60.

the fact that, as with Longbourn House, its existence as a family was indistinguishable from its life as a neighborhood. Not only did it function as a clearing-house for the next generation of Austens and their friends and lives, but the house itself was caught between its private and its public characters: it was originally built as an inn and after 1845 was divided into "tenements for labourers," retaining some of its original collective function.[10] "Very snug" they might have been at Chawton, but the outside world poured through it, and the pressure of people fed into the pressure of art, endowing a real female community with a power for which we must be grateful.

But it is on this very issue of direct female power that Jane Austen's novels are most equivocal. Beginning with such trivial incidents as the married Lydia's displacement of her older and more level-headed sister Jane at the head of the table, or the married Mrs. Elton taking precedence over the elegant Emma at a ball, there is an unnervingly arbitrary and grotesque quality to the assumption of power by women. If flabby fathers are to be deplored in the novels, strong mothers or mother-substitutes like Lady Susan, Mrs. Norris, and Lady Russell are almost always pernicious in their authority: as Mrs. Bennet's reign seems to testify, female power is effectively synonymous with power abused.

It was Mrs. Bennet's awful specter that led the Victorian feminist Harriet Martineau to back into an oblique apology for the little authority Englishwomen were allowed:

> I was asked whether it was possible that the Bennet family would act as they are represented in 'Pride and Prejudice:' whether a foolish mother, with grown up daughters, would be allowed to spoil the two youngest, instead of the sensible daughters taking the case into their own hands. It is certainly true that in America the superior minds of the family would take the lead; while in England, however the domestic affairs might gradually arrange themselves, no person would be found breathing the suggestion of superseding the mother's authority.[11]

Given such meager-minded despotism Harriet Martineau might have better understood why men looked with trepidation on the idea of female participation in the government of their countries. But despite Mrs. Bennet's aura of awfulness she is in league with her creator in driving her daughters out of a non-home into the establishments they deserve. Though in the case of the three most nubile the end crowns the whole, her government is shown to be at one with the usurpation that is the paramount characteristic of her counterpart in the larger social world —the supremely awful Lady Catherine de Bourgh.[12]

Unlike most of Wickham's statements, his anticipatory description of Lady Catherine seems quite adequate to the character we eventually meet: "She has

[10] James Edward Austen-Leigh, *Memoir of Jane Austen* (1870; rpt. Oxford: Clarendon Press, 1967), pp. 85–86.

[11] Harriet Martineau, *Society in America*, 2 vols. (New York: Saunders & Otley, 1837), ii, 276.

[12] For the delicate identification of Mrs. Bennet with Lady Catherine, see Marvin Mudrick, *Jane Austen: Irony as Defense and Discovery* (New Jersey: Princeton University Press, 1952), p. 103; and Joseph Wiesenfarth, *The Errand of Form: An Assay of Jane Austen's Art* (New York: Fordham University Press, 1967), p. 63.

the reputation of being remarkably sensible and clever; but I rather believe she derives part of her abilities from her rank and fortune, part from her authoritative manner, and the rest from the pride of her nephew, who chuses that every one connected with him should have an understanding of the first class" (p. 84). In other words, Lady Catherine's authority is not inherent but derived in arbitrary and misplaced fashion from accidents and contrivances outside herself; she is a pastiche of external pretensions, an embodiment of that power without selfhood that threatens to make all authority ridiculous. This monster of misgovernment is the only character other than Mrs. Bennet to deplore the exclusively male right of inheritance, which the sprightly, iconoclastic Elizabeth seems to accept as a matter of course: "I am glad of it; but otherwise I see no occasion for entailing estates from the female line.—It was not thought necessary in Sir Lewis de Bourgh's family" (p. 164). This interesting fact makes clear one role that Lady Catherine plays in the novel: she functions as an image of the overweening matriarchate that would result could widow and daughters inherit the estate Mrs. Bennet craves. In her futile confrontation with Elizabeth, Lady Catherine makes clear that her private great society runs on matriarchal principles:

> "I will not be interrupted. Hear me in silence. My daughter and my nephew are formed for each other. They are descended on the maternal side, from the same noble line; and, on the father's, from respectable, honourable, and ancient, though untitled families." [After this condescending inclusion of the lesser paternal line, Lady Catherine goes on to warn Elizabeth not to "quit the sphere" in which she was brought up.]
> "In marrying your nephew, I should not consider myself as quitting that sphere. He is a gentleman; I am a gentleman's daughter; so far we are equal."
> "True. You are a gentleman's daughter. But who was your mother?" (p. 356)

Lady Catherine's final challenge throws Elizabeth back on the female, matriarchal dream world she is trying to escape; in asserting the primary reality of men and patrilineal inheritance, she comes close to denying that she is her mother's daughter. Lady Catherine's withdrawal, and the reassuringly ardent Darcy's quick appearance in her place, suggests the salutary recession of the usurped power of all mothers before the meaning and form only men can bestow.

For the acknowledged center of power is the shadowy Darcy. "As a brother, a landlord, a master, she considered how many people's happiness were in his guardianship!—How much of pleasure or pain it was in his power to bestow!— How much of good or evil must be done by him!" (pp. 250–251). Looking at Darcy as his portrait immortalizes him, Elizabeth is overcome by a kind of social vitalism: she is drawn not to the benignity and wisdom of his power but to its sheer extent as such, for evil as well as good. What compels her in the portrait is the awesomely institutionalized power of a man; a power that her own father has let fall and her mother, grotesquely usurped. Loathing as she does the idea of any kinship to her mother, Elizabeth will doubtless be content not to have her own portrait displayed after her marriage. Thus Austen speculates: "I can only imagine that Mr. D. prizes any Picture of her too much to like it should be exposed to the public eye.—I can imagine he wd. have that sort of feeling—that mixture of Love, Pride & Delicacy" (24 May, 1813). After the clamorous anonymity of Longbourn, marriage waits for Elizabeth as a hard-won release into a privacy only Darcy can bestow.

But underneath this pervasive largesse Darcy has as shadowy a selfhood as his aunt Lady Catherine. If Elizabeth's childhood is obliterated in memory, Darcy's is a muddled contradiction. The man who caught Elizabeth's eye before audibly insulting her was, according to his "intelligent" housekeeper, a fount of virtue from the beginning of his life. He was merely too modest to declare his goodness and Elizabeth too prejudiced to see it: "I have never had a cross word from him in my life, and I have known him ever since he was four years old. . . . I have always observed, that they who are good-natured when children, are good-natured when they grow up; and he was always the sweetest-tempered, most generous-hearted, boy in the world. . . . Some people call him proud; but I am sure I never saw any thing of it. To my fancy, it is only because he does not rattle away like other young men" (pp. 248–249). A good deal of weight is put on this testimony, though it is oddly redolent of Mr. Collins extolling the condescension of Lady Catherine; and it meshes neither with the reliable Mrs. Gardiner's "having heard Mr. Fitzwilliam Darcy formerly spoken of as a very proud, ill-natured boy" (p. 143), nor with Darcy's own meticulous diagnosis of his past:

> As a child I was taught what was right, but I was not taught to correct my temper. I was given good principles, but left to follow them in pride and conceit. Unfortunately an only son, (for many years an only child) I was spoilt by my parents, who though good themselves . . . allowed, encouraged, almost taught me to be selfish and overbearing, to care for none beyond my own family circle, to think meanly of all the rest of the world, to wish at least to think meanly of their sense and worth compared with my own. Such I was, from eight to eight and twenty; and such I might still have been but for you, dearest, loveliest Elizabeth! What do I not owe you! You taught me a lesson, hard indeed at first, but most advantageous. By you, I was properly humbled. (p. 369)

Darcy the man is as muddled a figure as Darcy the boy. Is he indeed converted into humanity by Elizabeth's spontaneity and spirit, or was he always the perfection that maturity allows her to see? Oddly, Elizabeth herself prefers the latter interpretation, replacing her power over him with a reassuring silliness: "And yet I meant to be uncommonly clever in taking so decided a dislike to him, without any reason. It is such a spur to one's genius, such an opening for wit to have a dislike of that kind. One may be continually abusive without saying any thing just; but one cannot be always laughing at a man without now and then stumbling on something witty" (pp. 225–226). Elizabeth's selective memory serves her well here by erasing the fact that she had, and has, several good reasons for disliking Darcy; but she seems to need a sense of her own wrongness to justify the play of her mind. In choosing to emphasize her own prejudice over Darcy's most palpable pride, she can wonder freely at the power in his portrait while her own (if there is one) will be closeted away, invisible to all eyes but her husband's. Standing as a tourist before the solitary grandeur of his portrait, she recalls the young Jane Austen, a "partial, prejudiced, and ignorant Historian," willfully slicing off fragments from the magisterial pageant of Goldsmith's *History of England* in order to establish a private community of four between Mary Queen of Scots, "Mrs Lefroy, Mrs Knight and myself" (*MW*, p. 145). The power of silliness can yoke a country girl and a queen; but in the face of the magisterial and masculine parade of reality, there is safety in imaginative appropriation only if one is "partial, prejudiced, and ignorant." Objectivity, impartiality, and knowledge might endanger the cloak of invisibility which is so intrinsic a part of Jane Austen's perception of a woman's life.

The sanctioned power of management with which she endows Darcy allows him to prove his heroism in the third volume by taking over the mother's role: like the shadowy "Duke of dark corners" in *Measure for Measure*, he moves behind the scenes and secretly arranges the marriages of the three Bennet girls. The end of the novel finds the neighborhood of families that centers around Pemberley busily improving Kitty for a good match, leaving only the lumpish Mary still at home to be displayed by her mother, their alliance a fitting penance for the pedantry of one and the presumption of the other. The last page tells us incidentally that the war has ended, and, with Darcy's will to harmony, perhaps the waiting will as well. In becoming the novel's Providential matchmaker Darcy brings about the comic conclusion by an administrative activity for which Mrs. Bennet and Lady Catherine were, and Emma Woodhouse will be, severely condemned. In the end the malevolent power of the mother is ennobled by being transferred to the hero;[13] and the female community of Longbourn, an oppressive blank in a dense society, is dispersed with relief in the solidity of marriage.

## II. *Little Women*

> [P]ublishers are very perverse & wont let authors have their way so my little women must grow up and be married off in a very stupid style.[14]

In *Pride and Prejudice* a world without men is empty of effects. Lacking an inheritance the Bennet girls are only theoretically impecunious—unlike the March girls they have nothing to do with the kitchen, and clothes on call for any occasion —but physically as well as psychically they live in an empty world. The world of the March girls is rich enough to complete itself, and in this richness lies the tension of *Little Women* and its two sequels.

" 'Christmas won't be Christmas without any presents,' grumble[s] Jo, lying on the rug" (p. 2), to start the series off with a spiritual absurdity that will be contradicted by the almost immediate entrance of all-dispensing Marmee. The

---

[13] See Kenneth L. Moler, *Jane Austen's Art of Allusion* (Lincoln: University of Nebraska Press, 1968), pp. 75–108, for a discussion of the managing, marrying Darcy in relation to his god-like prototype, Sir Charles Grandison. It is part of Jane Austen's feminization of Richardson's material that in *Pride and Prejudice* it is initially the mother's "business" to get her daughters married, and Darcy merely replaces her in the job.

[14] Letter to Sam May, quoted in Madeleine B. Stern, *Louisa May Alcott* (Norman: University of Oklahoma Press, 1950), pp. 189–190.

Christmas gift that Marmee seems tenderly to offer her girls is hunger. First, each decides to give up her one precious dollar to buy a Christmas gift for their mother instead of a loved item for herself; Marmee then enters with a letter from father, who is nobly serving as a chaplain in the Civil War, admonishing the girls to "conquer themselves . . . beautifully" and making them all feel deliciously guilty; and on Christmas day itself, in response to their sacrificial gifts, she makes her famous request that the girls give up their holiday breakfast to a starving family. They go trooping through the snow with full hands and empty stomachs, "funny angels in hoods and mittens" who have learned that it is better to renounce than receive. And the book succeeds in making us believe that this hungry day is "A Merry Christmas."

When Ebenezer Scrooge gives Bob Cratchit a Christmas turkey as a token of relationship, we easily but rather abstractly accept the bird as a metaphor of Scrooge's change of heart; but we know that Scrooge could buy a wilderness of turkeys for himself had not his nephew Fred joyfully invited him to dinner. The March girls' pilgrimage to the poor quarter of town is significant only because they themselves are hungry, and the food that Marmee gently requests they renounce is vividly alive: I would surmise that their vanished buckwheat cakes, bread, cream, and muffins have been longed for by more female readers than the cold meat, cake, and pyramids "of all the finest fruits in season" that Elizabeth Bennet was served when she finally entered Pemberley. The largesse is Darcy's; the renunciation is the March girls' own, and their concert in performing it, *after* the narrative has established them as selfish little beasts who want all sorts of things they won't be permitted to have, is the sisterhood the novel is about.

In the richness of that uneaten breakfast it is easy to forget that the March girls are rewarded for their generosity by masculine bounty. That evening they put on a play Jo has written which is described in extended detail; after it is over all find waiting a splendid supper sent by wealthy Mr. Laurence next door, in appreciation of their good deed. But the supper is less important in itself than it is as a liaison established between the two houses that makes possible the friendship between the four girls and his grandson, rich, spirited Laurie. Laurie plays the role of Bingley in *Pride and Prejudice:* he is not only marriageable in himself but the cause of marriage in other men. Introduction to him indirectly makes possible the marriages of all the girls: Meg marries his tutor, Jo goes to New York to escape his importunity and meets Professor Bhaer there, and he himself finally marries Amy. In himself Laurie is like Darcy in that he has "good match" emblazoned all over him. The morning's renunciation aligns the March girls with the spirit of marriage, and Christmas is Christmas indeed.

But the treatment of this simultaneous savior and intruder is quite different in the American story. In *Pride and Prejudice* the sisters acted in joyous concert only at Mr. Bennet's wry announcement that he had paid a formal call on Bingley. In *Little Women* the sisters act in a concert that has no reference to Laurie, and in deference to its beauty he solicits access to it with only partial success:

*Laurie colored up, but answered frankly, "Why, you see, I often hear you*

*calling to one another, and when I'm alone up here, I can't help looking over at*
*your house, you always seem to be having such good times. I beg your pardon*
*for being so rude, but sometimes you forget to put down the curtain at the*
*window where the flowers are; and when the lamps are lighted, it's like looking*
*at a picture to see the fire, and you all round the table with your mother; her*
*face is right opposite, and it looks so sweet behind the flowers, I can't help*
*watching it. I haven't got any mother, you know"; and Laurie poked the fire to*
*hide a little twitching of the lips that he could not control.*

*The solitary, hungry look in his eyes went straight to Jo's warm heart. She*
*had been so simply taught that there was no nonsense in her head, and at*
*fifteen she was as innocent and frank as any child. Laurie was sick and lonely;*
*and, feeling how rich she was in home love and happiness, she gladly tried to*
*share it with him.* (p. 57)

The balance of *Pride and Prejudice* is inverted. It is Laurie who peers wistfully in
at the female family, "like looking at a picture," as Elizabeth did Darcy's. Real
plenitude belongs to the community of women, true hunger to the solitary man.
When Elizabeth's family inadvertently exposed itself to Darcy by a parade of
vulgarities at the Netherfield Ball, he could only flee in horror with Bingley; but
when the March family inadvertently exposes itself by leaving up the shade,
Laurie glimpses a carefully-poised fullness that draws him to its perfect self.

The March girls offer Laurie all the richness of interchange between art, taste,
and nature that Pemberley held out to Elizabeth Bennet. Even when he is not
present they are almost always perceived as a carefully-grouped pictorial composition. With characteristic abundance of detail the author sees it as her artistic
duty to give us, not the income, but the appearance of the March girls as soon as
possible: "As young readers like to know 'how people look,' we will take this
moment to give them a little sketch of the four sisters, who sat knitting away in
the twilight, while the December snow fell quietly without, and the fire crackled
cheerfully within" (p. 6). After an intimate survey of hair, coloring, carriage, etc.,
the author archly concludes with a mystery which is no mystery at all: "What the
characters of the four sisters were we will leave to be found out" (p. 7).

But we have already found their characters in their appearance: raised among
disembodied sages in Transcendentalist Concord, Louisa May Alcott stubbornly
clings throughout her novels to the primary reality of physical things.[15] In her
world people can decipher character and mood instantly by subtle shifts in faces,
bearing, eyebrows, clothes. Mr. Laurence's kindness speaks to Jo out of his
portrait before they meet, and when Jo becomes a writer, her jaunty cap communicates instantly to the peeping family the degree to which genius is burning.
When the physical body is so insistently alive and expressive there are no
barriers to intimacy but time and death; this accessible and familial world, where

---

[15] Ralph Waldo Emerson's *Journal* of 1856 lauds Bronson Alcott's ability to escape the very world of things to
which Louisa adheres: "The comfort of Alcott's mind is, the connection in which he sees whatever he sees.
He is never dazzled by a spot of colour, or a gleam of light, to value the thing by itself; but forever and
ever is prepossessed by the individual one behind it and all." Quoted in *Bronson Alcott's Fruitlands*, com-
piled by Clara Endicott Sears (Boston: Houghton Mifflin Co., 1915), p. 5.

character is a language all can read, contains no Austenian "intricate characters" who deceive by their appearance.

Alcott trusts what she can see, and nowhere is her reliance on the life in things more vividly apparent than in her delineation of the March haven: the expressive rattle of Jo's knitting needles, the high-heeled boots which crush Meg's feet, Beth's divine piano, Amy's plaster casts and the delicate "things" she dramatically sweeps off the bazaar table when she feuds with May Chester, Marmee's crooned-over slippers—throughout the novel the March women are defined in their primary relationship to the "things" that display their characters. The physicality of their community is not bestowed, but inherent and overflowing. Clothes in *Pride and Prejudice* were vaguely mentioned, usually in terms of some inane question from Mrs. Bennet about "style" which was cut short by her contemptuous husband. But Alcott slips her views about dress reform into the novel by forcing the female reader to feel Meg's agony when she is pinched and squeezed in her attempts at elegance. Letters in *Pride and Prejudice* were sparely-used and significant; either they were severe tests of character, like those of Mr. Collins and Darcy, or they conveyed necessary information, like Jane's and Mr. Gardiner's about Lydia's elopement. But *Little Women* spills over with letters that are given to us simply for the purpose of relishing their writers: "As one of these packets contained characteristic notes from the party, we will rob an imaginary mail, and read them" (p. 186). We learn nothing from these letters but the fact that Meg is Meg, Jo, Jo, Beth, Beth, and Amy, Amy, which has already been amply demonstrated; but if we are engulfed in their lives as a fifth sister, it is enough. The abundance in which we perceive the life of the circle dramatizes its message of the richness of poverty when Marmee's and Alcott's moralizing makes us wince; despite the girls' mechanical grumbling, it is difficult for the reader to believe in what they have given up when she finds herself surrounded by what they have.

The primacy of the female family, both as moral-emotional magnet and as work of art, is indicated by the quality of its appeal to Laurie: though he thinks he loves Jo best, his primary role is that of son-brother-squire to the family unit as he is mulled over by each of the girls in turn. Initially, the sophisticated Moffats and Jo herself link him to Meg, who is scornful about being matched to a mere "boy." Later comes Jo's famous rejection of him, the most talked-about part of the book from its own day to ours,[16] and Jo's private hope that a match with Beth will soften him and cure her lingering illness. Beth amazedly disabuses her, her characteristic "trouble" being that she must die and leave the family circle, with never a thought of love or Laurie; so Jo brusquely and pragmatically consigns him to the match he does eventually make: "Amy is left for him, and they would suit excellently; but I have no heart for such things, now" (p. 416).

---

[16] Patricia Meyer Spacks' students "resented the way Jo is finally disposed of" as clamorously as Alcott's first adolescent readers did (p. 100). In Spacks' rather grim view of the novel Jo is denied glamorous Laurie as punishment for her aggression; but Elizabeth Janeway gives her a sweeping cheer for holding firm: "It is worth noting that the two other adored nineteenth-century heroines who say No to the hero's proposal give way in the end, when circumstances and the hero have changed: Elizabeth Bennet and Jane Eyre. But Jo [like Melville's stubbornly American Bartleby] says No and does not shift." Elizabeth Janeway, *Between Myth and Morning: Women Awakening* (New York: William Morrow & Co., 1975), p. 237. Janeway was the first to make plain the high-spirited sedition that still draws mothers and daughters to *Little Women*; but both critics define Jo by her response to a proposal, which is not for Alcott a crucial area of definition.

Thus, before romance blooms for him, Laurie is rejected by each of the girls in turn. Impossible to imagine romantic heroes like Darcy, or even Bingley, being so bounced around the Bennet circle before settling on the one sister who is "left for him." Even in his marriage to Amy, Alcott seems to smooth poor Laurie's path for him by making Amy shed her artistic ambitions in favor of being "an ornament to society"—as Louisa's single-minded sister May never did—and by Amy's homesick vulnerability abroad after learning that Beth has died without her. With all his winsomeness, love, and money, Laurie's attempts to enter the charmed circle are continually frustrated until death makes a place for him.

But Amy's is not the only March marriage to take place under the shadow of death. Womanly Meg's love match to poor-but-honest John Brooke is colored for us by Jo's tragic sense that the wrench to the family it entails is more an ending than a beginning: "I knew there was mischief brewing! I felt it; and now it's worse than I imagined. I just wish I could marry Meg myself, and keep her in the family" (p. 224). Her equation of all life with the family circle echoes Louisa's own mournful love letter upon her older sister's wedding: "After the bridal train had departed, the mourners withdrew to their respective homes; and the bereaved family solaced their woe by washing dishes for two hours and bolting the remains of the funeral baked meats." [17]

But it is not just gawky unawakened Jo who sees Meg's marriage as a precious death; the structure of the novel reinforces this mournful tone. Even all-comprehending Marmee seems to view it with resigned acquiescence rather than joy, and their father's voice breaks as he performs the ceremony, as it will at Beth's and John's funerals. For Mrs. March allows her girls one great freedom that may explain why the book has been so unreasonably beloved for over a century: the freedom to remain children, and for a woman, the more precious freedom not to fall in love: "Right, Jo; better be happy old maids than unhappy wives, or unmaidenly girls running about to find husbands. . . . One thing remember, my girls: mother is always ready to be your confidante, father to be your friend; and both of us trust and hope that our daughters, whether married or single, will be the pride and comfort of our lives" (p. 110). The solemnity of the moment when Mrs. March oracularly reveals her "plans" endows the sisters with an independent selfhood which is a rare dowry in any century, and draws the circle even more tightly together.

Meg's marriage is placed alongside a series of calamities that darken the book irreparably: Mr. March's illness, Marmee's hurried departure for Washington, Beth's near-fatal illness, and father's return as a befuddledly noble center of reverence that destroys the family flow. The inclusion of young love among these upheavals implicitly defines it as more of a tearer of sisterhood than an emotional progression beyond it; and the equation between the departures of marriage and death continues in the last half of the book, where Beth's wasting illness and death run parallel to the marriages of the rest of the sisters. Both stress the loss of the childhood circle rather than the coming into an inheritance of fulfillment.

---

[17] Quoted in *Louisa May Alcott: Her Life, Letters, and Journals*, ed. Ednah D. Cheyney (Boston: Roberts Brothers, 1890), p. 132. Future references will appear in the text.

In their desire for perpetual sisterhood Jo and Beth are at the heart of the novel. Beth's long wasting is the waning of childhood and the collective death of the sisters; in a sense she dies so that the others can marry. Though she is usually recalled as a simpy domestic angel, the intensity of her yearning for home recalls that of the heretical Catherine Linton: "I'm not like the rest of you; I never made any plans about what I'd do when I grew up; I never thought of being married, as you all did.[18] I couldn't seem to imagine myself anything but stupid little Beth, trotting about at home, of no use anywhere but there. I never wanted to go away and the hard part now is the leaving you all. I'm not afraid, but it seems as if I should be homesick for you even in heaven" (p. 417). The spirit of home, Beth dies when it does.

In her last illness she has a dying room into which are brought all the favored relics of the family; for as long as she can hold a needle she makes "little things for the school children daily passing to and fro" which she throws out the window like utilitarian manna from Heaven. She dies when she relinquishes her hold on these "things" which are the quintessence of the family; the necessity of parting is the necessity of growing away from home completion and living despite the splitting of the circle.

Had Alcott written the Little Women she envisioned, Beth might have survived to preside over a self-sustaining sisterhood: "Girls write to ask who the little women marry, as if that was the only end and aim of a woman's life. I won't marry Jo to Laurie to please any one," she wrote after the appearance of the first half (p. 201). In fact, she did write a piece about non-diminutive women, at the same time that she began the book we know. As Ednah Cheyney shows, in her article "Happy Women," [19] "she gratified her love of single life by describing the delightful spinsters of her acquaintance. Her sketches are all taken from life, and are not too highly colored. The Physician, the Artist, the Philanthropist, the Actress, the Lawyer, are easily recognizable. They were a 'glorious phalanx of old maids,' as Theodore Parker called the single women of his Society, which aided him so much in his work" (p. 187). Here is the idyll lying behind Marmee's new wives' training school: a community of new women whose sisterhood is not an apprenticeship making them worthy of appropriation by father-husbands, but a bond whose value is itself. Jane Austen may have lived too closely to Chawton to write about it, but for Alcott the communal cottage itself, and not the roads out of it, would have been the palace of art that made her ideal subject.

The conjunction between sisterhood, art, and politics is more explicit in An Old-Fashioned Girl (1870) and in an untitled fragment of an adult novel that was never published.[20] In the former a chapter called "The Sunny Side" presents a community of woman artists as an oasis among unhappy families and dreary stylishness. Their spirit takes form in their collective daughter, a massive statue of the noble woman of the future standing monumental and alone, with a ballot-

---

[18] In fact, as we see them in the first part, none of the girls does think of being married: it seems to strike their aspirations unawares.

[19] The New York Ledger, 24 (April 11, 1868).

[20] Untitled manuscript, Alcott Papers, 59M–309 (21), Houghton Library, Harvard University, Cambridge, Mass. The manuscript is unpaginated after the first few pages.

box for her emblem but no husband or baby. In the fragment the sisterhood between two artists is aligned against the patriarchal family the March books claim to revere: "Do not look for [meaning] in marriage, that is too costly an experiment for us. Flee from temptation and do not dream of spoiling your life by any commonplace romance." Though the more feminine heroine marries and lets the paint on her palette go dry, she embodies their corporate dream in a long description of a group of her militant colleagues crusading for the right to draw from nude models. In the adult novel, then, the female studio of *An Old-Fashioned Girl* abandons its jollity for its demands. By contrast the March girls have to relinquish their artistic aims; though we learn in *Jo's Boys* that even placid Meg had once pined to be an actress, Jo speaks for all of them when she commemorates her latent love for "her Professor" by burning all her published stories. In Alcott's imagination, art, militancy and sisterhood seem to be one, but had she allowed the girls to embrace such a triad, her "little women" might, like the Amazonian statue, have grown beyond control.

*Work: A Story of Experience* (1873), an autobiographical adult novel on which Alcott worked for twelve years before she published it, attempts to resolve the conflict between the surging emotion and creativity of the female community and the "normal" tenderness and sacrifice of patriarchal marriage by reversing the order of the phases of *Little Women*. The novel is the story of strong-minded Christie's "declaration of independence," in which she vows to support herself as a man does. After a series of sobering adventures she marries the Thoreauvian David Sterling and they march together to the Civil War and to triumphs as soldier and nurse. Christie feels no sense of loss in the war's disruption of their life together: "I like it, David; it's a grand time to live, a splendid chance to do and suffer; and I want to be in it heart and soul, and earn a little of the glory or the martyrdom that will come in the end." [21] Her wish is fulfilled when her husband is brought in fatally wounded and she ushers him efficiently and skillfully into death. Her marriage has begun and ended with the Civil War, leaving her with memories of death and a daughter.

Like most picaresque protagonists Christie finds permanence at the end of the novel: through her new vocation as a public speaker at feminist rallies she brings together leisured and working women in political and loving sisterhood. Her private life has become the sisterhood she works to perpetuate historically, as she and her daughter Pansy live in a co-operative commune with David's mother and sister. By the end of the novel the private and the public communities are moving into a single unit that transcends in its embrace barriers of class, age, and race: "With an impulsive gesture Christie stretched her hands to the friends about her, and with one accord they laid theirs on hers, a loving league of sisters, old and young, black and white, rich and poor, each ready to do her part to hasten the coming of the happy end" (p. 442). In *Little Women* sisterhood was dissolved by its culmination in marriage. But here marriage is an interim episode at one with war, valuable in that it helps create the crowning community of women

[21] Louisa May Alcott, *Work: A Story of Experience* (Boston: Roberts Brothers, 1885), p. 376. Future references to this edition will appear in the text.

whose co-operative blend of private and public life heals all the divisions the Civil War embodied.

In the saga of the March family this militant vision of permanent sisterhood is a felt dream rather than a concrete possibility. Alcott seems to have chosen the name in deference to the maiden name of her mother, Abigail May: in endowing her sisters with another month name beginning with "M," she secretly makes them all the mother's children with nothing of the father, which would have warmed Lady Catherine's matriarchal heart. Along with its adhesion to the mother, "March" also suggests militancy, as when Louisa departed for the Civil War more as soldier than as healer: "I was ready, and when my commander said 'March!' I marched" (*Journals*, December 1862, p. 140). But with all this the month of March is an undeveloped anomaly, waiting for its consummation in summer: the suggestion is that the March girls will bloom only when they have lost their name in the warmth of a man's, as all but Beth eventually do. In the loss of this sisterhood the three remaining girls establish a matriarchy under Jo's aegis at Plumfield.

Only in the two sequels does Jo's refusal to marry Laurie become comprehensible: the reasons given in *Little Women* alone seem more rationalization than explanation. It is not that Laurie would "hate [her] scribbling," as she desperately claims: he is vigorously excited about her writing from first to last, while it is Bhaer's stern disapproval that makes her burn it.[22] The real rightness springs from the fact that Laurie can only make his comrade a lady, but Professor Bhaer, an educator, can make her a cosmic mother—the greatest power available in her domestic world. Poor Laurie is pushed into the background as "Lord" to Amy's "Lady," and spends the rest of the series compensating for his discontent in business by endowing all Jo's projects as her little empire spreads and spreads. By the time we meet her *Little Men* she has cast off the comfortable, clinging "Marmee" in favor of the grand "Mother Bhaer," the Goldilocks-like joke containing a tinge of maternal threat. At times she is simple "Mrs. Jo," a vessel of self-sufficient maternal power; and at times she and her husband are raised Germanically to the status of cosmic powers: "the mother," "the father."

Planted and harvested at Plumfield like crops, according to principles of co-operation and mutual help, the students belong both to a "great family" and a "small world."[23] Though stormy Jo now functions more as beacon than pilgrim —"I am not as aspiring as I once was" (*LM*, p. 367)—her influence penetrates the future. The school at Plumfield, which is also family, farm, and cosmos, bears a faint resemblance to the Shaker community which thrived in opposition to Bronson Alcott's short-lived Fruitlands in Harvard, Mass. Essentially matriarchal in its worship of its founder, Mother Ann Lee, the celibate Shakers lived on principles of sexual equality and co-operation; like that of the March family and

---

[22] Both M-G-M versions of the novel (George Cukor, 1933, and Mervyn LeRoy, 1949) soften Bhaer's role from censor to critic: the wise professor presents Jo with the old chestnut young writers in movies seem never to have heard before: "Write about what you know." Jo promptly writes about Beth and the book is a masterpiece. But the Professor Bhaer Alcott created is never so constructive.

[23] Louisa May Alcott, *Little Men* (New York: Grosset & Dunlap, Inc., 1947), p. 42, p. 369. Future references to this edition will appear in the text.

Plumfield, their greatest spiritual release was the ritual of confession. The Shaker society had an unusually large percentage of women who worked and governed equally with men, while in Bronson's neighboring Fruitlands, the men tended to do the thinking, and the Alcott women, the work. It was the crisis of Bronson's life when his partner, Charles Lane, defected to the Shakers, but if Louisa could not desert her father in fact, she did in art: in her later works she seems quite deliberately to shape her father's Utopian vision to the dimensions of her stoical mother and of the rival paradise that destroyed his own.[24]

But in establishing Jo's matriarchal reign Alcott has not forgotten her early dream of sisterhood. *Jo's Boys* sees a diminished reunion of the original circle, as Amy and Laurie and the now-widowed Meg move to the grounds of Plumfield where the campus of Laurence College now stands in virtuous opposition to nearby Harvard, Jo's dumping-ground for her "failures." The three sisters now direct the female students in an institutionalized version of Marmee's old sewing circle, over which Jo vigorously presides. But instead of repeating Marmee's lessons of suppression and self-conquest, hard-earned from her own experience, Jo gives "little lessons on health, religion, politics, and the various questions in which all should be interested," [25] reading copious extracts from the growing body of feminist literature and instilling in her pupils a greater respect for work and independence than for marriage. This little school within the school seems a greater success even than Plumfield: among the girls whose lives we follow, only poky domestic Daisy marries in the course of the novel. Meg's Josie and Amy's Bess go on to artistic triumphs and unseen "worthy mates," and "Naughty Nan," the school hoyden, becomes a doctor: "Nan remained a busy, cheerful, independent spinster, and dedicated her life to her suffering sisters and their children, in which true woman's work she found abiding happiness (*JB*, p. 338). Though the March girls themselves must compromise, they can at least create free women.

But though "Naughty Nan" grows up to create a healing sisterhood, only "A Firebrand" can institutionalize one: dangerous Dan, the black sheep Jo loves most. Always hovering on the edge of violence, Dan seems to embody all her own murderous rage which her mother called her "bosom enemy" and bade her "conquer." He grows up to roam the untamed west and dreams of founding "Dansville" there, a Utopian town run along the co-operative lines of Plumfield which would accommodate and enfranchise all dispossessed social groups: "You shall vote as much as you like in our new town, Nan; be mayor and alderman, and run the whole concern. It's going to be free as air, or I can't live in it" (*JB*, p. 71).

But the town that can be run by women never takes political shape: life tames Dan to self-sacrifice rather than self-perpetuation. He spends a year in prison for killing a rogue, has his legs crushed in a heroic mine rescue, falls hopelessly in

---

[24] For a description of the Shaker community see Charles Nordhoff, *The Communistic Societies of the United States*, with a Prefatory Essay by Franklin H. Littell (1875; rpt. New York: Schocken Books, Inc., 1965), pp. 117–255. For an account of Bronson Alcott's nervous collapse after Charles Lane deserted his community for that of the Shakers, see Sears, pp. 126–127, and Janeway, p. 236.

[25] Louisa May Alcott, *Jo's Boys* (New York: Grosset & Dunlap, Inc., 1949), p. 263. Future references to this edition will appear in the text.

love with Amy's snow maiden, and sacrifices his broken life defending the Indians. Jo's long relationship with him, half-envious and half-erotic, shows the irresolution behind the triumph of "the mother." The trilogy's final sight of her is of a wistful woman, "still clinging fast to her black sheep although a whole flock of white ones trotted happily before her" (*JB*, p. 337). Though she has achieved her position of matriarch, the roads are closed to the offices of "mayor and alderman." The family has been stretched to its limit.

Like the Bennet girls the women in Alcott's novels are finally forced into a posture of waiting, less for the entrance of the men than for "the coming of the happy end" which is the coming of the children: new little women who are allowed to be angry, study art, marry and create simultaneously, embrace spinsterhood; and the little men who may build towns for them to govern. Both the Bennet and the March households are finally defined by the incompleteness which is the source of their strength. The first, a non-world whose daily existence is "lop't and crop't" into nullity, is happily absorbed into the outside world of men, power, and history which gives it substance. The second, rich in its inter-twined world of games, duty, love and "things," manages finally to take almost everything to itself. At the end of *Pride and Prejudice* Jane Austen exorcises the specter of matriarchal tyranny her book has evoked by locating it in the ludicrous and obstructing Lady Catherine de Bourgh; in the sequels to *Little Women* Louisa May Alcott gives her matriarchy the dignity of community but forbids its final amalgamation with the history it tries to subdue. For this "happy end" the family is not enough; though with love or coercion it can train its daughters in the art of waiting, it cannot be both new woman's colony and new wives' training school. Its vacuity and its glory lie in the netherworld it establishes between them.[26]

[26] This essay was written with the help of a grant from the Ford Foundation, but all opinions and any mis-conceptions in it are my own. The Radcliffe Institute has provided me with incalculable support, for which this essay is partial thanks.

# VI.

## Language and Style

# "I Would Rather Have Written in Elvish": Language, Fiction and The Lord of the Rings

## ELIZABETH D. KIRK

That a three-volume novel by a distinguished medievalist should be as popular as J. R. R. Tolkien's *The Lord of the Rings* may be a little odd. That it should be popular with people who paint "Frodo lives!" on walls and wear pins that say "Go! Go! Gandalf" in elf script; with people who have never seen an English pub or walked more than two miles consecutively; with artists of the stature of W. H. Auden; and with respected critics who compare it to Malory, Spenser and Ariosto; and that it should achieve this with six appendixes and no sex is an event Aristotle would banish from any plot as an "improbable possible." That the trilogy should be a novel at least in being "a piece of prose fiction of a certain length" and yet show itself so different in kind from the literature on which our current tools for understanding and evaluating aesthetic experiences work best, makes the riddle one of real concern to the critic of fiction.

An admirer of the trilogy is inevitably haunted by the ghost of Ossian—or rather, by the fantasm of some urbane critic of the twenty-first century who will find our response to it as self-evidently ludicrous as we find the mid-eighteenth century's enthusiasm for Macpherson's pseudo-epics. We cannot even be sure that he will laugh at our enthusiasm rather than at our prudishness about admitting it. One way or the other, he will find in our behavior infallible symptoms of cultural malnutrition. But whether our response to Tolkien merely reveals, as the Ossian phenomenon did, an age's craving for a category of experience of which it is discovering itself to be deprived, or whether it shows the euphoria of discovering something intrinsically good which will go on appealing to audiences who come to it from widely differing experiences, we can certainly ask ourselves what sort of experience reading the Trilogy actually is. When we do, we see that it is as different from what happens to us in reading a novel, whether of the nineteenth century or of our own, as it is from most fantasy and most "escape" literature.

Tolkien himself has made it peculiarly difficult for his admirers to save face. The manifest discrepancy between the subject and manner of the trilogy and the works we take seriously as "literature" might be glossed over if we could interpret it allegorically and find that it is about everything it appears not to be about. But Tolkien has repeatedly insisted that the trilogy is not allegorical. Recently, in a preface to the paperback edition, he has gone so far as to admit that such a story may have "applicability" to other situations where related issues are involved, but he insists that his book "is neither allegorical nor topical. . . . I cordially dislike allegory in all its manifestations, and always have done since I grew old enough and wary enough to detect its presence."[1] Admittedly the sort of "allegory" many critics unearth after curtseying uneasily toward Tolkien's statements scarcely approaches "applicability" and amounts to little more than the assertion that, hobbits or no hobbits, the story is not without a theme, such as the triumph of life over death, or the importance of moral accountability, a rather thin justification for two thousand pages and half a volume of appendixes, and one which does not explain away the unlikeness of the trilogy to twentieth-century fiction and poetry.

But Tolkien is more difficult than that. When Edmund Wilson understood that Tolkien regarded *The Lord of the Rings* as a "philological experiment," he was exasperated into accusing all Tolkien enthusiasts of having "a lifelong appetite for juvenile trash" and Tolkien himself of achieving no more than "professorial amateurishness." To his publishers Tolkien had written: "The invention of languages is the foundation. The stories were made rather to provide a world for the languages than the reverse. I should have preferred to write in 'Elvish.' " He goes on to call the book an essay in "linguistic esthetic" and declares "It is not 'about' anything but itself. Certainly it has *no* allegorical intentions, general, particular or topical, moral, religious or political."[2] Tolkien's comment must be put into context. In his preface to the paperback edition he includes as a motive for writing "the desire of a tale-teller to try his hand at a really long story that would hold the attention of readers, amuse them, delight them, and at times maybe excite them or deeply move them" (p. ix). But even here he repeats that the central element which distinguishes the vast tapestry of the trilogy from the simple plot of its predecessor, *The Hobbit*, was "primarily linguistic in inspiration and was begun to provide the necessary background of 'history' for Elvish tongues" (p. viii).

It is certainly the case that the style is the main (or at least the overt) bone of contention between the enthusiasts and those who declare they could not get past the first twenty pages. A critic as sympathetic as Patricia Spacks deplores the "disastrous gap between the primitive and the pseudo-primitive" and apologizes for the style as "entirely an instrument of the story. When it demands attention in its own right, it is unlikely to justify the attention it receives."[3] Even a reader who clearly appreciates the trilogy as much as Burton Raffel can say of Tolkien's prose that "his objectives are limited and basically exclude what I here term literature."[4]

Raffel's essay, which analyzes the style of several typical "hobbit" passages from the early part of the book and goes on to find comparable qualities in

[1] New York: Ballantine Books, 1965, I, pp. x-xi.

[2] Edmund Wilson, "Oo, Those Awful Orcs!" *The Nation,* Vol. 182 (April 4, 1956), pp. 312–314; see also Charles Moorman, "The Shire, Mordor, and Minas Tirith" (1966), reprinted in Neil D. Isaacs and Rose A. Zimbardo, eds., *Tolkien and the Critics* (Notre Dame, 1969), p. 213. Essays reprinted in this volume, sometimes in revised form, will be cited from there for convenience (hereafter *Critics*).

[3] Patricia Meyer Spacks, "Power and Meaning in *The Lord of the Rings*" (1959), *Critics*, p. 98.

[4] "*The Lord of the Rings* as Literature" (1969), *Critics*, p. 218.

Tolkien's treatment of character and incident, is one of the best and most objective yet provoked by the trilogy. The shrewdness with which he describes the dynamics of this style is undeniable. For instance, Tolkien describes a room in the inn at Bree:

*They found themselves in a small and cozy room. There was a bit of bright fire burning on the hearth, and in front of it were some low and comfortable chairs. There was a round table, already spread with a white cloth, and on it was a large hand-bell. But Nob, the hobbit servant, came bustling in long before they thought of ringing. He brought candles and a tray full of plates.*[5]

Raffel comments:

*The operant words are* small and cozy, bit of bright fire, low and comfortable, white cloth, bustling. *The picture is clearly painted; one cannot mistake either the setting itself or the things about it of which Tolkien approves. And in the narrative these are the notes Tolkien needs to sound. . . . But to tell us, for example, that a room is "small and cozy," is to tell us only that the feeling Tolkien wants us to have about the room is one of comfortableness and modest size. "Low and comfortable chairs" tells us, again, what we are to feel about the chairs, not very much about the chairs themselves . . . he is writing as a narrative moralist. The social and aesthetic virtues of the room and the chairs are basic to his tale, but neither have independent existence, neither are experienced by us or for us.* (Critics, pp. 225–226)

In so far as this differentiates the functioning of Tolkien's "hobbit" style from other styles, it is illuminating. But one can quarrel with Raffel's idea of the effect such a style has on our awareness. It is a matter of definitions. If we expect a style that goes beyond the barely functional to show us, with both the immediacy of our own sharpest experience and the richness of artifice, the particularity of awareness in *a* time and *a* place, as does a novel by a great novelist who is also a great stylist, we will find the passages Raffel analyzes "limited." They attempt no such thing. On the other hand, the role of style in narrative is a matter of debate even among critics of the novel itself, and the very qualities that make Raffel declare the trilogy lacks style can be defended as those which make its style central to its achievement.

If we go back to Tolkien's remark about "linguistic aesthetic," remembering what language means to a man who is, in his academic life, not only a great philologist and a great teacher but a great critic, we can see that this phrase goes to the heart of the matter. Philology, in the technical sense, is obviously a precise science which observes the evolution of languages and formulates "laws" that describe them. But these laws are not prescriptive, in the sense in which we say that the "laws" of chemistry and physics describe what, given certain precisely known and controlled circumstances, will invariably occur. The laws of philology

---

[5] *The Lord of the Rings*, I, 166. All citations follow the hard cover edition, published in London and Boston, of which the first two volumes, *The Fellowship of the Ring* and *The Two Towers*, appeared in 1954, and the third, *The Return of the King*, in 1955.

serve only to make the mass of raw data intelligible; they do not explain why a given concatenation of circumstances produced a certain result, since they must always take account of the fact that the same situation, or what seems to us to have been the same, existed a few years later or a few hundred miles away and produced a different result or no result at all. Thus, even in its most scientific aspect, philology is part of the humanities which have been aptly defined as the study of those things human beings do not necessarily do. Yet Tolkien himself says of philology that such historical analysis is only a part of its charge: "the essential quality and aptitudes of a given language in a living moment is both more important to seize and more difficult to make explicit than its linear history."[6]

When we think of a language as having "quality and aptitudes," we are seeing it as more than a signalling system in which specific noises, gestures or shapes are equated with specific objects or acts. If such a signalling system constitutes language, many animals have it, and can produce specific behavior in each other by specific cries or movements; the "language" of bees and of jackdaws, for instance, can convey facts of some complexity. A language in the full sense of the term is the expression of—even, to a degree, the creator of—a network of consciousness that holds together an entire pattern of life. The individual word does not merely signal a specific thing, or neutrally reflect it. As Tolkien's Treebeard says of his own language, Entish: "Real names tell you the story of the things they belong to" (II, 68)—a "story" which includes the complex of values, functions and other objects to which any given thing is related. A "real name," then, will select certain features of a thing and of its relation to other things as those by which our consciousness of it is evoked. Many different words will evoke the given thing in different contexts, depending on the connections which its specific meaning sets up, and on the context to which it relates by sound, derivation and usage. Different languages may have additional perspectives on the object. A language is characterized by what it lacks words for, as well as by the words it has. A language that cannot distinguish, as ours is fast losing the power to do, between an "uninterested" and a "disinterested" attitude has to that extent diminished the consciousness of its users.

Grammar and syntax affect our capacity to take cognizance of and to evaluate our experience even more fundamentally if less obviously than our vocabulary. Grammar is the mechanism by which we can indicate the relationships that exist between things or events. Our thoughts, shaped by English and comparable western languages, take for granted that chronological relationships (past, present and future), whether an action is happening to the speaker or to someone else, and whether the subject is active or acted on, are the important things about any event which grammar should record. Other languages may take no note at all of these elements, or may blur them in order to analyze instead the degree of completeness, independence, certainty, or absoluteness of the action, or the nature or authority of the speaker.

---

[6] "On Fairy Stories," *Essays Presented to Charles Williams*, ed. C. S. Lewis (London, 1947; reprinted Grand Rapids, Michigan, 1966), p. 48. The essay was first delivered as an Andrew Lang lecture in 1938.

Grammar affects the order in which we take in an idea. When the English language simplified its grammatical endings to the point that it cannot indicate whether the man bites the dog or the dog bites the man except through word order, English also lost the capacity to make us see the bitten dog first and reveal to us in explanation, next, that the man bit him except by putting the whole event into a passive construction which would be static as well as more diffuse. We can only achieve such effects by elaborate circumlocution, or by highly literary styles, like Milton's, and only where the facts involved prevent ambiguity. "A mighty fortress is our God" creates a completely different experience than "Our God is a mighty fortress." Modern English, unlike Old English, is a language comparatively poor in the capacity to modify experience through order; Latin is extraordinarily rich, which is one reason why we find classical Latin so hard to learn, and why grammatical terms derived from Latin are so imperfectly adapted to describing how English really works. We may receive a momentary inkling of the relativity of language when we learn bits of etymological lore, but we do not become genuinely aware of the cloud of language that surrounds and pervades us unless we learn another language, preferably one quite different from our own, well enough that we no longer "translate" it semi-consciously but can respond directly to its capacity to reflect and shape experience and thought by its particular selective, evaluative and correlative possibilities.

Within a given language, however, there are "languages," the languages of groups and regions, occupations and avocations; the precise languages of specific studies and disciplines, tools kept artificially sharp for one purpose only; and the eroded hypnotic semi-meaningless words of advertising or propaganda, which influence by a maximum of association with a minimum of meaning. The "language" of a great artist is a highly individual synthesis out of all these possibilities; it is only in a limited sense his own creation, but to the extent that it is, it makes possible the particular kind of consciousness on which his works depend, and at the same time recreates and enriches the common medium. In this sense it is impossible to draw any hard and fast line between "language" as the raw material which makes style possible and "style" itself. Ordinarily critics confine themselves to what is individual about the use given to language by a particular artist, and philologists to the communal usage. But this distinction is pragmatically shaky as well as philosophically tenuous, and, as we have seen, Tolkien himself rejects it.

Judgments of Tolkien's style like Burton Raffel's reflect a comparatively modern assumption that the function of language in any work of art is to force the reader out of the reactions, awarenesses, associations of ideas, and value judgments which he shares with others and to substitute for them sharper, more distinctive, individual, and "original" modes of awareness. Good style is style which drags the reader out of his habitual derivative consciousness and makes him participate in a new one. This is a function of post-Romantic views of the artist as a privileged sensibility whose experiences are not only more intense than those of ordinary men but "original," that is, in degree if not in kind they are really different and more valuable. But this is by no means the only possible view of the artist. Keats himself told his publisher that poetry "should surprise by a fine excess and not by Singularity—it should strike the Reader as a wording of his own highest thoughts, and appear almost a Remembrance."[7] And it is perfectly possible for an artist's concern with language to be concern for language as a medium of communal consciousness and of certain modes of awareness and evaluation to which its existence *vis à vis* other languages testifies. The artist may dramatize language as the blood and sinews of a culture as distinct from other cultures. Many great novelists have combined this sort of interest in language with the kind Burton Raffel has in mind; one can read Joyce or Jane Austen for either reason. An artist can also be concerned with language almost purely in the second sense. This has been true of most "high styles" of the past, whether they represent the heightening of communal experience in the way that "primitive" formulaic styles do, or whether they involve the highly sophisticated artistry, which may or may not be formulaic, of literary epic.

What Tolkien has done is to attempt a story concerned with language in the communal sense, yet which is as different from epic as it is from the novel. *The Lord of the Rings* enacts the nature of language. Tolkien has created an entire world in its spatial and chronological dimensions, peopling it with languages which have, in a necessarily stylized and simplified version, all the basic features of language, from writing systems and sound changes through diction and syntax to style. By playing them against one another, he has created a "model" (in the scientific sense of the term) for the relationship of language to action, to values and to civilization.

One can readily see why the construction of an imaginary world of remarkably dense texture is necessary to such a process. But the choice of a "fairy tale" as the basic genre is at first sight more puzzling. Yet it is basic to Tolkien's view of language. In his illuminating essay on the fairy tale (see footnote 6), Tolkien argues that the process which he calls "sub-creation," the creation of worlds whose rationale has nothing to do with imitating experience as we know it, is inherent in the very nature of language:

> The incarnate mind, the tongue, and the tale are, in our world coeval. The human mind, endowed with the powers of generalization and abstraction, sees not only green-grass, discriminating it from other things (and finding it fair to look upon), but sees that it is green as well as being grass. But how powerful, how stimulating to the faculty that produced it, was the invention of the adjective: no spell or incantation in Faërie is more potent. And that is not surprising: such incantations might indeed be said to be only another view of adjectives, a part of speech in a mythical grammar. (p. 50)

Such an idea of the connection between language and invention centers itself on the relation of language to those experiences that are not peculiar to a given, specially sensitive individual. Instead, Tolkien sees one of the central values of the "fairy tale" as its capacity to bring about "recovery" of experiences so communal

---

[7] To John Taylor, 27 February, 1818, *The Letters of John Keats*, ed. Hyder E. Rollins (Cambridge, Mass., 1958), I, 238.

and basic that the individual loses contact with them as he becomes more sophisticated: "It was in fairy-stories that I first divined the potency of the words, and the
wonder of the things, such as stone and wood and iron; tree and grass; house and
fire; bread and wine" (pp. 74–75). So far from apologizing for this lack of particu-
larization, Tolkien sees it as central to the "recovery" process:

> The radical distinction between all art (including drama) that offers a visible
> presentation and true literature is that it imposes one visible form. Literature
> works from mind to mind and is thus more progenitive. It is at once more uni-
> versal and more poignantly particular. If it speaks of bread or wine or stone or
> tree, it appeals to the whole of these things, to their ideas; yet each hearer will
> give them a peculiar personal embodiment in his imagination. Should the story
> say "he ate bread," the dramatic producer ... can only show "a piece of bread"
> according to his taste or fancy, but the hearer of the story will think of bread in
> general and picture it in some form of his own. If a story says "he climbed a
> hill and saw a river in the valley below," the illustrator may catch, or nearly
> catch, his own vision of such a scene; but every hearer of the words will have
> his own picture, and it will be made out of all the hills and rivers and dales he
> has ever seen, but specially out of The Hill, The River, The Valley which were
> for him the first embodiment of the word. (p. 87)

Plain words lose their capacity to evoke vision and experience in this way, and one
answer is for the artist to picture a specific instance with such sharpness that his
hill takes the place of any other hill. But for Tolkien there is another answer: to
provide a context in which the reader's capacity to recreate is itself recreated: "By
the forging of Gram cold iron was revealed" (p. 75). It is significant that Burton
Raffel actually quotes this passage and yet shows by his comments that he takes it
to mean that the ingredients of a narrative—the bread, the hills—should have no
properties and no presence beyond those necessary to make incident follow
incident:

> It is a cog in some narrative machine: there was some reason for this person to
> climb a hill, there was some reason for him to see a river, and some conse-
> quences flowed therefrom. What were they, these reasons and possible conse-
> quences? Read on and discover. None of this has anything to do with what
> words as words can communicate. ... (Critics, pp. 226–227)

This is precisely the opposite of Tolkien's meaning. His friend C. S. Lewis, in an
essay "On Stories" published in the same volume as Tolkien's, makes this clear:
"To be stories at all, they must be a series of events; but it must be understood
that this series—the *plot*, as we call it—is only really a net whereby to catch something else" (p. 103). Perhaps, in a sense, this is true of any fiction, but in the art of
story proper, the "something else" is not character or criticism of social conditions
but "something other than a process and much more like a state or quality," the
state of seeing hill and valley in some generic, yet for each person intimate sense.
This is true even of suspense and *peripeteia*: "It is the *quality* of unexpectedness,
not the *fact* that delights us. It is even better the second time" (p. 103). Or, as

John Stevens comments of the *lais* of Marie de France, which he sees as structures based on focal "dramatic images": "if a ballad is a song that tells a story, a *lai* is a story that tells a song. . . . [Marie's] climaxes are climaxes of the expected."[8] Incident can have this power of mediating states with special intensity when the incidents are divorced from the role they play in actual life and from the ways in which we perceive our experience under normal states of consciousness. The gratuitous character of incident on which its poetic role depends is created by a non-realistic plot and by language which would be unsuited to the transmission of a realistic one.

In this insistence on the value of generic experiences and this recognition of art that does not sharpen the reader's awareness toward the particularized, Tolkien flies in the face of most modern poetics, whether of fiction or of poetry. But it should be noted that it is we, and not Tolkien, who are eccentric in the larger patterns of western history. The majority votes with Dr. Johnson when he condemns art—including some of the poetry we most value today—that particularizes experience past the point where it has generically human, as distinct from individual, relevance. The idea that the function of art is to make possible experiences that are not isolated or eccentric is as old as Aristotle. Even T. S. Eliot, who found himself, during most of this period, on the opposite side from Lewis in the debate on literature, says of the writing of poetry,

> There is only the fight to recover what has been lost
> And found and lost again and again: and now, under conditions
> That seem unpropitious. (East Coker, V)

It is by no mere aberration that Tolkien should be thus raising issues central to the twentieth century's critical debate over the role of language and the particular in art. In the very years when *The Lord of the Rings* was taking shape, C. S. Lewis, Tolkien's fellow medievalist, fellow member of the "Inklings" and fellow writer of fantasy, was defending Milton's style against T. S. Eliot, F. R. Leavis and I. A. Richards on precisely these grounds:

> [Dr. Richards's] school . . . talk as if improvement of our responses were always required in the direction of finer discrimination and greater particularity; never as if men needed responses more normal and more traditional than they now have. . . . Sensitive critics are so tired of seeing good Stock responses aped by bad writers that when at last they meet the reality they mistake it for one more instance of posturing. They are rather like a man I knew who had seen so many bad pictures of moonlight on water that he criticized a real weir under a real moon as "conventional." A belief . . . [is common] that a certain elementary rectitude of human response is "given" by nature herself, and may be taken for granted, so that poets, secure of this basis, are free to devote themselves to the more advanced work of teaching us ever finer and finer discrimination. I believe this to be a dangerous delusion.

---

[8] "The *granz biens* of Marie de France," *Patterns of Love and Courtesy: Essays in Memory of C. S. Lewis,* ed. John Lawlor (Evanston, Ill., 1966), p. 10.

As he goes on to say, "The whole art consists not in evoking the unexpected, but in evoking with a perfection and accuracy beyond expectation the very image that has haunted us all our lives."[9]

By creating a panorama of languages, and by recognizing that the very nature of language requires a plot for its exploration, Tolkien has created a counterpoint between different sorts of "images and expectations" as they relate to experience. It is basic to any such attempt that a series of different "languages" shall be used. To be "languages" at all they will have to have, on the one hand, differing physical characteristics, and, on the other, differing ways of evoking and evaluating experience. Short of writing a story in a series of distinct actual languages—what Tolkien presumably meant by saying he would have preferred to write in "Elvish" —it will be necessary to divorce the physical and stylistic qualities which in any real language are interdependent, and to represent the stylistic ones by variations of English, while introducing proper names and quotations of translatable size to give a sense of the language as a physical medium for thought. This Tolkien achieves by presenting his book as a translation and correlation of material from various languages; in the Appendix on languages he explains how, using modern English and its relationship to Old English and to other languages, he has devised an equivalent for the relationships between the languages of his "sources," explaining that the differences between them will necessarily be much less marked than those between the "originals." This device is reinforced by the narrative situation, in which most of the time the characters are supposed to be using the "common speech" rather than their own languages, since members of different species are present together, and their own languages are merely reflected in their manner of using the "common speech." Thus in practice, the counterpoint of "languages" is primarily a counterpoint of stylistic levels or of genres. The other aspects of the different languages are suggested not merely by names of places and people (especially by giving the name of a place in more than one language) and by quotation, subsequently translated, but by the Appendixes which, while explaining pronunciation, writing systems and the history and sociology of the different species, fill in the linguistic background with great verisimilitude.

It is difficult to do justice to this strategy by quotation, since the effect is by its nature diffuse and cumulative. The styles range through the classic spectrum from "low" to "high." The basic note, against which all the others play, is struck by the "hobbit" style Raffel quotes, which ranges from the consciously playful "nursery tale" tone of the trilogy's opening sentence—"When Mr. Bilbo Baggins of Bag End announced that he would shortly be celebrating his eleventy-first birthday with a party of special magnificence, there was much talk and excitement in Hobbiton" (I, 29)—to a spare and flexible "plain style" for action or business.

---

[9] *A Preface to Paradise Lost* (1942; reprinted New York: Galaxy Books, 1961), pp. 55–56, 58. See also Lewis's comments on the limiting character of visual images compared to words ("On Stories," p. 102). It should be noted here that Lewis has frequently insisted that any influencing was done by Tolkien to him and not the other way around ("No one ever influenced Tolkien—you might as well try to influence a bandersnatch," he wrote to Charles Moorman in an often quoted statement on the relations between the "Inklings"), and this is confirmed by Tolkien's own statements (see Moorman, p. 214).

The "high styles" include the highly decorated ("folded marbles, shell-like, translucent as the living hands of Queen Galadriel," II, 152) and the deliberately archaic, alliterative and sonorous, weighted with proper names from "other languages" and often inverting usual word order or adding, in apposition, information of no direct, utilitarian relevance. For instance, Gimli the dwarf ceremonializes his first glimpse of the mountains so central to the history of his people, using names in Dwarfish, Elvish and the Common Speech which have occurred elsewhere or will do so, and elements of which turn up as ingredients in other words:

> I need no map. . . . There is the land where our fathers worked of old, and we have wrought the image of those mountains into many works of metal and of stone, and into many songs and tales. They stand tall in our dreams: Baraz, Zirak, Shathûr. Only once before have I seen them from afar in waking life, but I know them and their names, for under them lies Khazad-dûm, the Dwarrow-delf, that is now called the Black Pit, Moria in the Elvish tongue. Yonder stands Barazinbar, the Redhorn, cruel Caradhras; and beyond him are Silver-tine and Cloudyhead: Celebdil the White and Fanuidhol the Grey, that we call Zirak-zigil and Bundu-shathûr. (I, 296)

But at its best, the high style is simple, though ceremonial, suggesting greater importance and wider perspective: "Only I hear the stones lament them: *deep they delved us, fair they wrought us, high they builded us; but they are gone*" (I, 297). Some long accounts in this style achieve great power, like Gandalf's account of his battle with the Balrog and his return from death, which concludes:

> Naked I was sent back—for a brief time, until my task is done. And naked I lay upon the mountain top. The tower behind was crumbled into dust, the window gone; the ruined stair was choked with burned and broken stone. I was alone, forgotten, without escape upon the hard horn of the world. There I lay . . . while the stars wheeled over, and each day was as long as a life-age of the earth. Faint to my ears came the gathered rumour of all lands: the springing and the dying, the song and the weeping, and the slow everlasting groan of over-burdened stone. And so at the last Gwaihir the Windlord found me. . . . (II, 106)

The primary impact of these various styles comes from their juxtaposition. Elements of high and low can play against each other in a single passage, to strike a certain balance of tone. Or speakers of different styles may be involved in the same event:

> "Welcome and well met!" said the dwarf, turning towards him. . . . "Gloín at your service," he said, and bowed still lower.
> "Frodo Baggins at your service and your family's," said Frodo correctly, rising in surprise and scattering his cushions. "Am I right in guessing that you are the Gloín, one of the twelve companions of the great Thorin Oakenshield?" (I, 240)

The same thing may be described in a variety of styles. The Ents are given direct, detailed physical description by the narrator. Then a hobbit tries to describe them to his friends:

"Ents," said Pippin, "Ents are—well Ents are all different for one thing. But their eyes now, their eyes are very odd." He tried a few fumbling words that trailed off into silence. (II, 167)

Later the same hobbit describes these eyes in retrospect:

One felt as if there was an enormous well behind them, filled up with ages of memory and long, slow, steady thinking. . . . it felt as if something that grew in the ground—asleep, you might say, or just feeling itself as something between root-tip and leaf-tip, between deep earth and sky had suddenly waked up, and was considering you with the same slow care that it had given to its own inside affairs for endless years. (II, 66–67)

Finally Gandalf describes the Ents to the King of Rohan:

"They are the shepherds of the trees. . . . You have seen Ents, O King, Ents out of Fanhorn Forest, which in your tongue you call the Entwood. Did you think that the name was given only in idle fancy? Nay, Théoden, it is otherwise: to them you are but the passing tale; all the years from Eorl the Young to Théoden the Old are of little count to them. . . ." (II, 155)

An event told consistently in one style may be juxtaposed with another in a different style. Or, presented realistically, an event may then be embodied in history, ritual or poetry. The final battle charge of Théoden, after shrewdly deploying his men, is action only slightly poeticized:

Suddenly the king cried to Snowmane and the horse sprang away. Behind him his banner blew in the wind, white horse upon a field of green, but he outpaced it. (III, 112)

Later an elegaic lament is chanted at his grave:

Out of doubt, out of dark, to the day's rising
he rode singing in the sun, sword unsheathing.
Hope he rekindled, and in hope ended. . . . (III, 254–255)

The same speech may be given in several versions that testify to different aspects of it. The inscription on the Ring is reproduced in its flowing elvin lettering (I, 59); it is presented in translation, and within the larger poem of which it forms one couplet:

One Ring to rule them all, One Ring to find them,
One Ring to bring them all, and in the darkness bind them. (I, 59)

And at Elrond's council it is read aloud in the Black Speech: "*Ash nazg durba-tulûk, ash nazg gimbatul, ash nazg thrakatulûk agh burzum-ishi krimpatul*" (I, 267).

The lyric "Snow White!" is complemented by an untranslated but closely related Elbereth lyric given only in Elvish. The elaborately decorated verse accounts of Luthien and Beren, and of Nimrodel, are followed by prose accounts and commentaries. Aragorn's coronation pledge is given in the original language of Elendil himself as well as in a formal translation, and then is played against the colloquial explanation of the ceremony being whispered by a bystander to a friend. Galadriel's lament is followed by an "art prose" reconstruction made by Frodo years later.

The primary function of the verse scattered through the narrative is to provide an intensification of the qualities of a given style which could not be so pronounced in the main narrative without overburdening it. The verse ranges from the comic doggerel, riddles, or drinking songs of the hobbits, and their simpler introspective lyrics, through the remote, filigree "fairy" narrative poems with their complex rhyme and assonance patterns that represent the lower level of Elvish lore as translated into the "common speech," and the gnomic "rhymes of lore," to the high ritual of certain elf songs that approach acts of worship, and the epic poetry of Rohan. These latter involve imitations of Old English alliterative, formulaic verse of a brilliance that can only be fully appreciated by someone who has had to confess himself defeated by the same task, and some actually scan by the strict rules of Anglo-Saxon prosody. A few of these poems, especially the elf song "Snow white! Snow white!" and perhaps the lament for Gilgalad, Bilbo's "I sit beside the fire and think," and Pippin's bath song, achieve, in addition to their narrative function, some independent poetic stature though not of a characteristically modern sort. Apart from that, most of them have a quality the twentieth century has long ceased to think of as proper to poetry: they are pleasurable.

This cross-referencing of styles is what distinguishes the trilogy most sharply both from other fantasy and from the novel—and lovers of the trilogy from its antagonists, who may dislike specific styles, find the whole business too complicated and self-conscious, or feel that the change from one style to another undercuts both. It is certainly true that such a strategy results in an interplay of perspectives as marked as that which, in modern fiction, we dignify as "narrative ambiguity," but its effect is the opposite of ironic. It attempts to build cumulatively an awareness of human perceptions as rich and as sharp as that which can be achieved by the subtle development of a single style. By the very nature of Tolkien's experiment, such complexity cannot characterize any one of his styles. The condition of creating such a panorama of "languages" is that each style shall be used not primarily to define the individuality of the given speaker or situation, but to enact the kind of consciousness he shares with others who have a comparable stance before experience. Each language selects from the complete range of awarenesses possible in that situation certain aspects which constitute an interpretation of the situation, an accommodation between what that speaker's cultural experience has been and what the situation "really" is. No artist can do this with a variety of "languages" and *at the same time* correct the reader's experience of the event itself toward "finer discrimination and greater particularity." The thing can be done well or badly. If it works, it works because the artificially simplified language evokes experience in the reader to complete it, and because a basic medium close enough to our own normal awareness is provided as a "least common denominator" style against which the others can play. The fairy-tale and nursery-tale style which embodies the hobbits' normal level of experience plays this role, supplemented by an admirable "plain style" where clear and vivid description of action or setting is needed. As Roger Sale shows so clearly, the mechanism ceases to work when the proportion of the "hobbit perspective" drops below some critical line.[10] As soon as that happens, the other styles must stand entirely on their own ability to draw sufficiently on elements already present in the reader's experience to complement their necessarily simplified and generalized character. They are, after all, not really styles so much as symbols for, or samples of, style. Probably this accounts for the fact that readers of the trilogy all seem to feel that the non-Frodo sections of *The Two Towers* and *The Return of the King* drag somewhere, without agreeing in the least about which sections are responsible.

It is for this reason that we cannot predict whether the "dynamics" of *The Lord of the Rings* will work for readers who come to it a hundred years from now. Even today it completely fails to work for anyone who actively dislikes the "hobbit style"; for anyone who does not share, or at least envy, the experience of landscape and weather and tramping out of doors; of beer and bread and fire; of puzzles and lore; of hierarchy with mutual respect; and of the camaraderie between friends and colleagues of the same sex. As Tolkien himself observes, "Fairy tales were plainly not concerned with possibility but with desirability. If they wakened *desire*, satisfying it while often whetting it unbearably, they succeeded" (p. 62). This is what *The Lord of the Rings* demonstrably does for an audience as diverse as it is large, and it does so largely by means of what we must call the magnificent precision of its language, though that precision is of a kind wholly alien to what we think of ourselves as valuing today. That this "desirability" should be so widely felt in an environment which would seem in many ways unpropitious testifies that the trilogy is not merely—though it may be also—an inkblot in which we find whatever we bring to it. The complexity of its linguistic and stylistic achievement is matched by its bold inversion of larger patterns, especially its transformation of the archetypal quest-plot into a quest to get rid of something, rather than to find something. As Roger Sale shows so well, its conception of courage is very much of our own time, not of romanticism or classical epic, though it is very like that which Tolkien's own major essay on *Beowulf* finds northern rather than Greek.[11] Its sense of history, of the cost and the inexorability of time, has its kinship with *Four Quartets*, and Tolkien's concept of "recovery" reminds one of the last section of *Little Gidding:*

> *We shall not cease from exploration*
> *And the end of all our exploring*
> *Will be to arrive where we started*
> *And know the place for the first time.*

[10] "Tolkien and Frodo Baggins" (1964), *Critics*, p. 263.

[11] "*Beowulf*: the Monsters and the Critics," *Proceedings of the British Academy*, XXII (1936).

The readers of Ossian were probably the very people least qualified to say whether their experience was a response to excellence or a sign of the direction poetry would take when new consciousness of certain qualities in human experience found major artists to shape it. Dr. Johnson saw through the whole business, and he was right; but then he had not fallen under the spell, nor was he prophesying the future. We can see clearly in the development of nineteenth-century fiction that as the novel defined a function for itself different from that which narrative had served in the past, and won respect for that function, it cut itself off from many of the possibilities available to fictional art. And at the very time that this was going forward, less respectable genres, fantasy, science fiction, horror fiction, the detective story, children's literature, were picking up some of the pieces and transforming them to the point that novelists of our century could begin to reintegrate them. To write *The Lord of the Rings* was certainly not "to ring the bell backwards" nor "an incantation to summon the specter of a rose." Sam, thinking about the nature of narrative as such, marvels:

*"Don't the great tales never end?"*

*"No, they never end as tales," said Frodo. "But the people in them come, and go. Our part will end later—or sooner." (II, 321)*

# Flaubert and Emma Bovary: The Hazards of Literary Fusion

LEO BERSANI

Romantic love has been one of our most effective myths for making sense out of our sensations. It organizes bodily intensities around a single object of desire and it provides a more or less public theater for the enactment of the body's most private life. In love, desires and sensations are both structured and socialized. The loved one invests the world with a hierarchy of desirability. At last we have a measure of value, and even the unhappiest lover can enjoy the luxury of judging (and controlling) his experience according to the distance at which it places him from the loved one's image or presence. Passion also makes us intelligible to others. Observers may be baffled as to why we love this person rather than that one, but such mysteries are perhaps more than compensated for by the exceptional visibility in which the passionate pursuit of another person places the otherwise secret "formulas" of individual desire.

Love is desire made visible, but it is also desire made somewhat abstract. We do not yearn merely for sensations in romantic desire; we seek the more complex satisfaction of another desiring presence. To desire persons rather than sensations is to indicate a certain predominance of mind over body. The sublime-sublimating nature of love is clearly enough pointed to by the notable fact that, as we see in Racine, even the most obsessive sexual passion can be adequately described with practically no references to the body. Indeed, the more obsessive the passion, the more insignificant the body may become; sexual fascination steals some of the body's vitality, and therefore partly dissipates physical energies. Love, like art, is a *cosa mentale*; like art, it systematizes, communicates and dilutes the fragmented intensities of our senses. But this is of course too one-sided. Even in passions as diagrammatic as those of Racine's protagonists, the diagram itself is initiated by a traumatic encounter with another body (*"Je le vis, je rougis, je pâlis à sa vue,"* Phèdre says of her first meeting with Hippolyte). And, even more decisively, the rich verbal designs which express the Racinian lover's passion never divert him from the single purpose of possessing another body. An abstract psychology of mental states constantly refers to an impossible and indescribable meeting of bodies. The dream of certain happy sensations sustains all speech, while the realization of that dream would be the end of speech. In its continuous allusiveness to both sensation and thought, love once again reminds us of art. They are both pursuits of sensual intensities through activities of sublimation. Love, then, can be considered as an ideal subject for literature; it is the most glamorous of dramatic metaphors for the "floating" of the literary work itself between the sensual and the abstract.

The various sorts of intelligibility which literature brings to the life of the body are Flaubert's subject in *Madame Bovary*. Character has an interesting superficiality in the novel. Flaubert's intention of giving a realistic and inclusive image of bourgeois provincial life—the book's sub-title is *Moeurs de province*—partly disguises a certain thinness and even disconnectedness in his psychological portraits. True, the portrait of Emma Bovary is eventually filled in with an abundance of psychological and social details, but, during much of the narrative, she is nothing more than bodily surfaces and intense sensations. Emma first appears in Chapter 2; her personality begins to be analyzed in Chapter 6. For several pages, Flaubert's heroine is a patchwork of surfaces: a "blue merino dress with three flounces," excessively white fingernails, a thick mass of black hair, the moving reflections of the sun through her open parasol on her face, a tongue licking the bottom of a glass.[1] (This attention to physical detail can of course be partly explained in terms of narrative strategy: Flaubert economically conveys the desires of the men looking at Emma by describing those aspects of her presence which stimulate them.) Not only do we thus see Emma as a somewhat fragmented and strongly eroticized surface; when we move to *her* point of view, we have an exceptional number of passages which describe the life of her senses. Mediocre in all other respects, as Brunetière wrote, Madame Bovary becomes a superior creature thanks to a rare *"finesse des sens."*[2] Emma's greedily sensual awareness of the world has often been noted. The dinner and ball at la Vaubyessard, for example, provide a feast of brief but intense thrills for all her senses: "certain delicate phrases of the violin" which make her smile with pleasure, the cold champagne which makes her entire body shiver, the dazzling gleam of jewelry, the warm air of the dining room which envelops her in a "mixture of the scents of flowers and fine linen, of the fumes from the meats and the smell of the truffles" (pp. 369–371).

At moments of more overpowering sensuality there even emerges a "formula" for Emma's sensual intensities, a characteristic style of sensation which, as we know from Flaubert's other works, wasn't invented for Emma alone but rather seems to be a basic formula for Flaubertian sensation in general. Sexuality in Flaubert is frequently expressed in terms of a rippling luminosity. "Here and there," Flaubert writes as part of his description of Emma's first happy sexual experience (with Rodolphe in the forest near Yonville), "all around her, in the leaves and on the ground, patches of light were trembling, as if humming-birds, while in flight, had scattered their feathers" (p. 472). The

[1] *Madame Bovary*, in *Oeuvres*, ed. A. Thibaudet and R. Dumesnil, 2 vols. (1951–52), I, 338–339, 341, 345. The translations in this essay are my own, although I have consulted and found helpful both the Lowell Bair translation in the Bantam Books edition of *Madame Bovary* which I edited (New York, 1972), and the Norton Critical Edition, edited with a substantially new translation by Paul de Man, based on the version by Eleanor Marx Aveling (New York, 1965). Subsequent page references to *Madame Bovary* are to the French edition, and will be given in the text.

[2] Ferdinand Brunetière, *Le Roman naturaliste* (Paris, 1893), p. 195.

moon, during Emma's last meeting with Rodolphe in the garden behind her house, "cast upon the river a large spot, which broke up into an infinity of stars, and this silvery gleam seemed to writhe to the bottom of the water like a headless serpent covered with luminous scales. It also resembled some monstrous candelabra, with drops of molten diamond streaming down its sides" (p. 506). While the experience of pleasure itself seems to include a vision of discreet points of light (the diamond light is perceived as distinct "drops"), the anticipation or the memory of sexual pleasure frequently diffuses these luminous points into a heavier, even slightly oppressive atmosphere. In the garden description the brilliantly decorated serpent and the candelabra plunging into the water are hallucinated participations of the external world in Emma's sexual pleasure. At a certain distance from sex the thought of pleasure, or the images connected with it, makes for a less dazzling hallucination, and light now suffused with color becomes softer and thicker. After that first day in the forest with Rodolphe, Emma feels that "she was surrounded by vast bluish space, the heights of feeling were sparkling beneath her thought" (p. 473). Much later, as she lies alone in bed at night enjoying fantasies of running away with Rodolphe, Emma imagines a future in which "nothing specific stood out: the days, all of them magnificent, resembled one another like waves; and the vision [cela] swayed on the limitless horizon, harmonious, bluish, and bathed in sun" (p. 505). A world heavy with sensual promise (and no longer blindingly illuminated by sexual intensities) is, in Flaubert, frequently a world of many reflected lights blurred by a mist tinged with color. As the carriage draws her closer to her meetings with Léon in Rouen, the old Norman city seems to Emma like a "Babylon" of pleasure. She "pours" her love into its streets and squares; and "the leafless trees on the boulevards seemed like [faisaient] purple thickets in the midst of the houses, and the roofs, all shiny with rain, were gleaming unevenly, according to the elevation of the various districts" (pp. 564-565). Purplish masses of trees against an even darker background, millions of liquid light reflections which both brighten and obscure the city's outlines: this typical Flaubertian landscape recurs frequently during Frédéric's idle walks in Paris early in L'Education sentimentale, and, as in the case of Emma's Rouen, it seems to be what Flaubert's "hero" finds in the world when he looks at it with sensual longing. Desire has (or rather makes) its own atmosphere in Flaubert.

Now as soon as we speak of a characteristic formula of sensation or desire we are of course giving a certain intelligibility to what at first seemed to be the discontinuous and fragmented life of the body. But the intelligibility is all for us; nothing in Madame Bovary indicates that Emma has the slightest awareness of a durable and defining style in her sensuality. Furthermore, in the passages quoted in the last paragraph, it's by no means clear whether the images are meant to express what Emma is actually seeing or hallucinating in the world, or whether they are Flaubert's descriptive and metaphorical equivalents for sensations or states of mind to which they allude but which in fact don't include them. Put in this way the question is unanswerable and irrelevant.

I ask it partly because, irrelevant or not, it is bound to occur to us, and partly because it is one way of formulating a problem I'll soon be looking at more closely: that of the relation between literature and sensation. For the moment, we can simply note that even if Emma does see the bejewelled candelabra in the river, that doesn't seem to be of any help to her in making sense of her sensations or in locating continuities in her experience. Of course, this is merely one aspect of her general mediocrity. She is inattentive even to that which makes her superior: the exceptional refinement of her senses. Emma's consciousness is intense, but it carries very little. She thinks in clichés, and, as far as her moral awareness goes, she is hardly less self-centered or more scrupulous than Homais. One has only to think how richly Jane Austen's and George Eliot's novels are nourished by all the ideas and principles of their heroes and heroines to appreciate the risk Flaubert takes in creating, to use a Jamesian term, such an insubstantial center of consciousness as Emma for his novel. (Indeed, James found Emma too thin a vessel to carry the weight of the novel's meaning.) But the most interesting fact about Emma, as I've been suggesting, may be precisely that she has so little consciousness. For in spite of the fact that she is, after all, part of a realistic fiction in which characters have names, social positions and personalities, she almost succeeds in existing without what the realistic novel generally proposes as an identity. When she is not having intense sensations she does little more than *long for* sensations. Her principal activity is that of desiring. But what exactly is there for her to desire? In what images will she recognize a promise of happy sensations?

Love sublimates and novelizes sensation. The literature of romance on which Madame Bovary gorges herself is the only spiritualizing principle in her life. The dangers of this literature are so emphatically illustrated in Flaubert's work that we may tend to overlook the service it performs for Emma's intense but random sensuality. For a moment during the performance of *Lucia di Lammermoor* at the Rouen opera house, Emma manages to smile with a "disdainful pity" as she thinks of all the lies which literature tells about life; "she now knew," Flaubert adds, "how small the passions were which art exaggerated" (p. 531). The next day, when Léon visits Emma at her hotel, they attempt, with the help of literary clichés, to recompose their past, to fit the quiet, uneventful love of the days in Yonville to an ideal of glamorously desperate passion. "Besides," Flaubert philosophically remarks, "speech is a rolling mill which always stretches out feelings" (p. 539). But what alternative is there to the exaggerations and the extensions of language? In this same scene at the Rouen hotel Emma and Léon finally stop talking: "They were no longer speaking; but they felt, as they looked at each other, a humming in their heads, as though something audible had escaped from their motionless eyes. They had just joined hands; and the past, the future, reminiscences and dreams, everything was merged in the sweetness of this ecstasy" (p. 540). In the same way Emma's sensual torpor as Rodolphe speaks to her of love on the day of the agricultural fair is a state in which "everything became confused" and the present merges with images from the past. Emma's consciousness is invaded by the odor of Rodolphe's pomade, the memory of a similar odor of vanilla and lemon which came from the viscount's beard as she waltzed with him at la Vaubyessard, the light from the chandeliers at that same ball, an image of Léon, and finally the smell of the fresh ivy coming through the open window next to which she and Rodolphe are seated (p. 459). As Jean-Pierre Richard has brilliantly shown, a fundamental theme of Flaubert's "material" imagination is that of a fusion between the self and the world, as well as among all the elements of consciousness. Contours are blurred, boundaries disappear, and the great danger in Flaubert's imaginary world is that of being drowned in a kind of formless liquid dough, in a sea of thick, undifferentiated matter.[3] I'll be returning to the dangers of fusion; for the moment I want to emphasize that even at moments of great sensual pleasure, as in the passage just quoted, the intense sensation tends *to break down differences* in *Madame Bovary*— differences between people, between the present and the past, and between the inner and outer worlds. Thus, not only does Flaubert present Emma as a patchwork of bodily surfaces; not only does he tend to reduce her consciousness to a series of strong but disconnected sensations; he also indicates that by its very nature sensation makes a mockery of the distinctions we invent in thought.

There is, however, the rolling mill of language to rescue us. Language *defuses*; its conceptual nature attacks the intensity of sensations, and words unwrap the bundle of sensory impressions and extend them, as distinct and separate verbal units, along the "lines" of space and time. More specifically, in the case of Emma Bovary, stories of romance raise her sensations to the level of sentiment. They replace the isolated and anonymous body with couples sharply characterized socially, and they provide spatial and temporal elaborations—that is, a *story*—for the ecstatic instant. But, interestingly enough, Emma re-charges literary language by retaining only its inspirations for visual fantasies. Probably every reader of *Madame Bovary* has noticed that Emma "thinks" in tableaux. Indeed, the sign of desire in the novel is the appearance of a tableau. The desire for an ecstatic honeymoon is a mental picture of driving in the mountains, to the sound of goat-bells and waterfalls, toward a bay surrounded by lemon trees; the desire for an exciting existence in Paris is a group of neatly compartmentalized images of the different worlds of ambassadors, duchesses and artists in the capital; and the desire to run away with Rodolphe takes the form of an exotic travel fantasy through cities with cathedrals of white marble and finally to a picturesque fishing village. These desirable tableaux could be thought of as halfway between verbal narrative and the hallucinated scenes of intense sensations. As she indulges in them Emma enjoys a tamed version of bodily desires. There isn't a single original image in these romantic tableaux drawn from literature, but, perhaps because of that very fact, all the books which Emma has read collaborate to form a satisfyingly consistent love story, a highly intelligible cliché which imposes order on ecstasy.

[3] See "La Création de la forme chez Flaubert," *Littérature et sensation* (Paris, 1954).

Given the immensely useful function of literature in Emma's life, it is, in a sense, merely snobbish to complain about the inferior quality of the books she reads. But something does of course go wrong with the function itself. Emma is extremely demanding. She wants the intelligibility of literature *in* the ecstatic sensation. At the risk of making things overly schematic, let's say that we have followed her from disconnected sensations to the sublimating stories of art; how will she now return from art to life? There wouldn't be any problem if Emma could be satisfied with transposing literature into desirable mental tableaux. She is, however, engaged in a much more complicated enterprise, one which literature itself, to a certain extent, encourages. Literary romance gives a seductive intelligibility to the body's pleasures; but it perhaps also invites its readers to expect the body to confirm the mind's fictions. The lie of which Emma's novels are guilty is their suggestion that the stories which in fact modulate and dilute existential intensities are equivalent to them. It is as if writers themselves were tempted to ignore the abstracting nature of language and to confuse an extended novelistic fantasy with the scenes of hallucinating desire and sensation. Emma welcomes the confusion: she waits for experience to duplicate literature, unaware of the fact that literature didn't duplicate life in the first place.

This fundamental error naturally leads Emma into considerable trouble. For example, the books she reads (like all literature) make use of a conventional system of signs. Flaubert enumerates several of the gestures and the settings which signify love in the novels Emma read when she was at the convent: "[These novels] were filled with love affairs, lovers, mistresses, persecuted ladies fainting in lonely pavilions, postriders killed at every relay, horses ridden to death on every page, dark forests, palpitating hearts, vows, sobs, tears and kisses, skiffs in the moonlight, nightingales in thickets, gentlemen brave as lions, gentle as lambs, virtuous as no one really is, always well dressed, and weeping like fountains" (pp. 358-359). To use favorite categories of contemporary French criticism for a moment, we could say that in this passage Flaubert gives us a list of the principal signs used in popular romantic fiction; and the referent for all these signs is love. The connection between the sign and the reality is of course arbitrary (as it is for individual words), although it is also necessary for the coherence of a specific literary system. Emma, on the other hand, sees the connection as inevitable, as a *natural* one. She consequently takes a short cut and dreams of "persecuted ladies fainting in solitary pavilions" and of "nightingales in thickets" as if they *were* romantic passion. It's as if some one expected to possess the object "chair" by pronouncing the word which designates it. Love seems impossible to Emma unless it appears with all the conventional signs which constitute a code of love in fictions of romance. Since Charles doesn't respond to the romantic clichés she tries out on him, Emma, "incapable . . . of believing in anything that didn't manifest itself in conventional forms," decides that his love for her must be diminishing (p. 365). (Rodolphe, incidentally, makes the opposite mistake on p. 500: unable to see "the differences of feeling under the similarities of expression," he doubts Emma's passion because she uses formulas he has heard from so many other women.) There are particular words, costumes, gestures and settings which, so to speak, manufacture passion. As Flaubert says of Emma: "It seemed to her that certain places on the earth must produce happiness, like a plant indigenous to that soil and which would be unable to thrive anywhere else" (p. 362).

In a sense, however, there is a subtle rightness in Emma's confusion. We can point to a tree or a chair to indicate what we mean by those words, but where is the object "love," the definite shape we might evoke each time we say the word? Like all abstract concepts, love is a phenomenon created by its own definition. It is a synthetic product (the result of a synthesis, and existing nowhere in nature), and its only reality is on the level of the sign. (And, like all conceptual codes, it is subject to historical change: twentieth-century love is not the same as love in ancient Greece.) But if love is a certain composition of signs, is Emma so wrong to feel that she won't have found love until she assembles the signs in the right combination? "In her desire," Flaubert writes critically, "she confused the sensual pleasures of luxury with the joys of the heart, elegant habits with delicacies of feeling. Didn't love, like Indian plants, need a prepared soil, a particular temperature?" (p. 379). But the concept of love does in fact "grow" only in the "soil" of romantic fictions. We should therefore qualify what I said a moment ago: Emma's mistake indeed *seems* to be to confuse the literary props of passion with its reality, but more profoundly she errs in thinking that passion is a reality which can be determined *at all* outside of literature. Now I don't mean that she (or anyone, for that matter) is "wrong" to use abstract words to describe concrete experiences; conceptual syntheses are as necessary outside of books as in books. The dangerous confusion is between the usefulness of a synthesizing vocabulary and a pre-existent reality which we often assume it contains. For if we make this confusion, our experience comes to have a crippling responsibility to our vocabulary, and people far more intelligent than Emma torture themselves with the vain question of whether or not certain relationships can "really" be called "love." Emma Bovary is an impressively rigorous if narrow thinker; having picked up certain words in literature, she refuses to use them a bit sloppily (which is the only way to use them) in life. " . . . Emma tried to find out exactly what was meant in life by the words *felicity, passion* and *rapture,* which had seemed so beautiful to her in books" (p. 356). But nothing is meant by those words in life; they "mean" only verbally, and especially in books.

Furthermore, in seductive (and treacherous) fashion, the books which Emma reads attribute duration to the rapturous instant. Romantic love in literature may end tragically, but it is not likely to run out of emotional steam and end in boredom. Of course, all literature not only makes sense of the instant; it also makes time from the instant. The life of the body sublimated in time is the history of a person. But in Emma's favorite books history is glamorized as a succession of intensities. Romance conceptualizes sensation; furthermore, it suggests that time never dissipates sensations. Emma does experience sensations which seem to her to live up to her definitions of romantic ecstasy; but she learns that romantic ecstasy doesn't last. And we find the dramatization of this banal fact interesting only because it is made through a character who, quite remarkably, refuses to make any compromise at all with time. While Flaubert gives detailed attention to the modulations of feeling in time (I'm thinking, for example, of the chapter which summarizes the change in Emma between her return from la Vaubyessard and the move from Tostes to Yonville, pp. 377–387, and of the few pages—418–425—which describe her agitated, rapidly changing feelings after she discovers that Léon loves her), his aristocratic heroine expects each moment to repeat the rapture of a previous moment. But Emma's thrilling excitements are quickly submerged in ordinary time, and it is this shattering absence of drama which wears her out, which leads her to complain bitterly about the "instantaneous rotting away of the things she leaned on" and to feel that "everything was a lie!" (p. 584).

Maurice Blanchot has suggestively said of Flaubert that he shows us "the horror of existence deprived of a world."[4] We might consider this remark in two different ways. On the one hand, as I've suggested, Emma finds in literature a world in which to place and to identify her sensations. One could say that without literature she has existence without essence: disconnected, unidentifiable sensations on which literature will confer a romantic being or essence. On the other hand, she returns from literature with everything except the physical world in which the romantic existence might be lived. And she is finally crushed by the weight of an insubstantial imagination which has been unable to discharge itself of its fables, which has never found a world. The gap between an excessively signifying imagination and an insignificant world occasionally produces attacks of acute anxiety in Emma. Boredom is a crisis in her life because it is the lie which experience gives to the constantly interesting stories of literature. Things continue not to happen; and even the most trivial sight or sound can provoke panic simply by not corresponding to the mind's expectations, by illustrating the indifference of the world to our fictions. Jean Rousset and Gérard Genette have perceptively spoken of certain "dead moments" in Flaubert's work, of descriptive passages which seem to have no dramatic function but merely interrupt or suspend the novel's action.[5] A Balzacian description, however superficially digressive, is never dramatically irrelevant; it either provides information necessary for our understanding of the story or metaphorically characterizes the people involved in the story. In Flaubert, on the other hand, descriptive detail often seems to be given for its own sake; suddenly the story is no longer "moving," and we have an almost detachable literary *morceau*. These apparently gratuitous descriptions have a relation to the rest of the story similar to the relation be-

---

[4] *La Part du feu* (Paris, 1949), p. 322.

[5] See Rousset, "*Madame Bovary* ou le 'livre sur rien'. Un aspect de l'art du roman chez Flaubert: le point de vue," *Forme et signification: Essais sur les structures littéraires de Corneille à Claudel* (Paris, 1962), and Genette, "Silences de Flaubert," *Figures* (Paris, 1966).

tween Emma's uneventful life and her action-packed imagination. They are the formal narrative equivalents of experience which fits into no design. A certain carelessness on Flaubert's part about the dramatic significance of description educates the reader into being somewhat casual about meaningful patterns. In *Bouvard et Pécuchet*, Flaubert will finally bloat his narrative with information which we can dismiss as soon as we have received it. And even in *Madame Bovary* there are signs of his wish to train us to experience literature itself as having some of that boring insignificance which Emma is so exasperated to find in life.

Of course, one could scarcely imagine a novel more likely to exasperate Madame Bovary than *Madame Bovary*. A striking peculiarity of realistic novels, as Harry Levin has emphasized, is their hostility to literature[6]—or, more specifically, to that continuously significant and fully designed literature of which the novels Emma reads are, after all, merely inferior examples. I'm thinking of the dramatically gratuitous and even boring descriptions in the later Flaubert, as well as Stendhal's affection for the random and unexpected detail, for a life and for books imaginatively improvised. Emma's distaste for Flaubertian art can be assumed from the way she eventually turns against even non-Flaubertian art. Literature has served Emma very poorly indeed. It makes sense of experience for her, but experience doesn't confirm the sense she brings to it. And this is especially disastrous since Emma can't really return to literature. If *Madame Bovary* is a critique of the expectations imposed on life by literary romances, it is also a critique of the expectations which those same romances raise concerning literature itself. Flaubert's novel is an extraordinarily subtle dialectic between literature and sensation; the movement between the two creates a rhythm less immediately obvious but more profound than the alternation between exalted fantasies and flat realities.

Emma indicates her impatience with the literary imagination when, in answer to Léon's remark (the evening of her arrival in Yonville) that verses are much more "tender" than prose and are better for making one cry, she says: "But in the long run they're tiring . . . ; and now, on the contrary, I love stories in which the action doesn't let up from start to finish, and which make you frightened" (p. 401). It's true that as disappointments accumulate in Emma's life, books provide her with the "up" she no longer finds in love; unable to feel any "profound bliss" in her meetings with Léon (p. 582), Emma turns to literature for a "quick fix." She stays up at night reading "lurid books full of orgiastic scenes and bloody deeds. Often she would be seized with terror, she would cry out" (p. 588). At these moments of terror Emma has, it might be said, finally achieved her ideal if unbearable equilibrium between mind and body. An organized activity of sublimation (literature) is providing her with extraordinary sensations. The intensities of a body left to itself are discontinuous and mystifying. Literature explains those sensations, but it also dilutes them in the abstract, somewhat ghostly time of verbal narrative. The explanations of literature don't work in life, and the intensities of life are

---

[6] *The Gates of Horn: A Study of Five French Realists* (New York, 1963), p. 51.

lost in the endless and tiring meanings of literature. Consequently, what else is there to do but cultivate a style of reading in which the mind would excite itself out of consciousness? To get the fantastic fables of romantic literature without the words of romantic literature would be to allow imagination to act directly on the body without the cumbersome mediation of language. In her nocturnal screams, Emma—however briefly and unviably—has resolved the paradox of seeking sensations in the airy fancies of imagination.

An unbearable and an unviable solution: in reading those wild stories, Emma is of course profiting from neither the originality of her own talent for sensations nor from the sense-making structures which literature invents for the life of the body. Now Flaubert seems more sensitive to the sin against literature than to the sin against life. Much of the force of a potential argument in *Madame Bovary* against literature's violation of experience is lost because experience hardly seems worth the trouble. The alternatives to literary romance in the novel are Homais' invulnerable self-sufficiency, the boredom and pettiness of provincial life, Charles's bovine mediocrity, Rodolphe's egoism and brutal sensuality, and Léon's pusillanimity. Indeed, even when, as in *L'Education sentimentale*, Flaubert broadens the social context of his fiction beyond the narrow limits of dull provincial towns, he is never even mildly tempted by the "serious" activities and institutions of adult life (such as marriage, political involvements, or even ordinary sociability). And the only characters who appear to have his unqualified approval are the inaccessible and vaguely outlined Madame Arnoux, and those mute, simple-minded, virtuous creatures, Dussardier in the *Education* and Félicité in "Un Coeur simple."

Flaubert's radical critique of almost all versions of sentimental, intellectual and political "seriousness" could be thought of as expressing a profound distaste for all those sublimating activities which organize life in society. And Flaubert seems to encourage this view of his work by the attention which he gives, as we have seen, to the variety of sensual contacts which his characters have with the world. Emma Bovary is a sentimentalist, but her creator de-sublimates her sentimentality *for us* by presenting her both as an exciting physical presence and as having an exceptionally refined talent for sensual responses. But Flaubert's attitude toward this aspect of Emma is ambiguous. He may be seduced by the physical presence he has created, but nothing in the novel suggests that Emma's moral and intellectual emptiness and her genius for sensations have been imagined as part of an experiment in de-structuring personality. That is, Flaubert is not trying out novelistically the viability of fragmented and de-sublimated desires in the specific time of an individual life. For Flaubert, I think, finds Emma's sensations both fascinating and terrifying. The dangers of losing the self in uncontrollable fusions with the world seem to deprive the Flaubertian imagination of the leisure necessary for disengaging what I have called the personal formula of Emma's sensual intensities and allowing her to test that formula in her history. It even seems as if Flaubert were anxious to avoid the slightest possibility of making that test. The powerful deadness of Emma Bovary's environment would defeat even the most energetically inventive desires, and, when the environment is perhaps rich enough to contain spaces not yet absorbed by established modes of feeling and thought (as in the Paris of *L'Education sentimentale*), Flaubert creates a hero without Emma's energy, a figure too weak to inscribe on *any* terrain the traces of his original desires.

The natural inclination of Flaubertian desire is toward dangerous fusions; in other terms, desire leads to the nightmare of a loss of form. There are, it's true, fusions as well as a kind of material and spiritual oozing which indicate ecstacy rather than panic: the "vague and prolonged cry" which Emma hears after she and Rodolphe have made love in the forest blends harmoniously "like a piece of music with the last vibrations of her throbbing nerves," and a few moments earlier ". . . something sweet seemed to emanate from the trees" (p. 472). But the hallucinated sense of substances breaking out of their forms is also a sign of terror in Flaubert. After Rodolphe refuses to give her money, and just before her suicide, Emma's very being seems to jump out from her body and explode in the air or sink into the moving soil:

> She stood there lost in stupor, no longer conscious of herself except through the beating of her arteries, which she thought she could hear escaping like a deafening music that filled the countryside. The earth under her feet was softer than the sea and the furrows seemed to her like immense dark breaking waves. All the reminiscences and ideas in her head were rushing out, in a single leap, like a thousand pieces of fireworks. She saw her father, Lheureux's office, their room in the hotel, a different landscape. She was going mad, she had a moment of fright, and managed to take hold of herself. . . . (p. 611)

Emma regains her sanity only to kill herself; how will *Flaubert* protect himself from these "escapes" of being?

Only art is saved from Flaubert's pessimism about sensation and the sublimating mechanisms of social life. The Flaubertian cult of art explains Flaubert's severity toward inferior art. The realistic claims of Emma's favorite novels depend on their ignoring their own mediating processes, on their attempt to hide the differences between the nature of the intensities they seem to exalt and that of the exalting narrative itself. As I've said, they encourage Emma to search in life for the abstractions invented in books, and they also invite her to expect that real time, like the printed time of a novel, can be an uninterrupted succession of intense passages. Emma contributes to the sins of literary romance and, in a way, skilfully dismisses art by trying to separate the romance from the literature and thereby ignoring the work—the effort and the product—of the writer. She brings to these books exactly what they require: a lack of imagination. She reads literature as we might listen to a news report. Emma Bovary parodies all the pious claims which have been made by realism in Western esthetics for the relevance of art to life. Down-to-earth even in the midst of her raptures, Emma "had to be able to extract from things a kind of personal profit; and she rejected as useless everything which didn't contribute to the immediate gratification of her heart,—being by temperament more sentimental than artistic, seeking emotions and not landscapes" (p. 358).

Flaubert's writing is a continuous correction, through stylistic example, of Emma's confusions. The book we are reading constantly draws our attention to its own nature as a *composed* written document. Flaubert speaks in his correspondence of moments when he himself is, as it were, so taken in by the realism of his own writing that he begins to experience the incidents he describes: he shares both Emma's and Rodolphe's sensations in the scene of their love-making in the forest, and he writes the section on Emma's death with the taste of arsenic in his mouth. Occasionally Flaubert thus tends to draw from his own writing something like the immediate "personal profit" which Emma demands from literature. But to spend a couple of weeks shaping a single paragraph hardly seems calculated to leave the writer capable of "seeing through" his writing to the experiences it describes. The painfully slow composition of *Madame Bovary* is much more likely to leave Flaubert with the taste of verbal agonies rather than with the taste of arsenic.

More importantly, Flaubert's language, unlike Stendhal's, calls attention to its own strategies, sounds and designs. Flaubert's text has kept traces of being continuously worked over; and while this gives something awkward and heavy to his writing (which, in my previous work on Flaubert, I now think I've tended to over-emphasize), we might also feel that a certain stylistic opacity is Flaubert's decisive refutation of Emma's confused argument for a literature of pure sensation. The very fact that, because of Emma's sensuality, Flaubert has so often to describe moments of intense sensation gives him frequent occasions for illustrating the "proper" literary use of sensation. And what Flaubert shows us is a detailed process of establishing intervals within sensations of fusion which seem to allow for no intervals. In the passage I quoted some time ago, which describes Emma and Rodolphe's last night together, Flaubert compares the reflection of the moon in the water to a "headless serpent covered with luminous scales," and also to an enormous candelabra with drops of molten diamond flowing down its sides. The sexual suggestiveness of these images is obvious. As I've said, they transpose Emma's sensual pleasure into a hallucinated scene in the external world. But also, by the very fact of being literary images, they are the sign, for us, of a certain distance from the sensations they describe. In her sexual exaltation, Emma may actually *see* the serpent and the candelabra; a much cooler novelist tells us that the moon's light "seemed to writhe to the bottom of the water like a headless serpent covered with luminous scales," and then, somewhat awkwardly, he starts the second comparison (in a new sentence) with: "It also resembled . . ." These last few words could have been eliminated; we might have had a single sentence, with the two images closer to each other. "It also resembled [*cela ressemblait aussi à*]" is a heavy but salutary reminder of the *work* of comparison. To make a verbal analogy is to bring together two things which may usually not go together, but at the very instant we say the second term of the analogy we establish a difference between it and the first term. We create a linguistic space which no similarity can abolish.

Writing is the creation of such intervals, spaces, and differences. To speak and to write are the sublimating activities which allow us to spread out sensations in time and in space. Flaubert, whose terror of sensual fusions seems to have made this a literally saving truth, makes the point for us in more extreme ways than most other writers. Comparisons can be particularly obtrusive in his work; a somewhat creaky machinery for making analogies almost mangles the object of comparison. In a famous and frequently derided analogy Flaubert compares Emma's memory of Léon to an abandoned campfire in the snow of a Russian steppe, and by the end of the second paragraph of an extravagantly extended comparison, there is some question of whether or not Emma's anguish is going to survive this exercise in Slavic meteorology (p. 438). Proust, in an often quoted remark, declared that there is not a single beautiful metaphor in all Flaubert.[7] But the presumed "real" point of departure for a Proustian comparison is, as in Flaubert, but even more frequently than in Flaubert, volatilised and absorbed into the imaginative logic of a process of composition. What is not "beautiful" in Flaubert is not the content of his metaphors but the glaring visibility of his literary strategies. He is far more concerned than Proust, perhaps because of those terrors of the sensual imagination which we have briefly looked at, in maintaining a sharp distinction between art and the rest of life. The heaviness of much of his writing could therefore be thought of as pedagogically useful: he is constantly demonstrating the extent to which literature renounces the immediacy of sensations in order to express them.

As an example of those fusions which take place in Flaubert at moments of great sensual excitement, I've spoken of the passage which describes Emma's sensual torpor in the city hall of Yonville on the day of the agricultural fair. Present and past, Rodolphe and Léon, the odor from the viscount's beard and the odor from Rodolphe's hair merge into a single swimming sensation. "The sweetness of this sensation [of smelling Rodolphe's pomade] thus penetrated her desires from the past, and like grains of sand in a gust of wind, they swirled in the subtle breath of the perfume which was spreading over her soul" (p. 459). Everything has merged into a single, indistinct, whirling sensation—everything, that is, except the only thing we are really given, which is this exceptionally complex sentence. And the coherence of the sentence depends on our moving carefully from one distinct unit to the other in order to follow the construction of Flaubert's metaphor. The sentence begins with a kind of abstract chemistry, suddenly switches to the concrete image of sand in the wind, which seems to authorize the verb "swirled [*tourbillonnaient*]" when we return, in the last part, to the penetration and dancing of past desires in a present sensation. As even these brief remarks indicate, the fusions of literature are always separations or articulations, and they invite the critic to even further articulations. The Flaubertian workshop is one in which a master craftsman—somewhat at the expense of his own craft—teaches us to read.

[7] "A propos du 'style' de Flaubert," *Chroniques* (Paris, 1927), pp. 193–194.

# The Word as Object:
# The Rabelaisian Novel

JERRY WASSERMAN

If we examine George Steiner's argument that the scientific revolution of the mid-seventeenth century marked the beginning of a "retreat from the word," a decline of humanistic confidence in the ability of verbal language to apprehend the totality of reality and experience, we discover an interesting paradox.[1] For within a hundred years the wordiest of all artistic forms, the novel, is a thriving enterprise. It is also true that by the eighteenth century a novelist like Sterne was questioning the efficacy of fictional language in ways that will continue to be common to novelists of our own day. But such questioning had already begun in the sixteenth century with Rabelais. So to understand better this ongoing problem of the novelist's confrontation with his medium, we must go back to the historical moment at which the novel as we know it had its inception—the birth of the age of printing.

The Gutenberg revolution transformed the primarily oral art of literature into a primarily visual one, replacing the spoken word with the printed word. Literature thus became largely a mode of silence, to be read to oneself rather than spoken or heard aloud. At the same time language became objectified, reified, mass-produced as part of a concrete and portable object, the book. For Marshall McLuhan the significance of Rabelais lies in his early awareness of "the gigantism that issues from mere additive association of homogeneous parts," that is, from "the uniformity and repeatability of the printed word." He is primarily referring to the homogenizing and democratizing effects of print on the reading public of Rabelais' day; but there is also the "gigantism" of Rabelais' prose style—particularly evident in his catalogues—which was influenced by the new typographical effects available to him. McLuhan goes on to say that Rabelais is a transitional figure, since the "earthy tactility" of his work was a throwback to the old audile-tactile manuscript culture at the same time as his visual verbosity prefigured the new culture of letters.[2]

It is somewhat misleading, however, to make an absolute distinction between the visual and tactile so far as the novel is concerned. For the accentuation of the visual aspects of the book has often gone hand in hand with a quantification and

---

[1] *Language and Silence: Essays on Language, Literature, and the Inhuman* (New York: Atheneum, 1967), pp. 14–24.

[2] *The Gutenberg Galaxy: The Making of Typographic Man* (Toronto: University of Toronto Press, 1962), pp. 147–150, 194.

concretization of reality on the printed page. Sterne, Joyce, Beckett, Butor, Robbe-Grillet and others make use of a fictional language which is sometimes less referential than objective, corporeal. Their verbal catalogues, especially, do not always transcend themselves toward a preconceived or conventional meaning, but rather comprise an autonomous and intra-referential structure which demands that the reader compose its elements and discover for himself the experiences signified for him on the novel's narrative level. Rabelais' doubts about the transcendent powers of language, doubts that are reflected in his satires of the abuses to which various forms of communication are subject, were increased by the mechanically identical printed pages that he saw come off the presses. Yet at the same time the printed page appeared to him as a revelation, an accomplishment of Plato's prophecy "that if the image of science and learning were corporeal and visible to the eyes of men, it would arouse admiration from the whole world." [3] Thus his impulse, and that of his successors, was to use the medium that objectified words to explore their weaknesses and possibilities, and create a new "language" of typographical objects indigenous to print. Rather than using words only to signify reality in a one-to-one referential relationship, the Rabelaisian novel also employs a mimetic fictional language that poses an *analogous* world of visual verbal objects in which the reader might participate and thereby experience the world as fully and freely and directly as do Gargantua and Pantagruel. In this sense Rabelais was the father of the "new" novel; for in Robbe-Grillet's words, "the author today proclaims his absolute need of the reader's cooperation, an active, conscious, *creative* assistance. What he asks of him is no longer to receive ready-made a world completed, full, closed upon itself, but on the contrary to participate in a creation, to invent in his turn the work—and the world—and thus to learn to invent his own life." [4]

I

When *Pantagruel* was published in 1532, the French printing industry was only about sixty years old. Rabelais had already been in close contact with the printers of Lyon for at least a year, having edited Latin medical texts for publication, and he kept up with developments in printing after he turned to writing fiction. One of the most important of these was the publication in 1543 of Vesalius' anatomy, a book with elaborate cross-references between the printed text and illustrations of the human body. Rabelais' own medical training was likely to have made him aware of the inadequacy of purely verbal means for disseminating this kind of information; and *Le Tiers Livre*, his work most concerned with the ambiguous nature of language, was published in 1546. The

---

[3] *The Histories of Gargantua and Pantagruel*, trans. J. M. Cohen (Baltimore: Penguin, 1955), p. 230. All citations of Rabelais in English refer to this edition and are accompanied with page numbers in my text. Citations in French are from *Oeuvres complètes*, ed. Pierre Jourda, 2 vols. (Paris: Garnier, 1962), indicated as *Oeuvres*. The passage in Plato paraphrased by Rabelais is from the *Phaedrus*. Cf. *The Dialogues of Plato*, ed. and trans. B. Jowett, 3rd ed. (New York: Oxford University Press, 1892), I, 457.
[4] *For a New Novel: Essays on Fiction*, trans. Richard Howard (New York: Grove, 1965), p. 156.

progress of what Rabelais called "the noble art of printing" is also evident within the fictive time span of his work. At the beginning of *Gargantua* the young giant has to copy out his lessons by hand, because "the art of printing was not yet practiced"; by the end of that book he has installed a printing-house; and by Pantagruel's time Gargantua can write to his son that "the elegant and accurate art of printing" has brought about a renaissance of learning (pp. 70, 194).

But even print may be liable to destruction. On the first page of the author's prologue to *Pantagruel* the reader is advised to learn the book by heart to insure its survival in case the art of printing should die out or all books perish. Perhaps the most serious threat to its existence is political repression: all of Rabelais' books were either banned or expurgated. In his dedicatory preface to *Le Quart Livre* he even asserts that he had decided, in the face of such intimidation, "not to write another word" (p. 437). Thus it has been suggested that the "silences" within his work were a form of political expediency. His critical truths would be embodied in the obscurity of his book, a form that would outlast his persecutors and allow the perceptive reader, by close and repeated scrutiny of the printed page, to bring the truth to light.[5] But upon close reading we find Rabelais' work to be less concerned with preserving the *meaning* of linguistic signs than with establishing their ontology. His book is in large part an exploration of the relationship between signifier and signified and the silences that lie between them, an examination of the ability of words to "mean" anything other than themselves.

Assuming that the problematical *Cinquiesme Livre* was written by Rabelais, his work opens and closes with images of embodiment. At the beginning we are told to learn the book by heart; at the end the verdict of the Holy Bottle is "Drink." The book is a flask and the priestess Bacbuc tells Panurge not to "read this chapter, understand this gloss," but "taste this chapter, swallow this gloss" (p. 704). Elsewhere Rabelais makes the same identification between his book and wine, and urges us to drink heartily (p. 286). To truly know a thing is finally to be it, to partake of its essence. Drinking in Rabelais is in one sense a function of the humanistic thirst for knowledge—the printing press, McLuhan points out, derives its name from the technology of the wine-press (*Gutenberg Galaxy*, 147) —and is most often associated with Pantagruel, who is an inspirer of thirst. He gets his name from a minor demon of oral tradition and the mystery plays who throws salt into the mouths of drunks, causing thirst as well as hoarseness —that is, difficulty of speech. His companion Panurge, on the other hand, is a direct descendant of Hermes, the god of speech, from whom he derives his mastery of language.[6] The whole novel is informed by the alternate modes of apprehension these two characters represent: the silent and corporeal, and the

---

[5] V. L. Saulnier, "Le Silence de Rabelais et le mythe des paroles gelées," *François Rabelais: ouvrage publié* . . . , Travaux d'Humanisme et Renaissance, VII (Geneva: Droz, 1953), pp. 241–245; and Michael B. Kline, *Rabelais and the Age of Printing*, Etudes Rabelaisiennes, IV (Geneva: Droz, 1963), pp. 47–53.

[6] Mikhail Bakhtin, *Rabelais and His World*, trans. Helene Iswolsky (Cambridge, Mass.: M.I.T. Press, 1968), p. 325; and Ludwig Schrader, *Panurge und Hermes: Zum Ursprung eines Charakters bei Rabelais* (Bonn: n.p., 1958), pp. 124–125.

linguistic. While Rabelais is not consistent in his identification of each character with his particular virtue, Panurge's search for answers eventually leads him away from language to the Pantagruelian drink, which is the book itself, whose printing is only made possible by the herb Pantagruelion (p. 427). The pervasive spirit of Pantagruelism is finally reflected in Rabelais' creation of a Pantagruelian language, a corporeal language embodying its own essence.

Even if we ignore *Le Cinquiesme Livre*, the climax of the fourth book is the confrontation of Pantagruel and his crew with M. Gaster, Sir Belly, "the true master of all the arts," who is silent and deaf, speaking only by signs (p. 571). The answer to all the crewmembers' questions is given by "signs, gestures, and demonstrations"—their own eating and drinking—which satisfy their hunger and thirst and enable them to know Gaster's truth (pp. 586–588). For Rabelais knowledge is primarily physical and sensational. Witness Gargantua's famous goose, which sends its sensations through the anus to the intestines and only then to the heart and brain. Consequently, audile-verbal communication, the least palpable mode, is often less effective than communication addressed to the visual and tactile senses, which approach more closely the essence of that which is to be known. Words, then, might be most meaningful in a visual and corporeal form—in the form of print. But what must first be examined is the ability of words to carry any meaning at all.

## II

The ideals of Renaissance humanism which permeate Rabelais' writings are nowhere more evident than in his attacks on the abuses of spoken language. The best speech is that which is natural and elegant, avoiding the archaic and the pedantic. The obscurity of scholarly and legal jargon suffers some of Rabelais' worst scorn and best satire. Early in *Pantagruel* we are presented with the ludicrous Limousin scholar who "murders" French and Latin by his affected vocabulary and accent. In response Pantagruel asserts that "we ought to speak the language in common use, . . . we should shun obsolete words . . ." (p. 185). Gargantua's letter to his son, which follows soon after this scene, encourages Pantagruel's concern for correct verbal behavior, and expresses a desire that he become "a perfect master of languages," primarily Greek, Latin, and Hebrew (p. 195).

But the next episode, Pantagruel's meeting with Panurge, casts serious doubt on any consideration of linguistic excellence for its own sake. When Pantagruel and his companions come upon the bedraggled Panurge, he is obviously in need of help. But the curious, ingenuous young giant first wants him to *tell* who he is, where he comes from, where he is going, and what he wants. Panurge responds to these portentous questions in German: what Pantagruel wants to know, he says, is a sad and pitiful thing and would make an endless story. Instead of responding to Panurge's physical condition, however, Pantagruel responds to his words. He does not understand them, and asks that Panurge speak another language. It is characteristic of Panurge that he can never resist playing a trick;

so in spite of his pressing bodily needs he begins rattling off one language after another. The first is nonsense—literally "un aultre langaige." Then come Italian, Scottish, Basque, nonsense again, Dutch, Spanish, and Danish, none of which Pantagruel or his friends understand. By the time Panurge gets around to the three classical languages that they do understand, they are so caught up in the forms of his speech that they fail to realize *what* he has been saying. Their failure to acknowledge his suffering until he finally speaks vernacular French is a serious abuse: a concern for language at the expense of the speaking subject. Perhaps this is the lesson that Panurge means to teach them. For what he has been saying in Dutch, Danish, Greek, and Latin is that the eloquence of his *physical presence* expresses his bodily needs and his need of their pity and charity, precluding any necessity for speech: "speeches and words are superfluous when the facts are evident to all" (p. 200, n. 3). The ease with which Pantagruel has been distracted by language suggests that speech may not be merely super-fluous in certain situations, but can also be seriously misleading, drawing attention away from where truth really lies. What Panurge represents in this sense is an alternative to the verbal sign—a physical and visual sign embodying both the signifying agent and the signified concept.

Following his meeting with Panurge, Pantagruel arbitrates the lawsuit between Baisecul and Humevesne. Their arguments and his judgment are all given in more or less simple language, the language in common use, and avoid obsolete or technical words. But it is all absolute nonsense, comprehensible only to the three participants. What the individual words signify is easily understood, but their peculiar combinations point to a reality beyond the normal range of human apprehension: "the court declares that in view of the quaking of the bat, declining bravely from the summer solstice to woo the trifles which have checkmated the pawn through the wicked vexations of the light-shunners that are in the meridian of Rome . . ." (p. 212). While Pantagruel's judgment is a great success, it is entirely limited to the narrowly-enclosed universe of discourse in which the nonsense language operates. No one else understands any of it and it has no effect except upon the attitudes of the litigants. As far as the reader is concerned it is as meaningless as the nonsense languages Panurge speaks. Pantagruel understands the linguistic principle that "languages arise from arbi-trary conventions and the needs of people" (p. 339). But in this case, while the conventions of the language of the lawsuit are no more arbitrary than those of any other language, it suits the needs of only a limited number of people in a singular situation. It is only a small step from here to what Leo Spitzer calls "*une création d'un monde verbal autonome,*" which evokes "*l'espace vide de l'irréel,*" destroying our belief in the thing behind the word.[7] The nonsense languages of Panurge, the Latin gibberish of Janotus de Bragmardo in *Gargantua* (pp. 77–78), the "Lanternese" poem of Panurge in the third book (p. 417), and his terrified babble of sound during the storm in the fourth book (pp. 492 ff.)—all these represent the obverse of Roquentin's problem, for they are names divorced

---

[7] "Le Prétendu Réalisme de Rabelais," *MP,* XXXVII (1939), 143.

from their things, signifiers which de-realize rather than evoke a signified concept. We are left with what Alfred Glauser calls a museum of verbal objects,[8] of which the chief exhibit, as we shall see, are the lists and catalogues that pro- liferate throughout the novel.

Even when the sense of a body of words seems apparent, its meaning often remains enigmatic. For a linguistic sign to be meaningful the relationship it signifies must be understood. Much of Rabelais' third book concerns the fragile nature of this linguistic convention and the difficulty of sustaining a common understanding through words. *Gargantua* ends with a riddle and the inability of Frère Jean and Gargantua to agree on whether it is about Divine Truth or a tennis game. This introduces the ambiguity which begins in the third book with Panurge's long praise of debtors. While in the humanistic tradition of the para- doxical encomium, the expression of a truth through the praise of folly, Panurge's argument also illustrates the susceptibility of language to sophistical manipula- tion, and raises serious questions about it as an agent of truth. The same is true of his next argument, "proving" that the codpiece is the principal element of a warrior's armor.

The rest of this book is concerned with Panurge's consultation of various authorities as to whether he should marry, and if so, whether he will be a cuckold. In every case the answer is interpreted in two diametrically opposite ways. Panurge's refusal to acknowledge the finality of any one answer can be attributed in part to his self-love and lack of courage to commit himself to an irrevocable course. But the inherent ambiguity of words certainly contributes to the inability of the friends to agree on the meaning of the oracles. Every prophecy but one is expressed in language which Panurge, who insists on getting a positive answer, manages to twist to his own interpretation. The judge Bridoye, knowing the deceptive language of lawyers to be an instrument of the devil, judges his cases by throwing dice and trusting to divine guidance (p. 411). But Panurge persists in pursuing linguistic certainty. Only twice is he unable to provide a positive interpretation. In his parodic Socratic dialogue with Trouillogan, the *reductio ad absurdum* of linguistic ambiguity, the philosopher uses words so evasively that no conclusion is possible. Panurge finally gives up in disgust. He is equally furious with the response of the deaf and dumb Nazdecabre, and concludes by threatening him with a beating. But this is because the silent prophecy Nazdecabre gives in physical signs and gestures is so clearly under- standable and so obviously negative that Panurge can offer no alternative. He can only stubbornly deny its truth. Pantagruel had recommended the counsel of a dumb person on account of the traditional truthfulness and dependability of oracles declared by gestures and signs, as opposed to verbal oracles which were often mistaken "because of the ambiguities, equivocations, and obscurities in the words" (p. 339). The response of Panurge proves him right and demands a closer look at the nature of non-verbal signs.

[8] *Rabelais créateur* (Paris: Nizet, 1964), p. 104. Cf. Jean Paris, *Rabelais au futur* (Paris: Seuil, 1970), p. 59 *et passim*.

## III

Rabelais introduces his discussion of the significance of Gargantua's colors with an attack on bad visual puns and those *"transporteurs de noms"* who would portray a sphere to signify hope (*"sphère/espoir"*) or a broken bench to signify bankruptcy (*"banc rompu/bancque roupte"*) (*Oeuvres*, I, 41). Such puns confuse linguistic convention with pictorial analogy and pervert the logic of both kinds of sign. As an ideal alternative Rabelais proposes the Egyptian hieroglyph, "which none understood who did not understand, and which everyone understood who did understand, the virtue, property, and nature of the things thereby described" (p. 58). One cannot understand the visual image of a thing without understanding its nature. Rabelais' conception of the hieroglyph is what Saussure would call a "symbol" and Wittgenstein a "pattern" as opposed to a word. Whereas words are arbitrary signs and give us no indication of the nature of the thing signified, symbols or patterns are always characterized by some rudimentary intrinsic link, some comparison between signifier and signified.[9]

Rabelais is here following Plato, who suggested that words may have originated as vocal imitations; but since the original namer may have had an erroneous conception of the thing named, and since the original word is usually severely distorted by the time it reaches us, the link between the word and the thing is really no less arbitrary than if it were purely conventional. Therefore we must look to the thing itself rather than its name to understand its essence. In the absence of language, Socrates says, we would express ourselves by bodily imitation of the nature of things.[10] And what is pantomime but a kind of existential hieroglyph, a living incarnation of the visual sign. So in *Pantagruel*, following his exposés of verbal communication, Rabelais presents us with the silent gestural debate of Panurge and Thaumaste. The matters to be disputed, Thaumaste explains, "are so difficult that human words would not be adequate to expound them to my satisfaction" (p. 231). But the absurdly comical debate that follows is understood by no one except the two contestants—and even Thaumaste does not really understand it. For again Panurge is playing a joke. His gestures are merely obscenities which Thaumaste and the spectators take to be profundities. Their meaning is lost on those who see them, just as we see the words in the preceding judgment of Pantagruel, as representative of nothing but themselves. They are purely and autonomously *there*.

Such visual and corporeal attempts at communication by pattern appear elsewhere in Rabelais in more successful forms. Shortly after his debate with Thaumaste, Panurge takes upon himself the interpretation of the empty envelope sent by a Parisian lady to Pantagruel. All his efforts are aimed at making visible what he takes to be invisible writing. The word must be seen to be understood. At last he discovers the phrase, "why hast thou forsaken me,"

[9] Ferdinand de Saussure, *Cours de linguistique générale*, ed. Charles Bally and Albert Sechehaye, 3rd ed. (Paris: Payot, 1955), pp. 100–101; Ludwig Wittgenstein, *The Blue and Brown Books* (New York: Harper and Row, 1965), pp. 27–28, 84.

[10] *Cratylus*, in *The Dialogues of Plato*, I, 368–387.

written on the ring enclosed in the envelope (p. 247) But it is only when he recognizes that the diamond is false, a visual symbol of Pantagruel's faithlessness, that the written message makes any sense, the motto and object reciprocally interpreting each other.[11] A more fully successful visual pattern is the picture that Panurge buys on the island of Medamothi. It represents the Philomela myth, a paradigm of non-verbal signification. Philomela had her tongue cut out by her brother-in-law so that she could not report his rape of her. In the absence of speech she wove a tapestry which vividly portrayed the event and brought about her revenge. The other paintings purchased by the crew also suggest the possibility of capturing reality in iconographic form: "a lifelike representation of Plato's Ideas and the Atoms of Epicurus"; and "a portrait of Echo in her natural shape" (p. 454). While it is almost impossible to visualize these two portraits, they are in line with Rabelais' continual efforts to concretize the abstract. In the next chapter Pantagruel sends his father a pigeon with a white ribbon, their pre-established sign of Pantagruel's safe passage. The visual-corporeal representation is no less conventional than words in this case, but it reaffirms the possibility of an unambiguous and effective alternative to verbal communication.

Rabelais follows Plato in putting sight at the forefront of all the senses. It is, he stresses in his prologue to Book Three, the dearest of God's physical attributes to man (p. 281). Without it, Rabelais knows, his book would not be possible, for the printed book is above all an object in visual space. In the prologue to *Gargantua* he uses as a metaphor for his book the Silenus, which he transforms into a "little box," frivolous on the outside but rare and profound within. Whether or not we take seriously his ambiguous injunction to seek out the "sublime sense" beneath his comical surface, we are left to deal with a visual object. His "Pythagorean symbols" either represent something other than themselves or they represent themselves (p. 38). Even if the box is empty it is still there. But since we are ultimately concerned with the words of the book, we must establish their visual significance. The key lies in the *"parolles gelées"* episode.

Sailing on the open sea, Pantagruel and his crew suddenly hear an uproar of words and sounds that have no apparent source. The ship's captain explains that they are on the edge of a frozen sea where a fierce battle had taken place the preceding winter. The sounds of the battle had frozen in the air and now with the coming of spring were melting and hence becoming audible. Pantagruel actually grabs a few handfuls of frozen words out of the air and throws them on the deck. They are of various colors and when handled by the crew they melt; but the resultant sounds are not understandable because they are "in a barbarous language." The frozen words are objects in physical space, to be seen and handled but not understood. When asked by Panurge to sell him some of the words, Pantagruel replies, "I'd rather sell you silence." And what are so many of the

11 For such signs Jerome Schwartz, following Capaccio and Mario Praz, uses the Renaissance term "device". "a visual sign which reveals to those who understand it a key to the intelligibility of the world." "Gargantua's Device and the Abbey of Theleme: A Study in Rabelais' Iconography," *Yale French Studies*, no. 47 (1972), 235.

words printed in Rabelais' book but visual and concrete silences, existing for us as pure presence? "Hin, hin, hin, hin, his, tick, tock, crack, brededin, brededac, frr, frrr, frrrr, bou, bou, bou, bou, bou, bou, bou, bou, tracc, tracc, trr, trrr, trrrr, trrrrr, trrrrrr, on, on, on, on, on, ouououon, Gog, Magog" are some of the sounds the melting words make (p. 569). But to us, reading the book, they are visual signifiers frozen on the page, signifying nothing but themselves. The same is true of many of the episodes we have discussed and some which we have not—the drunkards' "conversation" in *Gargantua*, for example, which consists of autonomous words and phrases with no sense of relationship to each other or to their speaking subjects. Glauser refers to that episode as *"un éloge de la parole pure,"* a visible effervescence, a liberation of matter.[12] This new language, liberated into a non-communicative, non-transcendent realm of pure substance, comprises a mimetic level of the novel which embodies both the characters' experience of language and the reader's experience of much of the fictional world.

## IV

Communication, as we have seen, is often extremely problematical for Rabelais. In spite of the fact that the ideal of natural, elegant speech is achieved at many points in the novel, it is undercut so often that we are forced to look to alternatives. One possibility is that language can better accommodate some form of communicable truth by taking on the attributes of the visual, the symbolic, by resembling the essence of the thing to be signified. But there is no guarantee that the result will be comprehensible. Even if words manage to penetrate the transcendent "abode of truth" from which Pantagruel hoped the *"parolles gelées"* had come (pp. 567–568), even if they embody the essences of the Platonic realm of Ideas, the chances are still good that the *"parolles degelées,"* "melted" as it were by the perceiving consciousness, will manifest themselves as absolute nonsense. There is, of course, much successful communication in Rabelais: for perhaps the greater part of his novel words serve the functional purpose of narration. We can follow his story and understand his satire. Yet in most of the sections we have discussed words embody nothing but their own essence, and express themselves as objects without "meaning." The distinction between these two modes of expression is the distinction Sartre makes between prose and poetry. Whereas the prose writer is concerned with signification, the poet is concerned with words as things rather than signs. But this is not to say that the poetic word-object has no value for Rabelais. On the contrary its value inheres in its integrity—its being what it is, in-itself—and in its ability as a physical object to provide the human agent with sensations of all kinds. For Sartre the reader always shares in the act of creation with the author: the reader "is required not only to disclose the object (that is, to make *there be* an object) but also so that this object might *be* (that is, to produce it). In a word the reader is

---

[12] Glauser, p. 108. Cf. his discussion of *"les paroles gelées,"* pp. 278–281.

conscious of disclosing in creating, of creating by disclosing." [13] For Rabelais
there is an even broader range of activities associated wi'h creating and apprehending linguistic objects. We can observe them as spectacle, play with them,
manipulate them, and finally "consume" them as we consume wine. They thus
become part of our experience of, and integration with the physical world.

Consuming, since Sir Belly is the master of all arts, leads to creation: the
"poetic frenzy" of the Pantagruelians at the end of Book Five, for example.
The final product of ingestion is usually not poetry but excrement. Yet Rabelais
is not very discriminating about value. Pantagruel creates little men and women
with his turds and farts; Panurge makes a kind of frenzied poetry out of his
feces at the end of Book Four, as does young Gargantua, who also turns ass-
wiping into an educational activity. To be a child, for Gargantua, is literally to
be immersed in the physical world (cf. pp. 62–63). Even the earthiest, non-
directed play has an educational function, a creative value.

A similarly positive sense of being immersed in things is what Rabelais creates
for us with his "non-functional," non-directed language. When he describes how
Gargantua spent his time "in drinking, eating, and sleeping; in eating, sleeping,
and drinking; in sleeping, drinking, and eating" (p. 62); or how some of Frère
Jean's victims "died without a word, others spoke without dying; some died as
they spoke, others spoke as they died" (p. 100), he is no longer using language
for strictly representational purposes. By continuing to build words upon words
even after the narrative situation has been exhausted, he transfers the activities
of organic life to a verbal plane in which words assume a life of their own as
imaginative *analogues* of the physical world, to be played with in all their possible combinations and permutations. Michel Foucault has argued that the
relationship of language to the world in the sixteenth century in general was
one of analogy rather than representation or signification. The symbolic function
of language resided not in the words themselves "but rather in the very existence of language, in its total relation to the totality of the world, in the
intersecting of its space with the loci and forms of the cosmos." [14] Faced with
the difficulty of signifying the world by means of an inexact and ambiguous
verbal language, Rabelais turns instead to its concrete existence, and through it
offers us the first-hand experience of his inexhaustible world of verbal objects.
Rabelais the writer, in Sartre's terms, defers to Rabelais the poet. "Rabelais'
entire effort," as Erich Auerbach says, "is directed at playing with things and
with the multiplicity of their possible aspects; upon tempting the reader out of
his customary way of regarding things, by showing him phenomena in utter
confusion . . ." The things he plays with and the phenomena he presents are
not merely *represented* by the words of his book; they *are* also the words
themselves. But while words are things, they are not ends in themselves. What is
finally important is that we join in Rabelais' play, and experience, in Auerbach's
words, "the freedom of vision, feeling, and thought which his perpetual playing

---

[13] *Literature and Existentialism*, trans. Bernard Frechtman (New York: Citadel, 1962), pp. 11–16, 43.
[14] *The Order of Things: An Archeology of the Human Sciences* (New York: Pantheon, 1970), p. 37.

with things produces, and which invites the reader to deal directly with the world and its wealth of phenomena." [15] It is precisely to the world outside the novel that Rabelais' mimetic language leads us.

The pure phenomenality of Rabelais' world of words is most clearly evident in his absurdly long, comically grotesque, and utterly gratuitous lists and catalogues. Each catalogue is ostensibly aimed at naming and defining a particular subsection of the Rabelaisian universe: the books in the library of Saint Victor, the games played by young Gargantua, the virtues of the fool Triboullet, the names of the cooks on the isle of Farouche. Unlike its predecessors—biblical genealogies, Homeric catalogues, military ordinances of the medieval marketplace—the Rabelaisian catalogue is not meant to provide historical legitimacy, versimilitude, and immediacy, or to impress its audience with the power and resources of the state. As is so often the case with words used to attempt communication in the novel, the elements of the Rabelaisian catalogue tend to break free of referential relationships with external reality and attain an autonomous existence as objects within the physical space defined by the page.

The first list in the first chapter of *Pantagruel* is atypical in many respects. The genealogy of Pantagruel, like the genealogies in *Genesis* or *Matthew*, is a closed system. It begins with the first giant, ends with Pantagruel, and follows a strict chronology derived from its generating principle. Each name must be the offspring of the preceding name and it must end with the name whose genealogy it is. Thus we should be able to work straight through the vertical list to its end, knowing that our expectations will be fulfilled. But there are obstacles thrown in our path at every turn. Whereas the first three names in the list are Rabelaisian inventions, we are soon introduced to giants from the bible, myth, medieval legend, and history. Historicity is denied not only by the impossible inclusion of such disparate "families" in the same lineage, but by its impossible chronology as well. Offot, for example, a medieval giant, is the great-great-grandfather of Sisyphus, while Hercules is the grandfather of a contemporary of Roland. Language, instead of naming the world, consumes it. "Where else could they be juxtaposed," Foucault asks about the elements of a list in Borges, "except in the non-place of language?" Even while defining the origins of Pantagruel's Utopia, Rabelais creates a linguistic *heterotopia* parallel to but distinct from it.[16] Furthermore, while the vertical dimension of this list is theoretically contained by its first and last terms (although, since the genealogy is imaginary, Rabelais could conceivably incorporate an infinite number of names within it), there is no necessary limit to its horizontal dimension. For the 1542 edition of *Pantagruel* Rabelais added descriptive phrases alongside some of the names. The variety of descrip-

---

[15] *Mimesis: The Representation of Reality in Western Literature*, trans. Willard R. Trask (Princeton: Princeton University Press, 1953), p. 276.

[16] Whereas *"utopias* afford consolation . . . *heterotopias* are disturbing, probably because they secretly undermine language, because they make it impossible to name this *and* that, because they shatter or tangle common names, because they destroy . . . that less apparent syntax which causes words and things . . . to 'hold together.' " Foucault, pp. xvi–xviii. Cf. Joyce's similar genealogy of Bloom in *Ulysses* (New York: Random House, 1961), pp. 495–496.

tions and their utter irrelevancy suggest both the arbitrary nature of descriptive language and the inexhaustibility of the additive principle in a linguistic field: Etion "was the first to get the pox through not having drunk fresh in summer," Enac "was very expert in taking little worms out of the hands," Gayoffe's "balls were of poplar and his tool of sorb-apple wood" (p. 173). And by leaving most of the names *unqualified*, it is as though Rabelais were asking us to lend our own creative imaginations to his raw material. This is the principle of "super-fetation" which Rabelais joyfully establishes early in *Gargantua* (p. 47): no situation, no matter how fertile, is ever so complete that we cannot add to it, though the end result may be made no more "meaningful" in the process.

Finally, the vertical structure of Pantagruel's genealogy further removes its component words from their ostensible function as signifiers. Each name is preceded by the words, "*Qui engendra*," arranged exactly beneath the preceding "*Qui engendra*" on the page. Visually, we are presented with a solid vertical column broken only by the descriptive phrases that run longer than a single horizontal line. One effect of this repetition is to objectify the words, to draw our attention from their sense to the visual *Gestalt* they comprise. The eye is more naturally drawn to their relationship with each other than to the relationship of each "*Qui engendra*" with the name that follows. A related effect is that we become numb to any meaningful differentiation between the senses of the individual lines. Such systematic repetition produces a "saturation" effect. After a point, even though we are aware of a closural principle in the list that guarantees its coming to an end, we find it difficult to sustain interest in the individual steps leading to the end. As we become bored with the banality of the repetition, our impulse is to seek variation in the activity of reading, to play with the words themselves.[17]

In subsequent lists Rabelais gives added emphasis to such methods of undermining the nominative properties of words. The next two major lists in *Pantagruel*, for instance, move toward greater openness. In the 1532 edition the library of Saint Victor had only a relatively small number of titles; by 1542 it had grown to a hundred and forty books, and these are only "certain books" that Pantagruel found most magnificent (pp. 186–187). Epistemon's somewhat shorter list of the damned is only a small portion of the "more than a hundred million of them" who, he can attest, suffer the pox (p. 268). Both these lists have paratactic, purely arbitrary structures, as do most of the others, and both are potentially limitless. The arbitrary number and order of the things named give us almost unlimited freedom to deal with them. So too do the particular qualities of the library catalogue. Mixing French with Latin, real names and titles with invented ones, real words with invented words, Rabelais again introduces us into a linguistic realm free from the strictures of external reality. The mixture of roman and italic type emphasizes the visual aspects of the list, as Rabelais

---

[17] See K. Koffka, *Principles of Gestalt Psychology* (New York: Harcourt, Brace, 1935), pp. 410–414; and Barbara Herrnstein Smith, *Poetic Closure: A Study of How Poems End* (Chicago: University of Chicago Press, 1968), p. 42 *et passim*.

reminds us that these manuscripts are being printed for publication (p. 192). The gigantism of the catalogue, in which words proliferate in objective form, parallels the proliferation of the books in print; and Pantagruel's education in the library becomes our education in the object-world of the printed page.

A brief survey of some of the other lists is sufficient to confirm their non-significative, mimetic function. Eusthenes' list of monstrous animals, which begins with

| | | |
|---|---|---|
| Aspicz, | Alhatrabans, | |
| Amphisbenes, | Aractes, | |
| Anerudutes, | Astérions, | |
| Abedissimons, | Alcharates, | |
| Alhartafz, | Arges, | (Oeuvres, II, 236), |

is grouped alphabetically by first letter. But all are things which, he says, "for the whole of to-day my spittle will do no harm to" (p. 588). Not only are the words themselves grotesque, but their grotesque relationship to the other terms within the sentence places them outside any normal realm of signification. The same is true of Xenomanes' descriptive anatomy of Quaresmeprenant, and Panurge's description of Frère Jean as a hundred and sixty-six different kinds of "ballock ball-bag" ("couillon"). In addition to the gratuitous internal relationships in these lists, structural repetition reinforces the visual dimension:

La nucque, comme un fallot.
Les nerfz, comme un robinet.
La luette, comme une sarbataine.
Le palat, comme une moufle.
La salive, comme une navette.  [etc.]   (Oeuvres, II, 128);

| | | |
|---|---|---|
| C. martelé. | C. magistral. | |
| C. entrelardé. | C. claustral. | |
| C. juré. | C. monachal. | |
| C. bourgeois. | C. viril. | |
| C. grené. | C. subtil.   [etc.] | (Oeuvres, I, 513). |

Notice, too, that in the "couillon" list the basic word is reduced to a mere visual cipher—"C."—so that the adjectives assume a kind of independence. There seems to be some organizing principle to this list. Words are grouped by rhyme, alliteration, assonance, or, tentatively, by subject. These groupings are not only arbitrary, however, they are also quite mobile. "Martelé" and "entrelardé" may form a pair, but so might "martelé" and "magistral" or "monachal." We might link "bourgeois" with "viril" or with "monachal." Any number of combinations is suggested by the placement, appearance, or association of the words; without syntactic connections they need not be read in any specific combination or order. Another list that functions this way is the celebration of the fool, Triboullet, by Panurge and Pantagruel. Here, however, the two vertical columns alternate between the two characters:

| Pantagruel | Panurge |
|---|---|
| F. d'azimuth, | F. de haulte fustaie, |
| F. d'almicantarath, | F. contrehastier, |
| F. proportionné, | F. marmiteux, |
| F. d'architrave, | F. catarrhé, |
| F. de pedestal, | F. braguart, |
| F. parraguon, | F. à XXIIII caratz, |
| F. celebre, | F. bigearre, |
| F. alaigre, | F. guinguoys, [etc.]  (Oeuvres, I, 563) |

Free of all constraints, making up their rules as they go along, the characters continue their game for more than three pages, playing with all the physical attributes of words as enthusiastically as Rabelais expects us to, and with no real concern for meaning.

V

Rabelais' world of language opens up new possibilities for us and for the Rabelaisian novelists who follow him. He uses all the opportunities of print to lay bare the contingency of language and reveal its independent physical existence. Communication is difficult enough, but words only add to the difficulty when we are not aware of their visual and corporeal properties. The world for Rabelais, as for Sterne, was a great sensorium, and intercourse was not primarily verbal intercourse. If words are to be truly useful, they must constantly reawaken us to an awareness of all our senses and creative potentials. Since his book cannot effectively tell us *about* the world, it will inaugurate us *into* it by way of its own physical world of verbal objects. As Pantagruel asks Panurge, in a passage that Sterne would use verbatim in *Tristram Shandy*, "What harm is there in gaining knowledge every single day, even from a sot, a pot, a fool, a stool, or an old slipper" (p. 331)—or, he might have added, from a bunch of nonsensical words? By embracing the autonomy of language and denying preconceived limits of closure or syntax, definition or signification, order or direction, Rabelais offers us freedom and continual renewal. Language for him is ultimately inexhaustible. New words can always be invented, new objects added to the verbal world. His lists do not, as Jean Paris suggests, play the documentary role of encyclopaedic lists which attempt to fix in their totality the elements of a world doomed to mutability (Paris, pp. 63–65). Rabelais' attitude toward such language is like that of Pantagruel, who refuses the narrator permission to preserve some of the "*parolles gelées*," "saying that it was folly to store up things which one is never short of, and which are always plentiful . . ." (p. 569).

Rather than store up Rabelais' words, we are asked to play with them. But "play," "nonsense," and "language games," all of which might be used to describe Rabelais' work, are bound by more or less strict rules.[18] The Rabelaisian game of language has its rule, too, but it is totally subject to the whims of the players. For it is the rule of the Abbey of Theleme:

*FAY CE QUE VOULDRAS.*

This is the freedom in which the basic, educative play of the child resides, and it is this sort of play that Rabelais asks of us. Childhood play is a free assimilation of the things of the world to the self. In Rabelais' terms we consume or embody our playthings, his verbal objects. The opposite of play is imitation, for by imitation the child accommodates himself to the world.[19] Analogously, language as play consumes or assimilates the world, while language as imitation, language that attempts to name, must accommodate itself to the world by whose rules it must be bound. By remaining "silent," non-referential, and creating its own reality, Rabelais' language escapes the abstractions and preconceptions that imitative language is heir to. We are invited to freely assimilate Rabelais' verbal universe through playful reading, and use our experience of its reality to see and feel the world as though for the first time.

[18] See Johan Huizinga, *Homo Ludens: A Study of the Play Element in Culture* (Boston: Beacon, 1955), pp. 11–13; Elizabeth Sewell, *The Field of Nonsense* (London: Chatto and Windus, 1952), pp. 25–27, 97; and Wittgenstein, pp. 90 ff.

[19] Jean Piaget, *Play, Dreams and Imitation in Childhood,* trans. C. Cattegno and F. M. Hodgson (New York: Norton, 1962), p. 87.

# Lawrence, "Being," and the Allotropic Style

*He turned in confusion. There was always confusion in speech. Yet it must be spoken. Whichever way one moved, if one were to move forwards, one must break a way through. And to know, to give utterance, was to break a way through the walls of the prison as the infant in labour strives through the walls of the womb.*

—Women in Love, p. 178[1]

## GARRETT STEWART

My central point about the style of D. H. Lawrence is augured by a single, mildly surprising turn in the grammar of the last sentence above, which teaches that "utterance" is apposite to "knowing" when (and only when, as we know from the rest of Lawrence) each is properly defined—blood knowledge spoken from the heart. This instruction comes linguistically, and takes as its subject the relation of language to life. As so often in Lawrence, the verbal and the psychological planes of his fiction intersect in the programmatic demands upon language to engage with the same rhythms of mutation and reissuance that it is struggling to transcribe on behalf of the spirit. The soul must bear witness to its own finer conception, the expunging of the old self and the germination of the new, and in so doing it must bear forth new words in which to clothe its dreams. No ordinary midwife in the rebirth of the spirit, language is itself refashioned along with the moribund values it has hallowed and entombed. And verbal freedom is not just escape, but new access. Twice repeated, the phrase "break a way through" alerts us by its own sonic contours to its dual role as both a verbal and a thematic paradigm, for in the self-dramatizing aural ambiguity of "away" and "a way," the second meaning (dependent on the preposition "through") seems to break away from the first as the ear moves from a designation of simple release to that of passage and arrival. Language has both said and done.

The want of a better term than "ambiguity" for Lawrence's fluid, elusive effects —of which this is the quietest, most evanescent sample—will soon be argued and, I hope, answered, but the loaded word is sufficiently heretical in Lawrence studies, and attention-getting, to do for now. Even a recent book by Roger Sale that follows a long section on Lawrence with one on William Empson as standard-bearers of *Modern Heroism*[2] makes no connection on the score of Lawrence's own

---

[1] Quotations throughout from *Women in Love, The Rainbow,* and *Sons and Lovers* refer by page to the Viking Compass editions (New York: 1960, 1961, 1958); from *Lady Chatterley's Lover* to the Modern Library edition; and from *The Man Who Died* to the Vintage edition, *St. Mawr and the Man Who Died* (New York: Random House, 1953).

[2] Roger Sale, *Modern Heroism: Essays on D. H. Lawrence, William Empson, and J. R. R. Tolkein* (Berkeley: Univ. of California Press, 1973).

daring types of ambiguity or the curious structure of his complex words—and wording. And yet for most readers it is immediately obvious that some kind of ambiguous intricacy is the essence of Lawrencian narrative at the level, at least, of situation and psychology. Stylistically, as Forster might have said, we need to "connect." Ambivalence and imprecision, of course, can also be a failure of language as well as an asset, as Birkin implies—along with something more— immediately after the summary attitudes about articulate expression set down by the narrator in our epigraph: "One shouldn't talk when one is tired and wretched. One Hamletises, and it seems a lie" (p. 179). One lapses at such times into solipsistic conversations that wither quickly to soliloquies; or even worse, one plays onanistically with language like the word-monger Loerke who, later in the novel, Lawrence so heatedly denounces. But the Shakespearean allusion is inevitably more pointed. Birkin has just been advocating a love that is "like death," a passion that will allow him to "die from this life" into a state that is "more than life itself" (p. 178). Surely this question-begging about sex and last things, this massive redefinition of death and love and their connections with more than one kind of life, is "Hamletising" in the very specific sense of an obsession with Hamlet's own central question—whether to be or not, and on what terms. One is reminded of the beguiling suicidal ironies of Paul Morel's imagination in *Sons and Lovers*, when "night, and death, and stillness, and in-action, this seemed like *being*. To be alive, to be urgent and insistent—that was *not-to-be*" (p. 287). And it is no accident in *Women in Love* that Loerke unconsciously travesties Birkin's "Hamletising" (in a French variant of "to be or not to be") with his own unhealthy, polyglot cynicism about love, however defined: "Yes or no, soit ou soit pas, to-day, to-morrow, or never, it is all the same, it does not matter" (p. 451).

For all the venom of his denunciation by Lawrence, Loerke is often in verbal matters merely the other side of the Lawrencian coin, Birkin's sly linguistic *doppelgänger*. Loerke's exchanges with Gudrun, as their weave and contour is described by Lawrence, sound in fact like a point by point perversion of the author's own probing rhetoric, "full of odd, fantastic expression, of double meanings, of evasions, of suggestive vagueness" (p. 445). The double-edged word is indeed a double-edged sword. Yet the whole question of Loerke's verbal affinity with the narrative habits of D. H. Lawrence seems premature at this point, since I am invoking an image of Lawrence whose linguistic profile is by no means taken for granted in criticism. I wish eventually to discuss the transcendental vocabulary and grammar of "to be" in Lawrence, emerging from the ambivalent counterpoise of life and death in his metaphysic, as one instance of his linguistic rigor and integrity and genius; but in the absence of received opinion about his place as "stylist," and even about the rightful place of language at all in the subjects he treats, my analysis must wait for some detailed remarks about the overall tenor of his style, or styles, long overdue in criticism. For what Mark Spilka wrote over four years ago in NOVEL is still true: that Lawrence "has his own kinds of precision and coherence and his own verbal resources for achieving them, but we have not even begun to assess their range and variety."[3]

Surely no other author in English of Lawrence's acknowledged stature and influence, and of so distinctive a prose voice, has had such scant attention paid, in the way of considered and sophisticated estimation, to the words he used to gain his leverage on the literary imagination. The earliest critics, taken by surprise, could seldom refrain from remarks against the rhetoric, and before long it went almost without saying, however partisan the omission, that Lawrence's language, great as he might be at character and event, was at best a noble effort on the side of overexertion. In its rash verbal gambles and extravagances, the jargonish Lawrencian rhetoric seldom seemed gainfully employed, and might well be arraigned, if not for mere sloganizing and artistic bankruptcy, at least for some criminal neglect of the law of diminishing returns. Though manifestly furious with old novelistic solutions to the problem of speaking truth, the offensive new style becomes rapidly insolvent, and fails to pay its way in meaning. Briefs for the defense are difficult to file when the charges and detractions are not articulated with any degree of attention to the habits they summarily berate. Contemporary reviews[4] lamented in passing Lawrence's "perfervid futuristic style" with its "morbidly perverted ingenuity," the "crazy iterations and benumbing violence" of its "curiously vicious rhythm," the "flinging about of heavy words" in a "turgid, exasperated" rhetoric, a "yelling" style rather than a telling one. This earliest dismay over the affronts and infelicities of Lawrence's expression has found its way, even if merely to be tamed and overcome, into much recent commentary, where the specter of the rhapsodic sermonizer, all rant and chant, is still vestigially with us, his rhetoric, for all its power at times, too often a shotgun marriage of cant and incantation. Quality in Lawrence's style is still a subject mostly for those who don't care for him, and who discuss it as an absence, with his defenders leaving the prose, unaided, to speak for itself when it honorably can. Yet certainly the best reply to the charges against Lawrence's style is not that it is sometimes wonderful, but that it is, and can be demonstrated to be, characteristically good, complex, and uniquely resonant.

The most recent attempt to do so at all systematically is Colin Clarke's study[5] of the language of paradox (arguably a special, exacerbated case of ambiguity) in the novels, especially *Women in Love*, and the effort has been rebuked, though with the best intentions of his own for the study of style in Lawrence, by Mark Spilka himself, who objects to Clarke's looking "*at* language rather than *through* it."[6] Consider how unthinkable this objection would be for recognized "stylists" and verbal manipulators from Sterne through Dickens to Joyce or Woolf, and one realizes what a special case Lawrence is thought to be by Spilka. He commends to our attention for its healthy, corrective approach, and for its note-

[3] Mark Spilka, "Critical Exchange: Lawrence Up-Tight," NOVEL, 5 (Fall 1971), 70.

[4] I have quoted in pastiche from a half dozen reviews reprinted in R. P. Draper, ed., *D. H. Lawrence: The Critical Heritage* (New York: Barnes & Noble, 1970), pp. 10, 93, 98, 101, 169, 258.

[5] Colin Clarke, *The River of Dissolution: D. H. Lawrence and English Romanticism* (New York: Routledge & Kegan Paul, 1969).

[6] Quoted from Spilka's review in NOVEL, 4 (Spring 1971) by Clarke in his own defense, "Critical Exchange," NOVEL, 5 (Fall, 1971), 65.

worthy contribution to the "meagre work on Lawrence's style," an essay by Alan Friedman[7] that he hopes will serve "as an antidote to Lawrencian style myopically misconceived as verbal paradox."[8] Yet Friedman's spirited, incisive essay is interesting here primarily for what it, too, leaves out of consideration. Isolating, as he thinks Lawrence did, "the nearly insuperable problem" as "verbalization" itself, yet recognizing that the "unsayable is stylistically embarrassing,"[9] Friedman sees Lawrence taking a crucially different tack from "Joyce's brilliant solution to the problem—*distorting* conventional verbalization in order to render preconscious and unconscious material."[10] Rather, Lawrence, "in order to take us elsewhere, into his own particular and very different region of the unconscious . . . distorts not words and not grammar, but the conventional signals for emotions."[11] That is, one must suppose, the distortions operate almost sub-stylistically, therefore eluding any definitive linguistic analysis. On the contrary, there is a natural latitude within both definition and syntax, a plasticity of usage and ligature that promotes, whether deliberately or not for a given writer, what we call ambiguity, and that Lawrence defiantly frees up, maximizes, and exploits. It is this decidedly un-Joycean but equally verbal experiment which Friedman seems closer to when he later characterizes Lawrence's style as "writing which runs roughshod over idiomatic English."[12] Where else could this bullying possibly be registered but in the "distortion" of "words" (meanings if not spellings), and "grammar"? I propose to look neither exclusively *at* nor exclusively *through* these components of Lawrence's unsettled idiom, and hope to avoid the far more common error of looking merely *around* them. Instead, I intend to look *with* style at the underlying reality it is meant to reveal, in the way I believe language was for Lawrence himself a way of seeing, the investigative license of his poetic means, the "way through" the opacities of deceit and self-delusion.

But is style so licensed in Lawrence? Is it genuinely empowered to go where Lawrence wishes to take it? Can language claim jurisdiction over the experiences Lawrence is trying to convey at exactly those moments when his writing seems most ambitious? The question has been broached in a more recent NOVEL article by Taylor Stoehr[13] that takes its unacknowledged place at the opposite end of a controversy about Lawrence's rhetoric from the early essay by R. P. Blackmur. "Lawrence," for Blackmur, "was the extreme victim of the plague afflicting the poetry of the last hundred and fifty years—the plague of expressive form,"[14] and Lawrence the poet was so crippled "only to a less degree as a novelist."[15] This plague is, as Blackmur sees it, catapulted into dogma, with Lawrence holding "that if a thing is only intensely enough felt its mere expression in words will

---

[7] Alan Friedman, "The Other Lawrence," *Partisan Review*, 37 (1970), 239–53.
[8] Spilka, p. 70.
[9] Friedman, p. 245.
[10] *Ibid.*, p. 246.
[11] *Ibid.*
[12] *Ibid.*, p. 248.
[13] Taylor Stoehr, "Lawrence's 'Mentalized Sex,' " NOVEL, 8 (Winter 1975), 101–22.
[14] R. P. Blackmur, "D. H. Lawrence and Expressive Form," *Form and Value in Modern Poetry* (New York: Doubleday, 1957), p. 255.
[15] *Ibid.*, p. 253.

give it satisfactory form." [16] The result is slovenly, stultifying, and indiscriminate. Approaching Lawrence's language from the standpoint of psychological rather than rhetorical dogma, however, Stoehr has suggested (in unmentioned agreement with Friedman on "verbalization" as the central problem) that no words can be felt honestly by Lawrence to be "satisfactory" for the erotic imagination at the heart of his prose and his poetry, that the very giving over of sexual experience into the expressive keeping of words "mentalizes" it to its inevitable detriment. Stoehr asks his leading question early in the essay: "Is it possible to render a scene of sexual feeling in fiction without indulging in 'mentalized sex' of the kind that he despised?" [17] The answer seems to be no, Stoehr claiming that Lawrence's avowed preference for the "unconscious against conscious life" was, in the most self-frustrating kind of "irony," a "stand against the novel." [18]

Stoehr does not mention Blackmur, who complains primarily about the poetry, and Blackmur's argument never anticipated Stoehr's irony that language itself would come under implicit criticism, not for its expressive laxity, but for the very dangers of articulate expression. Yet in refuting Blackmur, Harold Bloom has also suggested an answer to Stoehr's question. Bloom stresses, against Blackmur, "rhythmical mastery" and incantation[19] rather than architectural proportion as the expressive strength of Lawrence's verse. Wishing to rescue Lawrence for the mainstream of Romantic poetry and its visionary company, Bloom sees him as a poet "compelled by the conventions of his mode to present the conceptual aspect of his imagery as self-generated." [20] I would go further, and argue that as a prose writer Lawrence commands a vocabulary and grammar that are also self-generating. Hugh Kenner has said of Samuel Beckett that, unlike the great prose masters of the past, whose expressive province was the phrase, Beckett's revolutionary "unit of effect" is the sentence.[21] It would seem to me that Lawrence's essential prose span falls somewhere between; it is the phrase echoing off the walls of a sentence, a keeping underway—and under self-investigation—of diction, syntax, and imagery whose separate momentums reinforce and impel each other. Such self-generated rhetoric need not succumb to the fallacy of expressive form; not necessarily unshaped, its form can announce—and enunciate—itself as an evolution in process, and from that very evolution may derive, in Bloom's term, its "conceptual aspect" and its conceptual, though "unmentalized," power. Self-generation looms at such times in Lawrence, and they are frequent, as the elemental wedding of style and subject decreed and presided over by the flux of his language. Form is content, style becomes imitatively framed, and this is quite the reverse of a language believed to be so transparently expressive of its subject that it can be left unwrought. But if we grant this possibility of an imita-

[16] Ibid., p. 256.
[17] Stoehr, p. 109.
[18] Ibid., p. 116.
[19] Harold Bloom, "Lawrence, Blackmur, Eliot, and the Tortoise," Harry T. Moore, ed., A D. H. Lawrence Miscellany (Carbondale: Southern Illinois Univ. Press, 1959), p. 367.
[20] Ibid., p. 368.
[21] Hugh Kenner, A Reader's Guide to Samuel Beckett (New York: Farrar, Straus, and Giroux, 1973), p. 183.

tive, not a sloppily expressive form, the question remains what specific fluctuating process is most likely to be reproduced, and by what devices. Lawrence himself gives us the best lead in this direction in a flamboyantly suggestive passage strangely overlooked by commentators—even by Taylor Stoehr, whose central inquiry it would have gone far toward answering.

It is hard to imagine why a statement like the following at the close of Lawrence's foreword to *Women in Love*, candidly prefixed to the very novel in which the question of stylistic motive is so widely vexing and hotly debated, should have given such infrequent pause to the critics: "In point of style, fault is often found with the continual, slightly modified repetition. The only answer is that it is natural to the author; and that every natural crisis in emotion or passion or understanding comes from this pulsing, frictional to-and-fro which works up to culmination." The implication is, one would think, bluntly obvious. The rhetoric of incremental self-generation takes its metaphor from the generative act itself in this image of a "frictional" style, a useful way of labelling the sexual element in Lawrence's prose. Blackmur was looking for some of the right things in one of the wrong places, for a poetry of finish in a poetry of self-effectuation. As with Lawrence's verse, the language of his novels is also not a shaped but a process prose, working itself up and out as it goes. In his landmark study from the early fifties, an essay otherwise notable for a strong and accurate fix on the Lawrencian sensibility, Mark Schorer wildly misses the point of Lawrence's prefatory note: "The attempt," he regrets to say, "to duplicate, in syntactical movement itself, the dialectical flow of the theme is perhaps a mistaken aesthetic ambition." [22] If what Lawrence meant by frictional culmination was dialectics, then Hegel was the greatest pornographer of the nineteenth century. The truth is, of course, less oblique, and offers a rather straightforward way out of the dilemma in which Stoehr thinks Lawrence has trapped himself. Sex can be kept "out of the head" even when explored by prose discourse if it is embodied rather than overseen, intimately registered rather than analyzed. Sex does not have to turn cerebral simply by being said, for by what Schorer calls "syntactic movement" prose can attune itself to the vital rhythms it is meant more to approximate than to examine. That is, the dilemma of the verbal consciousness versus the anti-mentalizing sexual conscience, of aesthetic potential versus the staunchly guarded ethic of the instinctual life, is more thoroughly stylistic in its bearings than Stoehr demonstrates, though his textual evidence quite properly centers on *Lady Chatterley's Lover*. It is in that last novel where we find the most strenuous and prolonged efforts at that driven, insistent style which Lawrence's negative critics have felt, watching it develop through *The Rainbow* and *Women in Love*, illustrates the most injurious strain (both senses) in his exploratory technique. To give it a working label, we may call it for now the orgastic style, a prose that

[22] Mark Schorer, "*Women in Love* and Death," from *The Hudson Review*, 6 (Spring 1953), 34–47; rpt. in Mark Spilka, ed., *D. H. Lawrence: A Collection of Critical Essays* (Englewood Cliffs, N.J.: Prentice-Hall, 1963), p. 59. Since first lodging my complaint about the paucity of comment on this passage from the foreword to *Women in Love*, I have come upon Leo Bersani's interesting discussion of it, from a somewhat less stylistic perspective than mine, in "Lawrentian Stillness," *Yale Review*, 56 (Autumn 1975), 53–54.

paces itself to the rhythm and tempo of sexual climax while simultaneously investigating the psychic contours of such "dyings," answering once and for all, I think, the questions its own extremity of effect raises most acutely about the place of verbalization in sex and in love.

Repetition, apposition, parataxis, the ambivalences of syntactic elision, the patterns of echo and assonance, the functional shifts of diction within and between phrases, the thrust, swerve, and conversion of imagery—the whole lunging, unstable dynamic of Lawrence's style, never more furiously displayed than in the passage below from *Lady Chatterley's Lover*—substitutes for a mentalized portrait, certainly for any observations rationally derived or dialectically arrived at, a visceral rhythm that is the furthest development in English of the Romantic rhapsody. And it does this, here as elsewhere, in scenes that are themselves an account of the death of mentalized response. To disinfect sex from any taint of morbid intellectuality—or of pornography, as Lawrence defines it—to keep it clean and felt and intoxicated, even while casting it up into words, he had to let it speak for itself, rhythmic and half inarticulate, a pulse and not an exposition. To the formidable liabilities of this procedure the style of *Lady Chatterley* surrenders itself wholesale, like Connie to Mellors in this scene:

> *She yielded with a quiver that was like death. . . .*
>
> *She quivered again at the potent inexorable entry inside her, so strange and terrible. It might come with the thrust of a sword in her softly-opened body, and that would be death. She clung in a sudden anguish of terror. But it came with a strange slow thrust of peace, the dark thrust of peace and a ponderous primordial tenderness, such as made the world in the beginning. And her terror subsided in her breast, her breast dared to be gone in peace, she held nothing. She dared let go everything, all herself, and be gone in the flood.*

The ambiguity in "all herself" of "all by herself" and "her entire self" seems to propel, in company with the basic frictional momentum, the relentless unfolding of the next paragraph:

> *And it seemed she was like the sea, nothing but dark waves rising and heaving, heaving with a great swell, so that slowly her whole darkness was in motion, and she was ocean rolling its dark, dumb mass. Oh, and far down inside her the deeps parted and rolled asunder, in long, far-travelling billows, and ever, at the quick of her, the depths parted and rolled asunder, from the center of soft plunging, as the plunger went deeper and deeper, touching lower, and she was deeper and deeper and deeper disclosed, and heavier the billows of her rolled away to some shore, uncovering her, and closer and closer plunged the palpable unknown, and further and further rolled the waves of herself away from herself, leaving her, till suddenly, in a soft, shuddering convulsion, the quick of all her plasm was touched, she knew herself touched, the consum-*

*mation was upon her, and she was gone. She was gone, she was not, and she was born: a woman.* (pp. 196–97, my emphasis)

This may heave and plunge once too often, but like the phonic thickening of "deeps" into "depths" there is a progression and strategic deepening to be noted. Just before the turning point at "still suddenly," inversion shuttles to the end of the pivotal clause, slightly varied from its earlier appearance, the crucial pronouns of what we might call, borrowing from the physical death of Tom Brangwen in *The Rainbow*, "the stripped moment of transit from life into death" (p. 248). For as "further and further rolled the waves of herself away from herself, leaving her," she is finally divested, "her" stripped of "self," a "leaving" that in the second sense of this participle also leaves the essential "her" behind, freed of the self-reflective awareness which has until now blocked her sexual release. "Isn't Connie Chatterley just as self-regarding in this scene," [23] Stoehr asks, as any of the self-conscious, posturing lovers in the kind of pornography Lawrence detested? But the answer is not sought in the changes rung on the self-reflexive grammar in the actual sentences Lawrence gives us, especially as it is salvaged for a more genuine, tactile intuition of self that is not overly mentalized, when "she knew herself touched, the consummation was upon her, and she was gone."

With this most feverishly detailed and unalleviated sexual death scene in all of Lawrence's major fiction in front of us, we are in a position as never before to recognize the greatest of Lawrence's contributions to the literature of sexuality, and to its literary language. In his famous essay "Night Words," speaking about the necessary impoverishment of pornography as a genre, George Steiner notes that the "list of writers who have had the genius to enlarge our active compass of sexual awareness . . . is very small," and though he does not mention Lawrence, he does allude to the tradition of which the novelist's sexual vocabulary is the final flowering: "The close, delicately plotted concordance between orgasm and death in Baroque and Metaphysical poetry and art clearly enriched our legacy of excitement, as had the earlier focus on virginity." [24] Building on the earliest achievements of Richardson, Emily Brontë, and Flaubert in the novel, and of Keats and Shelley especially among the Romantic poets, Lawrence becomes the greatest modern representative on this increasingly small list of authors. By extending and cross-indexing the "concordance" in every direction, Lawrence matured the Metaphysical trope into a metaphysic, and, pushing the link between libido and oblivion to its logical extreme, reinterpreted life as an erotic continuity with sensual annihilation and brought into prominence as no writer before him the idea of a sexual afterlife—the new heaven and earth of the redefined self, the "to be" that arises, phoenix-like, from the ashes of the extinguished ego. But Lawrence has not only given us a number of subsequent entries in such an index

---

[23] Stoehr, p. 108.

[24] George Steiner, *Language and Silence: Essays on Language, Literature, and the Inhuman* (New York: Atheneum, 1967), p. 92.

and lexicon of sexuality, he has also bestowed on English prose a largely original grammar of orgasm, in which the posture and pace of his style, its stance and frictional mode of advance, are at once an exercise in, and an expression of through language, the sexual imagination. In the last sentence of that paragraph from *Lady Chatterley*, as in the one just before it, apparent serial grammar has the ambiguous feel of simultaneity at the moment of transit: "She was gone, she was not, and she was born: a woman." Looking back from this point over the entire passage, we realize that Lawrence's pulsing, frictional style, as described in the foreword to *Women in Love*, is readied for the mimetic approximation not only of a sexual climax, or negatively of that "terrible frictional violence of death" between Gerald and Gudrun in *Women in Love* (p. 337), but also of the oscillating rhythms of catharsis and parturition, emotional purge and rebirth.

I have begun by discussing the orgastic rhythms of Lawrence's prose because, as Stoehr shows, they offer the most graphic test case for the self-critique of verbalization. But they are to Lawrence's entire rhetoric as sex is to life: no more than an important part. And probably an even greater challenge is offered to expressive language in the simulation not of the sexual death but of the ensuing peace that is passed away to, and that in its turn passes understanding, and words. On the way to this voiceless transcendence of the redefined "being," it is necessary to see that language does not doubt its own legitimacy for emotional registration so much as insist on its unremitting self-analysis and revalidation. "To know, to give utterance" is never to rest complacent, but to "break a way through" the barriers of inexpressiveness itself. The most mistaken attacks on Lawrence's style are those that assume the rhetoric as subservient to, sometimes even abject before, the philosophy. Better to see the gradual building toward a philosophy of rhetoric, turning the style back on itself to produce an argument in and for a revisionist language of fiction.

Lawrence has to be the most polemical of the great novelists, and hence the most deeply rhetorical, more deeply than has yet been thought. Style looks beneath its own surface for the governing principles of anchorage and transformation. Lawrence writes a prose of tested, not flouted limits, most speculative where it is thought to be most cocksure and blustering, a style contesting its own rules. This self-mediated debate, with implications far beyond the linguistic purview of a writer's craft, is ranged and waged from the level of habitual diction to the characteristic scaffolding of whole sentences, from puns and paradoxical phrases, for example—that by pitting both ends against an unachieved middle cast doubts upon or ultimately fulfill the possibilities of synthesis—to the large-scale stationing of repetitions, incremental or not, that tax, and, by so doing, test the principles of recurrence and mutability. Lawrence's use of pronouns and reflexives at times suggests a quarrel with the whole idea of antecedence, continuity, and identity in a subjective flux, his deployment of singular and plural verbs a caution against crippling limitations on our ideas of unity and oneness. The disposition of voice, mood, and case—as in passive or transitive predicates, or in the balancing of nominative against accusative forms—serves to assess and at times demur from the received arrangement of subject, object, and agent in sexual relationships, the evident vectors of cause and effect. In similar fashion his serial syntax argues with the tyranny of rigid transitions and his revolutionary use of appositives becomes a debate over the lower and upper limits of the apposite, almost a redefinition of synonymy and metaphor, identity and transformation. Sprung so often from the concrete, the fleshed and blooded, the near tactility of Lawrence's best abstract diction is finally an indictment of evacuated categorical language, a brilliant willing of weight and texture upon ideality. And of special interest for this essay, the pressure Lawrence brings to bear on the verb "to be" and the declension, so to speak, of its gerund form, "being," goes beyond anything in our fictional literature in anatomizing the vocabulary and grammar of existence.

In Lawrence's renegade rhetoric, the most ponderous and idiosyncratic "deliberation" turns out to be just that: a self-adjudication. Not to make the writing sound falsely measured and cerebral, we must nevertheless hear it as an inquiry of passion as well as a cry. The metaphors of arraignment and judgment with which I began discussing the charges against Lawrence's rhetoric are rightly internalized for his prose, which becomes in more than one way trying. But the tables get quickly turned, and to hear Lawrence's style properly emerges as the hearing of a case against anything less flexible, his best effects constantly enlisted as exhibits for the new prosecution. We must begin weighing evidence for the expressive supremacy of Lawrence's non-orgastic rhetoric long before *Lady Chatterley's Lover,* and the book Lawrence thought of as his first sustained breakthrough in experimental techniques, *The Rainbow,* is a good place to start gathering testimony for Lawrence's deft, fertile ambiguities. In the first generation of the narrative, the Polish widow Lydia Lensky represents to Tom Brangwen that influx of foreign glamor that makes habitable again his annulled native ground after the death of his mother. She is the personification of the new and strange, and the pun on her national origin (Lawrence defecting to Joyce's camp?) made by the servant Tilly catches the antipodal magnetism to which Tom is eager to submit: "Mrs. Bentley says as she's fra the Pole—else she *is* a Pole, or summat" (p. 26). She is all three to Tom, a pole of experience to be felt and known, an epitome of otherness, indeed a "summit" to be reached.

I mention the Joycean—or call it Dickensian—touch only as a point of departure for the more thoroughly original and peculiarly Lawrencian effects to come, the syntactic latitudes and subdued punning, for instance, in the passionate betrothal scene of Tom and Lydia, as the increments of serial grammar overlap in a sequence of metamorphic stages impossible to mark off precisely: "And he bent down and kissed her on the lips. And the dawn blazed in them, their new life came to pass, it was beyond all conceiving good, it was so good, that it was almost like a passing-away, a trespass" (p. 41). Tom, whose worst trauma in grammar school arose from his inability to write "in the real composition style" (p. 11), now has his sexual fulfilment sung by Lawrence in a style schooled in the resolute dismantling of grammatical convention and compositional "commonplaces" (p. 11). The style's sliding transformation taxies past us in a paratactic sequence deliberately interknit and elided: not *a, b, c,* but *ab, bc, cd.* Does the modest, pivotal understatement "it was so good" attach backwards or forwards? "It was so good that it was beyond all conceiving" or "It was so good as to be like a passing-away?" Both, of course, especially when we recognize the calculated demolition of idiom taking place along with the syntactic detachments. The experience is "beyond all conceiving" because it is the post-conceptive birth throes of a new life, a life which "came to pass" both as an occurrence and a "passing-away." This ingenious fiddling with idiom reaches a climax in the appositional "trespass." In connection with Lawrence's first novel, *The Trespasser* —with neither explanation nor example, though it is one of the few mentions of Lawrence's word play anywhere in print—Frank Kermode alludes to the noun "trespass" as "a favorite French pun of Lawrence's." [25] The French "trépas" is "death," and what Lawrence has come upon, and made to seem a profound linguistic coincidence, is a single set of letters, approximately, that covers the central ambiguity in his sexual encounters, the transport that is a passing away, the exstasis that becomes a crossing to the unknown. One of the most complex of his fictional experiences is thus halved into articulation and fused again by the bilingual duplicity. Death in Lawrence, when it is other than extinction, is both a world apart and a transgression thereupon, the terminus and the transit, a bound as at once a limit and a leap beyond.

The genius and formal originality of *The Rainbow* resides in its tendency to render these leaps evolutionary. What results is the psychological internalization of the chronicle novel format, so that its three-tiered plot line, like so much of the syntax that locally articulates it, is elided, overlapped, the travails and achievements of one generation made to seem in spiritual apposition to its precursor—with (to adopt perhaps the only commonplace about Lawrence's style to the generational grammar of *The Rainbow* as a whole) new stages of the family biography becoming "incremental repetitions" of their predecessors. The narrative shape of the novel unfolds a composite and progressive psyche that is finally given the name "Ursula," after being designated "Tom" and "Anna" in their turn, but which is always some refraction of the central Brangwen spirit. I trust that a bit more evidence will make clear the rich correspondence between the overall logic of narrative transmutation in this novel and the self-augmenting transformations of Lawrence's rhetoric as they are carried beyond the experiments of *Sons and Lovers.*

To this end there is a vital document. Edward Garnett received the best known letter Lawrence ever wrote, quoted as often and as inevitably as a half dozen of Keats's most renowned letters in any discussion of their author's characteristic artistry. "You mustn't look in my novel," Lawrence both warned and boasted to Garnett, "for the old stable *ego*—of the character." [26] The hesitation at the dash, if it is more than emphasis, hints at a distinction between the stable ego of

[25] Frank Kermode, *D. H. Lawrence* (New York: Viking Press, 1973), p. 10.
[26] Harry T. Moore, ed., *The Collected Letters of D. H. Lawrence* (New York: Viking Press, 1962), p. 282.

character, which you won't find, and some other kind of stable ego which you will, rather than at something beyond or beneath the ego altogether, as this statement is often taken to mean. For the moment Lawrence seems explicit enough: "There is another *ego*, according to whose action the individual is unrecognisable, and passes through, as it were, allotropic states which it needs a deeper sense than any we've been used to exercise, to discover are states of the same single radically unchanged element." Here we seem to have a useful working metaphor for the segmented generations of *The Rainbow*, in which Tom, Anna, and Ursula are not separate egos but allotropes of the Brangwen element, as diamond and coal (to use Lawrence's analogies in this letter) are to the primary carbon. Yet a preceding passage in this letter has tended to mislead readers and confuse the issue. "I don't so much care about what the woman *feels*—in the ordinary usage of the word," says Lawrence, speaking generally about any woman in fiction, any character. "That presumes an *ego* to feel with. I only care about what the woman *is*—what she IS—inhumanly, physiologically, materially . . . what she *is* as a phenomenon (or as representing some greater, inhuman will) instead of what she feels according to the human conception." So the question is unavoidably twofold, if not contradictory. We must look beneath the ego in characterization for the vital phenomenon, and we must look beyond character for the phenomenon of the continuous ego. To give the theory local habitation and a set of names, we note that the truth about the first Tom Brangwen, for instance, as about his daughter and his granddaughter, must be probed for beneath personality and character; but what is found will not distinguish one human entity from the other so much as lead us back to the unifying phenomenon: the family ego, "as representing some greater, inhuman will." The biological dictum that ontogeny recapitulates phylogeny turns biographical in *The Rainbow* and holds for the special case of the Brangwens, where successive characters in the species undergo the metamorphic ordeals of their predecessors in order to trespass for themselves, through a kind of death and rebirth, upon the next evolutionary stage. The underlying continuity is thus both allotropic and hierarchical.

But where does this lead us with respect to style? The letter to Garnett, perused often and minutely, has never been read to suggest anything very specific about the language which, in one verbal experiment after another, aids in precipitating, as it were, Lawrence's new art of characterization. That metaphor from chemistry, on the large scale as well as the small, is just the one we want, for Lawrence's high-risk experimental idiom is precipitate and headlong in the hope that something will eventually settle out, isolate itself into unheard of clarity. Lawrence's revolutionary emphasis on allotropes of the self in fictional narrative thus mandates a change in the very nature of novelistic prose. In the pun on "trespass" we have an example of Lawrence's new elemental diction, whose isolable, separate meanings operate on this allotropic principle. But "trespass" is not simply a pun; it is also, when it suggests death, a metaphor of motion. In this regard it is no accident that another term for figure of speech, "trope," and the chemical term "allotrope" derive from the same Greek root for "turning," whether "aside" or "into," which is indeed the process tropes and allotropes can be seen to result from: figurative diversion and transformation, metaphoric revision in the one and radical metamorphosis in the other. "Trespass" is an especially good allotropic sample because one of its operable meanings names the transitional mobility it at the same time exemplifies, an entrance into or a transgression upon its own alternate definition. The scientific model also works for dubieties of syntax, where two seemingly different parsings of a grammatical arrangement can be resolved as allotropes of a twofold unity hitherto unobserved. So that syntactic ambiguities not only distribute allotropic diction but demonstrate the principle in their own mutable working out. Frequently set in motion by the presence of an unstable syntactic bond, a paratactic loosening of structure for instance, words are alchemized into their own ambiguous allotropes, phrases and clauses into their grammatical alter-egos. This is the eccentric chemistry of lexicon and syntax in Lawrence's style, and suggests a private linguistics in which ambivalence finds its model in chemical valence, paradox in nuclear polarization, and where the alternate possibilities of a pun or the repulsing poles of an oxymoron are discovered to be merely aspects "of the same single radically unchanged element," the unitary and harmonizing substance Lawrence is restlessly seeking beneath the play and fluctuation of his surface matter and which can only be made accessible to us if we develop a "deeper sense than any we've been used to exercising."

If this is a new verbal science, it is also a new poetry. Lawrence is the only major English novelist of this century, the first since Hardy, who is also a major poet, and yet next to nothing has been said about the fertile, shifting ground held in common by the poems and the novels as their eminent verbal domain. A single excursion into the ambiguous topography of one of Lawrence's better-known poems should begin to make clear some crucial similarities in his prose and verse styles. The poem is one of many about sexual death and regeneration, with the persona "carried by the current in death over to the new world"; it is called "New Heaven and Earth," and in her book *New Heaven, New Earth* it is singled out by Joyce Carol Oates as a poem whose language is "continually straining its boundaries in an effort to make the strangeness of his experience coherent." [27] Linguistically figured, these are the ultimate boundaries of life and death as they converge in a transformed new space that is simultaneously, on the far and near side of the mortal divide at the instant when the border vanishes, a new heaven and a renewed earth. The opening two stanzas compose one of the finest and most characteristic death "passages" in his verse, turning (as it happens) on that allotropic pun "trespass":

> And so I cross into another world
> shyly and in homage linger for an invitation
> from this unknown that I would trespass on.

27 Joyce Carol Oates, *New Heaven, New Earth: The Visionary Experience in Literature* (New York: Vanguard Press, 1974), p. 60.

*I am very glad, and all alone in the world,*
*all alone, and very glad, in a new world*
*where I am disembarked at last.*[28]

Lawrence is fond of the opening *in medias res* (to what is "And" conjoined?) and here he also opens *in medias legis*, halfway between two denotations of his second word, "so" (between "therefore" and "thus," or "consequently" and "in this manner")—the action described being not only the decisive choice or announced first move of the transforming experience but also the thing itself in process, a duality which the subsequent diction and grammar bear out. The play on "trespass" suggests again both an exit and a deathly accession, a transgression upon not "that unknown" but "this," not over there somewhere but right here, a surprising variant of what Lawrence identifies in a poem called "Silence" as "the great hush of going from this into that." In "New Heaven and Earth" the entire process of arrival is latent in the single demonstrative "this." It is a grammar of encroach and trespass. The chiastic syntax that pivots the next stanza —very glad, all alone, all alone, very glad—is a fitting instance of Lawrence's serial grammar passing over into apposition, fitted precisely to the evoked parallel and gradual identification between the two worlds at the moment of passage, with the mortal distinction between "the world" and "a new world" relinquished by the transfiguration. Even the willful formality of the passive "am disembarked"—instead of the transitive "disembark"—answers both to the grace of agency by which the easy transit is made and to the simultaneity of past and present tenses ("I am arrived," rather than "I have arrived") in this selfless, unassertive transport.

Such an argument for complexities of phrase in Lawrence's poetic language, too often read as an exercise in metrical vagrancy and uninstructed effusion, should attract itself by association to the prose of his novels, which attempts in its own curious motions to elicit certain underlying principles of transformation and identity. Only when Lawrence has provisionally convinced us that the two or more faces of an ambiguity may be stages of a definition in transit, allotropes of a single evolving unity, has he fully equipped his style to invoke and investigate his thematic preoccupations. "The ordinary novel would trace the history of the diamond," Lawrence wrote in that letter to Garnett, "—but I say, 'Diamond, what! This is carbon.' And my diamond might be coal or soot, and my theme is carbon." Life, what! This is being, and his version of life might be death or annihilation, yet his theme is the deeper principle of being. His grammar might seem paratactic or appositional, but his theme is transformation. His noun might suggest either "passage" or the French for "death," but his theme, "trespass," is what they have in common. This is the way Lawrence's imagination has begun, with *The Rainbow*, to explore the secret springs and surface currents of characterization, and I am submitting that it was only natural for a similar sense of

---

[28] Vivian de Sola Pinto and Warren Roberts, eds., *The Complete Poems of D. H. Lawrence* (New York: Viking Press, 1964), p. 256.

language to find itself evolving at the same time in the noticeably more mannered style of this fourth novel. For manner in the best of Lawrence is never sheer mannerism but an expressive means, in the case of *The Rainbow*, and especially of *Women in Love*, a breaking away from the traditional forms of *Sons and Lovers*—and a way through, to the poetry of refurnished "utterance."

The betrothal scene in *The Rainbow* with which I began this part of the discussion was preceded by another version of death and resurgence in the first passionate embrace between Tom and Lydia, during which the hero was struck almost unconscious. "He returned gradually, but newly created, as after a gestation, a new birth, in the womb of darkness. Aerial and light everything was, new as a morning, fresh and newly-begun" (p. 41). The actual moment of metamorphosis and rebirth is signaled by that pivotal grammar which transforms the probable "Everything was aerial and light" into its curiously inverted form. The unidiomatic inflection of the resulting clause lands an odd accent on the verb of being, partially displacing it from its equative status into a verb of simple predication, simple existence, as if to say that only by being so transmuted into the aerial and the bright can reality be honestly said to have come into being at all. Existence itself has been subjected to a limiting but beautiful redefinition by the ability of a single verb, and the syntax it governs, to hover between alternatives. It is indeed the Hamletized verb "to be" and its various deployments—especially the ambiguities loosed by its appearance as "being"—which I wish to concentrate on for the rest of this essay, a task which will seem, I trust, only as narrow as a modest passageway: an entrance, marked off and cleared away, into the enormity of Lawrence's stylistic innovation and the swarm of questions it raises about the role and perimeters of "utterance." This will be, I recognize, not so much a reading of Lawrence as a prolegomenon to one, not a circumscribed essay on his fiction but rather a prelude to any number of them—an article whose primary rewards will therefore be still only in sight, not yet visited upon its pages, when they have come to a close. I might have produced a roster of puns and syntactic uncertainties by way of confirming that Lawrence's style works in the way I believe it does—and works its strange, unexampled magic. Instead I have tried not to prove this, but to put just a few of these stylistic ventures to the proof by giving some hint of their full aesthetic power and authority. The main burden of what remains will fall on two crucial but little-discussed passages in *The Rainbow* and *Women in Love*, Ursula at the microscope in Chapter XV of the former, Birkin and Ursula on the night before their wedding in Chapter XXVII of the latter, scenes whose climaxes arrive, respectively, with the phrases "a consummation, a being infinite" (p. 441) and "a consummation of my being and of her being in a new one" (p. 361). Criticism, however sensitive, is necessarily less concise than poetry, even a novelist's poetry, and it is no fault of stylistics, only a testament to the evocative and concentrating powers of Lawrence's style, that it takes so many more words for analysis to bring the full reach of art to light. My hope is that when thus highlighted, the genius of Lawrence's often perverse style will stand revealed for what it is, an effort on behalf of that bright book of life, as Lawrence called the novel, to make it all the more lustrous and illuminating.

In the last important fiction Lawrence completed before his death, the use of an ambiguous "to be" variant is still part of his stylistic stock-in-trade, and is accompanied by a more obvious play with diction. When Isis first touches Christ's wounds in *The Man Who Died*, they are healed to ecstasy: " 'They are suns!' he said. 'They shine from your touch. They are my atonement with you" (p. 207). The noun "atonement," especially in connection with Christ's mortified flesh, is an ironic reinterpretation of the Christian "Passion," the suffering for and remission of sins. The sexual passion of the man who died is a unification by touch, here the touch of Isis, on the next page of the entire living and inanimate universe, not a reparation for so much as an atoning *with*, the deeper repair of the soul's sexless isolation: "This is the great atonement, the being in touch. The gray sea and the rain, the wet narcissus and the woman I wait for, the invisible Isis and the unseen sun are all in touch, and at one." The redefined grace of "atonement" is by this point a manifest pun on "attunement" as well, both allotropic nouns resonating, just as they do within the single spelling, within the larger harmony of passionate and universal concord. There is also an ambiguous glimmer in the appositive phrase "the being in touch." The immediate idiomatic sense of the words does not, if we are used to Lawrence by now, overrule the possibility of an alternate reading, so that the phrase as written is felt to have emerged from a blended resolution of two allotropic base sentences: "He is in touch" and "He exists only in touch." This is the atonement—the restitution that becomes a restoration—by which the man who died realizes that in touch and only in touch is predicated his true being.

The distinction between kinds of "being" has lasted through to Lawrence's last long story from an experiment with it in his first great novel, *Sons and Lovers*. That inching over of "to be" from copula to intransitive we saw in *The Rainbow*'s inversion, "Aerial and light everything was," had taken a small but moving part two years before in the subterranean verbal drama enacted at the end of *Sons and Lovers*, a schizophrenic dialogue between Paul Morel and the voice of his own despair over the death of his mother:

> *Then, quite mechanically and more distinctly, the conversation began again inside him.*
> "She's dead. What was it all for—her struggle?"
> *That was his despair wanting to go after her.*
> "You're alive."
> "She's not."
> "She is—in you."
> *Suddenly he felt tired with the burden of it.*
> "You've got to keep alive for her sake," *said his will in him.* (p. 411)

As if the psychological fissuring of the scene runs so deep as to divide not only voice but verbal structure as well, there is a movement toward ambiguity in this exchange from patterns of clear attribution ("She's dead," "You're alive") through an elliptical format, with "alive" understood, that takes a deceptively parallel track into pure predication as the verb of being breaks out from its contracted form ("She's not," "She is"). There is no contradiction, just a double perspective; the language of negation is not equivalent to the language of nothing, and this is a linguistic fact which Lawrence raises to metaphysical status. Granted that his mother is not alive, she can still be, exist, in him. This is the blessing and the burden of immortality through love. Death kills, yes, but it does not necessarily cancel, and after life there is still being by being loved. The meta-linguistic distance between "she is not alive" and "she is not" can be as great as eternity.

In *The Rainbow*, toward the beginning of the chapter called "The Bitterness of Ecstasy," Ursula Brangwen must face her own epiphanic quandary over "to be or not to be," and an earlier description of her mentality prepares us intriguingly for this scene by suggesting a clear kinship between the expressive bents of heroine and author, the disposition and pitch of their imaginations: "It pleased her also to know, that in the East one must use hyperbole, or else remain unheard; because the Eastern man must see a thing swelling to fill all heaven, or dwindled to a mere nothing, before he is suitably impressed. She immediately sympathised with this Eastern mind" (p. 275). This is also, of course, the very fiber of Lawrence's Western mind and of the verbal extremes of his New Testament, in the report of whose hyperbolic language Ursula is vouchsafed the former seeing—a vision of that infinite "heaven" to which being aspires. She is in her biology lab at college late one afternoon, studying a unicellular "plant-animal" as if it were the abstracted essence of organic life, struggling to comprehend its nature as a unit of selfhood. The powerful light projected on the slide and given off in turn by the nucleus seems absorbed into the vital tissue of Ursula's imagination, and the result, at last, is Lawrence's own Genesis text:

> *Suddenly in her mind the world gleamed strangely, with an intense light, like the nucleus of the creature under the microscope. Suddenly she had passed away into an intensely-gleaming light of knowledge. She could not understand what it all was. She only knew that it was not limited mechanical energy, not mere purpose of self-preservation and self-assertion. It was a consummation, a being infinite. Self was a oneness with the infinite. To be oneself was a supreme, gleaming triumph of infinity.* (p. 441)

The elusive gradations of the prose blend sexual and transcendental vocabulary in a "consummation" during which the participant has simultaneously "passed away," and the incremental tracking of the passage carries us from an external world that "gleamed" oddly, through the "intensely-gleaming" knowledge of such a world, to the "supreme, gleaming" sense of self into which this knowledge has lifted and transformed the spectator. Ursula *dies* into the knowledge of life, which is the paradox of transit and accession in Lawrence: a passing-away-into. By so doing, both life and her awareness of it fuse in the blinding heat of revelation, with important pronominal distinctions blurred stylistically and melted away. The "it all" she cannot at first understand is, of course, the vision of vital organic selfhood she has been granted, but also—by the magnetism of nearest antecedence—that "light of knowledge" in which she is bathed. The verbal fusion is threefold. Revelation and the twin objects of that revelation are transfigured into a complex unity; both objective and subjective life, brilliantly lit by the apparatus of her discovery, as well as her own shimmering intuitive apprehension of them—that knowledge of self at one with otherness without which there is no genuine life in Lawrence—are a "consummation" together, jointly "a being infinite." To use a term from elsewhere in this passage, it is that last phrase which "nodalizes" the symbolic connotations of the entire scene, and to put it more effectively under the critical microscope I must borrow the high-powered lens provided retrospectively by a minor episode in the next novel.

A dismissible bit of dialogue between Ursula herself and Birkin in the "Mino" chapter of *Women in Love* takes us self-consciously to the heart of the whole allotropic verbal imagination in Lawrence. When Ursula, disgusted with the male domination of the cat, repudiates its assertiveness as "a real Wille zur Macht" (p. 142), Birkin at once hurries the phrase into French, where he thinks he can ameliorate it. Mino's lordliness is not, he claims, a true will to power, precisely, but rather "a volonté de pouvoir"—meaning something quite close to "will to power," to be sure, but translated by Birkin as "a win to ability, taking pouvoir as a verb" (p. 142). Though Ursula may be right to dismiss such polyglot glibness at this juncture as hair-splitting "sophistries," still Birkin's linguistic acuity remains, the ear for double possibilities in language that can be turned elsewhere to better account than mere rhetorical duplicity and emotional double-dealing. Birkin's word-worrying imagination—as usual he is Lawrence's spokesman, though explicit about language this time in a way the narrator would never be—suggests to him that "pouvoir" can be either a noun, meaning "power," or an infinitive, meaning "to be able," in which capacity it is suitable for idiomatic transplant and variation. This indeterminate item of diction generates in the immediate context a syntactic ambiguity, in which two rather different meanings bear an allotropic relation to each other and to the elemental linguistic shape of which, with their varying suggestions of "enablement," they are divergent avatars. It is once again, and more analytically than elsewhere in the novels, the pun as allotrope, a phenomenon exemplified—in English this time, not in French, and with unusually vivid facets of implication—by that crystallized ambivalence in *The Rainbow*, "a being infinite," to which I come round again.

The phrase serves to refract at odd angles two separate linguistic impressions that turn out to be mirror images. Or, to return the metaphor to allotropic chemistry, we could say that the phrase submits to a kind of nuclear fission that explodes it into linguistic alter-egos that are only later discovered to approach the condition of identical twins. As Birkin might put it, you can understand "a being infinite" by taking "being" as either a verb (participle) or a noun, thus producing the chiastic mirror phrases "being infinite" and "infinite being"—where grammatical and logical distinctions are naturally transcended in a state of perfect stability and fulfilment in which the only action (i.e., gerundive) *is* a state of being (i.e., noun phrase). But this is to move too quickly toward a resolution of the ambiguity. The easy, apparently unschemed genius of Lawrence's idiomatic license at such times is to make the linguistic level of his prose a dramatic function of his theme, and though this phrase is what I would call a perfect Lawrencian ambiguity, the glory of which is to argue itself back into singleness, it takes us a while to see, at least to appreciate, this achievement.

Substitute anything but an adjective redefined or downright contradicted by "being" (as in "being alive" or "being dead") and an adverbial uncertainty sets in. "Being (momentarily?) ecstatic," for example, does not constitute the definition of "an ecstatic being." Only the adjective "eternal" can conquer this ambiguity of duration. And "a being infinite" embraces this atemporality while implying also its own redundant adverb of extent, something like "exclusively"; since there is room in the universe for only one infinity, a single instance of it exhausts the category. Carried to the religious plane, and surely this is where Lawrence's prose levels off at such times, it is the difference between Western and Eastern thought, and another index to those innate sympathies on Ursula's part for the hyperbolic reach of the latter. In Christianity, for example, countless eternal souls are subsumed by one infinite deity, whereas in its Eastern counterparts personal eternities are obliterated in a single achieved infinite. For Ursula, then, to accede to the knowledge of living selfhood is to participate with it in infinity, which in turn (as the circular logic of the ambiguity finally reveals) is to be synonymous with—or to use that finer Lawrencian phrase from another context in *The Rainbow*, "unanimous with" (p. 235)—infinity itself. With so much at stake, the interchangeability of the original phrases, "being infinite" and "infinite being," is no facile ambivalence but a hard-won linguistic victory, for the reader's interpretive energy expended only to "make no difference in the end" must, in the split second of getting there, transact and transfuse a unity. Like the Eastern man who "must see a thing swelling to fill all heaven, or dwindled to a mere nothing, before he is suitably impressed" (p. 275), Ursula has, through the aid of a microscope, recognized and occupied the macrocosm. That shining nucleus, the infinitesimal swollen to the infinite, becomes along with Ursula herself a monad of the absolute vastness in which all life dwells and of which it partakes. Under the most scientific scrutiny, the single-celled organism and Ursula's vital self are each discovered to be, in other and more central terms, an allotrope of infinity.

Our proof that the infinity glimpsed has been internalized is there in the idiomatic hyperbole of a single adverb in the sentence describing her new life: "Her soul was busy, infinitely busy, in the new world" (p. 441). Nabokov, in the voice of his novelist R in *Transparent Things*, writes that "the favors of death knowledge are infinitely more precious than those of love," [29] and this speaker too, waiting expectantly like Ursula on the brink of the infinite, has a mortal stake in his adverb. Ursula will not be spiritually equipped for this residence in

---

[29] Vladimir Nabokov, *Transparent Things* (New York: McGraw-Hill, 1972), p. 82.

"the new world," however, until *Women in Love*, where the language of "being" undergoes its fullest redefinition. The chapter we have been studying in *The Rainbow*, after all, is called "The Bitterness of Ecstasy," and not until Ursula sloughs off her present lover, Skrebensky, and comes into an ultimate harmony of "being" with Rupert Birkin in the "Flitting" Chapter of the next novel will her transformation of self be complete. I wish to hold off this climactic passage only long enough to discuss the preceding sexual encounter between Birkin and Ursula before their wedding eve, for what it can fix in perspective once and for all about the province and conduct of style in sexual matters. When Birkin and Ursula make love at the end of "Excurse," the new being they achieve is carefully articulated as the liberation into balanced mutuality, in a way that will serve to distinguish Lawrence from that other great verbal innovator of the twentieth-century British novel, James Joyce.

After an unidiomatic purification of something like "She had her will of him" in a sentence beginning "She had her desire of him" (p. 312)—whereby the assertiveness is replaced with simple longing—we move into a strategic balance of clauses first, then phrase against phrase: ". . . she touched, she received the maximum of unspeakable communication in touch, dark, subtle, positively silent, a magnificent gift and give again, a perfect acceptance and yielding . . . (p. 312). Were it not for the suggestive trammeling of idiom and the transmitted sense of a linguistic flux struggling for balance, this would be the kind of dazed, reeling style, slackening into the flaccid and abstract, which a certain kind of reader is bound to recoil from in Lawrence. The intercourse described, this "communication," is in the punning sense "unspeakable" not because of shame this time, but because of its "intolerable" perfection—beyond the reach, and beyond the necessity, of words, except those of the narrator, whose language is so engaged as to fall into the rhythms of simulation. This we will have to call Lawrence's post-orgastic style, the prose not of frictional rush to climax, but of the poise and reciprocal peace that ensues. Otherness must be grammatically respected, avoiding the strict subject and object relationship in sexuality, with mutuality and balance made syntactically evident.

Joyce, on the other hand, for whom most everything in sex is speakable, nothing mysterious, insists on a methodical erotic parity for the episode between Bloom and Molly on Ben Howth: "She kissed me. I was kissed. . . . Kissed, she kissed me." [30] Joyce is as preoccupied as Lawrence by the grammar of sex, but he conjugates it more baldly, as summed up in a different context further on: "Act. Be acted on." [31] And then, just four pages before Molly's soliloquy, there is the marathon passage (as far from Lawrence as it is possible to get) in which the essential grammar of active against passive sex is microscopically explored with a series of hysterically overblown euphemisms like "the natural grammatical transition by inversion involving no alternation of sense of an aorist preterite proposition (parsed as masculine subject, monosyllabic onomatopoeic transitive

---

[30] James Joyce, *Ulysses* (New York: Random House, 1961), p. 176.
[31] *Ibid.*, p. 211.

verb with direct feminine object) from the active voice into its correlative aorist preterite proposition (parsed as feminine subject, auxiliary verb and quasimonosyllabic onomatopoeic past participle with complementary masculine agent) in the passive voice. . . ." [32] In short: "He fucked her, she was fucked by him." For Lawrence, neither the parched, exhaustive formulation nor its common sense translation could be the ideal grammar of sexual exchange, for both are too much an acting *upon,* instead of that "magnificent gift and give again" in which the dictional "give" (what someone in another context has called word "play" in the engineering sense) acts out the sexual take and give. The allotropic noun and verb form represent at once the love received and its reciprocated bestowal, and even the subsequently conjoined noun and participle "acceptance and yielding," the latter taken to mean "giving out" as well as "in," document this erotic to-and-fro.

Writing about the "imperative need" of our race, in the most prophetic stretch of his postscript to *Lady Chatterley's Lover,* Lawrence identifies it as "a need of the mind and soul, body, spirit, and sex: all. It is no use asking for a Word to fulfil such a need. No Word, No Logos, no Utterance will ever do it. The Word is uttered, most of it: we need only pay true attention." [33] The question is not quite closed. Though the Logos is all but complete, perhaps it needs reinvigoration with a new voice, an heroic eloquence of the kind Lawrence is prepared to give us, that will round it out and bring us round. "But who will call us to the Deed," he goes on to ask, "the great Deed of the Seasons and the year, the Deed of the soul's cycle, the Deed of a woman's life at one with a man's. . . ." The Word is out, "most of it," but we must be recalled to its injunctions, to a "Deed" that seems both an act and a warrant of being, by some kind of rhetorical summoning. We must be roused, that is, by prophetic art, which is the circuitous paradox in everything Lawrence says about effective, effectuating speech: that it falls somewhere between the outmoded and the prerequisite, an essential last and first step, the agent of its own transcendence.

This is the climactic feat brought off in the seventeenth chapter of *Women in Love,* "Flitting," just before Rupert Birkin and Ursula Brangwen are married. It is a scene whose linguistic subtext is a marriage of Birkin's long-standing wariness about the restrictive grammar, "I love you," and about all the common words of sex and affection, with Ursula's abiding will toward hyperbole. The passage begins with an instance of a gerund/noun ambiguity similar to that in "Mino." Ursula has agreed to spend the night with Birkin, accepting his logic that "We're married as much to-day as we shall be to-morrow" (p. 360), and "he went across to her and gathered her like a belonging in his arms"—taking "belonging," as Birkin himself once said about "pouvoir," as a verb rather than a noun. Let there be love. This is the Lawrencian Word, and it devolves upon Birkin when he utters that declaration he has for so long resisted: "I love you."

[32] *Ibid.,* p. 734.
[33] Lawrence, "A Propos of *Lady Chatterley's Lover,*" in *Phoenix II: Uncollected, Unpublished, and Other Prose Works by D. H. Lawrence* (New York: Viking Press, 1968), p. 510.

Yet Ursula, champion and past mistress of hyperbole, "wanted proof; and statement, even over-statement, for everything seemed still uncertain, unfixed to her" (p. 361). Statement, however, is exactly what is impossible when there are no genuine words into whose shapes the Word can descend. "There were infinite distances of silence between them," and to bridge them with statement seems artificial. "He said: 'Your nose is beautiful, your chin is adorable.' But it sounded like lies and she was hurt. Even when he said, whispering with truth, 'I love you, I love you,' it was not the real truth. It was something beyond love, such a gladness of having surpassed oneself, of having transcended the old existence" (p. 361). As we have already been led to expect from earlier arguments between them, the unsatisfactory nature of the verb "love" resides more in the worn, outmoded pronouns that govern and are governed by it. Immediately, the failure of the lower-case word "love" to express Birkin's experience with Ursula leads him to thoughts of self-transcendence and to a rumination on the mutual failures of "I" and "you" as designations. Finally Birkin might remark about his "I love you," with Emily Dickinson, "Tell Her, I only said—the Syntax—/ And left the Verb and the pronoun—out!" [34]—a "star-equilibrium" without the clutter and drag of personality. After all: "How could he say 'I' when he was something new and unknown, not himself at all? This I, this old formula of the age, was a dead letter" (p. 361).

Armed with the hyperbole of his own verbal arsenal, the narrator now launches by counter-example a frontal assault on the spurious syntax of personal subject and object in one of the finest, most supple runs of abstract lyric writing in Lawrence's fiction. However outworn and predictable the formulation may at first appear, the native and inevitable ambiguities of the English language have never been in Lawrence more commandingly tapped and implemented:

> In the new, superfine bliss, a peace superseding knowledge, there was no I and you, there was only the third, unrealised wonder, the wonder of existing not as oneself, but in a consummation of my being and of her being in a new one, a new, paradisal unit regained from the duality. How can I say "I love you" when I have ceased to be, and you have ceased to be: we are both caught up and transcended into a new oneness, where everything is silent, because there is nothing to answer, all is perfect and at one. Speech travels between the separate parts. But in the perfect One there is perfect silence of bliss.
>
> They were married by law on the next day, and she did as he bade her, she wrote to her father and mother. Her mother replied, not her father. (pp. 361–62)

The mounting rhythms begin as "superfine" grades into "superseding" ("fine" into "better than"). Next, the singular verb "was" is used with the compound subject "I and you" as if the transcendence and negation of this duality justifies the solecism by anticipating the unity toward which it is moving, and which has been until now "unrealised" in both senses.

[34] Thomas H. Johnson, ed., *The Complete Poems of Emily Dickinson* (Boston: Little, Brown, 1960), p. 238.

They happen to be senses we are familiar with in Lawrence if we remember the moving near-death of Paul Morel in *Sons and Lovers*, the son nursed back to health by his mother after the death of his brother William. I turn to this in order to suggest the emotional force elsewhere imparted by such a seemingly minor ambiguity as the appearance of "unrealised" in the "Flitting" passage. After William's death, Mrs. Morel nearly dies herself, and when Paul answers her cries of "Oh, my son—my son!" (p. 139) she fails to acknowledge him. Yet when Paul too falls ill, she knows finally that she "should have watched the living not the dead" (p. 141), and the theme of emotional recognition comes into brilliant focus. I will quote the whole exchange on Paul's sickbed, to set the ambiguity in its full dramatic context:

> "I s'll die, mother!" he cried, heaving for breath on the pillow.
> She lifted him up, crying in a small voice:
> "Oh, my son—my son!"
> That brought him to. He realised her. His whole will rose up and arrested him. He put his head on her breast, and took ease of her for love.
> "For some things," said his aunt, "it was a good thing Paul was ill that Christmas. I believe it saved his mother." (p. 141)

Mrs. Morel knows that she has killingly ignored Paul by lingering with William in the land of the dead, and that only if she can make this other son "recognize" her loving presence at his sickbed, as she could not make William, will she be able to save him. Yet when this is brought about, Paul has not only "realised" her existence in this sense, and seen that she again acknowledges his, but he has also, and as a reciprocal result, "realised her" by *actualizing* her being, making real her life again after suspended animation, retrieving her along with himself from the borders of death. The abstract phrasing that may sound at first merely heedless of idiom, and needlessly so, is heard on a moment's consideration to reveal some profound latency for doubleness deep at the springs of our language and our life. Lawrence does not get this effect, he permits it, as if the ambiguity is found, not contrived. The two distinct meanings of "realised," in context movingly inseparable, exemplify in quite pure form the allotropic nature of Lawrence's best self-resolving ambiguities. To call the double life of "realised" a pun is only to emphasize that it has none of the artful sheen we expect from such literary contrivances; it neither glows brightly, as in Dickens, nor scintillates, as in Joyce. Somehow primal, it radiates from deep beneath itself the double truth enacted in both directions by the narrative which frames it—the truth that to love is to make live, and that acknowledgment of the other in love can, like a charmed incarnation, resurrect and "realise."

I am not speaking of a serviceable or even necessarily conscious allusion to *Sons and Lovers* on Lawrence's part when I suggest that some of this impact, muted to be sure, is conveyed by the adjectival component of "unrealised wonder" in the "Flitting" paragraph, and that the twofold force it brings is enough to explode the negative at the very instant when the transfiguration is at once envisioned for the first time and embarked upon. This dampened ambiguity modulates into the following long appositive phrase ("the wonder of existing . . .") and its own more resonant linguistic vibration in "a consummation of my being and of her being in a new one," the culmination in Lawrence of the "to be or not to be" motif.

Birkin himself would be disposed to note that in reading the phrase you can take "being" as either a noun or a verb, "one" as pronoun or noun, with the twin quiver of ambivalence perfectly accorded (both to and with) that alchemizing transition at which the two meanings are as coal and diamond to the underlying carbon. No sooner do we hear the phrase as "a joint consummation of our separate beings in a new one, a new being," than it reasserts itself as "a triumph of my existing, along with her, in a new One, a new unity"—as specified in the next phrase when the lovers are "both caught up and transcended into a new oneness." Since, on the first of the alternate readings, the new "being" is just such a coming into wholeness, the verbal distinctions, palpable enough in their own right and on their own separate terms, are risen beyond like the lovers themselves after the death of their separateness. Or they are factored down to their spiritual common denominator, like allotropes traced to their binding elemental source. A truth both deeper and higher is so arrived at. As the phrase "transcended the old existence" gets varied to "caught up and transcended into a new oneness," the repeated term, like the most potent of Lawrencian echoes, is an incremental step forward, the past participle "transcended" having been shaded off in its transition from the preterite form into a penumbra of double exposure. As a true passive, it would imply that something has transcended the "I" and "you," which have in the process "ceased to be," rather than that they are made in themselves transcendent. But the latter is also the point. By assuming redefinition, "I and you" are transcended and dwarfed by the new oneness and equilibrium, and therefore, not separately but together now, they are felt to transcend their former duality, with true and false passives thus subsumed as allotropes of the transfiguring linguistic chemistry.

It is, as I say, a matter of profound redefinition. What we find in this passage is not Western literature's canonical amorous mysticism of sex-as-fusion, the erotic transmogrification of two-made-one, precisely because what has come before in *Women in Love* has once and for all reworked the terms of healthy sexual merger. Lawrence is not talking in "Flitting" about two personalities made one, two traditional "I's," two "old stable egos," but about that subsisting identity deeper than the superficial, atavistic "self" which participates with another like it, under universal laws comparable to those of stellar physics, in a psychic gravitational field that makes the identifiable electromagnetic unit not each separately but the achieved and sustaining continuity between them. As personalities named Rupert Birkin and Ursula Brangwen they are still separate agents. But when they are "hung in a pure rest, as a star is hung, balanced unthinkably" (p. 311), when a sense of "being" apart from mere personality has been won over and above reason (as the adverb "unthinkably" half implies), above and beyond that "self-assertion" which Ursula saw transcended under the microscope, then the primary identity of the lovers is as the very equilibration, one constellated with the other, which they define in their astral balance.[35]

And so the "Flitting" passage manages not to seem anticlimactic, contradictory, or reductive; taking implicitly as its subject the new set of terms by which it is to be understood, it complements and completes the earlier notion of "star-equilibrium" by invoking a more pat rhapsodic formula for sexual harmony and transcendence only to rehabilitate it with powerfully ambivalent phrase. Along with the word "one" hanging, as if "balanced unthinkably," between pronoun and noun, Lawrence has kept fluid the demarcation between "being" as a state and as an act, between nominal and verbal forms, between the sense of a stabilized self and of a progression toward one, so that the word can function as a free register of presence or process, rather than as some fixed label for any of those falsifying categories into which "being" is habitually prodded. We might think of the "star-equilibrium," then, as a Lawrencian coinage, an original sexual metaphor, for the mutual relation between separate selves as those selves have more or less traditionally been defined, whereas "a consummation of my being and of her being in a new one" offers the other side of the coin, a time-worn metaphysical conceit bravely reconceived under pressure of the self's radical (in the chemical sense) redefinition. What results is therefore, at last, unfamiliar to the literary history of eroticism: it is indeed a *"new one . . . a new oneness."*

The finest syntactic transactions of this passage from "Flitting" have taken place at the very threshold of our verbal intuition, so low-keyed as to be almost off the linguistic register, as nearly speechless as hyperbole can get. For it is the prose not of sexual death but of the poise and starry calm of rebirth, a hush deeper than the grave's, in which "everything is silent, because there is nothing to answer, all is perfect and at one. Speech travels between the separate parts. But in the perfect One there is a perfect silence of bliss." Even the silence is imaged as the negative of a reciprocation, the absence of a reply in the face of "nothing to answer." Between "I and you" there were protestations and avowals, even Ursula's coveted "over-statement," but with "we" there is nothing, nothing to come or go between us. Hyperbole, in other words, is tangent to silence at zero and at infinity. When the next sentence brings us suddenly back to earth with "They were married by law on the next day," we realize not only that the Word has been uttered, but that the "Deed of a woman's life at one with a man's" has been both done and, in the contractual sense, signed. This has been possible only because of that redefinition of the vital self which reveals it, in the words of the letter to Garnett, as "representing some greater, inhuman will," the mutuality of "being in a new one" as it were. At the end, virtually, of Birkin's and Ursula's phase of the novel, before their equilibrium gives way to the libidinous deadlock

[35] In "Being Perfect: Lawrence, Sartre, and *Women in Love,*" *Critical Inquiry,* 2 (Winter 1975), T. H. Adamowski finds in the "star-equilibrium" of Birkin and Ursula "a relationship that is tantamount to the 'double reciprocal incarnation' that Sartre describes" (p. 366) in the balance between "being" and "nothingness"; the closeness of this to the spiritual achievement of the "Flitting" passage is further implied by the "being perfect" of Adamowski's title, for as verb resolves to noun and back again, the phrase might be taken to suggest the perfect "incarnation," together, of two previously discrete selves carnally renewed and perfectly conjoined.

of Gerald and Gudrun in the last hundred pages, and just before their story subsides into the marital formula of the legal service, the novel passes through one of the most deceptively traditional denouements in all Lawrence, an epithalamium remade in the image of its own terms reimagined. Utterance has helped break the way through, and now testifies to the achievement. For finally, in "married by law," I think we are being asked to recall the common etymological origins of "lexical" and "legal," with verbal consciousness once again instructing us in the power of language itself. After deeper, unspoken legitimizations, this epithalamic hymn to the silence of "being" is matter-of-factly given back to the secularized Word of law.

# Contributors

ROBERT ALTER, now a contributing editor for *Commentary*, teaches Hebrew and comparative literature at Berkeley. His Fielding essay was reprinted in *Fielding and the Nature of the Novel* (1968). He is the author also of *Rogue's Progress: Studies in the Picaresque Novel* (1964), *After the Tradition* (1969), and *Partial Magic: The Novel as Self-Conscious Genre* (1975).

NINA AUERBACH teaches English at the University of Pennsylvania and writes on Victorian fiction. Her essay on Austen and Alcott will appear in expanded form in her book on communities of women in fiction for Harvard University Press. It was written, she reports, "in the matriarchal community of the Radcliffe Institute" on a Ford Foundation grant.

JOHN ROSS BAKER, formerly of Lehigh University, is a victim of academic retrenchment. He resides in Bethlehem, Pennsylvania, and when last heard from had completed a study of the Chicago critics for his University of Illinois dissertation.

LEO BERSANI chairs the French department at Berkeley and writes frequently on modern literature. His essay on Flaubert appears also in *A Future for Astyanax/ Character and Desire in Literature* (Boston: Little, Brown, 1976). His book on Baudelaire and Freud will be published this fall by the University of California Press.

R. P. BILAN is writing a book on F. R. Leavis in which his *Novel* essay will reappear. He teaches at the University of Toronto and is presently co-writing the annual Canadian fiction review for the *Toronto Quarterly*.

WAYNE BOOTH, one of *Novel*'s advisors, holds a chair in English at the University of Chicago. His "second thoughts" essay reappears in *Now Don't Try to Reason with Me: Essays and Ironies for a Credulous Age* (Chicago, 1970). His most recent books are *A Rhetoric of Irony* (1974) and *Modern Dogma and the Rhetoric of Assent* (1974).

MALCOLM BRADBURY teaches American Studies at the University of East Anglia in Norwich, England. His essay on structure was amended and reprinted as "The Novel and its Poetics" in *Possibilities: Essays on the State of the Novel* (New York and London: Oxford, 1973). He has also published three novels, *Eating People Is Wrong* (1959), *Stepping Westward* (1965), *The History Man* (1975), and a collection of stories and parodies, *Who Do You Think You Are?* (1976). His first critical text, *The Social Content of Modern English Literature*, appeared in 1971.

GRAHAM GOOD is chairman of Comparative Literature at the University of British Columbia. He has previously published on Balzac and Mann and is working now on a study of the theory and practice of short fiction.

ELEANOR N. HUTCHENS teaches English at the University of Alabama in Huntsville. She is the author of two books, *Irony in Tom Jones* and *Writing to be Read*. Her latest of many essays, "O Attic Shape! the Cornering of Square," argues that geometry in *Tom Jones* is the playful demonstration of wrong.

FRANK KERMODE, now at King's College, Cambridge, is the author of such notable works as *The Sense of an Ending, Romantic Image, Wallace Stevens, D. H. Lawrence, Continuities*, and *Puzzles and Epiphanies*. He also edits the Modern Masters series for Viking Press.

ELIZABETH KIRK teaches medieval studies at Brown and heads the graduate program in English. She is the author of *The Dream Thoughts of Piers Plowman* (1972) and of essays on medieval poetics and the Pearl Poet. An ACLS fellow and a research associate at the Pontifical Institute of Medieval Studies in Toronto in 1974-75, she began work there on a book on Julian of Norwich.

DAVID LODGE holds a chair in English at the University of Birmingham in England. His most recent novel, *Changing Places* (1975), won the Hawthornden Prize. He is the author of *Language of Fiction* (1966) and *The Novelist at the Crossroads* (1971), in which his essay for *Novel* was reprinted. His new book on modes of modern writing will appear this year in England and America.

JULIAN MOYNAHAN is finishing a study of Anglo-Irish literature, 1800-1932, entitled *Irish Enough: The Literary Imagination of a Hyphenated Culture*. A Distinguished Professor of English at Rutgers, he has published three novels and has just completed a fourth. He is the author also of critical books on Lawrence and Nabokov and the editor of the recently published Viking Portable Thomas Hardy.

JOHN HENRY RALEIGH, former Vice Chancellor of Academic Affairs at Berkeley, is the author of *Matthew Arnold and American Culture* (1957), *The Plays of Eugene O'Neill* (1965), and *Time, Place, and Idea: Essays on the Novel* (1968). He has just finished a book on Joyce's *Ulysses* and is writing another on Scott's *Ivanhoe* and its times.

WALTER L. REED, now at the University of Texas at Austin, has published a book on the Romantic hero in nineteenth-century fiction called *Meditations on the Hero*. He recently won a Guggenheim fellowship for an "exemplary history of the novel" based on *Don Quixote* and the picaresque.

ROBERT SCHOLES, with *Novel* since 1969, runs the semiotics program at Brown and is currently writing a semiotics of fiction. He is noted for such books as *The Nature of Narrative* (with Robert Kellogg in 1966), *The Fabulators* (1967), and *Structural Fabulation* (1975). His essays on genre and on formalism and structuralism appear in revised form in *Structuralism in Literature* (1974).

PATRICIA MEYER SPACKS, now on *Novel's* editorial board, teaches English at Wellesley. Currently she is working on an interdisciplinary course in adolescent values at the National Humanities Institute in New Haven. An eighteenth-century scholar, her most recent books are *The Female Imagination* (Knopf, 1975) and *Imagining a Self* (Harvard, 1976).

MARK SPILKA, *Novel's* managing editor since its inception in 1967 is writing a book on literary quarrels with tenderness. He is the author of *The Love Ethic of D. H. Lawrence* (1955) and *Dickens and Kafka: A Mutual Interpretation* (1963).

GARRETT STEWART, author of *Dickens and the Trials of Imagination* (Harvard, 1974), teaches English at the University of California, Santa Barbara. He has written elsewhere on Keats, Austen, and Charlotte Brontë.

JERRY WASSERMAN teaches English and Comparative Literature at the University of British Columbia. He is the editor of a casebook on "The Grand Inquisitor" and has written articles on Lawrence, Conrad, Shakespeare, Beckett, and Afro-American fiction. His piece on Rabelais is part of a current study of visual and concrete mimetic form in the novel.

IAN WATT, another *Novel* advisor, is currently completing the first volume of a two-volume study of Conrad. His "second thoughts" essay was recently published in an Italian translation with *The Rise of the Novel*.

RAYMOND WILLIAMS, at Jesus College, Cambridge, is the author of two novels, *Border Country* and *Second Generation*, and of such notable social and literary studies as *Culture and Society*, *The Long Revolution*, and *The English Novel from Dickens to Lawrence*. His essay on George Eliot reappears in revised form in his recent book, *The Country and the City*.